Leo Strauss and the Crisis of Rationalism

SUNY series in the Thought and Legacy of Leo Strauss

Kenneth Hart Green, editor

Leo Strauss and the Crisis of Rationalism

Another Reason, Another Enlightenment

CORINE PELLUCHON

Translated by
ROBERT HOWSE

SUNY PRESS

Original translation: Corine Pelluchon—*Leo Strauss, une autre raison, d'autres Lumières* © Librairie Philosophique J. Vrin, Paris, 2005

Cover image / WikiPaintings.org / Red and White Domes by Paul Klee

Published by State University of New York Press, Albany

Printed in the United States of America

For information, contact State University of New York Press, Albany, NY
www.sunypress.edu

Production by Diane Ganeles
Marketing by Anne M. Valentine

Library of Congress Cataloging-in-Publication Data

Pelluchon, Corine.
[Leo Strauss. English]
Leo Strauss and the crisis of rationalism : another reason, another enlightenment / Corine Pelluchon ; translated by Robert Howse.
pages cm. — (SUNY series in the thought and legacy of Leo Strauss)
Includes bibliographical references and index.
ISBN 978-1-4384-4967-8 (alk. paper)
ISBN 978-1-4384-4966-1 (pbk.: alk. paper)
1. Strauss, Leo. I. Title.

B945.S84P4513 2014
181'.06—dc221 2013006634

10 9 8 7 6 5 4 3 2 1

Contents

Translator's Note

The original French-language work upon which this translation is based was the doctoral dissertation of Corine Pelluchon, a prominent contemporary French intellectual and philosopher who has since written a number of books and articles on subjects such as bioethics, environmental ethics, and animal welfare and was recently honored by the French Academy. The dissertation was published by Vrin in France in 2005 and won the François Furet prize in 2006. Professor Pelluchon chose not to revise the work for purposes of an English-language version, except the bibliography, which has been updated; it goes without saying that her thinking may nevertheless have evolved since it was written. I had Professor Pelluchon's full cooperation throughout the preparation of the translation; she was unfailingly generous with her time and patient, with a translator engaged in many other projects simultaneously. I learned much of value for my own scholarship on Strauss through our interactions.

Robert Howse
New York City, December 2012.

Introduction

> "Liberal education consists in listening to the conversation among the greatest minds. (. . .) The greatest minds utter monologues. We must transform their monologues into a dialogue. (. . .) Since the greatest minds contradict one another regarding the most important matters, they compel us to judge of their monologues. (. . .) Yet we must face our awesome situation, created by the necessity that we try to be more than attentive and docile listeners, namely, judges, and yet we are not competent to be judges. (. . .) Liberal education, which consists in the constant intercourse with the greatest minds, is a training in the highest form of modesty, not to say of humility. It is at the same time a training in boldness: it demands from us the complete break with the noise, the rush, the thoughtlessness, the cheapness of Vanity Fair of the intellectuals as well as their enemies. It demands from us the boldness implied in the resolve to regard the accepted views as mere opinions, or to regard the average opinions as extreme opinions which are at least as likely to be wrong as the most strange or the least popular opinions."[1]

The Crisis of Rationalism

In the text that reproduces an exchange that took place in early 1970 between Leo Strauss and Jacob Klein, both of whom were invited at the end of their careers to present their intellectual autobiographies before a select audience, Klein said of his old friend: "His primary interests were two-fold: first, the question of God; and second, the question of politics."[2]

Strauss was born in 1899 in a small town near Marburg, in a former county of the Hesse region that had become a Prussian province in 1866, and was brought up in a Conservative and even Orthodox Jewish home.[3] He was exposed right from high school to the message of German humanism. Furtively he read Schopenhauer and Nietzsche. "I formed the plan, or the wish, to spend my life reading Plato and breeding rabbits while earning my livelihood as a rural postmaster."[4]

Most of today's scholars think that the philosophical career of Strauss is confined to a series of commentaries on the great texts of antiquity. The incarnation of philosophical *Eros*, Socrates represents the problem that unifies the thought of Strauss: the possibility of philosophy, which implies a certain organization of society that allows thinkers the full liberty to write and teach, but which is not self-evident, even when one lives in a democracy that appears to have solved the theological-political problem. There is always a break between philosophy and the city, because philosophers substitute for commonsense opinions ideas that embarrass other human beings and undermine any authority other than reason, which the political authorities perceive as a menace against established order. Finally, modern presuppositions prohibit us from really philosophizing, that is, returning to Plato or Aristotle—through Maimonides, one should add (and here one indicates Strauss's contribution to philosophy).

This portrait of Strauss is that of a man who lived through the twentieth century exactly as if he had remained in Germany raising rabbits. His 1921 thesis on Jacobi[5] the philosopher of the Anti-Enlightenment who provoked the pantheism debate, where what is at stake is in part the critique of modern rationalism, would have been a mere accident. The fact that this thesis was supervised by Cassirer would be entirely circumstantial; for reasons of geographical proximity, Strauss was going to study philosophy at Marburg, home of the neo-Kantian school founded by Hermann Cohen. The dialogue that Strauss pursued, from the beginning to the end of his career, with this representative of the synthesis between Judaism and German philosophy would be a mere reflection of his nostalgia for an Enlightened Judaism that history had made problematic. It would not be a genuine debate concerning the troubling heritage of the Enlightenment, setting up a confrontation between Spinoza and Maimonides, two essential moments of philosophical inquiry. Strauss, who studied at Paris and Cambridge in 1933 and 1934, respectively, would have lived almost without any spiritual development and would have been found, from 1938 until his death in New York in 1973, telling his contemporaries that "one must experiment with Plato,"[6] because, for the ancient philosophers, ethical and political questions are situated at the core of philosophy, while modern science and the distinction between facts and values have distanced us from these questions in favor of the Will to Power and the reign of technology. Strauss would be a partisan of the return to antiquity and someone who despises modernity, which means that his contribution to philosophy would be no greater than if he had stayed at home and read Plato, writing commentary after commentary and not bothering to publish his thought. And this is something he would have done, since, if one clings to this interpretation that reduced the work of Strauss to a defense of antiquity, one would think that he achieves that through an art of writing between the lines designed to preserve his thought from vulgarization or distortion. However, this focus on Straussian esotericism is of little interest to anyone except for a small number of disciples.

I think, to the contrary, that through his place in the history of philosophy and through his distinctive preoccupations, Strauss provides strikingly new perspectives with a view to thinking through the crisis of our times. This requires an explanation of what the crisis consists of, where it comes from, and what the circumstances are that have made it particularly intense in the twentieth century. I seek to prove that it is this crisis that "provoked" the philosophical inquiry of Strauss. Is this crisis still ours, and how is it that this philosopher provides an orientation that operates at the levels of both theory and practice? All of these questions revolve around a pivotal point that gives this work its meaning and, to begin with, explains its title. This work, which is a work that takes Strauss as its point of departure and is not a presentation of his "doctrine," is focused on his critique of the modern Enlightenment, which is responsible for the ideological and philosophical confusion[7] that we experience, and the various historical manifestations that he analyzes, in collective life as well as in ideas. This crisis of modernity is essentially a crisis of rationality, as Nietzsche and Heidegger saw. But, contrary to Nietzsche and Heidegger, Strauss claims that nihilism comes from the forgetfulness of the meaning of Law or of a certain articulation of politics and religion that explains the status that Strauss wants to give to political philosophy.

The possibility of philosophy and the status of first philosophy bestowed on political philosophy are thus a result, a consequence of the thought of Strauss, more than its unifying feature. Strauss's thought is constituted by two problems that never ceased to haunt him: the religious problem and the political problem.[8] These two problems assume that one confronts a reality that exists outside of pure thought and that resists it. This requires a different sort of inquiry than that in place since the Cartesian cogito right up to the neo-Kantians and phenomenologists, but there is also a linkage, an interconnectedness, since, in political matters, thought and reality, philosophy and action are blended. And, further, given his historical fate, to live as a contemporary the great upheavals of the twentieth century—through his German birth, his social and religious origins, and his place in the history of metaphysics, Strauss confronted all his life this problem. He devoted his intellectual energy to this problem, in awareness that not all problems permit of a solution, as he said concerning the Jew lost in a non-Jewish world, then in a secularized world where the question of his identity no longer presents itself in terms with which his ancestors would be familiar. This problem, soluble neither by Zionism (of which the adolescent Strauss was an adherent) nor by assimilation (which did not bring redemption in the century where one expected it, and which, after the Second World War, poses again the question of the impossible abandonment of his origins by a human being), is the symbol of the human problem. Strauss examines the problem as such, as that which reveals the problematic character of the liberal solution, of the separation of the theological and the political. The result is an articulation of the tradition as well as of modernity that deviates from the scheme supported by the modern Enlightenment, judged to be defective and with questionable foundations.

Two Historical Shocks and a Threat

Thus one cannot understand why "the West has become uncertain of its purpose"[9] without returning to the genesis of modern thought. The critique by Leo Strauss of the modern Enlightenment allows us to reconsider the principles on which is founded this project of civilization that has led to liberal democracy, based on individual liberty and the establishment of a universal and just society aimed at eliminating intolerance and promoting peace. It is as historian of philosophy and as political philosopher that Strauss, in his discussion on the heritage at the same time positive and negative of the Enlightenment, makes a constructive critique of civilization.

The work that he has handed down to us is all the more valuable given that he began his philosophical career in the mid-1920s. He was at that time "a young Jew born and raised in Germany who found himself in the grips of the theologico-political predicament."[10] Not only did the weakness of the Weimar Republic underline the impotence of democracy to suppress discrimination, but also the tradition is experienced, in religion in general and in Judaism in particular, as a crisis. It is as if the critique of religion undertaken at the beginning of the modern Enlightenment had led to the choice between the return to orthodoxy or atheism, without there being any middle way between reason and Revelation. Did the Enlightenment destroy what it enlightened? What Strauss calls the moderate Enlightenment represented the possibility of a reconciliation of reason and faith. The moderate Enlightenment was overtaken by the radical Enlightenment. The latter will detach religion from knowledge and make the distinction between facts and values a criterion of objectivity, condemning religion and politics to be nothing more than objects of study that provide a "decent burial" to religious traditions and to classical political philosophy. The destruction of metaphysics, the disenchantment of reason, and the exclusion from the domain of politics of all reflection concerning the meaning of the good life have led to a rationalism characterized by the reign of technology and the progressive dehumanization of an atomized society where individuals do not really participate in political life and are deprived of any relation to transcendence that depends on something other than purely subjective experience. These phenomena are accompanied by all kinds of irrationalism. Is it that modern rationalism reverts back to its opposite and prepares with the undermining of reason—which is the final gesture of surrender to nihilism—the ground for tyranny? "I began therefore to wonder whether the self-destruction of reason was not the inevitable outcome of modern rationalism as distinguished from pre-modern rationalism."[11]

This question, which is the nerve of the Straussian critique of modernity, is *the* question of the twentieth century. It is provoked by the successive collapses of traditional morality and rationality. There are two shocks that mark, in a decisive fashion, twentieth-century man, tearing him away from the old world to which Hermann Cohen still belonged: "Cohen's thought belongs to the world preceding World War II. (. . .) The worst things that he experienced were the Dreyfus scandal and the pogroms instigated by Czarist Russia: he did not experience Communist Russia and Hitler's Germany. (. . .) Catastrophes and horrors of a magnitude hitherto unknown, which we have seen and through which we have lived, were better provided for, or made intelligible, by both Plato and the prophets than by the modern belief in progress."[12]

Strauss, referring to the Davos debates that occurred in 1929 between Cassirer and Heidegger, concludes that "ethics had been *silently* dropped: Cassirer had not *faced* the problem. *Heidegger did face the problem*."[13] This remark should be juxtaposed with what Strauss wrote about Cohen. Because he believed that the modern synthesis is superior to its premodern components, Cohen the neo-Kantian philosopher was not aware that he was dealing more with a problem than with a solution. Cohen and Cassirer do not face the problem because their belief in reason hides the reality from them. They do not see that beyond consciousness is the abyss. Husserl also lacked this radicalism: he did not look behind the pure consciousness to the morality and finitude of man. If, according to Strauss, Heidegger is "the only great thinker in our time," this is because he has seen that "rationalism is based on a specific understanding of what being means" and that "this basis of rationalism proves to be a dogmatic assumption."[14]

In order to confront the crisis of our times, it is necessary to return beyond modern assumptions and ask ourselves *who* can enlighten us: Is it necessary to dare to think in a new way, an ultramodern thinking, like that of Rosenzweig or Heidegger? Or, rather, is it the pre-modern thinkers who are more likely to ask the true questions and show us the path by which we can escape the crisis? The problem is to know how to rehabilitate a civilization that is contested both within itself and from the outside.

Communism and Nazism put in radical doubt the project of civilization that characterizes the world of modernity and the Enlightenment. These two phenomena are not historical accidents. Further, they are reactions one to the other. When Strauss considers Nazism and delivers in 1941 a lecture entitled "German Nihilism" and when, in 1962, in "The Crisis of our Times," he analyzes communism, he considers these developments as expressions of the crisis of the West: these are the most violent forms of the revolt against Western civilization within modern man himself. On the one hand, communism puts in question certain of the claims on which the hopes of the modern project were founded: communism showed itself to be radically opposed to the way in which Western man thought that "this universal and just society should be established and managed. The antagonism between the West and Communism leads to the consequence that no possibility of a universal society exists in the foreseeable future."[15] This experience of conflict requires a political restructuring and reconsideration of three characteristically modern beliefs: the belief in the superiority of universalism and globalism to particularism and patriotism; the belief in a causal relationship between affluence and happiness, prosperity, and virtue; and the idea that science ought to serve human power, which may be a "degrading delusion."[16] For its part, Nazism is the most extreme form of a return to a pre-modern ideal that rests on the refusal of a materialist society to which, according to the young Nihilists, the world of modernity would condemn us. When Strauss examines the non-nihilistic motivation that animates the German nihilists who would later become inflamed by Nazism, he writes that at the beginning it was a matter of young people revolting against the prospect of "cultural Bolshevism" and the scenario of men incapable of self-overcoming and sacrifice; this made the young open to the warrior-like values exalted in the German militarist tradition. "German militarism is the *father* of German nihilism. The young nihilists rallied to Nazism because they thought communism was ineluctable and that there was no other alternative to communism than the violent destruction of civilization. They thus chose 'the nothing, the chaos, the jungle, the Wild West' over a communist future and the establishment of a society of peaceful nations sustaining Cities of Pigs. They said 'No' and this No proved however sufficient as *the* preface to action, to the action of destruction."[17]

History, far from being the unfolding of reason, is in the twentieth century the spectacle of this internal critique of Western civilization. Strauss is less concerned with denouncing the modern forms of barbarism than with understanding the nature of the opposition to the West that they express. His philosophical project leads him to analyze the destructive logic of the West, because "the delusions of communism are already the delusions of Hegel and even Kant."[18] The resistance that the world of modernity inspires should be taken seriously. It is not the work of deviants, but the idea according to which it reveals that the humanity of the inhuman or the banality of evil isn't sufficient for understanding its specific character. It is a matter of considering the profundity of the crisis of the West and providing oneself with the means to correct that which, in modern rationalism, is destructive. The question is whether the Enlightenment itself played the role of sorcerer's apprentice.

The third danger which diminishes the claim of the moderns to embody the progress of freedom is mass democracy. This theme is present between 1835 and 1840 in a writer of whom Strauss does not speak, but to whom he is close in spirit. Tocqueville, in his *Democracy in America*,[19] describes the kind of despotism that can exist within the shadow of democracy and threaten it from the inside. The republic is a political regime that presupposes the citizen's interest in the public good. Originally, it opposed democracy, which is defined by the sovereignty of the people and excludes a priori the elitism required to have competent representatives acting on their behalf. This opposition between republicanism and democracy, reflected in the Chavalier de Jaucourt's article[20] in the *Encylopedia* in which democracy is viewed as dangerous and without a future, and in Rousseau, whose critique of representation goes hand in hand with the ideal of citizen participation, tends to disappear with the revolutions at the end of the eighteenth century. Democracy presents itself as the legitimate and irreversible regime, characterized by increasing equality of condition. This universalization of equality and its extension above the civic realm transforms it into a passion, a malleable aspiration, where imaginary discontents are even more important still than real-world inequalities.

A new type of man appears on the scene, rebellious against hierarchy and natural authority, an individual inclined toward contractual relations and driven more by vanity than by honor. This type of man, who is neither aristocrat nor priest nor soldier but rather bourgeois, is the subject of that which we will come to call, without any more seeing the oxymoron, liberal democracy. He is described by Tocqueville as an individualistic and materialistic being, oriented toward the private sphere and concerned with the increase of material wealth. He threatens the very system that gave birth to him when his passion for equality is not compensated by a sense of freedom permitting him to fulfill his duties as citizen. Nietzsche identified this type in the prologue to *Thus Spake Zarathustra* and designated him the "Last Man." Strauss is thinking about this type of man when, reflecting on the consequences of mass democracy, he defends education for excellence.[21] If the domains of public discourse and education are degraded, then democracy is in peril, because participation, even relative, of the citizen, including through voting, assumes a certain political culture. Permissive egalitarianism, which brings about the moral decline of a society where freedom doesn't rest any longer on the responsible citizen, but rather on the individual with his "pressing wants," is an important phenomenon that Strauss takes into account in his analysis of the contemporary world. It underpins not only his critique of relativism, particularly in *Natural Right and History*, but also his polemical usage of the concept of nature in the confrontation between ancient and modern natural right.

The idea that the passion for equality can turn against liberty tends to a hardening in certain of Strauss's positions and gives them a dogmatic flavor that becomes a caricature at the hands of some of his heirs: taking as points of departure the notion of nature, which we believe often serves a function of critique, the theme of the necessary return to the Ancients, the critique of relativism, and esotericism. The awareness of the fragility of democracy cannot but reinforce the notion of an unbridgeable gap between philosophy and the city. It will lead Strauss to apply more and more his discovery of the esoteric art of writing to all the philosophers and to practice this art of dissimulation in his own writings in the name of the gap between the few wise and the many unwise.[22] Not only is it not excluded that, contrary to the notion of a transparent dissemination of knowledge, there is a kind of censorship with a view to encouraging conformity—which can be conformity to modernity—but, moreover, there is by nature a tension between knowledge and opinion. This gap between philosophy and the city justifies an art of writing between the lines practiced by thinkers who know that their arguments will inspire the hostility of their contemporaries. Mass democracy, where public opinion is all-powerful, should be counterbalanced by the maintenance of education for excellence based on reading of the classics and the development of individuals' critical capacities. This idea is in the context of the painstaking studies that Strauss undertook, in particular in the last part of his life,[23] of the great authors, devoting himself with zeal to the interpretation of the classic texts and encouraging in his circle an education where the pupil was formed based on the pedagogical ideal of the Ancients.

Elitism, which is a constant in Strauss's thought, although we would not place it either at the origin or at the center of that thought, is at the same time a tendency connected with his extraordinary erudition and a reaction against leveling downward, that is, a way of fighting the modern enemy of liberty. It is Strauss's intellectual engagement that supported his assiduous reading of texts and gave to him the habits of a scholar in an age when the greatest intellectuals try to stand out by virtue of their extreme behavior and ideas. It suffices to think of Sartre and his famous "any anti-communist is a dog," which brought its author at least as much renown as his books. Strauss, at a moment when feverish partisanship dominated the world of ideas and when the universities resembled boxing rings, chose another path and openly opposed ideology in the name of political philosophy. If we want to understand the crisis of contemporary rationalism and find the means of solving it, then the thought of Strauss is more instructive than the study of doctrines that are, in varying degrees, the symptoms of this crisis or mere reactions against modernity. It is equally useful to consider Strauss's analysis of the common assumptions shared by the warring ideologies of modernity, capitalism, and communism. Does not the radicalism of philosophical inquiry consist in putting into question such assumptions by digging beneath ideological differences? We can then equally ask whether it is necessary to examine the alternatives for the West in considering, like Heidegger, the origin of metaphysics with Plato and Aristotle, or whether the destructive logic of modernity is instead linked to philosophical choices made at the beginning of the Enlightenment.

Whether or not this scholarly peculiarity of Strauss's takes pride of place over ideological engagement, we ought not to be misled as to the concerns that structure his thought and orient its problematic; we must use his work and draw from its very core in order to illuminate the problem posed by the crisis of rationality. This crisis challenges the West even in the very definition it has of itself. At its core is the theological-political problem, or rather the avoidance of this problematic through modern assumptions and the *doxa* derived from the Enlightenment. These opinions made needful a careful reading of the texts. Because our understanding of the Enlightenment frequently depends on a caricature, as Strauss said of Voltarianism, "Voltaire is always in our face,"[24] but we do not have genuine knowledge of his thought. This knowledge supposes that we have understood a thinker as he understood himself, and not on the basis of our own assumptions or as if what he said was self-evident. It is possible that we will fail to be enlightened and that we will have access neither to Maimonides nor to the modern Enlightenment itself. We could be less enlightened than Cohen, who still saw that which was not obvious in the modern Enlightenment. We would be still further from Maimonides than was Cohen the neo-Kantian. In order to think through the crisis of our times, a rigorous methodology is thus necessary. This is the way of Strauss when he interprets the classics, but also when he sometimes uses certain polemics and certain authors for purposes of his *own* problematic and preoccupations.

The relationship that exists in Strauss's thought between his own concerns and the problems is highly original, because in philosophical knowledge, we have the tendency to consider that the theoretical problems come first and to derive from them those concerns that can be decisive in practice. Our thesis is that the theological-political situation of which Strauss took stock is such as to impose on him this style of thinking and to lead him to put first the history of philosophy. The latter is indispensable for Strauss, who does not want to be a mere link in the chain that connects philosophical assumptions to social prejudices and makes the philosophers of the eighteenth and nineteenth centuries who were heroes into ideologues.[25] The urgency is due not only to history, but also to philosophy itself, to the fact that the crisis of the West has at its roots certain philosophical options that are generally accepted and that require reconsideration and debate.

The Crisis of Political Philosophy

The three historical elements that constitute the context of Strauss's thought are the weakness of liberal democracy, its failures, and its consequences. This weakness is at the same time a given reality and a challenge. It is not historical events that determine and contextualize the thought of Strauss;

rather, certain historical shocks call for probity[26] in the sense of intellectual probity that requires, in philosophy, the suspension of religious belief and ideological commitment. Contemporary man is caught in a vice that makes him perplexed in the religious and political spheres and requires him to rethink the relationship between tradition and modernity. This situation makes the philosopher a contemporary of Nietzsche, thinking and writing in the full presence of nihilism and susceptible of falling into a sort of critique that reduces systems of thought and theoretical stances to acts of will and to reactive moves by the disempowered and resentful. Aware of these conditions, Strauss decided not to add to the human heritage a work that would be a further expression or symptom of the crisis of our times.

While the thought of Husserl and Max Weber is important, it does not provide the means necessary to think through the crisis of our times. The former thought, which is confined to the "humanism" articulated in *The Crisis of the European Sciences*, interprets the crisis as a problem of method.[27] Husserl thinks, like Strauss, that the European crisis is rooted in a certain error of rationalism.[28] But his solution is fidelity to the contemplative character of Greek *theoria*: Husserl wants *more* reason, while Strauss seeks *another* definition of reason that reconnects the fundamental teaching of Plato with political philosophy. As far as Max Weber is concerned, one cannot avoid Strauss's judgment in *Natural Right and History* that, in inviting every individual to obey his own god or demon,[29] Weber stands behind relativism, that is, decisionism. And the opposition between these two thinkers concerns the nature of modernity as a rupture or break with the tradition. Strauss develops the thesis of a twofold revolt against the ancient idea of nature and revealed religion, setting himself off from the interpretation of Weber. The latter, true to German idealism, thinks that modernity comes from the rationalization of Christianity: traditional values cease to be authoritative once religion and politics acquire a certain autonomy. Strauss rejects this schema of continuity. For him, Christianity is not, so to speak, at the right level for thinking through the rupture between Ancients and Moderns. It will be necessary to reopen the quarrel between orthodoxy and the Enlightenment, returning to the level at which the conflict is originally joined, that is, in putting in question whether modern biblical criticism has refuted orthodoxy and in scrutinizing the rationalism that underpins the Enlightenment critique of Revelation.

It is thus not against Weber that Strauss will measure himself but rather Heidegger. The latter alone has responded to Nietzsche and undertaken a critique of modernity, but his notion of "resoluteness" will come to explain his adhesion to National Socialism.[30] Moreover, Strauss does not find in the Hölderin-inspired notion of the last god[31] the solution of the crisis. His beginning hypothesis is equally different from that of Heidegger: he considers that the current difficulties have their origin in *modern* political thought and not in the metaphysics that emerges from Greek philosophy.

Strauss does not imagine a return pure and simple to the Ancients, but asks what ancient philosophy can provide to us, what we can learn *from* it and not simply about it. What is the meaning of the freedom and membership in a collectivity that we have lost and that Aristotelian rationalism could permit us to rediscover? The question of the return of Strauss to Maimonides is more complex, in that the latter thinker is the representative of orthodoxy for the Jewish religion and Strauss, contra Guttmann, that modern Judaism is superior to the Jewish philosophy of the Middle Ages. This goes to the heart of the thought of Maimonides and is the basis for its pertinence, namely the notion of Law as the totality of social, political, and religious life. To take up this question again is for Strauss a way of restating the theological-political problem, rescuing it from the forgetfulness that began with the first wave of modernity.

The originality of Strauss is to claim that modern tyranny, which threatens democracy militarily from the outside and corrupts it from the inside, has its origin in a concept of the political that is detached from reflection on the end of man, on what is good or bad for purposes of a human existence that is worthy of the name. In other words, "the crisis of our times is a crisis of political philosophy." It is linked to the replacement of classical political philosophy, inseparable from the question of the end of man, with a political teaching where justice is based on the rights of the individual and is a matter of guaranteeing these rights and reconciling the rights of each with those of all in order to achieve civil peace. But this external harmony may be accompanied by an individualism and an unsociability that sap the foundations of the republic. Thus, in the political thought inaugurated by Machiavelli and Hobbes, the state serves to guarantee the happiness of man, not to teach and provide him with the means for excellence.[32] There is a break between Ancients and Moderns. Modern thinking is characterized by a forgetfulness of the question that, in the tradition, belongs at the same time to religion, philosophy, and politics. It is thus not a matter of finding an alternative to nihilism by declaring, "Where danger is, Grows the saving power also"[33] but of displaying the archeology of nihilism in order the grasp it at the roots and extirpate it.

Strauss understands nihilism as the result of the Enlightenment, which is a historical path of modernity that began in the fifteenth century and presented itself in three waves. To deconstruct the modern religious consciousness and bring to light the assumptions of political liberalism constitute the first chapters of this archeology of nihilism. The confrontation with the pre-modern way of things makes it possible to be aware of these assumptions and to see where lies the rupture between the Ancients and the Moderns. The history of philosophy is thus an indispensable means. It permits an escape from the second cave[34] that was dug below that of Plato: not only is our initial condition that of the prisoners of the cave described in Plato's *Republic*, but, in addition, modern thinking prevents us from noticing the assumptions on which our claims depend. The horizon of the history of philosophy is a propaedeutic to political philosophy. The latter is, for Strauss, the future and the beginning of philosophy.

Besides the aspect of deconstruction and critique, Strauss provides a positive contribution to philosophy. It consists in the studies that he undertook on the notion of Law in the Jewish and Arab philosophers of the Middle Ages. Representing a totality of human life at the same time social, religious, and political, this notion is precisely what has been forgotten by the Moderns.[35] The reopening of the quarrel of Ancients and Moderns is always, for Strauss, an occasion for engaging in the critique of modernity, but his profound knowledge of the Jewish and Arab philosophers of the Middle Ages permitted him to revise his understanding of the gap that exists between modern and ancient rationalism. The notion of Law, originating with Plato's *Laws*, supposes a rationalism that is welcoming to Revelation, or that reason is not in opposition to that which is *supra rationem*. This rationalism leads to a questioning of the modern belief in the capacity of man to take care of himself all alone, without the aid of the tradition. The Moderns thought that a society based on the individual pursuit of pleasure was possible. At a moment in history when this belief is considered an illusion, it is possible to ask whether Enlightenment might not be medieval. What should one think, then, of a rationalism that is equally a critique of the limits of reason? Does it really offer the possibility of linking tradition and modernity? While the interest of Strauss for Maimonides and Farabi, for whom political philosophy is an aspect of prophetology,[36] is not motivated by the defense of theocratic state, it is possible that the difficulties encountered by liberal democracy could be clarified through thought that would appear alien to the modern world altogether.

The reformulation of the theological-political problem is thus the occasion for connecting the ethical, the religious, and the political in a new way that affirms the political character of philosophy. The originality of Strauss in relation to the main currents of thought that characterized his century derives precisely from the status conferred on political philosophy. From Descartes to Husserl, it is the isolated individual who provides the key to the intelligibility of the world. Of course, the ego for Descartes is not the foundation of being and depends on God, and in Husserl, transcendental subjectivity, distinct from ordinary subjectivity, is in the last analysis intersubjectivity. But these philosophers never speak of the city as a matrix[37] from which human beliefs derive. By contrast, Strauss, who begins his career in opposing the idea of method that is dear to neo-Kantians, challenges the status afforded to consciousness in all modern philosophy. To concentrate on the figure of Socrates, and to adopt his mode of questioning, is to think of man in relation to his community. The political is primary in the sense that is the point of departure.

The great thinkers of the twentieth century did not build systems in the sense that Hegel built one, integrating human history into a greater logic that illuminates reality as a whole and renders it completely rational. Continuing to interpret the world in order to be able to express its logic, a world that appears more and more resistant to the need for coherence that animates our reasoning, they developed paths of access to reality. Consciousness, experience, and existence were dedicated as the privileged sites of access to reality. The phenomenologists, in breaking with the neo-Kantians, who thought that first awareness of things was determined by science, deepened the role of consciousness as Descartes had first understood it. The successors of Husserl had the ambition to describe more radically than he the way in which things are given to us, insisting on the relation with another or on the strict interdependency that exists between body and soul, man and world or history; they wrote books differing in style, but that in the last analysis constitute a collective project. Whether the phenomenologists distill experience as it is lived by a subject or they deconstruct, along with Heidegger, the metaphysics of subjectivity in bringing out the temporal dimension of our *Dasein*, analyzing its finitude and facticity, it remains no less true that, for them, philosophy does not in the first instance integrate the political into its sphere of activity, but rather refines the perception each individual has of the phenomena. Even if the phenomenologists no longer think of man in terms of an individual who makes a representation of the world, they do not conceive of man's being in the world in terms of primordial belonging to the city.

Phenomenology is capable of having a political orientation. One could even create, beginning from a philosophy such as that of Levinas, an ethics that is open to the political. One can also say that the fact of conceiving man as alone and without an external justification for his existence (Sartre), because there are not a priori any norms that transcend the individual that could constrain his action, and that he is only "that which he makes," encourages engagement with the forces of historical revolution. But, contrary to appearances, this connection between philosophical positions and political orientation is not essential; we are dealing with political opinions that can be legitimized by philosophy rather than political philosophy. Because the point of departure of phenomenology is not the individual as embedded in the community, its questioning is not, like that of Socrates, a questioning-together concerning our living-together, as Strauss wrote in "Cohen und Maimuni" ("Cohen and Maimonides"). The phenomenologists did not go down into the Platonic cave. They themselves began with the roof, not with the foundation.[38] They did not make philosophy into an exercise that examines what happens in the city, where opinions and interests compete with one another. Their reality derived from a world reconstructed by abstraction and more homogenous than that of the city, where individuals do not have direct access to the universal. They failed to imagine that prejudices woven by history would impede access to the truth or that the philosophers themselves would be incapable of thinking through the modern world.

By contrast, Strauss asserts that the task of theory is inseparable from the elaboration of a political philosophy whose precondition is the putting in question of modern assumptions. It is a matter of examining the manner in which he undertakes a critique of liberal democracy that does not, however, lead to the rejection of liberal democracy or of the entire heritage of the modern Enlightenment itself.[39] While Schmitt, in his critique of liberalism, does not succeed in overcoming the nihilism that he condemns, Strauss invites us to ask whether it is not in dispassionately confronting non-modern thought that we will be able to undertake a constructive critique of modernity. Far from conceiving of a return to the past pure and simple, Strauss indicates what in the tradition is able to provide *us* with illumination and how we can save liberal democracy from itself.

Modern Rationalism as the Destruction of Reason

The task of philosophy is delineated through reflection on the relationship that exists between political philosophy and the opinions that prevail in the city. Philosophy is political because is first: it is the point of departure for a reflection that transcends it and puts in question a large part of its claims. Man belongs to a community that is the site where his opinions as well as his attachments are formed and the source from which all knowledge is born. Two questions drive our inquiry: To what extent is the problematic of Strauss our own? Is it true that the future of the West depends on its capacity to reexamine the heritage of the Enlightenment and to connect modernity and tradition?

Let us begin from the confrontation of Strauss with the theological-political problem as taught by Spinoza. The relation to Spinoza, the origin of the Enlightenment that recognizes itself in his thought, is displaced when the quarrel between Ancients and Moderns cannot be definitively resolved in favor of the Moderns. What have we gained by Spinoza's critique of superstition, and what have we lost in that separation of religion and knowledge that relegates the former to a political instrument useful in achieving civil piece? Is religion really useful only from the point of view of the state? Is faith merely the refuge of the ignorant?

This questioning of Spinoza provides an occasion for Strauss to confront the Jewish thinkers who preceded him, in particular Mendelssohn and Cohen, but also contemporaries like Rosenzweig and Guttmann. Mendelssohn, who represents the middle road between tradition and modernity, belongs to the Moderate Enlightenment. For Strauss and his contemporaries, this middle road is a dead end. The Moderate Enlightenment sooner or later yields to the radical Enlightenment. The engagement with Cohen is of central importance, to the extent that Cohen represents the synthesis between German philosophy and Judaism and his defense of the religion of reason underlines his adherence to the Enlightenment and to the intellectual universe with which Strauss parted company early in his career. Cohen affirmed the primacy of the ethical, for which Strauss criticized modern philosophy more generally. But if Strauss, like other Jewish philosophers of his time, belonged to a movement critical of modernity and is convinced of the necessity of a return to the tradition, he must be distinguished from Franz Rosenzweig. The latter could be said to represent the "new thinking," the promise and possibility not only of an alternative between orthodoxy and atheism but of another way, novel and liberating, at least for those caught between modernity and a return to the faith of their fathers, between the subjective experience of God and belonging to a community that is held together by history, text, and ritual. The problem of knowing where to look to in the tradition remains in its entirety: Must one turn toward mysticism, as did Scholem, or, instead, toward rationalism? Does knowledge remain, like in the case of Maimonides, the site of one's relation to God, or instead do the philosophers, in their appropriation of the tradition, always begin from a human experience of the Absolute, the meaning of which they decipher in light of Talmudic and biblical texts (Levinas and Rosenzweig)?

The background of these philosophical investigations concerning Judaism is related to the debates surrounding Zionism and assimilation, which are two strictly human solutions to the Jewish question that one finds in the *Theologico-political Treatise* of Spinoza. The thought of Strauss rapidly goes beyond the specific context of Judaism. It then becomes a matter of posing the question of the future of liberal religion, that is, of a religion that identifies itself as an ethical teaching. The analysis of the critique of religion by Spinoza and Hobbes, who are the representatives of the radical Enlightenment and whose differences are of as much significance as their similarities, provides the opportunity to gauge the heritage of the Enlightenment, its permanent legacy, that is, its impact on the entire religious consciousness, including on the new orthodoxy. But the heart of the debate concerns rationalism. What is the demarcation line between Ancients and Moderns? What is the conception of reason and of man that underpins ancient rationalism and the sustained tension between reason and Revelation that is the basis of the philosophical critique of reason that one finds in Maimonides? What is at the core of the modern belief in reason, and how do the fundamental positions of the Moderns, which Strauss calls assumptions, come to lead to the destruction or the hatred of reason? Here we make the transition to Part II, which is at the same time a decomposition of the modern political consciousness, an examination of the assumptions that follow the reconstruction by Strauss of the logic of modern thought unfolding in three waves, and an indication of the way in which he understands the challenge of the crisis of the West. We shall see to what extent Strauss's thought is an introduction to the political philosophy of the future.

Having deconstructed the modern religious consciousness, Strauss shows the assumptions on which the modern conception of the state and the political depends. Machiavelli inaugurates the first wave of modernity and removes from the domain of the political all philosophical reflection on the best regime (*politeia*), which is the regime that allows man to achieve excellence and lead the good life, in conformity with his proper end. Hobbes is at the origin of two fundamental currents in modern politics: liberalism and absolutism. The priority accorded to subjective rights and to liberty as the absence of constraint characterizes Hobbes's analysis of political obligation and distinguishes it at the same time from the classic tradition and from modern republicanism. As for absolutism, it has its source in Hobbes's theory of sovereignty. Finally the character of the law changes beginning with Hobbes: it no longer has as its function to guide human beings towards virtue, but only to create the conditions under which the subjects can pursue their individual objectives in order to attain an exclusively earthly and private happiness. The state has as its function to create what Constant would call much later "modern liberty."[40] It is at the core of this critical reflection on political liberalism but also on the type of life and society that it promotes that the question of secularization arises as utilization of biblical morality for ends contrary to the spirit of the Bible. The confrontation between Schmitt and Strauss, both of whom reconsider Hobbes and who regret the fate of the political in liberalism and the appearance of a new barbarism coinciding with the era of technology, allows us to indicate the specificity of Strauss's thought and what is really at stake in his reopening of the theological-political problem.

Here we see what distinguishes Strauss from the decisionism of Schmitt, and also from the thought of Heidegger, with whom Strauss had a lifetime confrontation. The criticisms Strauss addresses to these thinkers are so many ways for Strauss to probe how one can stand up to the challenge of nihilism, from which no thinker since Nietzsche has been able to escape. Strauss thinks, like Schmitt, that a critical reflection on the role of the state and the political demands an in-depth study of the philosophical, political, and anthropological stances of Hobbes. But the question is above all that of the connection between theology and politics. While Revelation goes hand in hand with a conception of man as an ambiguous being, the Enlightenment defends the idea of man's rational autonomy. Secularization achieves a process in the course of which the ideal of the infinite potency of the free self-determination of man is affirmed as an unquestionable principle. We must see what kind of man and what society the modern political thinkers wrought in refusing to link political decisions to philosophical inquiry. This question leads us to interpret the opposition between classical political philosophy and modern political thought. What did the study of the Jewish and Arabic philosophers of the Middle Ages bring to Strauss's understanding of classical political philosophy and his interpretation of Plato and Aristotle? How is it that Maimonides and Farabi are more faithful than we are to the Greek heritage? How can one understand the enigmatic formula according to which liberal democracy, which was born in the theological-political tracts of Spinoza and Hobbes, has its foundations in pre-modern thinking and will be saved by pre-modern thinking? Does that mean that there was a forgetting, a forgetfulness of an essential dimension that is akin to the soul of liberal democracy, that prevents liberty from degenerating into license and that provides the foundation for a just political community, one not characterized exclusively by external liberty or by the simple defense of human rights? What is lacking in human rights so that they can promote a truly just society?

The question of rationalism, which emerges with the debates over pantheism and the French Revolution, and which is, with Jacobi, the beginning point of our study, is revisited in Part II. We attempt to understand the logic that leads to the foundation of liberal democracy and its destruction by communism and fascism, which have their origins, respectively, in the first two waves of modernity and in the last one. In this history, which is the history of self-destruction, something essential has been forgotten. And this forgetfulness, characteristic of modern political thought, which consciously breaks with modern political philosophy, will become in the successors of Machiavelli, Rousseau, and Nietzsche a sort of blindness. This process, inseparable from the acceleration of modernity, leads to ever-greater divergence with political philosophy.

The Archeology and Overcoming of Nihilism

Heidegger thinks that technology is our destiny, the end point of metaphysics, that is, a forgetfulness of Being, which retreats. The essence of Being, the coming-into-presence and its essential origin since the *aletheia* as Event (*Ereignis*), recedes. The essence of the *aletheia* becomes inaccessible to perception and incapable of representation.[41] This retreat is evident since Plato. Strauss is not wrong to think that Heidegger is a historicist or that his thought is a symptom of the decline of the West, assuming that what he means by that is that Heidegger, who thinks that Being itself is subordinate to history, has a certain obsession with the fate of the West. Heidegger reverts to poetry, because poetic speech avoids the way of thinking characterized by calculation, in thinking Being in relation to the Entity (*Seiendes*) or being blind to ontological difference. But the solution that Heidegger provides is not a victory over nihilism. In maintaining the distinctiveness of philosophy from any form of *Weltanschauung* and in defending political philosophy, does Strauss allow us to emerge from the crisis of the West and to overcome nihilism?

We think that Strauss, in reconstructing the history of modernity beginning from the quarrel between the Ancients and Moderns, and in characterizing this history as the forgetfulness of the meaning of Law as the philosophers of the Jewish and Arab Middle Ages understood it, suggests a possible alternative to nihilism. That is the meaning of the political philosophy whose method and some aspects of whose substance we examine in the final chapter of this book. This chapter occurs in the second part, because Strauss himself did not elaborate a political philosophy for the future, but rather indicated its foundations and prepared it. To take apart the modern religious and political consciousness and to indicate, through the analysis of Maimonides's rationalism and an examination of the meaning of the Socratic turn, what has been forgotten, is what constitutes this preparation. But if modernity is self-destructive because something essential has been forgotten, this means that the return to pre-modern thinkers can be the occasion to reexamine and to bring to life that very thing that was forgotten and considered to be surpassed, and to rethink it.

Such an interpretation suggests that the thought of Strauss already offers a positive contribution to the foundations of a political philosophy of the future. This requires that we understand the Straussian reading of the history of philosophy as nonfatalistic. This is why the difference between Heidegger and Strauss is of capital importance. Strauss engages with Heidegger because it is Heidegger who took seriously Nietzsche's critique of rationalism and the modern belief in reason. We shall have to see to what extent political philosophy accomplishes the Nietzschean aspiration of an overcoming of nihilism, while not speaking in terms of the end of metaphysics or proposing a solution that is to be found outside the West.

Strauss reconstructs the debates of the Enlightenment at the same time that he cultivates an openness to Greek thought and the discovery of the Jewish and Arab philosophy of the Middle Ages. But why is he concerned with the Jewish and Arab Middle Ages rather than the Christian Middle Ages? The rejection of liberal theology is a common preoccupation of Jewish (F. Rosenzweig) and Christian (K. Barth) thinkers. This debate is the context that allows us to understand the Straussian critique of the Enlightenment, but also the dialogue of the deaf with Cassirer, the rejection of neo-Kantianism, and the disagreement with Spinoza. Does not the latter, in rebuilding religion on the foundation of morality, justify Nietzsche in speaking of Christianity as a morality of *ressentiment*? Like the author of *Joyful Wisdom*, Strauss critiques Christianity, viewed as the origin of nihilism. But does nihilism have the same meaning for Strauss than it does for Nietzsche? And if Strauss's tone is less polemical than Nietzsche's, does this mean that his attack against the universe of thought responsible for modern prejudices is less radical in its attack on the morality of the New Testament? This "attack" occurs at the end of a lecture titled "Cohen and Maimonides," when Strauss opposes the Pauline conception of Law in the *Epistle to the Romans*, I, 20, to that which is common not only to the Jewish and Islamic world but also to that of the Greeks. There is among the Jewish and Arab philosophers and in Plato the idea of a divine Law that is rational, because it is capable of rational understanding, but that has a suprahuman origin. Does Strauss think that nihilism is a consequence of Christianity—the result of the application of categories originating in Christianity, such as subjectivism and the separation of the temporal and the spiritual, to a world where Christianity and even the spiritual have lost their authority?

What is the meaning of the notion according to which forgetfulness characterizes modern thought and can explain the destructive logic of the Enlightenment? If Strauss does not believe that a return to a perfect political order is possible, and if he continues to defend liberal democracy, he thinks nonetheless that modern religious consciousness and the modern conception of the political must be deconstructed. There is, in the modern Enlightenment, a notion that is of Christian origin that has estranged us from Plato, but also from political philosophy. We must examine this judgment and ask what it is that Strauss calls the pre-modern Enlightenment. Strauss wrote in a letter to Scholem[42] that his book on Hobbes was an introduction to *The Guide for the Perplexed*. Does this entail that, after having analyzed the assumptions of the Moderns in the religious and political domains, we believe that we can attain Enlightenment from Maimonides?

We examine thus the tension between Athens and Jerusalem, that is, the philosophy that Strauss wants to promote. Maimonides is the representative of this tension between two opposite poles of our culture. What kind of relationship between tradition and modernity does Strauss have in mind? Not only does the distance between Strauss in relation to other thinkers of his times achieve its ultimate clarification, but also Maimonides implies that we have to pose again the question of esotericism. We rediscover, but not as an assumption or an a priori methodology, at a stage where the relationship between the problems and what is at stake has been analyzed, the question of esotericism, which is that of the ambivalent status of philosophy but also of the truth. What gap between man and the city, the philosopher and the man of action, knowledge, and power, follows from the philosophy of Maimonides? Can a society do without religion, or, alternatively, does the gap between a small number of wise men and a large number of non-wise require a noble lie? Finally, once the task of thought has been elucidated and the foundations of a political philosophy have been laid, can one say that philosophy is the best form of expression of the truth? How to speak to the city? How can the philosopher who, following Socrates, returns to the *endoxa*, can communicate to other human beings a thought that is the transformation of their opinions and experiences? Will this not seem strange and dangerous? What is poetry for a human being who is invited to "live with Plato"? Is it simply a cloak for thought, a pedagogical tool, and something that should be subject to political control? Or would it be surprising if poetry *also* were a site of truth, to the extent that, at Jerusalem as at Athens, truth is rational and suprarational, and that poetry participates in the exposition of the truth, just as do historical fables, discourse, and narration?

Part I

The Dissection of the Modern Religious Consciousness

But while man takes pleasure in this honest and legitimate search for well-being, it is to be feared that he will finally lose the use of his most sublime faculties, and that by wishing to improve everything around him, he will finally degrade himself. The peril is there, not elsewhere.

Legislators of democracies and all honest and enlightened men who live in them must therefore apply themselves relentlessly to raising up souls and keeping them turned toward Heaven. It is necessary for all those who are interested in the future of democratic societies to unite, and for all in concert to make continuous efforts to spread within these societies a taste for the infinite, a sentiment of greatness, and a love of immaterial pleasures.

—Alexis de Tocqueville, *Democracy in America*,
trans. H. C. Mansfield and D. Winthrop
(Chicago: University of Chicago Press, 2000), pp. 518–519

Introduction

The Perplexity of the Modern Religious Consciousness

The modern religious consciousness is perplexed. Religion means at the same time a tradition linked to texts and rituals, a community of believers, and a personal relationship to transcendence. And we have been witnessing, since the beginning of the nineteenth century, a movement toward the internalization of faith that empties religion of all content and that is able to live off the most peripheral forms of tradition, reducing Judaism to a Jewishness without content or merely folkloric in character and Christianity to a morality of respect. The result of the separation of public and private spheres, which emerged in 1670 in the *Theological-Political Treatise* of Spinoza as a solution to religious war in Europe and one of the pillars of liberal democracy, is not only that freedom of thought and scientific progress have been protected from religious censure. Religion itself has been detached from knowledge to the point of being identified with superstition, a resort of the ignorant, or a morality that is a panacea that serves to keep the ignorant in security and under control. This internalization of the content of faith can equally accompany irrationalism—because the believer no longer has the support of the knowledge of texts and the practice of rituals—and bring about new forms of religious syncretism where individuals explore in a random way various mystical traditions. Ultimately, those who maintain the content and form of Revelation have difficulty believing in miracles, and they presuppose a notion of God different from that of the Bible, which means that they allow the Enlightenment to triumph, and they have absorbed the biblical criticism of the Enlightenment. In this path of a compromise between reason and Revelation, one is compelled to say that the former has more to gain than the latter, which acquires a constrained meaning, as in Mendelssohn.

Everything occurs as if believers were in an untenable position, which condemns them to a compromise between the tradition and their conscience. The latter is a thoroughly modern notion.[1] It is, contrary to classical thought, ancient cosmology, and the ideal of the prophets, the departure point or the Archimedean point of modern thought, including when it concerns God, which is already a way of reducing to nothingness the question of Revelation. The latter supposes that one does not understand everything beginning from the human. God becomes a reality postulated by consciousness, even when the latter is constrained to make its own critique and to recognize that certain objects are relative to the subjective conditions of its functioning and that the question of their existence remains unanswerable. The content of consciousness is as given to it by the Enlightenment and its rationalism. It is no, then, surprise that atheism would be easier to defend than faith. It is more in conformity with the method and presuppositions of the modern consciousness. Moreover, Strauss, after Nietzsche, refers to an atheism from probity in order to designate the refusal of the Moderns to base morality, science, and philosophy on transcendent values. But this refusal is the proof that the Moderns have elevated science to the rank of an absolute value.

The birth of the philosophy of religion in the nineteenth century bears witness to this need to justify religion and the religious consciousness before the criteria generated in the name of science. Beginning with Schleiermacher, religion is considered as a product of human culture. Liberal protestant theology is an attempt to reconcile divine Revelation and human culture. But in humanizing and secularizing the original meaning of Revelation, it leads to what Rosenzweig, in 1914, called an "atheist theology."[2] To make Jesus into the incarnation of human perfection or the chosen people into a symbol of the ideal community of humanity is to weaken the meaning of Revelation. Secularization already implies atheism, because the moral autonomy of man is affirmed as against "the endlessly renewed miracle of Revelation." Like the author of the *Star of Redemption*, Karl Barth, in his preface to the second edition of his *Commentary on the Epistle to the Romans* in 1922, will make unconditional adherence to the word of God the heart of his theology. For Strauss, secularization leads necessarily to atheism in virtue of a destructive dialectic specific to modern Enlightenment. Like Rosenzweig and Scholem, he is part of that movement of return to the tradition that begins by contesting that in modernity and scientific reason which is threatening for this tradition. It is thus a matter of dissecting the modern religious consciousness and revealing its presuppositions in order to know whether the modern

Enlightenment has definitively won the battle and if it is true that religion has been surpassed or, rather, if it is not the form of modern rationality that has buried it. Is atheism part of the fate of the West, is it the sign of an achievement, or, rather, is not the result of an unconscious choice, that is, of a prejudice? Is the death of God progress or denial?

The *Theological-Political Treatise* of Spinoza had opened up the path to liberal democracy and religious tolerance, and the French Revolution had been followed by the emancipation of the Jews who believed themselves assimilated and recognized by other nations. It nevertheless remains true that the principle of interpretation by the Enlightenment of the religious phenomenon condemns the latter to disappear. Such is the meaning of the critiques that Strauss addresses to *Wissenschaft des Judentums*, which, transforming Judaism into an object of the understanding, is not adequate to assure its continuation. This is what is at stake in Strauss's rejection of historicism and progressivism in the social sciences. The rejection of the philosophy of culture, dear to Cassirer, and the fact that, for Strauss, the work of the historian cannot be divorced from a philosophical interrogation implying judgments of value, are marks of this reflection on the dialectic of the Enlightenment. These questions, which concern the Christian as well as the Jewish world, are equally at the center of the debates concerning Zionism and assimilationism. The discussions that took place concerning the Jewish problem, Strauss's abandonment of the Zionist solution, then his effort to think through, like Rosenzweig, but also, against him, a return to the tradition, which would not be a forgetting of this tradition, are a playing out of this questioning of the problematic legacy of the modern Enlightenment.

Believers cannot return to the religion of their ancestors because of the changes that have occurred between their own time and that of their ancestors.[3] The new orthodoxy that appears at the end of the 1920s and serves as a context for Strauss's questioning is incomprehensible without the debate concerning the Enlightenment. It is at the same time a questioning concerning the legacy of the Enlightenment, a means of incorporating certain critiques addressed to the old orthodoxy, and a struggle against the excessive internationalization of the content of the faith that prepares the way for atheism. But the task of a reflection on the legacy of the Enlightenment presents itself also to the atheist camp. Even if one is a progressive, one cannot deny one's origins.[4] Reflection on the survival of a culture in a secularized world is all the more relevant given that the secular society of which Lessing dreamed does not seem to exist. Not only did assimilated Jews like Karl Löwith[5] discover in 1933 that, whatever they might do, they would always be outsiders, but as well one can ask if "a country where there would be neither Jew nor Christian" (Lessing) would be desirable. If differences can lead to discrimination, does the homogenization of society and the absence of all reference to transcendence allow human beings to live in peace and participate in collective life with a feeling of solidarity with the fate of their fellow citizens? The possibility of a secular society is not obvious. Secular morality is not obvious, because the question of knowing whether a human being can do good when he or she does not believe in God has remained unanswered since Nietzsche, even while, as a political matter, one thinks, like Bayle, that a republic of atheists is possible. Similarly, the question of whether human rights are adequate to guarantee respect of the values that make just the lives we lead, individually and collectively, retains all its relevance and makes it legitimate to reflect on the weaknesses of humanism. The examination of the ideals of the Enlightenment and of the relationship between reason and Revelation that it proposes is at the same time a putting in question, at least in part, of humanism and the effectiveness of human rights and a way of bringing to light the philosophical assumptions on which the freedom of the Moderns[6] depends.

This threefold questioning is what is at stake in the pantheism controversy, which is a radical attempt to return to the source of the problem, that is, to Spinoza. What has changed between ourselves and our ancestors, whether Jews or Christians, believers or atheists, is that there was Spinoza. What have we won and what have we lost with Spinoza? What conception of reason guides his philosophy? What is the rationalism of the Enlightenment? Is modern rationalism, false rationalism, a misconception of the notion of reason itself? These were the questions that from 1785 were at the center of the philosophical debate. They allow one to proceed to a critical examination of the legacy of the Enlightenment. Jacobi opened this debate in a period when all the philosophers of the Enlightenment seemed to say that Spinoza had won. This is why it is necessary, in order to understand the Straussian critique of the Enlightenment, to begin by discussing the legacy of the Spinozist Enlightenment as it appeared in the time of Jacobi, with Lessing and Mendelssohn. Because it is this legacy that Strauss inherited, in working on Lessing and Mendelssohn and in encountering Cohen and Cassirer, and it was on Jacobi that Strauss chose to write his dissertation.

Strauss went on to conduct an examination of modernity on the basis of a reconstruction of the Enlightenment that brings to light the break between Ancients and Moderns. This perspective explains his focus on Spinoza, whose definition of reason and of the human being is more likely to underline the break between Ancients and Moderns than, for example, thought like that of Hume or Reid. And Jacobi saw that. This is why, to understand Strauss, it is necessary to begin with the philosopher of the Anti-Enlightenment and with the debates that took place in this domain of German thought. Further, Strauss develops his thought in reaction to the reading of the Enlightenment by the neo-Kantians and by the German Idealists; he discusses at the same time their appropriation of certain ideas originating in the Enlightenment, such as the synthesis between philosophy and religion that one finds in Mendelssohn, and in radicalizing their doubts concerning the problematic heritage of the Enlightenment, doubts expressed by Hermann Cohen, from whom Strauss borrows the idea of a return to the tradition that requires the overcoming of Spinoza. And all these questions are at the heart of the pantheism controversy provoked by Jacobi.

Chapter 1

Enlightenment and Anti-Enlightenment

The Jacobi Question

It is not by accident that Strauss begins his philosophical career with an interest in Jacobi (1743–1819). His thesis on the problem of knowledge in Jacobi is a way of countering the analysis of Cassirer and undertaking, starting in 1921, a critique of the rationalism of the Enlightenment that allows him to propose a different path than that of neo-Kantianism. Moreover, Jacobi attempts, beginning from the pantheism debate and the controversy concerning the Spinozism of Lessing, a theory of philosophy itself. This means that the concepts and the names of the philosophers themselves will serve, as in Nietzsche, as devices for thinking through the crisis of the West and nihilism. This also means that Jacobi represents a problem or a set of problems that concern the critic of reason.

Far from being, as for Kant and Cassier, a representative of anti-rationalism, Jacobi is, in Strauss's eyes, the decisive and original figure of the internal critique of rationalism. This is why his analysis concerns, in the first instance, Jacobi's concept of reason: instead of making Jacobi into one of the *Schwärmerei* or a partisan of illuminism, which would be to conflate the German and French Enlightenments, Strauss sees what is at stake in Jacobi's distinction between understanding and reason. The understanding (*Der Verstand*) thinks objects, but it is not their source. By contrast, reason (*Vernunft*) is the locus of the revelation of being. It is, along with perception (*Wahrnehmung*), a mode of knowledge where reality is received, as we are reminded by the verb *vernehmen*.[7] The object, far from depending on our understanding, which only organizes that which is given outside of it, is transcendent.[8]

The authentic rationalism that Jacobi wants to advance is opposed to the false rationalism of the Enlightenment, where reason is a flame that illuminates experience. The Enlightenment, which makes perception into an intellectual construction and belief in the reality of the object into a conclusion of reason, does not see the function of revelation and the receptivity of reason. It collapses into speculative egoism and idealism. These are philosophies of representation. By contrast, he who says, "I am not Cartesian" defends a hypercritical irrationalism and affirms as against Kant the existence of the thing-in-itself, but this philosophy of belief or non-philosophy goes hand in hand with realism, in which it is experience that illumines reason. This dimension distinguishes the Anti-Enlightenment of Jacobi from illuminism.[9] His concept of reason is not only a weapon against the Enlightenment, but is a way of suggesting that reason is related to revelation and supposes it. Reason feels that which it grasps, for is already there. It is not the site where being pronounces itself in the logos but rather where it trusts in feeling. Reason and understanding suppose sense, and reason designates the sense of the suprasensual.

In forging this notion, Jacobi radicalizes the conflict between the Enlightenment and orthodoxy, rejecting the Kantian solution. The rationalism of the Enlightenment, the conception of reason which is that of philosophy since Aristotle, where it is assimilated to the understanding, leads to atheism. The strategy of demonstrations of God's existence is nothing but a last resort, masking the fact that the consequences of a coherent rationalism, just as appear in Spinoza, are the negation of human freedom and the critique of the biblical conception of God. Natural theology, of which Lessing appears to be the outstanding example, is a mirage. In Straussian terms, it signifies that there is no such thing as the moderate Enlightenment, or that the moderate Enlightenment, represented by Mendelssohn, is destined to be captured and overcome by the radical Enlightenment. And it is in the guise of a conflict between Jacobi and Mendelsohn that the pantheism controversy will break open and put in the center of philosophical debate the system of Spinoza. This is because the problem is that "Orthodoxy could be returned to only if Spinoza was wrong in every respect."[10] Ultimately, it is a matter of knowing to which orthodoxy one should return. Is revelation internal, existential (Jacobi/Kierkegaard), or must it be based on biblical Revelation (Wizenmann)? Likewise, one could ask oneself if the return—or *teshuvah*—is a return to the Torah or simply to the culture that was founded by the Torah. Is it necessary to recognize that the new orthodoxy, in the end, has internalized the Enlightenment in opposing itself to the God of the tradition

(Cohen, Rosenzweig) or to revisit the teaching of Maimonides and the prophets (Cohen, Strauss)? Finally, one can pose the question of the place of mysticism (Scholem) in religious experience, which is the experience of a transcendent Call, to which religious doctrines give more or less adequate expression. For purposes of dissecting the modern religious consciousness, it is a matter of returning to Spinoza and the Enlightenment critique of orthodoxy.

Jacobi holds a threefold interest for Strauss. He demonstrates how the conflict between the Enlightenment and orthodoxy is a conflict between atheism and orthodoxy and that the debate has not been definitively resolved in favor of the Enlightenment. He avoids the Kantian solution of a religion within the limits of reason alone, permitting Strauss to overturn the neo-Kantianism of Cassirer. Finally, Jacobi stands for an internal critique of rationalism. In asking what conception of reason is at work in the Enlightenment, Jacobi is the first to say that philosophers of the Enlightenment have their own presuppositions and to put in question the truth of their system. This questioning opens up into a comparison between modern and classic rationalism, that is, into the question of knowing whether there is not a pre-modern Enlightenment. Thus "the Jacobi question" permits Strauss to reopen the quarrel of the Ancients and Moderns and ask whether Enlightenment is not essentially medieval.

After having discussed this heritage of the eighteenth-century Enlightenment at the same time as the pantheism controversy, and having shown the failure of the moderate Enlightenment, it will then be a matter of examining Strauss's reading of Spinoza's and Hobbes's critiques of Revelation. What is the legacy of this critique of the Bible? To what extent has it been accepted by the advocates of the new orthodoxy? Finally, what conception of reason and of man is at the foundation of modern rationalism and the theological-political problem as identified by the modern Enlightenment? All of these questions lead to an examination of the Straussian critique of the Enlightenment: What is it that permits Strauss to call the modern Enlightenment an obfuscation[11] and to say the modern rationalism has destroyed reason? Is it that Jacobi, because the task consists in securing and fully fathoming the problematic object by the reduction to the unquestionable conditions of its possibility,[12] grounds a philosophy of nothingness, fatalism, and atheism, and that only the *salto mortale* of faith and the heroism of belief will save man? Or, rather, is it necessary to return to the rationalism of Maimonides and an articulation of the theological and the political that the Moderns have forgotten?

The Pantheism Controversy

The Critique of Natural Religion

On the eve of the pantheism controversy (1780–1815), three positions were represented in the German Enlightenment: Lessing's theory of history, Kant's critical philosophy, and Mendelssohn's popular philosophy. Jacobi will attack these three figures and claim that their rationalism is unreasonable. The origin of the pantheism controversy is the religious philosophy of Lessing, whose *Education of the Human Race* appeared in 1780. Mendelssohn considers Lessing a partisan of rational religion who wishes to integrate Revelation into the exercise of reason and to reconcile finite consciousness with the divine Absolute. The stories of the Bible, dogmas, and rituals are the steps that allow man to understand, little by little, natural religion in its purity. Lessing explains, in paragraph 73 of his *Education of the Human Race*, that the concept of the Trinity is a way of grasping the idea of a God who does not exclude plurality. Natural religion, far from being identified with the content of a positive religion, conforms to reason. No revealed truth is definitively suprarational. The particular historical forms of religion are simply connected to the historical conditions of this rational religion.

This metaphysical humanism, where the taking into account of finitude does not exclude the search for the absolute, goes hand in hand with the message of tolerance in *Nathan the Wise* (1779). Inspired by Boccacio, the parable of the three rings invites us to recognize the equal legitimacy of the three monotheistic religions and constitutes an appeal for the respect of man as man. But this text, in which the principal character was inspired by Mendelssohn, breaks somewhat with Lessing's philosophical doctrine and his attempt to resolve the antimony between Leibniz and Spinoza. Lessing seeks a fully rational, fully coherent concept of God, thinkable and accessible by the finite mind. If God is absolute and infinite, how does He permit of being conceived by man? To this problem relating to the system of Spinoza, Lessing adds a difficulty represented by every conception of a transcendent God: how God the creator, the transcendent God of the Bible, can conform to the concept of absoluteness required by reason?

Lessing believed he had found the solution to this antinomy in the notion of subjectivity: the unity of the subject or of substance does not exclude the plurality of thinking. This solution would cause Mendelssohn to say that the Spinozism of Lessing is a "purified Spinozism" (*geläutert*), compatible with morality and religion. In Lessing, the system of Spinoza leads to the God of Leibniz, understood as monad of monads. Returning to the metaphor of the city, which one finds in paragraph 57 of the *Monadology*, if one conceives the divinity on a subjectivist model, one can think the totality of points of view without falling into pantheism, because this conception reconciles the unity of consciousness with the multiplicity of representations. Likewise, in Leibniz, human reason is a part of divine reason and revealed truths, which, *supra sed non contra rationem*, can be reconciled with the rationalism of natural religion. The problem is that Lessing denies to Revelation the heteronomy that constitutes its real meaning. Not only is this natural religion disembodied, but as well Mendelssohn—like Lessing and Spinoza—believes that reason is capable of self-grounding. He denies the irrational moment at the heart of reason itself that Jacobi calls Revelation. There is, says Jacobi, an abyss between this natural religion and positive religion. It is this abyss that is brought to light in addressing the "authentic Spinozism" (*authentisch*) of Lessing.

Jacobi met Lessing at Wolfenbüttel in 1780. It was in the course of a conversation with Jacobi that Lessing confided in him something he had not revealed to anyone, not even to his friend Mendelssohn. Jacobi read to him a poem by Goethe titled *Prometheus*. The rebellion of Prometheus is associated, according to Jacobi, with the Spinozism and pantheism of Goethe. What could be the religion of a free people? Could one believe in a transcendent God, creator of the world and benevolent, or is the God of Spinoza alone tenable? Lessing, in making Goethe's ode his own, said of Spinoza: "If I must put a label on myself, I don't see any other." Jacobi reported this statement of the late philosopher in a letter to Mendelssohn dated November 4, 1783.[13] Lessing would have said: "There is no philosophy but the philosophy of Spinoza." He denounced the heteronomy of positive religion and affirmed that man must put himself on the path of an authentic religion, in which progress will be characterized by the union of transcendence and immanence. He denied that there was a transcendent God, Providence, or salvation.

The revelation by Jacobi of Lessing's Spinozism launched the pantheism debate and provoked the indignation of Mendelssohn. Jacobi saw in Lessing a "convinced Spinozist": he is aware that the consequence of rationalism is a critique of the concept of the biblical God, the negation of human freedom or fatalism—which follows from a system that has eliminated final causes—and pantheism, which is the result of nihilism or constructivism that dissolves the object and subject of knowledge. Mendelssohn, for his part, had referred to a "purified Spinozism," cleansed of those elements undermining morality and religion.

Jacobi's revelation of the Spinozism of Lessing necessarily served to destroy the skillful compromise that the German Enlightenment had struck between philosophy and religion. And Moses Mendelssohn (1729–1786), German philosopher and Jewish thinker, incarnated this synthesis between the Western Enlightenment and Judaism. He was the greatest "model" for those Jewish thinkers who sought to give a modern expression to their tradition. Mendelssohn attempted to translate the elements specific to the Jewish tradition into the German language: he accommodated the thinking of the Law and of Revelation, which is at the foundation of the Jewish religious tradition within the framework of Western thought, and translated the Bible from Hebrew to German. Mendelssohn, who was close to the Wolffian theologians, in particular Baumgarten, sought to reintroduce the study of the Bible into a curriculum until then dominated by the study of Talmud and kabbalah. He privileged historical knowledge of the Bible, without neglecting the fact that religion served to console, to "edify," as he said by employing the term *Erbauung*, which is dear to Protestant thought and which assumes, among the supporters of the religious Enlightenment, a reconciliation between faith and reason.

Mendelssohn is part of that movement of the Enlightenment that seeks to construct the personality of the individual, in feeling as well as in reason, at the heart of a reasonable and tolerant religion. It is in his first work, *Philosophical Dialogues,* published in 1755 with the aid of Lessing, that he makes a synthesis between the philosophy of Wolff and religious belief. The three ideas of natural religion (belief in God, immortality of the soul, and Providence) are the core of this rational system, which includes a metaphysics, an epistemology, and an ethics. The existence of God is presupposed by this philosophy, but it is equally possible to demonstrate by reason. Finally, this "Socrates of Berlin" is also a man born at Dessau, one of the main centers of the *Haskala* movement. Moise Dessau Mendelssohn, the Germanized patronymic of Moses, son of Mendel, was an eminent representative of the Jewish Enlightenment. Concerned with liberating Ashkenazy Judaism from the intellectual ghetto in which Talmudic casuistry and the kabbalah had enclosed it, in particular after the Reform, he set for himself the task of encouraging the study of contemporary science and philosophy and promoting a rational comprehension of Jewish texts. Appearing in the third quarter of the eighteenth century, *Haskala* borrowed from the Enlightenment many of its forms and categories while drawing its substance from Jewish thought and biblical exegesis of the medieval Andalousian tradition. Mendelssohn embodies this original borrowing and adaptation of the Enlightenment problematic to the situation of Judaism. It is on account of this that the debate opened by the pantheism controversy is hurtful and worrying for him: it puts in question the confidence he had in Lessing. And the latter is no longer there to reassure him that differences of religious denomination will not be an obstacle to philosophical friendship and the progress of the Enlightenment. It was a "brother in Leibniz" that Mendelssohn felt he would lose if Jacobi succeeded in imposing his notion that Lessing was really a Spinozist.

The *Morning Hours,* only the first volume of which was published in Mendelssohn's lifetime,[14] focused on Lessing and could only allude to the debate with Jacobi. Mendelssohn wanted to reconcile Leibnizian-Wolffian philosophy, Judaism and English empiricism, from which his concept of common sense derives. After writing the first volume of *Morgenstunden,* he feared that the moderate Enlightenment could be compromised by materialism on the one side and by the *Schwärmerei* on the other. But the publication, at the same time, of the letters of Jacobi to Mendelssohn on Spinoza's doctrine was a shock. For two years, there had been exchanges of letters between Mendelssohn and Jacobi. The latter, through Elise Reimarus, had informed Mendelssohn concerning the Spinozism of Lessing. Herder, Hamann, Goethe, Lavater, and Reimarus were also immediately active in this discussion, either in suggesting that rationalism had shown its true colors (that is, the most scandalous atheism) or in minimizing the problem, reducing it to a minor accident on the Enlightenment journey. It is in this context that the *Berlinische Monatsschrift* published in 1784 articles by Mendelssohn and Kant on the question "What is Enlightenment?"

In publishing his correspondence with Mendelssohn, Jacobi brought this case before the public. His objective was to force everyone to choose his side and thereby to divide the Enlightenment against itself. He used Kant, who had limited the realm of knowledge in order to leave room for faith, to denounce the consequences of Lessing's rationalism and to unmask the contradictions in Mendelssohn's dogmatism (1785–1786). Then he went on to attack Kant himself as an inconsistent idealist (1786–1789). Finally, the *Pantheismusstreit* turned into the debate concerning the French Revolution (1789–1790). Until the beginning of the nineteenth century, the intellectual world would be under the shock of what Hegel described as a "thunderbolt," because a blow had been struck against the authority of the Enlightenment. The consequences of this upheaval, which will contribute to a reshuffling of the deck, both politically and philosophically, can be felt every time the meaning of Kant is reconsidered, for example, between Heidegger, who views the Kantian finitude as a break from the metaphysics of subjectivity that is the legacy of the Enlightenment, and Cassirer, who believes that Kantianism is the fulfillment of the Enlightenment. Ultimately, the question of the legacy of this critique of the Enlightenment will be posed by Nietzsche, a radical *Aufklärer*, who rejects the Romantic reaction against the Enlightenment as *ressentiment* and seeks a "new Enlightenment," but whose notion of "life" recalls the heroism, condemnation of doubt, and contempt of fear that are present in Jacobi.

There Is No Such Thing as Moderate Enlightenment

The debate that Jacobi provoked in speaking about the Spinozism of Lessing is an attack against the Enlightenment of Mendelssohn and his attempt to reconcile reason and Revelation: the natural religion of Lessing is disembodied, and the meaning that Mendelssohn assigns to the notion of Revelation is too weak. The natural religion of Lessing and the Judaism that Mendelssohn confines to legal obligation, which leave full freedom to the exercise of reason, have in common with Spinoza the belief that reason can be self-grounding, without the need of Revelation. The latter, in the strict sense, is heteronomous: it is received from the outside and is not immanent.

This is precisely Strauss's own objection to the moderate Enlightenment. In Mendelssohn, Revelation has a weak meaning: his God is a God who can be demonstrated by reason and who does not *require* Revelation. Soon one would be able, like Cohen, to speak of a religion of reason and to claim that Judaism was the fulfillment of Kantian morality. Messianism will have become the hope of a humanity progressing in moral goodness. Religion will be retained, thanks to the dimension of hope that it carries with it and that sustains the individual's striving toward goodness. It will be a complement to morality, but it will have been overcome as Law. This disappearance of religion as Law, which follows from the disappearance of the strong meaning of Revelation, is what Strauss rejects in the proponents of the moderate Enlightenment. The latter were playing with fire, because between the weak meaning of Revelation and its negation there is but a single step. Actually, there is no true moderate Enlightenment: it is to Spinoza that Mendelssohn's argument leads. Mendelssohn had sought to reconcile Revelation with reason, and he weakened the former to the point of making it useless. He had attempted to create a synthesis of the Jewish tradition with the Enlightenment, and he denied to his religion the notion of Law, which is the core of its distinctiveness. He wanted to reconcile

Judaism and the West, and he transformed the faith of his fathers into a particular cult, tied to a past epoch, and revealed by Moses to a tribe that no longer exists. Mendelssohn wanted to preserve Judaism and win it recognition. And on each occasion, he betrayed it. He was victim of an illusion, which was to believe that one could create a synthesis of reason and Revelation, of Judaism and the West, and that there was continuity between modernity and the tradition. Where Mendelssohn saw continuity, Strauss saw a rupture. Thus, the quarrel between reason and Revelation is taken to its climax, thanks to the pantheism controversy, which permits Strauss to show that this conflict reduces to the radical divide between atheism and orthodoxy, and then between modern and classical rationalism, that is, to the break between the Ancients and Moderns. Finally, where Mendelssohn speaks of a synthesis between Judaism and the West, Strauss speaks of a tension between Jerusalem and Athens.

Mendelssohn says that Judaism is a religion of Law that asserts no dogma and that, for this reason, approximates natural religion, but his way of limiting Law to positive laws valid only for a single nation makes Judaism disappear as a religion. It becomes a mere culture or designates the remains of a culture, connected to the Old Testament's conception of God, but fated to merge with the universalism of reason, that is, to blend into morality. To speak of natural religion is to say that there is no necessity for positive religions, and that a wise man "does not remain where chance of birth has cast him."[15] This way of relativizing the content of Judaism arguably opens into the Spinozist critique of particularist religion, the prescriptions of which ought to be abandoned in favor of a minimalist credo connected to whatever of universal morality there is in the Old and New Testaments. Is it not the theological-political problem that is specific to Judaism that is buried with Mendelssohn? Finally, what distinguishes Mendelssohn from Spinoza's rejection of a tribal religion, belonging to a bygone era and addressed to a people living in particular conditions? If these conditions are no longer present, because the Jews were readmitted to Berlin after 1671, and if people today are less inclined to idolatry than the people to whom Moses addressed himself, must one not reform Judaism in the direction of the modern Enlightenment and the West? Is not this the way to make Judaism relevant for the present and the future?

Mendelssohn thought that orthodoxy was an anachronistic form of religiosity but that Judaism could be preserved. He was mistaken, according to Strauss: once one says that orthodoxy is over, one makes Revelation in the strict sense disappear and one buries religion. The latter becomes a mere expedient, without doubt indispensable for the common people who, believing in salvation, try to make themselves worthy of it by their virtue, but completely useless for the true wise man, for the philosopher who has read the *Ethics* of Spinoza and knows that the truth belongs to the third kind of knowledge. In the era of the Enlightenment, religion is but the last resort of ignorance. It is an illusion that still has a future, but one should wish for it to end.

The moderate Enlightenment of Mendelssohn is apt to be confused with the radical Enlightenment. Thus Strauss chooses to go back to the source: from the beginning of the 1930s, he works on Spinoza's critique of religion instead of analyzing Mendelssohn's writings about God, such as *Jerusalem*. Strauss is interested in the *Philosophical Dialogues* of Mendelssohn and in the *Phaedon*, where the characters of Lessing, Socrates, and Plato are presented, but he focuses above all on the *Morning Hours* because the debate provoked by Jacobi obliges the moderate Enlightenment to confront the legacy of Spinoza. And for Strauss, as for Jacobi, this confrontation reverts to the examination of the concept of reason underpinning Spinoza's system. It is, first of all, the belief in the sufficiency of reason that Strauss discovers at the heart of the modern Enlightenment critique of Revelation. This belief marks a true break between the philosophy of the Enlightenment and orthodoxy, which supposes that man cannot make his salvation alone, without the assistance of Revelation, and even without the assistance of a religion. This break deprives the intermediate position of Mendelssohn of all credibility and shows that the real problem is that of a discontinuity between classical thought and the modern ideal of the progress of humanity through science and reason.

Just as Jacobi shows that "purified Spinozism" does not exist, Strauss shows that the conflict between the Enlightenment and orthodoxy is a conflict between atheism and orthodoxy. The latter supposes a notion of Revelation that affirms its heteronomy, its transcendence rather than its immanence. It is here that Jacobi takes issue with Kant, to whom everyone turned at the beginning of the pantheism controversy. In a parallel fashion, Strauss is going to think this conflict between reason and Revelation, which is the opening chapter of his reflection on the legacy of the Enlightenment, in bringing to light the quarrel of the Ancients and Moderns, that is, in refusing to believe that the problem has been solved by critical philosophy.

With the pantheism controversy, it is the entire modern Enlightenment that Strauss seeks to oppose to classical rationalism. No Modern, not even Kant, can pretend to have solved the conflict between orthodoxy and Enlightenment. No modern philosophy can claim to have surpassed the Ancients and to be superior to them. The only weighty thinker will be Heidegger, who will speak of a necessary return to the Greek sources of knowledge. Strauss will borrow from him this idea while choosing a return to Socrates and Plato rather than to the pre-Socratics. He will also borrow the idea according to which Western history is characterized as a forgetting. This notion of a forgetting, conceptualized differently by Heidegger and by Strauss, is exactly what separates the latter from the Kantian schema of Enlightenment. For Kant, the Enlightenment designates a slow and never entirely complete process of the dissemination of positive knowledge, as with the Encyclopedists, but it is above all a matter of the capacity of individuals and peoples to think for themselves without submitting to any authority external to reason itself. In Strauss, there is neither this idea of general progress of the Moderns in relation to the Ancients nor this privileging of autonomy. Strauss rejects autonomy in the technical sense given to it in Kantian philosophy, and which is taken up again by neo-Kantianism with its primacy of the ethical, but he also dismisses the current sense of the term, which suggests that most human beings do not require guidance on the spiritual front and in the conduct of their lives. Strauss is a philosopher, but at the same time he affirms that human beings need Law conceived as heteronomy.[16] This is the meaning of his return to Maimonides. The latter represents an attempt to think the idea of philosophy before the Law and to justify the Law by philosophical reason, which has nothing to see with the synthesis of philosophy and Judaism proposed by Mendelssohn.

Strauss rejected Kant and turned upside down the position of the neo-Kantians thanks to Jacobi. In order to address the refutation by Strauss of the moderate Enlightenment, from Mendelssohn to Kant, we must know how Jacobi turned Kantianism on its head, attacking it from within.

The Rejection of the Kantian Solution

At the beginning, Jacobi utilizes Kantian critical philosophy to oppose Mendelssohn. In his *Responses to the Accusations of Mendelssohn in his Letter to the Friends of Lessing* (1786), he said that philosophy does not permit the demonstration of God's existence and that all philosophy leads to atheism. In his *Letters to Mendelssohn*, he deploys the Kantian idea of the thing-in-itself, which supposes that human beings are receptive to that which is given. Because there is no logical proof of the higher truths of natural religion, and human beings therefore are not able to arrive at any systematic conclusions, either a priori or a posteriori, concerning the existence of the thing-in-itself, Jacobi will say that our conviction concerning the existence of things outside of ourselves is a belief. The Jacobian concept of belief explained in *David Hume* derives at the same time from the empiricism of Hume himself and from the Kantian idea according to which the reality of objects is not addressed by reason. This thesis will permit Jacobi and his young friend Wizenmann—proponent of the heteronomy of Revelation and convinced that the tradition alone can provide it with a stable content—to say that rationalism, which purports to deduce the existence of the concept, leads fundamentally to an atheism. The concept of God undermines itself. Religion rests on a dangerous leap. Whoever would say that the infinite being thinks, as Spinoza saw, would be saying something no less absurd than if he affirmed that the infinite is finite. The response from Mendelssohn, who had treated Kant as a destructive force and who did not in the beginning receive his assistance, remaining in retirement up to then, was to have recourse to "common sense": common sense is not able to choose between and give its assent to one or the other position. But this solution is a subterfuge: there is a conflict between Spinozism, that is, atheism, and fideism. The middle position that critical philosophy believed itself to occupy was untenable.

Jacobi takes up also the Kantian argument concerning the dogmatism of Spinoza by showing that his rational system rests on that which we call today a performative contradiction: it cannot explain how someone like Spinoza is possible. If we are nothing but modes of thought, how was Spinoza able to construct a system that begins with the definition of substance and purports to encompass the whole? Similarly, Strauss writes that "the clear and distinct account of everything that it presents remains fundamentally hypothetical. As a consequence, its cognitive status is not different from that of the orthodox account."[17] Spinoza hides the nonevident character of his premises by the success of his results. This critique of system and of the pretension of human reason to grasp the whole allows Jacobi to hone in on the misunderstanding of the philosophers. Not only have they confounded reason with the understanding in reducing it to the constructivist principle, but as well they thought reason did not need Revelation or a suprasensual realm given from the outside. The use of Kant opens up into an objection to Kant, as is shown by the conflict concerning the thing-in-itself.

Jacobi is going to make use of that which Kant discovered as positive in the dialectic of pure reason—that is, the privilege accorded to practical reason—because of the idea of freedom that allows the application of certain ideas found only a priori in reason. Jacobi borrowed from Kant in the first stage of the pantheism controversy in order to attack the dogmatism of Mendelssohn and Lessing. But, with the publication of his *David Hume and Belief or Idealism and Realism* (1787), he accused Kant of being an idealist who denies the existence of the thing-in-itself. Jacobi seeks to be more consistent than Kant himself. It is not only because Mendelssohn is dead that Jacobi turns against Kant from 1786, but also because he wants to prove that the solution to the conflict between reason and Revelation is not a religion within the limits of reason alone.

Kant understood that Jacobi's attack was against him. No longer was the opposition between rationalism and fideism, but rather between critical reason and dogmatism. In claiming that reason is the meaning of the suprasensible, Jacobi and Wizenmann succumbed to rational dogmatism. If they had reflected on the need for the Absolute that was part of the subjective functioning of our reason, they would not have taken their ideas for real objects. Jacobi falls into irrationalism, into *Schwärmerei*, into the virtually unavoidable tendency of reason to confuse its Ideas with things or to make hypostases and to enter into antinomies that critical reason or the consciousness of the boundaries and limits of our faculty of knowledge allows us to avoid. According to Kant, Jacobi and Wizenmann represent a regression in relation to the progress that critical reason has made in human rationality, progress that depends on awareness of the limits of the power of knowledge. This assimilation by the Kantian Enlightenment of rationality, Enlightenment, and critical reason is the strategy of the work titled "On a recently prominent tone of superiority in philosophy."[18] Belief cannot have any theoretical significance, and Jacobi's dangerous move leads to mysticism, which for Kant is hard to distinguish from madness. The dogmatism of Spinoza that dooms Jacobi and the *Schwärmerei* derives from the same negation of the finitude of reason: Jacobi is a dogmatist. The pantheism debate merely reveals what Kant already knew, namely that this is the dialectic of reason: these doctrinal conflicts are manifestations of the antinomies of reason. The only solution is to limit the ambition of human reason to grasp the suprasensible and to guarantee belief in the supersensible as a presupposition of practical reason. And Jacobi turns this idea against Kant himself in suggesting that Kant is not consistent: the rationalism of Kant, like the rationalism of the Enlightenment, derives from absolute idealism, because it reduces everything to the subjective principle of representation. In the domain of religion, this means turning God into a moral idea.

To dissect the modern religious consciousness and to explain that modernity evolves irresistibly toward secularization, toward the reduction of religion to a morality where the respect of the other is the only vestige of a relation to transcendence, as a relation to something other than oneself, Strauss returns to the moment where the Enlightenment decided our fate. He returns to Kant, who belonged to the moderate Enlightenment, and opposed the latter to the radical Enlightenment, represented by Hobbes and Spinoza. And if the radical Enlightenment buried all revealed religion, if Spinoza is more dangerous than Mendelssohn, the moderate Enlightenment represents nevertheless a real danger. It conceals the problem and pretends to preserve something that it destroys. Kant is thus more formidable than Mendelssohn: the relation between transcendence and immanence that follows from his thought concerning finitude and that is manifest in his morality based on the immanent law of reason signifies that the heteronomy of the Law and Revelation are not necessary to morality and that religion is subordinate to morality. This attack against religion as Revelation is all the more effective in appearing to be gentle. While the radical Enlightenment uses the weapons of mockery and derision against orthodoxy, thus limiting the consequence of its critique and allowing the idea of a conflict—then of a choice between two stances, two opposite *interests*—to remain, the Kantian Enlightenment pretends to preserve that which, at bottom, it annihilates: with Kant, religion becomes the auxiliary of morality, and the path toward secularization is assured. Strauss is thus required to avoid the Kantian solution and, to do that, to say that it has been discredited. Such is the role of Jacobi. Awareness of the danger that the Kantian Enlightenment represents for religion explains in part[19] Strauss's silence on Kant.

Strauss doesn't speak of Kant, but this silence is eloquent. It has a function and a precise significance. Further, it is not a matter of genuine absence: Kant is indirectly addressed by Strauss, because the critique of the relation between transcendence and immanence is at the source of the pantheism controversy and the debate concerning the French Revolution, and because Kantianism distinguishes Strauss from Cohen. The impasse of the Kantian solution first appears, in Strauss's view, in Cohen, who, in *The Religion of Reason Derived from the sources of Judaism,* interprets the morality of the prophets as if it culminated in Kantianism. This method of interpretation, linked to the Kantian scheme of Enlightenment, prevented Cohen from seeing what was distinctive in Judaism and in the articulation of theology and politics specific to the notion of the Law. In the philosophy of Cohen, which asserts the primacy of ethics, religion appears as a complement that supports man's striving toward the good, and not as a Law expressing a particular relation between God and humankind, considered at one and same time individually and collectively.

Strauss implicitly criticizes Cohen for having pursued the task of the destruction of religion for which Cohen himself had reproached Spinoza, who was guilty of reducing the religion of his ancestors to a mere national religion. With Cohen, one no longer knows whether one is really dealing with a religion. He thus is closer to Spinoza than he admits. What distinguishes the Kantian philosopher who makes of God an atheistic concept? If religion is to have meaning, and not collapse, like natural religion, in a sort of hidden atheism, revelation must be thought of as divine Revelation.[20] Cohen belongs to the movement for a return to tradition, but that tradition escaped him because he was too Kantian. Cohen was a man of the Enlightenment, that is, a man who, in the very reflection on the relationship between immanence and transcendence, rejected the heteronomy of Revelation and the Law. His mistake derives from the Kantian theory of the moral law. When Strauss writes that the alternative between orthodoxy and the Enlightenment is an alternative between orthodoxy and atheism, he equally wants to say this: the Kantian solution and the idea of the suprasensible, of which I have no experience than by my reason, which is practically oriented, and because there is in me a moral law that gives me a priori the sense of good and evil, could never provide the means for the Jews to save their tradition or for the modern religious consciousness to transcend the paradoxes of secularization.

Here it is worth underscoring the originality of Strauss's philosophy in a time when most philosophers thought that the truth of the Moderns was to be found in Kant or Hegel. Strauss breaks with both of them through his use of Jacobi. Through his critique of the system of Spinoza, the exposure of its contradictions, and the scrutiny of rationalist dogmatism, Jacobi showed the way to Strauss for the rejection of Hegel's philosophy. As for the German Jewish philosophers of his generation, the idea that reason could grasp the totality of the real seemed difficult for him to admit, at once for the concern with existence that is at the heart of Jewish rationalism—and that would be the beginning point for Rosenzweig—and because the point of view of the philosophy of history, which justifies all of reality, even the unjustifiable, seems to be a way of writing an official history, which is in fact the story of the conquerors, as Walter Benjamin had suggested. But in showing that the Kantian solution to the conflict between Enlightenment and orthodoxy is only in appearance one of successful conciliation and mediation, in suggesting that Kantianism derives from Spinozism, Jacobi further permitted Strauss to return to the sources of the problem, that is, the conception of man and of reason that is at the core of the modern Enlightenment, whether radical or conservative. And, moreover, this conception represents a total break with the kind of wisdom defended by the ancient and medieval philosophers. It is possible that reflection on religion is the occasion for reopening the quarrel of the Ancients and Moderns and showing the faults of the latter. What was destructive in the attack of the modern Enlightenment against religious orthodoxy? What is the reason that itself was lost and that Kantianism, despite appearances, was unable to rediscover?

The debate between orthodoxy and Enlightenment was not yet, at the start of the twentieth century, truly decided. The revealed religions were not rejected once and for all in an overturning of the past, and the remaining adherents to their tenets did not have to have recourse to subjective will. The debate over the kind of orthodoxy to which to return was opened. It was already present in the dispute over pantheism in the dialogue between Jacoby and Wizenmann. This debate concerning the content of Revelation is taken up by Strauss. Strauss invoked Jacobi in questioning the rationality of the Enlightenment, but he would not continue to be concerned with Jacobi, this purpose having been served. Strauss will have assimilated once and for all what had been gained through the pantheism debate, that is, the reversal of the neo-Kantianism of Cassirer, the return from the Moderate Enlightenment of Mendelssohn to the radical Enlightenment of Hobbes and Spinoza and the rejection of criticism. But Strauss would never become a man of the Anti-Enlightenment, because the return to orthodoxy that he proposes is less a struggle against the Enlightenment in the name of faith than a return to another type of Enlightenment, exemplified above all by Maimonides. This abandonment of Jacobi was foreseeable from the beginning, because Strauss never embraced on his own account the idea according to which individuality and existence are the true sites of Revelation. This idea, which appears in Kierkegaard, but also in Rosenzweig, is contrary to the sensibility of Strauss, who is not interested in religion for the sake of understanding his own faith. His interest rather is motivated by an inquiry concerning the necessity of transmitting a tradition and on the question of knowing the possibility of this transition in the present time. Considering the specific relationship of the biblical religions to the tradition, Strauss poses the question of how to know whether a tradition, in the sense of a nation or culture, can survive the Enlightenment critique of Revelation and the Bible.

Because he opposes an excessive internalization of faith, Strauss does not believe that subjectivity is the measure of all things. He seems closer to Wizenmann than to Jacobi. The young philosopher, who died in 1787, held that the tradition offered the best guarantee of difference, to the extent that stories, ceremonies, and rites constitute a genuine religious life. One finds in Wizenmann a reflection that will be at the core of Rosenzweig's *Star of Redemption*, which is situated between Jacobi and Wizenmann. The pantheism debate is really the spark for all of the questions that concern Strauss. The debate concerning Revelation, the final stage of the *Pantheismusstreit*, reveals the political agenda that is at the heart of the abstract critique of the rationalism of the Enlightenment. It equally permits us to understand the connection between the critique of the heteronomy of Revelation and the affirmation of a political teaching that differs radically from the political philosophy of the classics. Finally, it gives its full meaning to the theological-political problem, that is to say, the connection between religion and politics, which was considered as definitely solved by the modern Enlightenment and the advent of liberal democracy.

The Controversy over the French Revolution

The controversy over the French Revolution reproduces at the level of politics the first attack against the Enlightenment that occurred in the *Pantheismusstreit*.[21] Burke and Rehberg have in common with Jacobi and Wizenmann the resort to empiricism and the critique of the abstract ideal of the rights of man.[22] Rehberg (1757–1836), who already played a role in the pantheism debate, saw in the French Revolution and in Kantianism a rationalism that distorts reality and reconstructs it being from seductive but completely impractical ideas. Kantian morality and Rousseau's theory of the general will failed to close the gap between the universal and the particular. If the distinction between duty and particular duties is meaningful because it underscores the essence of morality and does not rely on conformity with conventions and existing commands, it still allows for particular duties to arise through the articulation of what is right and wrong in a specific situation. The content of right cannot be determined except in relation to a complete system of positive laws, that is, the state, as Hegel suggested in taking the example of theft, which has no meaning except in relation to the right to property.[23]

This reference to experience will be still more evident in the political domain. This is why the critique of the abstraction of human rights occupies a central place in the debate concerning the rationalism of the Enlightenment. Conversely, the link between the debate about the Revolution and the pantheism quarrel or the integration of this political question into a philosophical reflection on the claims of rationalism means that the critique of human rights has in the first instance not the polemical function that it would possess among certain French counterrevolutionaries such as Joseph de Maistre. Jacobi is not Joseph de Maistre, because that which he criticizes in the Revolution is first of all the idea that one can make a tabula rasa of the past and reconstruct the entire political edifice on an exclusively rational basis. The motivation of Jacobi, like that of Burke, who says, in reading the former, "I believed I was reading myself," is not to attack the idea of the republic or to defend absolute monarchy and the divine right of kings. It is rather to underline the unreasonable character of the revolutionary enterprise and its absurdity in showing that it is impossible to ground politics on abstract ideals and that such an enterprise is doomed to impasse, because it is profoundly unaware of that which is political life. Experience is not determined by the categories of our understanding, but rather is that from which we begin. It is not reconstructed but described. The point of departure, for thinking the political, is life, not the understanding and its a priori principles. Before establishing political right based on abstract principles and on the respect for man generally, it is necessary to begin, say Burke and Arendt,[24] from particular human beings and the concrete level where this question of respect of the person has to begin with a sense, that is, the nation.

The intention of Jacobi is thus not in the first instance polemical, even if his critique of the rationalism of the Enlightenment has political consequences: it leads the Anti-Enlightenment to naturally oppose itself to the Revolution or to the idea of a radical rupture with the past. Similarly, if the conception of reason as a function of revelation goes hand in hand with the rehabilitation of experience, it also signifies that the traditions and customs that are the empirical function of a society constitute the spirit of the laws. The abstract and universal principles of right thus cannot be applied without taking into account that particular instance that is the community. The source of right, far from being reason or the autonomy of the will, is history.

The reason at work in the project of the foundation of right and politics which is that of the Revolutionaries is a reason cut off from experience. It has "neither heart nor guts."[25] It is "arrogant" in setting itself up as the sole legislator. And reason is "not legislative, nor executive but purely juridical." It serves exclusively to apply given determinations to given objects. The reason that is at work in the revolutionary project corresponds to the understanding. It stems from the pretension of man to reconstruct the real according to his principles alone. This pretension Jacobi had already denounced in the idealist metaphysics that is situated at the heart of revolutionary humanism. The latter can assert a purely human conception of right, thus a certain metaphysical modesty that contrasts with the foundation of right in the ancien régime and the absolute monarchy based on the divine right of kings, but upon closer examination this modesty turns out to be false. It goes hand in hand with the pretension to be able to construct the world beginning from purely rational ideals. The consciousness of human finitude supposes that one is envisaging a purely judicial, not legislative, function of reason and that one accepts the idea that man is not man except as he manifests him in belonging to a concrete world, to a community.

If man is finite, it is because the existence of the world precedes philosophical concepts. Man is not capable of total mastery in the domain either of speculation or of action. The relation between theory and practice must not be thought of in the way that philosophers have done up to now, because there is within immanence an element of transcendence that is irreducible, whether at the level of knowledge or of action. In both cases one must take a dangerous leap: one must give up applying to all societies an abstract philosophy—whether it is the apparently universal rights of man that are considered as more universal than cannibalism. In other words, the question is that of knowing whether human rights are one social ideal like others or whether they should be considered the content of modern natural right.[26] The fact that they serve as criteria for judging positive law and measuring the legitimacy of existing laws in our societies does not resolve that problem. This reveals the difficulties relative to the principles on which modern natural right depends, because it is not certain that these principles are as universal as they claim.

The impasse and the contradictions of the rationalism of the Enlightenment thus concern also the content of this humanism, that is to say, the utilitarian principles that are the foundation of the rights of man. Right is defined beginning from the "desire to be happy." Jacobi sees here a form of Spinozism: the confusion between practical reason, duty, and happiness is a way of reviving the *conatus* of Spinoza, which is the tendency of each to seek his conservation and the improvement of his conditions of life. And this *conatus*, which alone can assure the universality of human rights, is neither right nor something that demarcates the specific difference between man and other sentient beings. Man is defined by desire, and this cannot produce duty or obligation other than in a fleeting and illusory way. This modern notion of natural right leads to the concession that "whales, codfish and herring have rights in the same manner as human beings. One says that, if these animals do not have like us a valid right to existence, it is because their natural organization is inferior to ours and they do not possess that which we are accustomed to understand under the name of reason?" But if that is the case, it supposes that "the rights of man are in proportion to his intellectual capacities."[27] With such a definition of natural right, how "could one regard it as inexcusable for Aristotle to defend natural slavery?" The desire or the quest for happiness, far from producing right and justice, could lead to the affirmation of the right of the stronger, which we wanted to eliminate. And this is the contradiction in the project of the Constituent Assembly. "It is the project to ground rationally the universality of human rights that exposes rationalism and juridical humanism as endlessly entering into contradiction with themselves. The aporias of the Declaration manifest the inherent absurdity of wanting to attribute to reason a legislative or executive power that it does not possess."

The rationalism of human rights, blind to what separates is from ought, fact from right, the animal from the human, amounts to political nihilism. The subject, the particular human being, and the object, right as effective in the world, are equally destroyed: "By means of the abstract term 'human being' one defines concrete human beings, 'him' and 'me' and one denies to each one the right to affirm for himself what he denies for the other. But it suffices to substitute 'him and me' with 'human being and animal' in order for the 'equality of rights and duties' to disappear instantly, thus illustrating the superficiality and impracticability of the rational process of abstraction on which depends in the end all juridical humanism."[28]

Abstract reason is impotent to define human rights that are truly juridical and authentically human. One must search for another source of right than abstract reason and autonomy of the will. For Jacobi, this source is history. The romantic genesis of the critique of the abstract rationalism of the Enlightenment ends up reducing to nothing the idea of natural and universal human rights, but is it all the same a reactionary critique? And what is the position of Strauss? Does he embrace the historicism of the Romantics, following them in their critique of natural right thinking as such, or, rather, does he use Jacobi for his rejection of the Kantian solution of the grounding of right, starting from reason and in order to propose a reinterpretation of natural right in light of the rupture between Ancients and Moderns?

For Jacobi, human existence is not given universally or a priori, but only in its concrete or particular conditions or manifestations. Similarly, the form of government must not violate the particularity of a people but be in conformity with the spirit of this people and the present state of their imagination. This is a living and dynamic reality, but it is not the abstract principles of the understanding or the rationalism of the Revolution that will transform it. Genuine human rights must be effect, not abstract rights. Far from imposing a systematic equality, which is at once impossible and contrary to equity, one must instead seek "inequality of the right kind," which alone is the basis of a just state, while equality at any price leads to tyranny. In 1790, Jacobi's critique of the rationalism of the Enlightenment is the same as in 1785. In politics as well as in the realm of ideas, the Enlightenment leads to nihilism and to a certain violence, to dogmatism. It does not avoid the kind of injustice that it condemns. The solution is to return to experience in order to reconnect to concrete existence. Political science, as Burke wrote, is an empirical science and cannot be learned a priori.

The connection of Strauss to Jacobi is evident and right from his 1921 dissertation. The rehabilitation of empiricism by the Anti-Enlightenment corresponds to the way in which Strauss thinks political philosophy as a reflection on the prevailing opinions in the city. And just as there is in Jacobi a methodological preference for description, there is in Strauss a return to the things themselves, a phenomenological reduction. Nevertheless, the things to which one returns are not the data of consciousness or the homogenous world reconstructed by the Husserlian cogito, but the opinions of human beings living in a community. To begin with the foundation is to begin with that primal layer of experience, which for Strauss goes back to Plato's cave and which Jacobi calls life. This methodological approach, which Strauss associates more and more with the return to Socrates or an appropriation of the thought of Socrates, a paradigm for the return to the political, leads more to a reconnection of the present to the past and the tradition than to thinking of the future in terms of a rupture with the past. There follows a putting in question of the schema of interpretation of the Enlightenment as a rejection of the illusions of the past and a denunciation of the progressive prejudice.

In Jacobi, as with Burke and Rehberg, practice should be based on observation of the times, of place, of social relations of the history and morality of the people. As is well known, Kant entered into this debate by publishing an essay in the *Berlinischer Monatsschrift* on the relation between theory and practice. Similarly, Fichte replied to Rehberg in his

Contribution to the Rectification of the Public's Judgment of the French Revolution, where he accuses men like Jacobi of being capable only "of borrowing and imitating" and judging "the future only in light of the past" in denying "man's freedom and his creative power."[29] Must one say with Fichte that "what one chooses as a philosophy depends on the man that one is" and that somersaulting man is afraid of change?

There is a difference between Jacobi and Romantics like Müller and Gentz, who in breaking with the Enlightenment and Protestantism, converted to Catholicism or explicitly invoked de Maistre. If all of them thought, as Rabaut Saint-Etienne suggested, that "our history is not our code," nevertheless Jacobi's contestation of the submission of right to abstract principles of reason does not necessarily imply that one must "restore religion" or "restore it as Law. Because it is only as law that it can be the basis for a faith of obedience,"[30] Jacobi stops short of Gentz and Müller. Jacobi's attachment to the individual consciousness—and not to tradition—as the site of the revelation of truth is what paradoxically underlines the limits of his religious response to the political problem and that which prevents him from being a philosopher of reaction.

One finds the same paradox in Kierkegaard.[31] Strauss's observations to Löwith allow us to understand why neither Jacobi nor Kierkegaard is a reactionary and to see the nature of Strauss's interest in Jacobi, which is different from that of a representative of the Anti-Enlightenment. Strauss notes that Kierkegaard, who is aware, despite his existentialism and his philosophy of subjectivity, that the human problem is a political problem, provides a religious answer to this problem. Löwith deems this answer "authoritarian and reactionary," while, for Strauss, it is merely a manifestation of the "Christian difficulty of finding a definitive solution to the problem of "order" or of political life.

The failure of Kierkegaard's project is that "his departure point," writes Strauss, is the "dissolution of the human being," his radical nakedness, which is accompanied by "the loss of his human content." The consequences of this response can be reactionary, but the response itself is not. In his letter to Löwith, he does not use the expression "political philosophy," but this is what is involved when he writes about a response inspired more by Greek thought than by the Christianity to which Kierkegaard and all the thought of the nineteenth century belonged. Strauss rejects the purely human response to the political problem and shows that "one is in agreement with Kierkegaard on the fact that the Christian difficulty to find a final solution to the problem of order can be overcome in a Christian manner; and that, in any case, the politics of modernity since

Hobbes and passing through Rousseau and Marx, commits the logical error of trying to solve a Christian problem in an Atheistic fashion."[32] But Kierkegaard's solution and his point of departure, which is also that of Jacobi, does not satisfy Strauss, who invites a return not to consciousness but to the opinions that prevail in the city, political philosophy being the reflection on those opinions and their rational articulation. Strauss's critique of Kierkegaard applies equally to Jacobi.

Having used Jacobi's critique of metaphysical humanism and of the rationalism of the Enlightenment, Strauss is going to distance himself in order to lay the cornerstones of his political philosophy, of which the foundations depend on Judaism, in particular medieval Jewish philosophy and its notion of the Law. Jacobi allowed Strauss to break with the Kantian solution, according to which the source of right is the subject. The grounding of right on history in Jacobi as well as in Burke goes hand in hand with a challenge to the claims of reason and with a certain conservatism. Unlike the reactionary, who favors a return to the past, the conservative thinks that modernity destroys the conditions of its own existence and brings about that which it wished to combat.[33] This political sensibility corresponds to the spirit of the Straussian critique of modernity, to the way in which he shows the destructive dialectic of Enlightenment. It sets the tone also for Strauss's reflections on the internal threat to mass democracy. But in proposing an interpretation of the notion of natural right, which illuminates, by a comparison of modern and ancient natural right, the political assumptions of the Moderns, Strauss breaks with Jacobi. Jacobi, in contesting the authority of modern reason, that is, the autonomy of the will, showed to Strauss the path through which he could break with contractarianism, metaphysical humanism, or the philosophy of the subject without thereby becoming an agitator for the return of the ancien régime or embracing the failure of politics, as with existentialism. For Strauss, the challenge to modern rationalism did not lead to the contestation of ancient rationalism but rather led toward ancient rationalism. In the end, this position allowed Strauss to radically distinguish himself from Hegel, who, against Jacobi, made life, thought of as the self-deployment of the unity of being and non-being, the very structure of the concept. Hegel conceives rationality as actualization, as history. This thinking does not seduce Strauss, who invites us not to overcome the crisis of rationalism by a philosophy of self-confidence,[34] but to think what is unthinkable for modern rationalism and to appreciate that which was forgotten by the Moderns in their so-called overcoming of ancient rationalism. This reference to ancient rationalism does not make Strauss a Romantic, or a figure of the Anti-Enlightenment; rather, he believes in a different Enlightenment.

There is another difference between Jacobi and Strauss. This difference illuminates their respective philosophical projects and allows us to see what sets Strauss apart from all positions that belong to the scheme of interpretation derived from the same universe as that of Jacobi, namely Christianity. Strauss begins with the city, while, for Jacobi, subjectivity is untranscendable and remains the locus of truth, revealed by belief and existence. It is possible to see the origin of this difference—which allows us also to understand why Strauss conceived a political philosophy instead of rallying to Heidegger's existentialism—in Strauss's fidelity to a motif inherited from the Jewish tradition. In Judaism, the individual him- or herself is thought of as belonging to a tradition that precedes him or her. This tradition is not merely a culture, a history, or the representation of what links each to his or her ancestors. It designates a religion and a belonging to a people of which the history, from its beginnings until the end of time, is an alliance with God, and through God, with the rest of humanity. Jacob, as in his fight with the Angel, struggled with God as he did with human beings: "I saw God face to face and my life was spared." Later he said to Esau, soon after, that he looked at him as he looked at God, with the same fear. The other, who is almost as distant as God, as Levinas thought, is the link between God and man.

It is impossible for a Jew to believe that his identity results from the relation of the self to itself, as with Kierkegaard, or even of the self with God.[35] In Judaism, one cannot dispense with the relation to the community, which is the mediation of the relation to self and the relation to God. This specific dimension does not in the least attenuate the fact that Judaism is a religion where the transcendence of God is affirmed in a radical manner, even if some thinkers tended to associate the primacy of morality with the nontranscendence of God, who becomes an idea, as, for example, Cohen, who, in his theory of the double correlation, makes of the relation of the *Nebenmensch* conceived of as *Mitmensch* the site where one seems closest to God. This and the subordination of politics to morality are counterbalanced by the messianism of Cohen. Cohen's messianism is certainly very different from that of classical Judaism and displays a certain secularization of religion, but it also betrays the impossibility for the Jewish thinker of completely separating politics, morality, and religion. The individual is always already caught in the relation to the other, to the community. He is not alone with God. For the Christian, man is alone *before* God and alone with his conscience in his relation to others. Politics and the community are secondary when the beginning point is the "nakedness" of the individual, who can implicate in his definition the relation to humanity,[36] but not in the first instance and essentially to his community. In this respect, Christ is the mediator between myself and God but also between myself and others. He also removes in respect to God and others the dimension of fear that is present in Judaism.

What separates Strauss from the Christian universe appears clearly when one confronts him with a thinker whose philosophy is the thematization and the dramatization of the concept of subjectivity, which is that of the twentieth-century existentialist but also of Jacobi. In the *Treatise on Despair*, which is also called *Sickness unto Death*, subjectivity is a relation to oneself that is constituted by the relation to God. As in the *Confessions* of St. Augustine, existence is the site of the overcoming of an inwardness or a "me" that is ontologically linked to the Creator but that must, within time and various stages of life, reconfirm this relation, converting itself. The travails of life confront the existing being, whether he is conscious of it or not, with the following alternatives: hopelessness or faith, love or evil. In fact, these alternatives reduce to one. Our relation to others and to ourselves depends, in Kierkegaard, on this original or ontological relation to God, which explains why faith alone can eliminate despair. Despair is the beginning point for consciousness and constantly challenges it. And just as this anxiety does not reduce to a psychological condition, but designates a category of freedom, defined as "the anxious possibility of power,"[37] which makes each act a qualitative leap, so is despair the fact of relating to oneself while fleeing oneself, refusing oneself, wanting too much to be oneself, or not being able to bear being oneself. The concrete situations of life, relation to others, and psychological suffering are the site where that fundamental relation to the self plays itself out, which is healthy and avoids despair only if it plunges its full transparency into the power that created us,[38] that is, if one has faith. This definition of identity explains the deepest meaning of Kierkegaard's declaration that "if I had faith, I would have stayed with Regine." Only faith, passion, and absolute relation to the Absolute, or a personal relation to God, allows one to be oneself, to love oneself and others.

One sees in this thinking that the relation to God is what in the first instance engages subjectivity, the individual before God, as Kierkegaard says, the Singular (*den Enkelte*), the Unique, of which Christ is the model. The relation to the other derives from a relation to the self that places the consciousness before God. Faith intensifies this reality. The community is out of the picture. The divinity of Christ, the second person of the Trinity and the Incarnation, do not attenuate the affirmation of the transcendence of God and the humanity of Christ such that he who harms his neighbor also harms Christ. But we are in the first instance alone in our relation to God.

In comparing Strauss with Kierkegaard, who was one of the first to oppose himself to systemic philosophy and Strauss, one appreciates the distance that separates an existentialist teaching, originally and essentially Christian, from a political philosophy the fidelity of which to Judaism will become all the clearer with a deeper understanding of the theological-political problem and the constitutive role of the nature of Law in Judaism. Strauss, taking into account his definition of man in terms of belonging to a community, is led to affirm the primacy of the political, while Jacobi locates truth in the subjective sphere of individual experience, belief, and existence. The tension in the work of Strauss between the world of thought and philosophical method and his fidelity to a conception of time and of man inherited from Judaism explains the unease, the lack of satisfaction Strauss feels whenever one of the two models dominates to the detriment of the other.

From Jacobi, Strauss takes the internal critique of rationalism and the rehabilitation of experience, which he encounters in the phenomenology of Husserl and Heidegger, which provided the conceptual tools of young scholars trained in Germany in the 1920s. Strauss uses the Anti-Enlightenment to show that the conflict between reason and Revelation is not definitively resolved, and to reopen the quarrel of the Ancients and Moderns. But he breaks from Jacobi when it is a question of determining the content of the orthodoxy to which one returns; not only is subjectivity not the site of Revelation, but, furthermore, the Tradition cannot be thought of as a mere compilation of texts, rites and dogmas, as in Barth, or the Theology of the Cross, because man in his relation to God is in a sense more alone than the Christian, who has a mediator, and less alone, because the individual, according to the Greeks, does not exist except as a philosophical abstraction. Man is from the outset this or that man, in a "cave" where there is this or that reality of power and where there is a set of opinions that have themselves been deformed by the existence of a second "cave." This second "cave" was constructed from modern presuppositions, and it coincides, according to Strauss, with the appearance of revealed religions.[38] For all these reasons, it is necessary to reopen the quarrel between Ancients and Moderns from a perspective outside of Christianity.

A critique of Enlightenment is not enough. Or, rather, in order to do justice to the Enlightenment, it must be informed by an awareness of a genuine break between the Ancients and Moderns concerning the conception of man. Jacobi and the Anti-Enlightenment saw the problem, but they did not know how to address it adequately because they were too influenced by the central notion of modernity, that of subjectivity, which comes from Christianity. Jacobi was not Cartesian, but he was Christian; thus he remained too modern for Strauss. One must thus open the debate at a point prior to the appearance of modern presuppositions: one must try to think outside of categories originating from Christianity. Examining the difference between Strauss and Jacobi is a bridge to the confrontation between Ancients and Moderns and the analysis of the reasons for which the modern Enlightenment is in fact a form of obscurity, whereas the Jewish and Arab medieval Enlightenment is the genuine Enlightenment.

The Crisis of the Tradition

The Science of Judaism and the Dialectic of Assimilation

The crisis of the tradition is in the first instance a crisis concerning its transmission. The Torah is of course there, but as in the tale of Kafka,[40] there are a thousand doors prohibiting access, and before each door there is a guard who discourages the ordinary man from entering. This man waits for years and dies before having dared to confront the obstacle other than by attempting to corrupt the guard. Is the Law accessible to him who has the daring to interpret it? For Strauss, as for Scholem, it is a matter of knowing how to bring to life the tradition. But this question supposes that one knows what broke the chain of tradition and the link between the word of man and the word of God. What happened *in between* Maimonides (Strauss) or the kabbalah (Scholem) and the science of Judaism?

The reflection on the return or *Teshuvah* is in the first instance, in Strauss and Scholem, a critique of the generation that preceded them: "*Teshuvah* sometimes means . . . a return to Judaism on the part of many Jews who, or whose fathers, had broken, with Judaism as a whole."[40] Now these men who were estranged from the house of their fathers belonged to the first generation of the science of Judaism: Samson Raphael Hirsch (1808–1888);[42] Leopold Zunz (1794–1886), Moritz Steinschneider (1816–1907), and Abraham Geiger (1810–1874). Whatever their differences, it is important to emphasize their common ground in order to make manifest the destructive dialectic of assimilation and integration of Judaism into the Enlightenment.

In turning the Law into an object of science and in applying to Judaism progressive methods of historiography, they destroyed Judaism as religion and lost a tradition that they wanted to save. This treason, which leads Strauss to remark that the emphatic sense of the expression *Teshuvah* is repentence,[43] is already contained in the expression *Wissenschaft des Judentums*. The term *Judentum* is formed on the model of *Deutschtum* and *Griechentum*, which designate, respectively, German nationality and Greek culture. Judaism is considered as a culture or a cultural experience, not as Law. In this translation, there is the influence of the paradigm of Pietism. That is to say, one finds the idea of an internalization of faith and the reduction of Revelation to its pedagogical function. When Zunz, in a work published in 1818,[44] outlined the program of *Wissenschaft des Judentums*, he situated it in the continuation of the Lutheran Protestant universe, where there is a secularization of theology through hermeneutic science. Judaism, which was looking for new keys and methods for interpreting its own history, encountered in Germany a philology marked by Protestantism and by a hermeneutic relation to the text and by philology.

It is a misunderstanding between this community that has need of a principle of description for its own culture to obtain universal recognition and the science of hermeneutics. The builders are the destroyers, Rosenzweig said in speaking of Zunz and his type. If Judaism experienced an internal evolution in virtue of the principle of accommodation, if one must interpret the Law in order to save it from oblivion, this does not prevent the reconstruction of the stages of the manuscript, its historical study, and its transformation into a simple object of scientific inquiry being in contradiction with its revealed character. Science, which desecrates its object, is not the right way to enter the Law. This contradiction between Judaism and science comes from the fact that Judaism is structured by the idea of return, while science is associated with progress:

> When the prophets call their people to account . . . they accuse their people of rebellion. . . . Man who understands himself this way longs for the perfection of the origin, or of the classic past. He suffers from the present; he hopes for the future. Progressive man, on the other hand, looks back to a most imperfect beginning. The beginning is barbarism, stupidity, rudeness, extreme scarcity . . . he is certain of the superiority of the present to the past . . . , he lives unqualifiedly toward the future. . . . What others call rebellion, he calls revolution

> or liberation. To the polarity faithfulness-rebellion he opposes the polarity prejudice-freedom.[45]

Progressivism derives from the modern Enlightenment. The science of Judaism, in separating what is valuable for the modern epoch and what was only worthy in the past, is a selective reappropriation of the tradition. The problem is that the founders of *Wissenschaft des Judentums* undertook an epistemological rupture with the past. They no longer read the Talmud in thinking of the intention of the successive authors who drafted these texts in violating the prohibition against writing down the oral Law. Far from imagining that there is a timeless truth necessitating several levels of reading, they embraced historicism, the prejudice of the Moderns. This is perspectivism, or the idea that all truth is relative to a particular historical period. Progressivism, which is its crudest version, presupposes that the Moderns are more advanced than the Ancients and that we are more capable than our fathers of understanding the texts of the tradition. Historicism and progressivism govern the interpretation of the tradition by the Moderns. The illusion of the scholars who followed the program of Zunz is to have believed that one could save the tradition in objectifying it and to have forgotten that the divulging of truth requires certain precautions, above all when it concerns the secrets of the Torah, and other explanations, which, at the beginning, were transmitted to individuals only orally. The adepts of the science of Judaism broke with the manner in which the authors of the tradition understood themselves. The more they advanced in their sociology of Jewish life in their historical-juridical project and in their science of language, the more they distanced themselves from the house of their fathers, to the point that the door to the Law was completely closed, as at the end of Kafka's tale, when the guard tells the man from the countryside, who senses that his death is imminent: "here only you could enter, because this entry was made for you alone. Now I'm leaving and closing the door."

This is thus the idea of rupture with the tradition that governs the various currents of *Wissenschaft des Judentums*. Scientific objectivity is thought as being the best means to gain the recognition of other nations. But the fact of cutting oneself off from awareness of what is at stake and abstaining from value judgments disenchants knowledge. This is why, in a letter to Cohen which is at the origin of the creation in Berlin in 1919 of the Akademie fur die *Wissenschaft des Judentums*, Rosenzweig insists on overcoming the narrow positivism of the first generation. Cohen and Rosenzweig lay the first stones; then Guttman continues the construction in welcoming the works of Scholem and Strauss. The latter preserve the monumental character of the German historiography of the nineteenth century, but, in working on a reflection on the forms of Jewish experience, they seek to escape the moribund atmosphere of *Wissenschaft des Judentums* of the first generation that led to a burial of Judaism. The fathers of the science of Judaism committed an error of judgment in ignoring that destructive dialectic whereby science destroys the very objects it seeks to illumine. They were not aware of the fragility of their object. They also misunderstood that essential dimension of the Jewish tradition that is oral instruction. This is because there is a break between the model of interpretation of the Ancients and that of the Moderns, which makes the Law indecipherable.

The Discontinuity of the Ancients and Moderns

Contrary to Amos Funkenstein,[46] who thinks that science is a "secularized theology" and who is inscribed in a sort of continuity of successive adaptations in rabbinic Judaism, Strauss asserts the discontinuity of the Ancients and Moderns and puts Jewish philosophy of the Middle Ages on the side of the Ancients. For Strauss, the return to Judaism specific to *Wissenschaft des Judentums* leads to a break with Judaism, a break that was considered as progress beyond Judaism[47] and was linked to Spinoza. Far from engaging in the prolongation of the Middle Ages and the enterprise of justifying the 613 commandments that characterized Book III of the *Guide of the Perplexed*, Spinoza denies the truth of the religion of Revelation.

Funkenstein adopts the language of accommodation, according to which the Torah speaks the language of human beings. He presents this a principle that exists throughout Jewish history. Favoring the rule taught by Rabbi Ismael, he thinks that the incongruities and incoherencies of the Bible are explained by their adaptation to the many and opposes the principle of an intransigent hermeneutics as at first defended by Rabbi Akiba. The latter thought that each word, each letter, each literary flourish of the Torah has a meaning and a necessity, and this language of God, impenetrable to human understanding, requires that the interpreter neglect nothing. According to Funkenstein, it is the principle of Rabbi Ismael that prevailed in the history of Judaism, for example in the manner in which allegory, in the Middle Ages, served to explain anthropomorphic forms of expression, which permitted the accommodation of the commandments of God to human intelligence. This principle is taken up by

Maimonides in Book I of the *Guide*.[48] This version of the principle of accommodation served to address the problem of the consistency between biblical cosmology and modern science.

Funkenstein returns to the minimalist thesis of Ibn Ezra (1055–1135), who (according to Funkenstein) foreshadows the Spinozist critique of the Bible. This tour de force is connected to the separation of Scripture and science that characterizes the minimalist conception of the principle of accommodation. Genesis is not read as an account of the creation of the world out of nothing, as was conceived by the theologians, but as an explanation of the nature of celestial bodies, that is to say, facts that have a relation to man and his status. The Torah speaks the language of human beings, and in his writing, Moses, who is a man, addresses himself to other men. Funkenstein sees in the exegetic principle of Ibn Ezra the beginning point of the Spinozist thesis according to which the Bible is a purely human document; there is already in Ibn Ezra a sort of secularization of Scripture. But if the Bible is a book written by human beings for human beings, that means that there is no question of an esoteric meaning. Strauss disputes both points.

Far from being the conduit between the minimalist principle of accommodation of Ibn Ezra and the biblical criticism of Spinoza and also in the science of Judaism, Maimonides is conscious of the dangers implicated in divulging the secrets of the Torah without an art of writing. Allegories are not simply attributable to the nature of language but also to the esoteric character of the Law. There are several levels of decoding for allegories, because there is a time for each thing and a way of relating to religion that depends on the level of intelligence of each. This awareness of the different levels of reading of a text and the idea that, for political reasons, not everything can be disclosed, are what separates the Ancients from the Moderns.[49]

When Funkenstein, and before him, Schlomo Pines, see in the meaning of the ceremonial laws of the Old Testament a prefiguration of the philosophy of history and interpret the graceful ruse of which Maimonides speaks as an anticipation of the Hegelian cunning of reason, they commit a twofold error. According to Strauss, one must not read an ancient text in applying to it modern categories. The interpreter must also be attentive to the hidden meaning of the text, which requires that one give up the notion that there are neither political censorship nor secrets to preserve. The writers of the past ought to be understood as they understood themselves. The reader should pay attention to the political context, which explains certain precautions, and the apparent disorder of a book like the *Guide of the Perplexed*, written by an author renowned for his capacity for organized thinking and codification of Law. Funkenstein did not see that the doctrine of Providence in Maimonides was inserted in the political part of the *Guide* and that prophetology was the site of Maimonides's political philosophy. And this attention to context makes evident the difference between the Hegelian cunning of reason and the graceful shrewdness of the *Guide*.[50]

The transgression of the prohibition of writing the *Michna Torah* is explained by the fear that the Law would otherwise be forgotten. It is thus necessary to transmit the tradition and its secrets, which had only been divulged orally and in a way that veiled them. The subtle art of veiling and unveiling explains in part the art of writing of Maimonides. According to Strauss, the chain that connects tradition to action was broken sometime between Maimonides and the science of Judaism. In order to understand the relation of a religion with its tradition, it is necessary to rethink, in addition to its confrontation with another culture and to the link between identity and appropriation it implies, the relation between the word of God and writing as a material record. These circles of interpretation are characteristic of all religions of the Book. In the case of Judaism, there is the additional difficulty of the duality of the written and oral Law. And the Talmud alone is proof that the Jewish tradition does not construct itself on the paradigm of progress, but the page is enlarged each time that a generation adds a commentary to a commentary. These concentric circles are opposed to the notion of progress as rejection or transcendence of the past. In misunderstanding this aspect of the religious tradition that demands several levels of reading and that is accentuated in Judaism by the oral Law, have the Moderns not condemned themselves to betraying the tradition that they had wanted to reinterpret?

Instead of articulating the conservation of the past for the future in fidelity to the concept of time, which is evident in the way in which the Torah is thought as inheritance and promise, the thinkers of *Wissenschaft der Judentums* ended up at an impasse. The idea of the oral Law that actualizes the written Law and underscores the creativity of interpretation is an invitation to the reappropriation of the past. The Moderns, like Kafka's man from the countryside, missed out on the possibility they had to enter through the gate of the Law because they had concentrated on what they had thought was the principal obstacle to the survival of Judaism: they believed that to have an identity, they had at any price to be recognized by the other nations and be assimilated. They adopted the linear conception of time specific to Christianity and to science, and transforming the

Law into an object of study they forgot the principle that should guide the translation of Judaism into another culture. Because it is in beginning from sight, from looking, according to Rosenzweig, that one can unlock language. This question goes back to the relation between language and the Law and introduces the difficulties surrounding Zionism. And if Strauss and Scholem are in agreement in their critique of *Wissenschaft des Judentums* and assimilation, their disagreement concerning Zionism reveals that they do not have the same interest in the critique of the modern Enlightenment or the return to the tradition: Scholem, a Zionist from 1911 on,[51] seems preoccupied with Jewish identity, with a certain nationalism, which explains his defense of Hebrew as the language of the Jewish people in Israel, whereas Strauss goes beyond the framework of Judaism toward an understanding of the theological and political contradictions that beset humanity and of which the Jewish problem is emblematic.[52]

The Aporias of Zionism

From the start constituted as a political and social phenomenon (Moses and the Judges), Judaism, through the experience of exile, reinforces itself around religion in order to preserve itself, by a kind of speculative work on itself, in the diaspora and in its encounter with Western culture. The diffuse influence of Hellenism during the period after exile gives way, in the Middle Ages, in the encounter in Spain with the Arab world, to teaching like that of Maimonides that would shape later Judaism. The Alexandrian period, which was marked by Philo and then by the golden age of the intellectual and philosophical reconstruction of Judaism (Saadia, Halevi, and Maimonides), permitted survival in the diaspora and the reinforcement of Jewish life. All of this is prior to the outbreak of the first crisis related to Spinoza. Beginning with Spinoza, the chain of tradition is undone and the meaning of study, that is, the connection between reading and action, was lost. The history of Judaism after the seventeenth century revolves around an axis situated between destruction and reparation. Mendelssohn and his circle of *Maskilim*, but also all the Jewish thinkers preceding Strauss and Scholem, attempted to reconstruct Judaism while being caught in the dialectic of the Enlightenment. In his *History of the Jews from Remotest Times to the Present,* Grätz shows that there are two main poles: religion and the relation to the Law and the social and political domain. He does not say whether Judaism has to choose one or the other of these poles. This indecisiveness resulted in this book being admired in the first instance by assimilationists and Zionists before being rejected by both in the subsequent generation, which is distinguished by its taking fixed, opposed positions.

The issue was whether Judaism was an anachronism if, as Hegel said, it had died with Christianity. Whether it is considered as a religion or a culture has decisive consequences. One can think that Judaism is overcome as religion but that it is alive and well as the law of a state. One can say that the reward for observance of the commandments concerns not individuals but the people. Zionists think that Judaism, thus understood, is a religion of the future more than the present. But can one have a political or cultural Zionism that is not also at the same time a religious Zionism?

Scholem criticizes *Wissenschaft des Judentums* for having created a politics of cultural assimilation while it should have supported the nationalist project. It should have taken from Romanticism its political orientation, not only its historiography. Scholem would have endorsed Romanticism had he known how to connect it to the modern movement for Emancipation and its relation to the world and to history. The return to the past, to historiography, was an anti-modern reaction, but the method arrived at only reinforcing progressivism, the certainty that the present is superior to the past. Finally, the German Jews who live their double identity and venerate Goethe[53] do not see that the philosophy from which they borrowed their categories has a political dimension that by definition would exclude them.

For Scholem, *Wissenschaft des Judentums* was a sort of Marronism, but its apolitical character was in reality a politics of assimilation. The Jew, in liberating himself from his tradition, breaks free of the yoke that holds him back. It was in abandoning their particularity that Jews hoped to avoid a terrible fate. But this assimilationism, inherited from the *Haskala*, led to collective suicide. Scholem opposed Rosenzweig, who in 1926 titled a collection of essays *Zweistromland* ("land of two currents"), alluding to the dual sources of Jewish and German culture, dreaming of German as a "New Babylon," irrigated by two rivers. Rosenzweig, who insists that the assimilationism of *Wissenschaft des Judentums* had privileged the German component and that it is necessary to rebalance the mix with a kind of "dis-assimilation," is against Zionism. He opposes the politics of rootedness advocated by Scholem and is hostile to the idea that the state of Israel can choose a sacred language like Hebrew for everyday use. This opposition is not simply due to the fact that Rosenzweig, who died in 1929, would not witness the catastrophe that Scholem did, but it can be explained by the return of Rosenzweig to the thought of Jehuda Halevi (1085–1140) and the famed "Parable of the Seed."

> God has a secret and wise design concerning us, which should be compared to the wisdom hidden in the seed which falls into the ground, where it undergoes an external transformation into earth, water and dirt. (. . .) It is, however, the seed itself which transforms earth and water into its own substance, carries it from one stage to another, until it refines the elements and transfers them into something like itself, casting off husks, leaves, etc., and allowing the pure core to appear, capable of bearing the Divine Influence. The original seed produced the tree bearing fruit resembling that from which it had been produced. In the same manner the Law of Moses transforms each one who honestly follows it, though it may externally repel him. The nations merely serve to introduce and pave the way for the expected Messiah, who is the fruition, and they will all become His fruit. Then, if they acknowledge Him, they will become one tree. They will revere the origin which they formerly despised.[54]

The Jewish people is like the seed which falls into the ground. It is obliged to remain in the diaspora because its mission is to live among the nations of the world as a witness to the truth of monotheism. The anti-Zionism of Rosenzweig is metaphysical. But when he said that "my return to Judaism made me not a worse but a better German," he could not convince Scholem. For Scholem, born in Berlin in 1897 and already living in Israel in 1923, this German-Jewish cultural symbiosis is a dangerous illusion. Scholem adopts the formula of Herzl: "We are a nation: the enemy makes us a nation, whether we like it or not."[55]

Zionism is, for Scholem, the solution to the problem of discrimination against Jews. Nevertheless, this solution is not without difficulties, because Judaism does not reduce itself to the political sphere. Strauss's and Scholem's critiques of *Wissenschaft des Judentums* are related to the affirmation not just of the cultural but also of the religious dimension of Judaism. If one wants to extend Zionism to the limit, one must be prepared to imagine a religious Zionism, a theological-political order instituting a common way of life. This tension explains why Strauss would not remain a Zionist, while Scholem, although aware of the difficulty, would make mysticism into a symbolic interpretation of the history of Judaism from its origins to his own time.

As a modern movement, Zionism is strictly political. Theodor Herzl in *The Jewish State* (1896) and Leon Pinsker in *Autoemancipation* (1882) began from the failure of the liberal solution to eliminate the problem of discrimination "but continued to see the problem to be solved as it had begun to be seen by liberalism," that is to say, without thinking that the destiny of the Jews was linked to a divine punishment and without envisaging "the building of the third temple and restoration of the sacrificial service."[56] The Jewish nation should "establish a modern, liberal, secular (but not necessarily democratic) state . . . the land which the strictly political Zionism promised to the Jews was not necessarily the land of Israel."[57]

This project presupposes that one gives up the traditional hopes of the Jewish people. Pinsker chose the motto "If I am not for myself who will be?" Strauss remarks that he omitted a phrase at the center of Hillel's notion: "And if I am only for myself, what am I?" Strictly political Zionism goes hand in hand with the representation of the Jewish people as a nation like any other and able to realize its destiny on its own, by natural means. The idea of a spiritual community, not just a cultural one, which is connected to Revelation, is discarded here along with the key phrase of Hillel. This strictly political Zionism is related to the urgent need for action and the refusal to wait for a solution coming from God. This is why Strauss juxtaposes the passage from Pinsker with one from Spinoza's *Theological-Political Treatise*: "If the foundations of their religion did not effeminate the minds of the Jews, I would absolutely believe that they will at some time, given the occasion (for human things are mutable) establish their state again." Religion is an obstacle to freedom; it makes the Jewish people passive. This aspect of political Zionism is positive and explains the adhesion of the young Strauss, who wrote much later, referring to Scholem, that Zionism, in bringing about the establishment of the state of Israel, "procured a blessing for all Jews everywhere regardless of whether they admit it or not."[58]

Nevertheless, this solution did not resolve the Jewish problem, because a community of blood that is not at the same time a community of spirit remains "an empty shell."[59] This is why the Zionists reacted to this frustrating situation where "the substance of . . . intellectual life" was not at all concerned with "Jewish matters"[60] by countering political Zionism with cultural Zionism. Cultural Zionism was thought to have found the medium between politics and divine Revelation, but in reality it transforms itself into religious Zionism: "the rock bottom of any Jewish culture is the Bible, the Talmud, and the Midrash."[61] And these works do not present themselves as products of the Jewish mind, as culture literature or history, but as "ultimately 'from Heaven.' ": "When religious Zionism understands itself, it is in the first place Jewish faith and only secondarily Zionism. It must regard as blasphemous the notion of a human solution to the Jewish problem."[62] Whatever the importance of the establishment of the state of Israel, this event does not coincide with the coming of the messianic age. It does not mean the end of the Galut (or exile), nor does it constitute Redemption. The return to Judaism is a return to the faith of the fathers. The problem is that this religious Zionism excludes Jews who are not able to believe in what their fathers believed in: "while religious Zionism is the only clear solution, it is not feasible, humanly speaking, for all Jews."[63]

The awareness of the tensions with Zionism explains why Strauss abandoned it. It is impossible not to remain a Jew and it is impossible at the same time to return to the original faith, because of Spinoza. The liberal solution is nothing but an expedient. There exists nothing better than this uneasy solution, which implies legal equality accompanied by discrimination in the private sphere. This response not only concerns the status of a single minority, but also underlines the constitutive difficulties of liberal democracy, which is, itself, a problem without a solution. Defined at the beginning in the theological-political writings of the seventeenth century by opposition to medieval society and based on the distinction between the private and public spheres that would bring about a world where the Inquisition and wars of religion would disappear, liberal democracy does not in fact eliminate discrimination and allow the expression of opinions contrary to its spirit. Finally, it confines religion to subjectivity.

This question of the internalization of faith imposes itself on the Jewish world along with the difficulties born of assimilation, that is, the fact that the Jews, in assimilating the culture of other nations, could have forgotten the specificity of their tradition. This was the case for the thinkers of *Wissenschaft des Judentums*, but the secularization of biblical morality and the internalization of the content of faith have provoked among Christians a perhaps still more radical disappearance of religion, of the identity and culture of the West of which it is the source. Everything operates as if the consciousness of belonging to a minority were a counterweight to this trend of secularization and uniformization of spirituality that results from liberal democracy, founded on a universal human morality. The common challenge for both Christians and Jews is whether a religion can survive when it is left to individual choice or whether one must return to tradition to preserve it from oblivion and to prevent its descent into superstition.

This is the thrust of the return to tradition as conceived of by Strauss and by Scholem. It involves a return to the study of the texts of the tradition. Because the danger that Judaism will be lost is connected to assimilation, persecution, and genocide, but also to secularization, Scholem believes that mysticism can bring to life the connection to religion and offer the Jews the key to the interpretation of the Law and their own history. His Zionism takes on its full meaning through his preoccupation with mysticism. What *Wissenschaft des Judentums* lacked, besides ideology, was openness to understanding the mystical texts of the tradition. When Scholem undertakes a historical analysis of mystical texts, he does not limit himself to identifying with the project of a renewed science of Judaism, but rather integrates this historiographical work into a metaphysical interpretation of the destiny of the Jewish people. He ceases to believe that Hebrew should be the language spoken in Israel and finds in the study of the kabbalah a means to hold fast to his Zionism without getting entrapped in its difficulties. Because Scholem is not an advocate of a theocratic state and because he is well aware of the dangers of messianism when transposed to politics, he constructs an approach that provides Jews throughout the world with a way of reading that permits them to recover a connection to the tradition that is not simply intellectual but also existential and that connects interpretation and action. Because of Strauss's awareness that the problems affecting Judaism are revealing of the destructive logic of the modern project, he will return to Maimonides as an emblematic figure of pre-modern rationalism and reopen the theological-political problem, considering what it is necessary to retain or reject in the Spinozist or Hobbesian critiques of religion.

Chapter 2

The Critique of Religion and Biblical Criticism

Spinoza's critique of religion presents the classic modern vision of the world. But this is not self-evident. This is why "interest necessarily reverts from [the] . . . classical exponents of the modern world view to the men who laid the foundations of this "world view," namely, to Descartes and Hobbes."[1] Before studying the specificity of Spinoza's critique, one should see the connection between modern natural science and the critique of religion, being aware that this connection is not as evident as might first appear, given that for Descartes, Newton, and Leibniz modern science does not exclude religious faith.[2] Among the thinkers who preceded Spinoza, such as Uriel da Costa and Isaac de La Peyrère, Thomas Hobbes is the thinker who best exemplifies the foundations and spirit of the radical Enlightenment.

Representative of the Epicurean motivation of the critique of religion, motivation that is the "first line of attack of the Enlightenment" and father of modern politics, based on the notion of sovereignty and the question of justified and necessary obedience by human beings to the Leviathan, Hobbes incarnates even more radically than Spinoza the break with the thinking of classics, whether of Greek, Aristotelian, or biblical origin. It is a matter of grasping the foundation of this critique of religion, which is at the same time more radical[3] in Hobbes than in Spinoza because it is a condition of his politics, and less definitive philosophically than for Spinoza, whose *Ethics* contains the notion of the intellectual love of God and separates the religion of knowledge from piety, which is inferior. The consideration of the differences between Spinoza and Hobbes is at least as important as the examination of what they have in common. It illuminates the revival by the Enlightenment of the Epicurean critique of religion. It is a matter of asking whether the war on revealed religion destroyed orthodoxy as such or rather whether it merely destroyed certain claims of a particular kind of orthodoxy, perhaps not genuine. In the latter case, the *interest* in Revelation would remain intact, which would give complete freedom to maneuver to the movement for a return to tradition to which Strauss subscribes.

The Critique of Religion and Revelation in Hobbes

Epicureanism[4]

The Epicurean critique of religion, which is connected to concern with human happiness and peace of mind, the idea that man can take his life in hand without worrying about Stoic fatalism or imagining that the gods have any concern with him, is the most important source of the critique of religion in the seventeenth century. "We understand by Epicureanism not first of all the *doctrine* of Epicurus and his school, but rather an interest natural to man, a uniform and elementary *outlook* [Gesinnung] . . . the will to free man from fear, determined by nature, of the divine and death, so that on the basis of a prudent calculation of the chances of pleasure and pain that present themselves to man, . . . one might lead a thoroughly happy life."[5]

Nevertheless, the modern Enlightenment modified the arguments of Epicurus in his *Letters to Menoeceus*. The precursors of Spinoza rejected religion because it was consoling, while, for Epicurus, it was connected to the fear of divine punishment. This has nothing to do with the argumentation of Spinoza, who considers revealed religion as superstition, deriving from fear of the unknown. According to Spinoza, this fear drives men to believe in the existence of revealed Laws and in miracles. But the rejection of this superstitious fear, which is really a purely human fear that Spinoza does not distinguish from the authentic fear of God, is linked to the certitude, central to Epicurus, that human happiness depends on liberation from false representations of the deity and of life after death. This is because these products of a false imagination prevent men from dedicating themselves to the only good that belongs to them: this life. The difference between Epicurus and the Moderns is that, for the former, religion is terrifying, while for the latter, it is a form of alienation and comfort, the opium of the people. It puts men to sleep, in making them believe that after their life of misery, they will experience eternal happiness; they are not pushed to change the course of things or the course of history, which is the rule of the powerful, including the Church. Moreover, religion has nefarious consequences for civil peace: "Emphasis falls now on liberating human society from its worst enemies (the "priests") by political action."[6]

The Epicurean motivation (the quest for a safe pleasure as a foundation of the critique of superstition) as it was exploited by the predecessors of Spinoza thus reconnects the affirmation of human responsibility and freedom, the belief in progress through science, and the condemnation, as a political matter, of the usurpation of authority by the Church. And it is Hobbes who will best articulate these elements. The analysis of his thought allows one equally to understand why this critique of religion is, in the seventeenth century, a critique of Revelation and depends on the unknowable character of miracles and biblical criticism. This is based on a principle of biblical interpretation that is linked in Hobbes to his rejection of a dual authority of Throne and Alter or the claim that spiritual authority should be subordinate to political authority.

Hobbes, in *De Cive* and *Leviathan*, explains religion on the basis of human nature, as defined by the passions. Man's desire, far from limiting itself to a quest for transitory pleasures, is also augmented by the desire for recognition, or vanity: each man desires that his personal worth be recognized by the others. This vainglory, which is linked to anticipation of the future, puts men in competition with one another and is reinforced by a desire for power. Pleasure, the source of immediate contentment, should be certain, that is, it must be secured against the cupidity and envy of others. Each desires what his neighbors desire and seek, in coveting the goods of others, to confirm his feeling of superiority. The individual, in order to continue to enjoy what he has, has to increase his power and, achieve ever greater power and ever greater honor. And because his power is the condition for the possibility of certain and continuing enjoyment, the desire for power[7] takes precedence over the desire of enjoyment and the desire for recognition or vanity, which is the origin of the war of all against all. This anthropology is the foundation of the political philosophy of Hobbes and his theory of a state, which, taking into account the naturally querulous character of human beings, stays above all possible contestation in order to be able to guarantee the civil peace. This conception of man implies that the religion cannot be the right way to guarantee peace and happiness. Science, which is *propter potentiam* and which is orientated toward the relief of man's estate, is the means for cultivating nature, realizing the hoped-for progress, and promoting civilization.

Revealed religion is in the first instance rejected by Hobbes because it is incapable of realizing human happiness: religion is the "issue of the search for causes that process without method." "The gods originate as an offspring of human fear."[8] Strauss links this critique, according to which dreams are the main content of the representation of divinity, to the teaching of Lucretius. Instead of seeking to know the true causes of bad things and providing oneself with the means, through science and technology, to address them, men are abused by prophets who pretend to be divinely inspired and who assign illusory and uncontrollable causes to events. Religion opposes itself to the progress of civilization. By contrast, the religion of Hobbes and its Epicurean spirit imply a materialist mechanistic physics: "If nature must be understood in such a way as not to be troubling to man, . . . only corporal substances could be acknowledged as substances and only local motions as alterations."[9]

But this critique of superstition, of which the causes are fear and ignorance, is reinforced by a condemnation of religion as responsible for increasing human unhappiness. Far from being a mere consequence of his natural philosophy and supplementary to his political philosophy, Hobbes's critique of religion is necessary for his political teaching. "Hobbes' politics is at any rate indissolubly connected with his critique of religion: religion is *the* enemy for this politics."[10] Effectively, religion is the product of vanity and men's underestimation of their own power.[11] This condemnation does not really apply to pagan religion, which had as its aim to educate men for peaceful life and which was an aspect of politics: opposition to authority was a sin. By contrast, revealed religion "makes politics an aspect of religion." It thus constitutes a menace to peaceful political life. The *gloriatio*, the basis of prophesy, has as a consequence the assertion of divided authority, which is harmful to politics. Religion based on Revelation claims spiritual authority and subverts politics, which is linked to the notion that human beings, who are in permanent conflict, need to obey a single authority, which will protect each against the others.

The critique of revealed religion is more radical in Hobbes than in Spinoza: contrary to Spinoza, religion is not useful to bring about political obedience. The latter is based upon a rational calculus of each human being, who recognizes a fundamental equality: anyone is capable of killing anyone else, regardless of mere difference in physical power, of inflicting the greatest of ills and violent death. The submission to a political authority that protects us thus does not require religion. Spinoza is closer than Hobbes to classical philosophy because he thinks that those beings who understand the necessity of things are wise, while others are driven by the fear of the unknown and the hope of life after death. By contrast, in Hobbes obedience derives from fear and self-interested calculation, and it is this calculation that constitutes reason. Everyone is equally endowed with it and its basis is human nature, the passions, while for Spinoza, reason is oriented toward *theoria* or contemplation, which implies the gap between the small number of the wise and the vulgar. Reason according to Hobbes is modesty,[12] and it is the equality of all men that contradicts prophecy. But Hobbes's rejection of the religion of Revelation is ultimate due to its political dangerousness; basing its legitimacy on the Bible, it claims an authority that rivals that of the political and contradicts the idea of political absolutism. The critique of divided authority is thus the core of the Hobbesian critique of the religion of Revelation. Scientific criticism of the Bible is the means that Hobbes uses for attacking at its foundation the legitimacy of spiritual authority. It is here that the Epicureanism of Hobbes shares certain traits with the Socinianism that one finds in Isaac de La Peyrère.

The Interpretation of the Bible

The political is, according to Hobbes, the key to understanding the Bible. If the clergy maintained a teaching that Scripture requires obedience to secular authority and did not demand piety,[13] there would not be a conflict between science and religion or between the state and religion. Hobbes opens up the possibility of modern biblical criticism, particularly that of Spinoza, to the extent that he echoes his judgment concerning the origin and form of the Old Testament, but the center of his thought is the problem of authority. Spinoza interrupted his writing of his philosophical masterpiece the *Ethics* in order to write his *Theologico-Political Treatise* because the counterreformation threatened the lives of free thinkers, in particular philosophers. This urgent situation brought him to action, but once calm is reestablished *theoria* regains its priority. The free and solitary exercise of contemplation that characterizes theory remains the most important thing for Spinoza, and his religious position and political engagement are secondary. Another manifestation of the difference between Spinoza and Hobbes is that the latter, instead of being concerned with the people of Israel, begins by questioning pre-Mosaic authority—it begins with Adam, not Abraham—in order to emphasize what are the foundations of political community.[14] What is essential is not to combat religion because it is false and contemptible from the perspective of the philosopher, but because it is prejudicial to public order. It is not because it persecutes philosophers that religion is nefarious, but because interpreted and co-opted as it is by priests, it threatens the state and contests the terms of the social contract.

By contrast, if ecclesiastical power is limited to teaching and remains in submission to state-determined parameters, then the Christian, far from being faced with two authorities, remains faithful to the contract he has made with the civil authority of his nation. A Christian living in a country where his religion is prohibited must submit to civil authority while preserving his interior faith. Because the external manifestations of piety are, for Hobbes, *adiaphora* or matters of no consequence, this nicodemism, being similar at first glance to marronism, is a question of civic duty. It is not only a prudential measure aimed at avoiding persecution, but for Hobbes an affirmation of the supremacy of the political and a consequence of his theory of sovereignty. Finally, the status of ecclesiastics, who are turned into ordinary civil servants, is based on an interpretation of the role of Christ and his apostles. Far from being kings who possess unmediated sovereignty, Christ and his apostles are not able to make laws that are real and valid, but merely propose a new teaching of morality.

This indifference to the external manifestations of faith and this moral character of the teachings of Christ are part of the modern religious consciousness, which is characterized by the fact that religion designates an autonomous cultural domain. It is connected to the subjective sphere and detached from the public sphere (Spinoza) and must not interfere with collective political decisions (Hobbes). It must not constrain progress, the right of each to control his own body and the freedom of morals, which are only unacceptable when they are in tension with the respect for others and human rights. In his analysis of the seventeenth-century critique of religion, Strauss emphasizes the assumptions of the modern religious consciousness. Rather than a digression through Hobbes, this inquiry is the occasion for grasping, within the continuity of the Epicurean critique that relates to something natural in man, that which separates us from classical thought of biblical origin, that is, from the Middle Ages, and for asking ourselves why this critique seems to have won the day, at least among most twentieth-century people.

The English version of *Leviathan* contains the most open presentation of Hobbes's critique of religion.[15] This does not mean that Hobbes expresses there his true teaching but that he presents himself as a believer in order to be credible when he deduces from his interpretation of Scripture that Revelation itself puts no limit on the duty to obey secular authority. It is here that the critique of the Bible takes the place, in the critique of religion, of the analysis of human passions: "To the arbitrary, private opinions of the theologians . . . Hobbes opposes the binding teaching of Scripture and the Church. And since the Church is also exposed to spiritual errors, he appeals not merely from theology but also from the Church to Scripture *alone*."[16] Divided authority derives from a defective interpretation of Scripture, just as eschatological dualism, which supports belief in Satan as well as in eternal life, results from an erroneous pagan Greek conception. The scientific criticism of the Bible is the means of rectifying these errors, propagated by the clergy. This provides a severe critique of the Roman clergy, originating in the Roman Empire.

Hobbes criticizes religion, namely theology and the Church, by turning to Scripture. Miracles are thus no longer considered as the criteria for or the sources of the knowledge of divine commandments. Moreover, there can no longer be prophets. Public Revelation alone, the transmission of the word of God through a text, will be recognized. But the problem is that the books of Scripture are written in a foreign language: "in case of doubt, [who] should decide which translation and explication ranks as authentic?"[17]

In order to ascertain which books have canonic status, Hobbes does not revert to the Church, not even to the Church of England, to which secular authority bids him to submit, but he interprets Scripture and establishes its political teaching "according to his own rational estimate." Thus he considers the Bible to be like any other literary work. The work of Hobbes is situated in a cultural context that is the extension of the Renaissance. That is, the Bible is no longer read as history but as a literary text. Philological criticism gains priority over the student of the content of the holy book. The pillar of the tradition—the Church and its theology aimed at explaining the commandments—is suppressed and replaced by the study of the sources and the context in which different books of the Bible were written. Far from minimizing the inherent contradictions of the Bible, it is a matter of unpacking the internal and external difficulties of the text, which give rise to philological work but also to geography and dating. Finally, it is a matter of reflecting on the status of the Holy Scriptures: What theological positions are expounded in the Bible, and by what means have they been transmitted? If the Bible has been written by men directly inspired by God, must one consider each book as a whole or rank the various books and say, for example, that Moses could not have written the account of his own death? The problem is that of authenticity of texts.

In the footsteps of Isaac de La Peyrère, Hobbes undertakes a critical reading of the biblical text and shows that, if one relies on the declarations in the Bible, one can see which books, for example, have been written by Moses (the book of the Law contained in Deuteronomy) and which books have been penned by other authors. The principle, in conformity with what Spinoza will call an immanent reading of the Bible, is to follow the indications given by the holy text itself. Thus one does not attribute anything to Moses that has not been attributed explicitly in the text of Scripture. Distinguishing between the subject and the author of a book, this principle of interpretation, which has as its object to combat falsifications and fabrications of Scripture, assumes a confidence in the authenticity of the holy text itself. The critique of the Bible does not put in question but assumes the revealed character of Scripture: "the meaning of the words used in Scripture can be ascertained neither from the vulgar nor the scientific use of speech, but solely from Scripture itself. The advancement of this principle in Hobbes has its ground . . . resting on the belief in the revealed character of Scripture, to validate the pure word of God against all human falsifications or fabrications."[18]

This concern for the sacred character of Scripture explains that in the case of a conflict between reason and Scripture, one will not interpret the biblical text as having rational meaning. If one admits that the Bible is not intended to teach philosophy or science, acceptance of its literal meaning does not pose any difficulty. The interest of the interpreter thus ought to be directed toward "the guiding intention of the Bible as a whole." It is through starting with clear passages that the interpreter "is able to advance an understanding also of the dark passages"[19] and to resolve the problem of the internal contradictions of the Bible.

In Hobbes, the study of the Bible conforms to a historical theory of the composition of the scriptures, as a compilation, where from the fourth century on there is a distinction between authentic and apocryphal books. This gives rise to a radical critique, because the authority of the Church is not the basis for judging the holy text. But, on the other hand, Hobbes, no more than La Peyrère or Spinoza, is not interested in establishing a new exegesis. And despite the late establishment of the canon; the distinction between the author and the subject of a book; and the limitations on the meaning of words such as "prophecy," "immortality," "word of God," and "spirits and angels," it is the authority of the Bible that makes a book canonic, not its author.

Nevertheless, the theological-political problem of the Enlightenment at the end of the seventeenth century is such that one can only imagine the separation of the theological and the political, of Church and state. This finds its clearest expression in Spinoza's *Theologico-Political Treatise*. The attack on the usurpation of power by priests and the rejection of theocracy are common to Hobbes and Spinoza and would become a leitmotif in Voltaire, Nietzsche, and Marx. The discrediting of the spiritual authority of the Church, accused of manipulating minds, denounced as avaricious and held responsible for intolerance, provides even today a justification for atheism and is a determining feature of the modern religious consciousness. This consciousness, whenever it is perplexed, is not deferential to the clergy and chooses for itself the dogmas in which it believes and the prescriptions that it follows. It creates a synthesis between what is declared by the representatives of spiritual authority and what it considers right. The theological-political writings of the seventeenth century and the scientific criticism of the Bible thus opened the door to an internalization of the content of religion. In attacking superstition and downgrading claims concerning the supernatural, scientific biblical criticism changed the relation of the Moderns to faith: Could the learned still believe in miracles, and could they imagine that the Bible was inspired by God and the prophets? And if there is a difference between magic and religion, into which category does one place dogmas like the Trinity and incarnation that are at the heart of Christianity? Can one even still speak of faith in God and in Revelation when one denies miracles and prophecy? These concerns lead to Hobbes's modification of Socinianism in light of a philosophy characterized by a "theology" and an ontology that are specific to the radical Enlightenment.

Socinianism and the Radical Enlightenment

Faust Socinus (1539–1604) was concerned with what he saw as the excessive harshness of the Mosaic Law and its failure to address immortality. For Socinus, immortality is central to Christianity; in the Epicurean tradition, Socinus's critique of religion is out of concern for human happiness. Socinianism thus will challenge those prescriptions of the Mosaic Law considered anachronistic and contrary to the spirit of love prescribed by Christ and the promise of eternal life revealed in the New Testament.[20] This return to Epicureanism is connected to the conception of a benevolent God that comes from the New Testament: as with Hobbes and La Peyrère, one is dealing with a post-Christian modification of Epicureanism.[21] The adherents of Socinianism are strongly committed to the separation of the Old and New Testaments, opposing the notion of a God who inflicts terrible punishments on his creatures and adhering to the doctrine of Marcius.[22]

The modern Enlightenment attacked earlier religious teachings by invoking the compassionate goodness of God.[23] Hobbes follows the

Socians in opposing the idea of eternal damnation and asserting that the destruction of the wicked after the Resurrection contradicts the Scripture. He takes up the central teaching of Socinianism concerning the guarantee of immortality but modifies it through interpreting this guarantee of immortality in a truly Epicurean spirit, as a mere guarantee against fear of death, and not in relation to righteousness and sin; it is a matter neither of the forgiveness of sinners nor of a life after death in the beyond, but for Hobbes salvation and hell are found on earth.

Hobbes's critique of religion is a "complete radicalization of Socinianism along the lines of Epicureanism."[24] The ecclesiastical tradition is rejected and the testament of the Holy Spirit is no longer considered necessary for the understanding of Scripture. As is implicit in the Socian faith, the only norm of belief is the Bible itself, the understanding of which is a matter for the reasoned judgment of the individual, a modern principle that governs religiosity after the Enlightenment. The Enlightenment also takes up the distinction between that which, in the Bible, is essential for salvation and that which is not. This distinction is Socinian and derives in Hobbes from the idea according to which the Bible teaches salvation and not philosophy or science. The replacement of "Greek" theology with biblical theology, the interpretation of eternity as an endless period of time, and the being of God as having power over us come from Socinianism. The negation of natural immortality and the idea that between physical death and resurrection there is no life are equally Socinian and are found again in the manner in which the modern religious consciousness has secularized most biblical concepts. Natural religion, the innate knowledge of God acquired by the contemplation of creation, is rejected in conformity with the Socinian teaching. This means that the critique of the Enlightenment, as we have seen with Lessing, does not preserve the question of natural theology except in an exoteric manner. The negation of the divinity of Christ, a key aspect of Socinianism, and the importance accorded to the function and not in the first place to the person of Christ, are found in Hobbes, as in most of the thinkers of the Enlightenment, who, without being completely atheistic, did not adhere to Christianity and whose belief is hard to distinguish from agnosticism.

What was critical for Socinus was to affirm the immortality of the soul, made certain by "the historical fact of the resurrection of Jesus Christ."[25] Similarly, it is not the sin of Adam that led to man's physical mortality: "The outcome of Adam's sin is that natural morality took on the character of a punishment and thus became necessary. . . . What is needful if a man who was created mortal is to attain immortality is a change of his nature, a second creation. This change is the fulfillment of the promise given by Jesus and vouched for by the resurrection of Jesus himself."[26]

One sees this idea in La Peyrère. But Hobbes accelerates this process of transformation of Christian teachings and empties them of any transcendent reference, interpreting salvation as earthly. This same radicalization of Socinianism characterizes his interpretation of miracles.[27] As with Revelation, miracles are not recognizable as such. Hobbes tacitly puts in question their possibility.[28] If Revelation is not identifiable, the revealed Law lacks constraining force. Belief in the Bible and in miracles is prejudices, because the difference between miracles and deceptions (*Betrug*) is difficult to establish. Thus for Hobbes the authority of Scripture is merely an artifice; it is only maintained because it allows him to attack the Church and to assert, by refutation of divided authority, his theory of the state. But once theological politics has been rendered impossible, Hobbes challenges revealed religion as such and undermines the authority of the Bible. This is the intent of his teaching on miracles, the centerpiece of his critique of religion that is central to his philosophy, not only because it is the condition of the possibility of his political theory, but also because it is in line with the conception of man and the world that is specific to the radical Enlightenment. The idea that there is no difference between nature and miracles, which is found in Calvin, leads Hobbes to say that the miracle, which is not identifiable as such, is only valuable to those who lack scientific understanding. Modern science does not refute the possibility of miracles, but it opposes them in asserting that this belief belongs to a prescientific stage of humanity.[29]

The denial of the possibility of miracles, Revelation, and prophecy goes hand in hand with Hobbes's view that we can only know for certain the objects of our representations and not things-in-themselves. It isn't that Hobbes denies the existence of things-in-themselves, only that they are knowable. Moreover, we only know what we make: science itself is dependent on our tools of analysis. Our grasp is limited to art, which is not the imitation of nature but invention. Hobbes uses the Cartesian teaching that self-consciousness is the foundation of philosophy, but, distinguishing between error and prejudice, he denies the possibility of a rational theology and excludes knowledge of things-in-themselves.

Hobbes differs from Socinianism in that his God is not the compassionate God of La Peyrère or even Locke. The notion of a compassionate God is used by Hobbes merely for purposes of rejecting the idea of eternal punishment and reinforcing the anti-spiritualist critique that comes from

Epicureanism and leads him to reject the idea of evil forces operating on us. Relying on the English version of *Leviathan*, Strauss shows that Hobbes abandons the notion of a compassionate God, common to the Moderate Enlightenment and Socinianism, and radicalizes the Cartesian device of the "deceiving God." Strauss also reveals the "moral orientation" specific to the radical Enlightenment and explains in what sense the critique of religion is, in Hobbes, "that which orients his entire philosophy."

The sympathy of Hobbes for the Cartesian notion of an evil demon is characteristic of his rejection of the biblical concept of God. Moreover, "this possibility of a *Deus deceptor* is only a peculiarly pointed expression of the possibility of a fully incomprehensible God."[30] This is the "inversion of the belief in providence."[31] The world was made by a totally incomprehensible God. It is thus in itself completely incomprehensible. Consciousness can be a protection against the deceiving God, but it cannot assist us "with an orientation in a world that is completely incomprehensible."[32] The retreat (*Rückgang*) to consciousness, writes Hobbes, who uses military language to evoke the defensive character of Cartesian philosophy, is not adequate. The work of civilization is necessary not to improve the human species but to save it. The radical Enlightenment is connected to a certain pessimism within its struggle for its own project, which is the furthering of civilization. There is no guarantee that man is fit for survival in this world. Nothing guarantees that the world is adapted to our powers. The God who created the world and man did not have the understanding that would have exposed him to several possible worlds in order to choose the best. The radical Enlightenment is that of Hobbes, not Leibniz. Finally, man himself is bad, and without the artifice of the state, men would destroy their own species. Only science and politics allow man to survive in conquering nature and in knowing himself sufficiently to accept the constraints required to live in peace.[33]

The Need to Reconsider the Radical Enlightenment

According to Hobbes, man's salvation depends on his capacity to engage his own forces in order to contribute to his security and the progress of civilization. This "philosophy of civilization" is divided between a theory of the state of nature and a doctrine that concerns the civil state. Yet if man believes in a God who can do anything, he will not think that the means he has to orient himself in a hostile world depend exclusively on himself. Given the obstacle posed by religion, the affirmation of human progress depends on science *and* politics. After Hobbes, the Enlightenment remained faithful to his belief in science, but did it not neglect the political philosophy, the necessity of which he asserted because his pessimistic anthropology made impossible the moral progress of humanity?

The philosophers of the Enlightenment thought that general human progress at once material, health-related, medical, and also aesthetic, moral, and political would follow from progress in knowledge and its diffusion. In the nineteenth century, this belief in science had a tendency to become itself a religion. The scientific became the criterion of all truth, relegating all other kinds of knowing to the infancy of mankind. Knowledge should be free of value judgments. Morality and reflection on the ends of human reason are exiled to the sphere of pure subjectivity, and this goes hand in hand with value relativism, each individual choosing on his own among various life possibilities those that seem agreeable to his or her. Finally, in the nineteenth century, one will see the emergence of philosophies of history that express serious reservations about this belief in man's progress through reason. And this belief in the general progress of humanity through technology, science, and the rationalization of collective life would crumble in the twentieth century.

Similarly, the death of God is not accompanied by the creation of new values reestablishing faith in man. Rather, the death of God defines a new kind of nihilism more dangerous than the earlier kinds, which designates the alienation through religion condemned by the Enlightenment. This nihilism is the reign of the last man. The last man is satisfied, while degrading all things. He wills for the sake of willing; he lacks both desires and ideals.

> "We have invented happiness," say the last men, and they blink. They have left the regions where it was hard to live, for one needs warmth. One still loves one's neighbor and rubs against him, for one needs warmth . . . One still works, for work is a form of entertainment. But one is careful lest the entertainment be too harrowing. One no longer becomes poor or rich: both require too much exertion. Who still wants to rule? Who obey? Both require too much exertion. No shepherd and one herd! Everybody wants the same, everybody is the same: whoever feels different goes voluntarily into a madhouse.[34]

Like the type of person characteristic of democratic society described by Tocqueville, the last man is individualist and self-absorbed.

He restlessly seeks small pleasures for himself. For Strauss, who thinks that we are at the crest of the third wave of modernity, this situation is the result of the Enlightenment and the manner in which the successors of Hobbes vulgarized it, transforming it into an ideology. Of the critique of religion, what remained was the condemnation of superstition and alienation, but they totally forgot its corollary: man's badness makes politics necessary, and the crisis of our time is a crisis of political philosophy. The eclipse of political philosophy or its relegation to a marginal status is a symptom of the essential forgetfulness that intervened between the radical Enlightenment and our times. We are separated from the Ancients by Hobbes and Machiavelli, who broke with classical political philosophy in replacing the question of the best regime capable of perfecting man's humanity with a political teaching concerning the state that is aimed at guaranteeing security. But we are equally distanced from Hobbes himself today. We are even further than he was from the truth of the political.

In order to be able to imagine a return to the Ancients, we must first revisit the modern ideology of the radical Enlightenment. This detour by the radical Enlightenment by the pessimism of Hobbes is facilitated, so to speak, by the events to which Strauss is a witness, which put in question the idea of progress. The God of Hobbes, of whom Leibniz said that he lacks goodness and who is characterized by his unqualified absolute power,[35] is reminiscent not so much of the fearsome God of the Old Testament as of the experience of evil that led to the Straussian reflection through the self-destructive logic of the West. In the human history, anything is possible. It is not that God can make human beings suffer as he pleases, but that humans inflict on each other undeserved suffering. The notion of absolute power is never put in question, whether one is dealing with God, of whom Maimonides underlined the wisdom, or human beings, on whom the technology confers the power of demigods.

The belief that the progress of civilization is a product of man alone turns religion into an obstacle, but this belief in itself does not lead to man's improvement. What is one to make of the optimism of the nineteenth century, including that of Cohen? Cannot even Spinoza provide more clarity on the crisis of our times? The challenge is to find a substitute for religion (Tocqueville) or to overcome it through political philosophy. And Spinoza here is equipped with a political realism that his successors would lack. This is why the critique by Strauss "of the hard-headed, not to say hard-hearted disciple of Machiavelli"[36] is not entirely negative. Strauss's critique of the Enlightenment is not purely an attack or a rejection. The originality and complexity of this critique of modernity is apparent even from the particularly subtle way in which he studies Spinoza, an essential figure to confront both for those who seek to return to orthodoxy and also for the heirs of Enlightenment, like Cohen.

Spinoza's Particular Contribution to the Critique of Religion

Three tendencies of different origin inform the seventeenth-century critique of religion. These three tendencies are represented by Epicurus, Averroes, and Machiavelli. The concern with civil peace is the motivation that unites them and explains, in a context of struggle against religious intolerance, that religion would be held responsible for human ills. In Spinoza, there is a merging of these three tendencies. The objective of the *Theologico-Political Treatise* (hereafter *TPT*) is to advance the goal of a liberal society, where the distinction between Jews and Christians no longer results in discrimination, where human beings are no longer persecuted for their religious opinions, and where philosophers are left in peace. The universal religion that Spinoza founds, beginning from his interpretation of the Bible and his rehabilitation of the figure of Christ, serves to defend tolerance and democracy and protect Spinoza himself from persecution. Accused of atheism and the resident of a Christian country where the Anti-Remonstrants used the Old Testament to legitimate their theocratic ambitions, Spinoza seeks to prove that the Bible itself advocates religious tolerance, that republicanism is the regime most in concert with the nature of man, and that freedom of thought and expression is favorable to civil peace.

Strauss shows the strategy behind these positions of Spinoza by situating them in the theological-political context in which they were elaborated. In so doing, he counters the severe judgment of Cohen against Spinoza, whom he condemned as "humanly incomprehensible" and for being "the accuser *par excellence* of Judaism in an anti-Jewish world." Nevertheless, Strauss is not deceived about the impact of Spinoza's criticism, which "makes all religions untrue." His "opposition to Spinoza is, on certain points, still greater than" that of Cohen, in particular when he analyzes the link between religion and superstition and the radical separation between religion and philosophy, of which the ends and purposes are different. Religion is aimed at obedience and uses the Bible to control the common people. Philosophy is aimed at the truth and is based on an elite intellectual community. The universal religion is a morality adapted to the common people and their passions, particularly fear. It does not realize the sovereign good, but it facilitates political stability and salvation in the weak sense of the term. The goal of philosophy is beatitude, the sovereign good or the intellectual love for God, knowledge of the third kind,[37] contemplation *sub specie aeternitas*. One could ask if Spinoza, in separating religion from knowledge and regrounding it in morality in order to found the liberal state, does not anticipate the Nietzschean critique of religion as a tool of the weak and the morality of resentment. Finally, is not Spinoza the founder of an extreme form of liberal Judaism that renders impossible any return to orthodoxy in requiring the adversaries of liberal religion to confront scientific biblical criticism?

Persecution and the Art of Writing

Cohen, in his 1915 work titled *Spinoza, on the State and Religion, Judaism and* Christianity,[38] accuses Spinoza of providing arguments to anti-Semites in contrasting the universalist teaching of Christianity with the particularistic and national—indeed nationalistic—character of Judaism, which "commands "the hatred of the enemy." Spinoza ridiculed his people and engaged in blasphemy in making the God of Moses a carnal and tribal God to which he opposed a completely idealized spiritual Christianity. He raised the suspicion that the Jewish religion was merely the doctrine of the Jewish state, while Christianity, where one was required to render unto God what is God's and to Caesar what is Caesar's, and the Pauline dogma are perceived as allowing Christians to avoid the mixing of religion and politics. Spinoza operates in bad faith, according to Cohen. He is motivated by the desire for revenge against the *Herem* that was pronounced against him. This becomes even clearer when he contradicts himself, in other places in the *TPT*, in recognizing the universalist character of the Old Testament, such as in chapter 14, where he sets forth the credo of the universal church, based on both the Old and the New Testaments. Finally, this man, indifferent to messianism and the notion of humanity that it implies; this disciple of Machiavelli who thinks of the state in terms of power, without any reference to morality; this philosopher who reserves true salvation for an elite is, from Cohen's socialist perspective, an unlikely democrat. "Cohen comes to the conclusion that far from deserving to be celebrated, Spinoza fully deserved his excommunication."[39]

When Strauss reconsiders this judgment, he shows that the accusations by Cohen against Spinoza are not the same as those alleged by the tradition. Cohen does not reproach Spinoza for having denied that Moses was the author of the Pentateuch and being opposed to the Ceremonial

Laws. Cohen, the neo-Kantian philosopher who takes for granted the scientific criticism of the Bible, knows that not all commandments have the same status or force and the importance of eliminating idolatry. This enlightened Judaism even explains his interest in Maimonides and his reading of book 3 of the *Guide*. If Cohen has a problem with Spinoza, it is not because the latter failed to distinguish between the historical and the mythical elements of the Bible, but rather because Spinoza is psychologically incomprehensible. How could a man whose ancestors were expelled from Portugal give arguments to those who hate the Jews? Spinoza had to be possessed by an "evil demon."

This understanding displays, according to Strauss, an inadequately precise reading of Spinoza. Spinoza is no more anti-Jewish than he is pro-Christian. Cohen should have asked himself why Spinoza treats Christianity and Judaism differently and says that the Mosaic Law excludes the practice of philosophy while that of Jesus seems to call for it. A careful reading of the *TPT* reveals that the liberal society that Spinoza wants to bring about is neither Christian nor Jewish: the purpose of the treatise is to show the way toward a liberal society. "The establishment of such a society required in his opinion the abrogation of the Mosaic Law (. . .) since Moses' religion is a political law, to adhere to this religion as he proclaimed it is incompatible with being a citizen of any other state, while Jesus was not a legislator but only a teacher."[40] Strauss recognizes the benevolence of Spinoza, who was not an enemy of his own people but a friend of the human race. His Christianity is a strategy to support the founding, based on the Bible, of a political regime characterized by the separation of theology and politics, Church and state. This distinction is for Strauss clearly evident, which is no small thing coming from someone who saw in Farabi's and Maimonides's understanding of prophecy the key to a political philosophy able to respond to the challenges of contemporary democracy.

A different strategy dictates the "choice" by Spinoza of Christianity and his disavowal of the Mosaic Law. This strategy relates to an art of writing to which the heirs of the Modern Enlightenment are not attentive. Spinoza's statements concerning the Old Testament can be explained by the context of persecution. He practices an art of writing that explains the inconsistencies between the *TPT* and the *Ethics* and certain contradictions with the *TPT* itself. The Christianizing reading of the *Treatise* is an exoteric reading. Cohen neglects to consider the forces of persecution operating at the time of Spinoza. He projects twentieth-century conditions onto Spinoza: he reads Spinoza too literally because he has not read him literally enough. One must be less literal than Cohen and not assume that the apparent order of his statements represents a rigorous demonstration. Similarly, if one tries to read the text in a more literal fashion than Cohen, one has to look beyond the order of demonstration, the order that is in reality implied by Spinoza's statements, which must be understood in light of the art of writing. It is a matter of understanding what the author wanted to say, rather than attacking him, as does Cohen, on the basis of an illusion, that Spinoza was writing the *Treatise* in peace in a tolerant society.

Once one adopts this rule of reading, where one takes account of the literary stratagems that the author employs to avoid persecution while achieving his intent, one distinguishes the exoteric and esoteric meanings of the text. The *TPT* is above all a political book: one must read Spinoza as a philosopher concerned with assuring the political conditions of freedom of thought. And this freedom to philosophize was threatened in Spinoza's time from numerous quarters—the Calvinist theologians, the Anti-Remonstrants who had as their principal adversary not the Jewish community but the Christian mainstream, friendly toward Spinoza and trying to get out from their grip. In 1665, Spinoza provisionally put aside his philosophical writing, where he deals with human liberty and the Sovereign Good, in order to write and publish anonymously a polemical text devoted to the defense of philosophy and the struggle against intolerance and persecution. In 1670, this was a struggle of Christians against other Christians, who were partisans of theocracy and used the Old Testament to justify their political ambitions. The surface of the *TPT* shows the concern of Spinoza not to lose the support of those resisting the Calvinist orthodoxy and thus friends of philosophy. Spinoza is no more anti-Jewish than he is pro-Christian, but when he writes the *TPT,* he addresses Christians: "In the *Treatise*, Spinoza addresses potential philosophers of a certain kind while the vulgar are listening. He speaks therefore in such a way that the vulgar will not understand what he means. It is for this reason that he expresses himself contradictorily; those shocked by his heterodox statements will be appeased by more or less orthodox formulae."[41] It is thus that he only reveals his refusal to recognize the possibility of miracles in a sole chapter, while "he speaks of miracles throughout the work without making it clear in the other chapters that he understands by miracles merely such natural phenomena as seemed to be strange."[42]

The meaning of the *TPT* is not exhausted in this interpretation of its exoteric meaning: there is an esoteric meaning in this work, which is not solely a tract for the time, but a bold project addressed to posterity.

The understanding of esoteric meaning allows us to see that the critique of Spinoza is in fact a rejection of the religion of Revelation. Spinoza expressed himself *ad captum hodiernum vulgi* because, even if he was addressing posterity with his concept of religion, he had to do it in an idiom that his contemporaries could tolerate, that is, in the language of a Christian committed to the testament of Christ. Understanding the esoteric meaning of the *TPT* allows us to properly evaluate the "Christianity of Spinoza" and recognize that Spinoza is not really a Christian, but its usefulness is above all to bring to light the mode of reasoning that underpins the radical Enlightenment. For in his affirmation of the self-sufficiency of reason, which provides the backbone of the modern critique of religion, Spinoza is more radical than Hobbes. This is the underlying argument of Strauss's 1930 book on Spinoza.

The major contrast is that between Spinoza's and Calvin's notions of human salvation. These are two opposed positions: Spinoza defends the idea that reason is sufficient for man's salvation, while for Calvin, Revelation is required. Strauss refers to a life-and-death struggle in the name of truth, because each side denies all validity to the position of the other. Spinoza and Calvin are incapable of understanding each other. Calvin identifies the belief in man's self-sufficiency to vulgar self-satisfaction and pride and stands upon the testament of the Holy Spirit. Spinoza attributes religion of Revelation to man's experience of powerlessness: man seeks to transfer to a being above himself that power over events that he does not have. There is a radical divide between philosophy and theology, a divide that deprives of all significance the attempt by Maimonides to view the Bible and theory as a united whole. Not only is there no reconciliation possible between the Enlightenment and orthodoxy, but, moreover, there is a conflict of opposing *interests*. But this means at the same time that the critique of religion does not constitute a refutation of religion.

The Religion of the Ignorant and Weak

While the interest for Revelation is based on the conviction that human life is by itself lacking in guidance or direction, the idea that human understanding suffices for the perfection of theory deprives Revelation of all utility. The radical Enlightenment of Spinoza is in opposition to the enlightened Judaism or rationalism of Maimonides. Maimonides presents the truths of Revelation as in unity with those of reason and justifies in this way the allegorical interpretation of Scripture, but he does not believe that Revelation is without value. For Spinoza, the incapacity of man to conduct self-sufficiently his own life derives from weakness and encourages servility. This is the argument of the Preface of the *TPT*: the critique of the religion of Revelation is *preceded* by a critique of the experience as derived from human fear. Religion is the product of an impotent desire to control fortune and an incapacity to love fate. Instead of seeing the world *sub specie aeternitas*, that is, the reality of casual necessity, human beings imagine that events are the product of an intelligence that acts, as they do, with an end in view. Aware of their drive to self-preservation, they find inside and outside the means of self-preservation. They believe that another being has provided them with these means and thus form the idea of God the creator and of Providence. They are naturally more inclined to hope than to fear, but when life is difficult they are overcome by fear of the future. And when fear dominates over hope, all the conditions are present for the birth of religion. The religion of Revelation is the rejection of a life governed by the imagination and the passions that are substitutes for action and thought. A man who is free and strong is not a believer; he is beyond hope and fear. He loves fate and is happy in understanding it: "Both the multitude, which by reason of superstition is in subjection to kinds and priests dominated by their thirst for power and glory, and their rulers are remote from the supreme aim of human perfection, which is the man strong and free, whose love is given to fate and to the contemplation of the eternal order of nature."[43]

Theoria is the certain good, the possession of which assures one eternal joy. Faith is a desire, a hope nourished by the expectation of things external, that is, what is uncertain and is beyond hope, and this desire and hope are augmented by the torments of fear and despair. Thus the two opposing positions, theory and religion of Revelation, *sapentia and superstitio*, both find their basis in human nature, in one and the same desire, the desire for self-preservation. But while *theoria* is a desire for preservation that is coherent and fulfilled, religion is an obscured desire for preservation that "lost itself in happiness that is susceptible to worldly goods."

The identification of religion with superstition comes from Epicureanism. But this connection between the rejection of the truth of religion and the rejection of its value for life is specific to Spinoza. Spinoza radically separates religion from knowledge, affirms the sufficiency of human reason, and makes faith the expression of impotence and ignorance. These tendencies will resurface in Nietzsche, whose Enlightenment is of Spinozist provenance from his definition of man by the *conatus* and the idea that there are strong and free men and his affirming of life through creation and play, which are ends in themselves, while the weak take refuge in faith. But in any case, Spinoza does not speak of reaction, the desire for vengeance, or resentment. Thus the thought of Spinoza does not allow for the presentation of religion as a morality of resentment. This aspect of Spinoza's critique follows from the reduction of religion to morality that Spinoza prepares with his universal religion, but it cannot be deduced directly from his thought.

By contrast, the critique of prejudices and the notion of two opposed attitudes toward life would become received truths for the modern Enlightenment, leading to the proclamation in the nineteenth century of the triumph of the positivist spirit. This attitude, privileging facts and direct experience, is the legacy of the sensibility that fed the positivistic critique of religion. This explains the rejection by Spinoza of Revelation as a mode of immediate presence: the rejection of miracles and the biblical conception of God as lawgiver is linked to the assertion of the identity of will and understanding in God[44] that makes Revelation impossible, but also to his interpretation of the natural law, that is, to the modern science of nature that understands "law" as a casual chain and not a normative order. Just as the interest in Revelation is prior to the belief in Revelation, the spirit of modern science precedes the rejection of the religion of Revelation. This spirit goes hand in hand with a conception of man as a superstitious animal who needs to liberate himself from fear and hope. These passions connect to the times and can engender the religious illusion when the imagination and habits, influenced by the discourse of priests, are not corrected through knowledge. Knowledge is a weapon against illusion. True knowledge is clarity and action, happiness or beatitude. It is false ideas or prejudices that lead to human suffering and alienation.

The idea that religion is about consolation for misfortunes and the God the creator is a projection, constructed on the model of a man who would have a power that he lacks, is the core of Feuerbach's analysis of the Christian religion. Christianity is a form of alienation: it is the projection, on an external and transcendent being, of attributes that belong to man and that need to be recuperated by him with a view to a religion of humanity that confers on the human species what the individual lacks. By contrast, for Spinoza, true salvation or beatitude is the fruit of contemplation, which is a solitary activity where the action, the dynamism lacks any promethean dimension. Spinoza is a Modern in his rejection of the religion of Revelation and at the same time faithful to the classical conception of the *summum bonum*, which does not exist in Hobbes, who knows only the greatest evil, violent death. The idea that religion is the resort of the ignorant and that a man educated by science and liberated from superstition would not believe in a revealed God, even less so in miracles, is a notion that comes from Spinoza and that has formed modern thought. To believe in the God of the Bible is for many persons today a proof of ignorance, psychological weakness, or the consequence of social misery that explains taking refuge in the idea of a life after death where the poor and the just will be redeemed. Feuerbach, Nietzsche, and Freud, who think that the religion of Revelation is an alienating illusion and who define man by desire, are the heirs of Spinoza. But the weapon that Spinoza uses to counter the religious illusion is no psychoanalysis, the genealogy of our concepts of good and evil, or historical materialism, but rather the scientific criticism of the Bible.

Religion is a combination of elements deriving from reason and from superstition. Spinoza's critique of religion begins with a critique of Revelation and then continues with the scientific criticism of the Bible. The interpretation of Scripture is a way of countering the theologians and the philosophers who do theology and of showing that the content of Revelation, once one separates out that which is useful for morality and serves obedience to the laws of the civil order, is a matter of imagination. Thus, we are led to the question of the social function of religion. Certainly, Spinoza derives the state from the natural right of human beings and the interest to exit the state of war to which the natural right over everything leads. Human beings do not need religion to understand that it is in their interest to live under civil laws. Does this mean that religion is useless once one has achieved the Republic?

*Biblical Criticism (*Bibelswissenschaft*)*

Biblical criticism permits Spinoza to found a universal morality that encourages human beings to obey the laws of the Republic. It is necessary to prove in the first place that Scripture is not able to be divine *everywhere* but only where it teaches in an unequivocal manner and then to show that this teaching is a moral one. The interest in Revelation is prior to belief in Revelation and justifies allegorical exegesis. The divine Law revealed to the entire human race by the prophets and the apostles is nothing other than what is taught by human reason. Where the Scriptures are contradictory, there is, strictly speaking, no teaching. The contradictory parts are rejected as solely intended for the people of that time, who were likely crude human beings for whom a metaphorical language was appropriate. Not only does Spinoza seek to liberate philosophy from the tutelage of theology in showing that the Bible has no authority except in matters of faith, but he uses the Bible as a basis for the freedom to philosophize. Thus he distinguishes the texts from which one can derive a rational morality—as with many passages in the gospels—from the precepts of the Sermon on the Mount, which are valuable only for a people living in a corrupt and declining state. This unsparing exegesis recalls the way in which believers could "falsify" the text. As for the question of the fourfold meaning of Scripture, Spinoza argues that the true meaning is that which the reader can understand regardless of whether or not he is a believer. This argument already constitutes a refutation of orthodoxy, for which only faith can illuminate the meaning of the Bible. Spinoza's biblical criticism is in the name of reason.

But unlike Maimonides, who affirms both the Law and the limits of reason, Spinoza rejects the principle of allegory. This principle is as follows: all the passages of the Bible where the literal meaning contradicts rational intelligence need to be interpreted in an allegorical manner. This principle allows Maimonides to assert, as against the *kalâm*, the law of reason and to reconcile it with Revelation in showing that the end of philosophy and the end of the Torah are the same,[45] but it also has a philosophical meaning. The idea of allegory assumes that there are different levels of understanding of the Bible, the secrets of the divine Law, which means that human reason and the teaching of philosophy, far from being constrained by Revelation, receive their motivation from it. Spinoza and Maimonides are in agreement concerning the determination of the divine Law without reference to the particularistic character of the Mosaic Law but instead based on a reflection concerning human nature. But Spinoza stands in radical opposition to the idea of Revelation, rejecting the idea of a hidden God. For this idea justifies the status of theology as a science distinct from the others. This explains also how allegory can be considered as the sole means of interpreting texts with a hidden meaning. As Maimonides indicates in the introduction to the *Guide*, allegories and riddles are necessary. Only the sub-lunar world is truly accessible to man. This conviction that human reason is insufficient in certain domains, related to Aristotelian science, is prior to the introduction of the central theological supposition that leads to the turn toward Revelation. By contrast, the idea that human reason is sufficient for the knowledge of all things, and Spinoza's concept of God, which deprives of all relevance the notion of Revelation and of a Law that can be transgressed, hold that allegory no longer has meaning and only the immanent interpretation and the letter interpretation of the Bible have a foundation.

From a rationalist perspective, "divine legislation" is nonsense. The ceremonial law serves only to legitimate a monarchical regime, which was necessary for a people in its infancy who needed a leader in order to obey the laws and respect morality: "The Israelites accustomed to the superstition of the Egyptians, untutored and exhausted by miserable bondage, were incapable of rational understanding of God, incapable also of grasping the internal necessity of moral teachings. . . . [Moses] elaborated the ceremonial law in order to train his people to unconditional obedience, since they were not ripe for freedom."[46] Spinoza treats the Old and the New Testaments in the same way, but he assumes that there has been progress over time based on human history and the conditions of human life. The evolution of Judaism into Christianity is logical and continuous. It is not a matter of a rupture with regard to substance but a change in form: a law that men can understand and that is inscribed in the human heart replaces written laws that were adapted to the Jewish nation at a particular historical time. The teaching of the entire Bible is a matter of morality, but it is the apostles who expressed it best and who perfected the moral law initiated by the prophets. This approach to interpretation is endorsed by Cohen, who asserts that the truth of the teaching of the prophets is Kantian morality. There is an idea of rational progress, of a religion more and more purified of the particular, the superstitious, which must be given its adequate expression as a rational morality.

The truth of religion for Spinoza is not pure philosophy—which tends to knowledge of the third kind—but popular philosophy, that of St. Paul. Solomon and Paul are philosophers, Spinoza suggests in chapter 4 of the *TPT*, to the extent that they are familiar with the internal meaning of the divine Law purified of anything related to obedience. Far from depending on prophecy, which for Maimonides is related to the intellect acting upon the understanding and the imagination and which is superior to philosophical knowledge, the moral teaching of the Bible is for Spinoza rationalist in its essence. If everyone were a philosopher, the Scripture, which is a work of imagination from which Spinoza tries to derive the rational teaching, would be useless.

Before examining the social function of religion, we must first consider the most original aspect of Spinoza's scientific biblical criticism. Spinoza's knowledge of the nature of the Hebrew language is the basis of his understanding and immanent reading of Scripture. Because the Bible should be studied as a literary text and because it consists of several different books, composed by different authors for different periods and different audiences, it is matter of determining the range of possible meanings for each story. Spinoza's method is to start with the common meaning of the Hebrew words without mixing theological or philosophical considerations related to the content or the object of study. The literary analysis, in order to be rigorous and objective, must be formal and linguistic.

We are not in the presence of an immutable truth, an inviolable text, but the letter of the text is the beginning point for understanding meaning. This meaning depends on the context and supposes a plurality of interpretations and points of view. This notion, which will be taken up by Diderot in the *Interpretation of Nature* and which illuminates the project of the *Encyclopedia*, should govern the reading of the Bible. It is a matter of ascertaining the meaning of the discourse contained in Scripture. Interpretations range from the more universal to the more particularist. Obscurities that might seem to be obstacles to a historical understanding of the Bible have in part their root in the peculiarities of the language in which it is written: "1. In Hebrew, consonants are often interchanged for other consonants of the same class, for instance one guttural for another guttural; 2. many particles have several meanings, sometimes even contradictory meanings; 3. the tenses of verbs are not sharply differentiated; 4. there are no vowels; 5. there are no punctuation marks employed to elucidate meaning, or separate the clauses."[47]

These rules of interpretation should make possible "an understanding without prejudices" of the Bible. The historical inquiry with respect to sources and philology and the spirit of objectivity that requires that the interpreter abstract from "his own convictions" and take "the Bible as it presents itself" resurfaces in the definition of objective knowledge by the Moderns and in the science of Judaism. For Spinoza, "natural science and the science of the Bible have the same goal": objective knowledge. Thus Spinoza is the father of the fact–value distinction, which is the hallmark of the scientific creed.[48]

Up to now, Strauss had affirmed that belief in self-sufficiency of reason preceded the critique of Revelation. Biblical criticism of the Bible is a means to strengthen this critique and reinforce the political regime guaranteeing civil peace and freedom of thought. It was a secondary aspect of Spinoza's teaching and depended on his rationalism, of which the clearest expression is the *Ethics*. Then attentiveness to the original version of biblical criticism led Strauss to recognize that it is not presupposed by the critique of religion and that its importance is not related to it. What it contributes to the modern religious consciousness becomes manifest when one understands that it presupposes only the positive critique of religion, not the metaphysical. Nothing can be presented as being taught by the Bible that is not taught literally. This requirement of objectivity thus understood is not connected to Spinoza's metaphysics. This is why the biblical criticism will have an impact and be recognized by "men who were anything but Spinozists."[49]

This question leads to an examination of the legacy of this critique of the Bible among atheists and partisans of liberal religion but also for those who, while wishing to return to orthodoxy, do not share the faith of their fathers. Similarly, when one studies a sacred text as a literary work through a philological, historical, and linguistic analysis, using context for explanation, does this not discard *in advance* the fundamental theological notion on which allegorical interpretation is based, namely that of the hidden God? Can one still speak of Revelation if the substance is entirely comprehensible by reason alone? What becomes of our relation to divine transcendence if the Call that characterizes it is not irreducible to any of its expressions? These are the questions that are at the heart of the inquiry of Strauss and his contemporaries of the possibility of maintaining the tradition after the accomplishment of Spinoza. But to evaluate correctly the heritage of the Enlightenment, it is useful to consider the way that Spinoza himself analyzes the role of religion in the liberal state.

The Social Function of Religion

The Universal Religion and the "Christianity" of Spinoza

The objective of Spinoza in the *TPT* is to deduce from the interpretation of the Bible the idea that it is favorable to religious tolerance, freedom of thought, and republicanism. He uses exegesis to establish the existence of a universal morality that is favorable to liberal society and even perhaps indispensible to civil peace. This is the function of universal religion and the meaning of the "Christianity" of Spinoza.

The aim of religion is to encourage the obedience of ordinary people, who are moved by fear of punishment. Spinoza's definition of piety is illuminating: it is not faith in Paul's sense of the word, that is to say a theological virtue that justifies man, but respect for the norms of collective existence established for the greatest good for all, civil peace. Private obligations to one's own are subordinated to public duty.[50] Spinoza has in view more the interests of community than those of the human individual, and this is his interpretation of the teaching of Christ: faith is what makes possible obedience to the laws of the state.[51] The motives that lead men to the social contract are not of a religious nature: religion is not necessary for the *establishment* of democracy. The universal religion that Spinoza invents seeks to make a good use of religious impulses, rendering them politically inoffensive. It could only be invented by a philosopher and is intended for those who are in a state of ignorance and servitude to their passions. Similarly, Christ "was used as foil to Moses,"[52] whom he was intended to eclipse. Spinoza, following in this respect Maimonides, who had asserted the intellectual character of the prophecy of Moses, presents Jesus as a philosopher in certain passages of the *TPT*.[53] In reality, Spinoza never returns to the fact that faith has as its end obedience and not truth, but this image of Christ the philosopher serves to legitimate the philosophical interpretation of religion. The contradictions of Spinoza can be explained by his political strategy: in endorsing Christ in the role of philosopher, he expects to confer authority on his universal religion, eliminate persecution, and show that philosophy does not threaten the community.

When he elaborates the seven dogmas of his minimum credo in chapter 14 of the *TPT*, Spinoza insists on the fact "that faith does not require true dogmas so much as pious ones, that is such as move the spirit to obedience . . ."[54] Pines suggests comparing these article of faith with what Maimonides[55] believes enable "the well-being of the city or the abolition of mutual harms." The preference of Spinoza for James, not Paul, that is, the justification by good works and not faith, conforms to this logic. Like Machiavelli, it is a matter of taking men as they are and understanding that the universal morality founded upon the teaching and imitation of Christ allows them to subject their impulses to discipline, to be tolerant, and to escape being manipulated by those who pretend to religious truth. But why does Spinoza write "how salutary and necessary this Teaching is in a Republic, so that human beings might live peacefully and harmoniously. . . ."?[56] Pines illustrates clearly the function of the universal religion and its role as an antidote to superstitious passion, but he does not consider whether its content is necessary. Did Spinoza think that belief in God the Creator and Providence were indispensible to piety, understood as obedience to the state and as morality?

Who will do what is right when they no longer believe in anything, when the idea of Providence and divine justice as a corrective to the frailties of human justice no longer exists? Spinoza knows that respect for the laws cannot be based on fear of human punishment alone. The exercise of democracy, the stability of the state, and social harmony require morality. And the respect for morality is not obvious among men who are inclined by nature to suspicion and intolerance. What does obedience to the laws of a state mean when it is not supported by ideals that encourage it? To say that belief in a transcendent God and in Providence supports civil peace and social consensus, is this not to suggest that civic spirit and morality based on reason alone are impotent to guarantee a stable order? Is not the analysis of the civil function of the universal religion of Spinoza an occasion to rethink the limits of the morality of human rights, that is, of an abstract and secular morality based on humanism?

The Ambiguity of Spinoza

The definition of piety that Spinoza provides is not self-evident, especially in a democracy. It is a matter of respecting other human beings, their persons, their property, and their religious opinions, because these acts or particular duties reinforce the state of which the end is individual liberty and the realization of democracy. A state in which criminality and law-breaking are frequent, writes Spinoza, is not one where human beings are more wicked than elsewhere due to race or geography but a state where the laws are not infused with an adequately wise spirit. This is a question of the pedagogical virtue of the laws, which help human beings to become citizens and form a type of individual more or less adapted to community life. What will give men the love for justice? How can one combat the impression that, in an imperfect and nonideal democracy, the just suffer while the wicked prosper? Who will be able to understand that it is better to submit to injustice than to commit it? The universal religion, support for the universal morality necessary to the proper functioning of liberal democracy, does it not enter into this political project, and does it not constitute a chapter in man's civil education?

If Spinoza, in the *TPT*, takes pains to cite the seven dogmas of the minimal credo and to propose a universal religion that is opposed to the philosophical conception of God expounded in the *Ethics*, is it not because he believes the common people would not be able to behave reasonably without the fear of heaven and that right, which merely requires the conformity of external actions with law, legality and not intention, nevertheless requires morality? It seems, at first glance, that Spinoza is close to Kant here, which makes Pines right to emphasize that the importance for both of obedience and rational duty and the idea that general duty—for Spinoza, obedience to the state—takes precedence over particular duties. But in the *TPT* does not Spinoza have a message concerning the majority of men, which he addresses to posterity? Spinoza would belong to a universe of pre-modern thought, with its notion of the noble lie and the idea of maintaining a tradition linked to a certain way of interconnecting morality, religion, and politics. His universal religion would be a hybrid that compromises between rational morality, prejudice about God—wrongly thought of as transcendent and as a lawgiver—and the official religion of his country, Holland. It would serve to base obedience to the laws of the democratic state on tradition, on the shared opinions to which the laws are addressed. The universal religion would equally be a step in the education of humankind, the vocation of which is to live in accordance with reason. Philosophers would not have need of religion, but it would provide a support for all the other citizens.

Religion plays no role in the *establishment* of the democratic state, but it has a role, in as in pre-modern thought, in the functioning and the *life* of democracy. This role, which is not simply negative, but pedagogical, is analogous to that which Homer and myths play in Plato. They are not true; philosophizing requires their rejection; and also, because they can be made to stand for contradictory things where they are invoked in politics, they constitute the tradition that cannot be put in dispute by anyone in any old way, as Plato emphasizes in the beginning of the *Laws*.

These questions are not directly raised by Strauss, but they are not foreign to his questioning of contemporary relativism. Strauss reads Spinoza in thinking about what our world, which he fashioned, has become. He is persuaded that the contradictions of modernity emerge for the first time in Spinoza. The distinction between the public and private spheres, which is central to the political regime defended by Spinoza in the *TPT*, has the result that liberal democracy cannot prevent the emergence of parties and tendencies of thought hostile to its own spirit, as was the case during the 1930s in Germany. It "cannot provide a solution to the Jewish problem, for such a solution would require the legal prohibition against every kind of 'discrimination,' that is the abolition of the private sphere, the denial of the difference between state and society, the destruction of the liberal state."[57]

One could even ask whether the maintenance of a *living* Christianity would not have been the sole means of preserving the moral values to which it gave birth and the rationalism of human rights, which borrowed from these values but was unable to defend them against National Socialism. "The victory of National Socialism became necessary in Germany for the same reason for which the victory of Communism became necessary in Russia: the man who had by far the strongest will or single-mindedness, the greatest ruthlessness, daring, and power over his following, and the best judgment about the strength of the various forces in the immediately relevant political field was the leader of the revolution."[58] Is atheism not too harsh for human beings, too politically dangerous to the extent that, with the exception of a small group of men capable of facing the death of God, most men are unable to find any ideal that could be a counterweight to the ideology of power?

The Limits of Secular Morality

It is as if, at the outset, the Enlightenment occurred in awareness of all the essential problems, but its evolution and the increasing rigidity of the position of the philosophers toward religion resulted in a regression and an obfuscation. The universal religion of Spinoza contains at the same time the premises of an entirely rational morality and a secular state and the possibility of a reflection on the ineffectiveness of the morality of human rights. The idea of respect of persons is too abstract for ordinary mortals, for the human being who has not assimilated the philosophy of Kant and is not habituated to it, due to either a religion education or even a traditional education emphasizing the solidarity between generations, and the *feeling* of being connected to the rest of humanity. Religion was a long-standing and indispensible complement to morality and to civic spirit, which gave effectiveness to the modern regime of rights on which democracy is premised. Without these values, the sentiments that underpin the respect of persons are no longer felt. It is thus that the morality of human rights now leads the individual to defend persecuted minorities that he does not know rather than show solidarity to his neighbors.

This is a paradox that Tocqueville emphasizes. He does not oppose the irreversible process of democratization but asks what must be done to prevent democracy from bringing about an unprecedented form of tyranny. And the remedy for this evil is not institutional but spiritual, moral, and psychological: whereas human beings "in aristocratic societies were connected to something beyond themselves and thus had a capacity for self-forgetfulness," the kind of individuals who appear in democracies have fairly clearly established duties toward humankind, "but devotion toward others becomes in fact rather rare." Human rights provide for the protection of everyone, but "human connection is diluted and weakened." Moreover, there is a tendency to live in the here and now. The individual whose self-affirmation goes along with equalization of conditions does not think of his forbears. This tendency is exacerbated with the decline of religion and is accompanied by a growing indifference of people toward their progeny: "Not only does democracy make each man forget his ancestors, but it hides his descendants from him and separates him from his contemporaries; it constantly leads him back toward himself alone and threatens finally to confine him wholly in the solitude of his own heart."[59]

And religion serves to counterbalance the individualism and materialism that arise in democracy, but that threaten it from inside, to the extent that popular sovereignty depends on the interest of the citizen for the public good, his capacity to inform himself of the issues facing his community and to participate in the life of the political community. Without this civic spirit, which requires that each not define himself exclusively in terms of the private sphere and that each feels a concern for the future of the nation, democracy is nothing but a word. This is why individualism, which is "a learned feeling" and not like egoism an instinct linked to self-preservation, and which "inclines each citizen to (. . .) withdraw into his circle of family and friends," viewed as the only human beings to whose fate one is not totally indifferent, undermines the foundations of democracy, its very spirit. Connected with materialism, which evokes the notion that individuals are absorbed "entirely in the search for permissible pleasures" and no longer seek those goods that constitute "the greatness of the human species," individualism generates a "self-indulgent" human type far removed from philosophical concerns but also from the kind of obedience required, according to Spinoza, for public harmony. No one wants to command, and no one is predisposed to obey. Indifference has become public virtue. Indifference to evil is the most banal evil, and it goes hand in hand with everyone's assertion of their rights, with that tendency to regard justice as only right and not law[60] and to eradicate the notion of duty that is part of the social contract. Does this mean that religion and the appeal to transcendent values are necessary to the maintenance of a minimal morality that insures respect for the laws and civil peace?

Tocqueville, who lost his faith at sixteen, held that religion is necessary because democratic man, who is content with the search for personal happiness and profit, can degrade himself of his own accord. To avoid this danger, it is necessary to spread, particularly in these societies, "the taste for the infinite, the sentiment of greatness, and the love of immaterial pleasures."[61] Christianity allows the possibility of maintaining "spiritualistic views." Governments should act as if they themselves were believers in order that their citizens learn to know, love, and respect this religious morality "in everyday life" and their personal relations. God is in a sense a postulate of practical reason, a moral necessity. Marcel Gauchet, when he raises the question of religion in a democracy,[62] regrets that Tocqueville did not go in the direction of a secular conception of democracy, which he thinks would be the best guarantee against totalitarianism. There is much at stake here, and the ambiguity of Spinoza, who expounds in the *TPT* universal religion in which he does not believe as a philosopher, is of interest, and is comparable with that of Tocqueville, agnostic but spiritual and a supporter of maintaining Christianity. What is the value of the substitutes for religion, philosophy of history, art in Malraux's sense, sects that are the product of religious syncretism and the ideal of performance and happiness brought into being by modern individualism and materialism? How to avoid the two pitfalls of religious fundamentalism and a nihilism that puts morality aside and gives men a taste for the right of the stronger?

Spinoza, who turns toward Christianity and breaks from Judaism in order to show that the Bible itself is favorable to religious tolerance and that republicanism is the regime best adapted to the nature of man, finds equally in this religion reduced to a moral teaching and its necessary postulates a remedy to the evils of disorder and license. For historical reasons, he always has in mind the dangers of theocracy and religious fanaticism, but his political realism and also his anthropology inclined him to consider that evil that follows from man's misuse of his liberty and the consequences of seditious opinions, including civil war.

Tocqueville, who feared the success of Spinozist pantheism in democratic societies,[63] wanted to temper the emergence of democratic individualism and materialism with the preservation of Christian morality. Thus it is a matter not of putting in question the cause of the Enlightenment, but of preventing modernity from turning on itself. This is the meaning of the liberty–equality dichotomy in Tocqueville: the cultivation of the sentiment of liberty—which for Strauss is a matter of liberal education—allows for the correction of that which is destructive in the passion for equality. The latter can modify the very meaning of justice, which is no longer linked to the reciprocity of rights and duties. It can lead to a violent society, characterized by the intolerance of difference, the rejection of authority, and the hatred of natural inequalities in ability. Such a society risks becoming a tyranny that would be a "soft and organized form of servitude" arising in the shadow of the sovereignty of the people and democratic practices such as the right to vote and freedom of expression. This threat, which is accompanied by the rule of sellers of ideas"[64] who establish in the culture the spirit of industry and commerce, is one that is internal to democracy. It is a pathology that destroys democracy from the inside and makes it harder to preserve it against external ills. The reality described by Tocqueville[65] was experienced by Strauss. The Straussian critique of the Enlightenment is a critique of what the Enlightenment has become, in part because of the irreversible process of equalization of conditions. If Strauss believes that Spinoza is an obstacle to the return to orthodoxy, because he distanced himself from Judaism and his critique of the religion of Revelation deprives the latter of any claim to truth, it is wrong to suggest that his critique of Spinoza is not nuanced.

The Enlightenment of Spinoza

The ambiguity of Spinoza, who separates religion from knowledge but preserves it as morality, is what also makes him a heroic figure. Even if the radical rupture with classical political philosophy and its concern with the end of man was already present, and hence the modern exclusion of the question of the good life from political reflection, the idea of universal religion shows the superiority of Spinoza to his successors.

Spinoza had understood that the truth cannot be divulged without precautions. Because Spinoza's Enlightenment excludes the egalitarian diffusion of knowledge and takes into account the dangers that can exist, including for the state, of the denial of any gap between philosophy and opinion, it is superior to the Enlightenment from the eighteenth century on, which defends the ideal of transparency. This leads in the twentieth century to a paradox foreseen by Tocqueville, which we call today political correctness. It entails the leveling and homogenization of thought, because the criterion is not the judgment of those who are wise but the approval of the greatest number. Freedom of expression turns against freedom of thought, producing a new kind of censorship with the complicity of the media. To reconsider with Strauss the legacy of the Enlightenment is to appreciate the depth of Spinoza's thought, whose conception of *theoria* is borrowed from Maimonides and the Ancients, including the implication that there is a gap between the few sages and the ignorant masses.

If religion is fated to disappear, if the irreversible process of modernity is that of secularization, then, nevertheless, as long as religion exists, the trend toward individual autonomy, individualism, and materialism that characterizes the human type to which democracy gives rise is counterbalanced by a morality informed by the idea of Providence and a benevolent God as understood by Spinoza. This universal morality and minimalist religion were still present in Voltaire and Rousseau in the eighteenth century and among the majority of the population in liberal democracies until the beginning of World War I. Those philosophers in the Enlightenment tradition in the nineteenth and early twentieth centuries viewed this religiosity with a certain condescension and awaited the end of this illusion, but the ordinary man was still a believer. With World War I, universal morality and religion collapsed, and in this sense, so did the Enlightenment of Spinoza. In this respect, Hobbes is more of a contemporary than Spinoza. The greatest evil exists, and God, if ever he exists, is a God lacking goodness and benevolence or a God who has withdrawn from the world. Moreover, man does not attain his true potential until he is able to bear the death of God.[66]

Today's Enlightenment is that of Nietzsche: it is a matter of overcoming the last man, who is low, without reverting to the transcendent ideals of the tradition. But the reality in Strauss's time, just as in Spinoza's, is not the Enlightenment but what it is struggling against. The reality with which Strauss is confronted is nihilism in the second sense of the term. Strauss thinks that philosophy was atheistic from probity, but he suggests that struggle against nihilism demands a morality based on a religion, at least as a noble lie. However, he does not accept the "Christian" solution of Spinoza, because Spinoza destroyed the Jewish tradition and prepared an extreme form of religious liberalism that is almost indistinguishable from atheism. Moreover, this idea of a separation of private and public spheres that is of Christian origin leads to an impasse: it eventually brings into being a political teaching based on the mere management of the welfare and security of human beings, while religion becomes increasingly moribund.

The Straussian critique of the Enlightenment is directed toward the affirmation of a political philosophy based on the question of the best regime, that the consideration of the perfection or the end of man should be the horizon of thought and action. And the idea of a separation of religion and politics is an obstacle to the assertion of this political philosophy based on the Greek model and to which the Maimonidean conception of the Law is essential. The latter is the essential challenge of Strauss's thought; it is the most important dimension of his constructive critique of democracy.

In considering all that separates Strauss from Spinoza, we understand the meaning and orientation of his decision to rethink the theological-political problem. But, just as Spinoza makes a radical break with the Jewish tradition and with Maimonides, even if seeming in certain respects to belong to the universe of pre-modern thought, Strauss wishes to overcome the "obstacle" of Spinoza and to return to classical rationalism, at the same time as giving their due to his political realism and anthropology. These two dimensions have in effect disappeared in the post-Spinoza Enlightenment, when the *political* dimension of the critique of religion is forgotten. Spinoza and Hobbes put in place the foundations of the modern state through the subordination of religion to politics, but they have not dispensed with the religious question as such. This way of channeling the religious impulse and making it serve civil education was a great achievement and a weapon against the political ambitions of the clergy, but also a sign of clarity. The dismissal of the religious problem by the heirs of the Enlightenment goes hand in hand with a naive, even angelic conception of human nature. And it is this conception that Soviet and Nazi totalitarianism as well as Islamism would eventually destroy.

The Legacy of the Critique of Religion

The Critique of Revelation Has Not Destroyed the Interest in Revelation

Not only does Spinoza's critique of orthodoxy not constitute a true refutation of the religion of Revelation, because it leads to a moral antagonism between two positions, but, moreover, it above all suppresses "the self-understanding of religion."[67] Thus, the religion of Revelation can take something positive from this critique: "If orthodoxy claims to know that . . . every word of the Bible is divinely inspired . . . Spinoza has refuted orthodoxy. But the case is entirely different if orthodoxy limits itself to asserting that it believes the aforementioned things."[68] The premise of orthodoxy cannot be refuted either by experience or by the principle of contradiction. And the truth of orthodoxy is precisely that this idea of a mysterious God is not an object of knowledge but a matter of faith. It is indeed this that distinguishes the wisdom that belongs to the Bible from philosophical wisdom,[69] which is based on the principle of knowledge through unassisted reason that excludes from the outset the biblical principle of obedience to an unfathomable God. Strauss does not leave matters at indicating that the proof of the impossibility for the Enlightenment to refute orthodoxy was its resort to mockery. Of course, this leads to a crucial concession: the impossibility of miracles and Revelation can no more be proven than their possibility. The debate is thus not between science and philosophy on the one hand and ignorance and superstition on the other, but between two ways of defining the meaning of life based on opposite assumptions, between two kinds of wisdom. Strauss returns from the antagonism between atheism and orthodoxy to that between

Jerusalem and Athens and proposes an interpretation of the Bible that does not attribute to it alien concepts or criteria of proof. It is a matter of reading the Bible following the principle of objectivity defended by Spinoza but going further than Spinoza by avoiding the attribution to the Bible of the criterion of truth applicable to a philosophical work.

"The improbable character of the Biblical faith is admitted and indeed proclaimed by that faith itself."[70] There is a fundamental difference between the God of the philosophers, who is understandable, and the God of Abraham, Isaac, and Jacob. Between Athens and Jerusalem, there cannot be a synthesis. The tradition upon which modern culture is based is grounded on the opposition of reason and Revelation, and this opposition reveals a difference in how one defines the meaning of the human: it is matter of two opposed kinds of *wisdom*. One cannot say that the "fear of God is the beginning of wisdom," the latter being based on obedience, that is, on the idea that human beings have a need of limits in order to guide their conduct and that reason is not sufficient, and *at the same time* make philosophical knowledge the only mode of access to truth. There is a genuine antagonism between Plato and the prophets, because the former makes the salvation of man dependent on the existence of the ideal political community, where philosophers are kings, while the prophets announce the unpredictable designs of an unfathomable God and put themselves in his hands.

It is not because the coincidence between political power and philosophy is improbable that the perfect society sought by Socrates is impossible: it is, in theory, conceivable even if there are many obstacles that make its realization impracticable. By contrast, the coming of the messianic age announced by the prophets depends on divine intervention and is something "unexpected, humanly unpredictable." The philosopher is only wise in the sense of human wisdom.[71] Even if the mission of Socrates was pronounced by the Delphic oracle, who was, according to him, that of the god Apollo, he did not submit without examination to this pronouncement, which he interpreted as an exhortation to philosophize.

The result of this antagonism is that the enterprise undertaken by Spinoza and Hobbes to interpret the Bible as an ordinary book depends on a prior, specifically philosophical assumption. If one proceeds by avoiding taking in advance a position in favor of Athens against Jerusalem, one necessarily understands that "the Bible rejects the principle of understanding by unassisted reason and everything that goes with it. The mysterious God is the last theme and highest theme of the Bible. Given the biblical premise, there cannot be a book in the Greek sense, for there cannot be human authors who decide in the sovereign fashion what is to be the beginning and the end, and who refuse admission to everything that is not evidently necessary for the purpose of the book."[72]

One thus comes to a conclusion that has nothing to do with that of the founders of the critique of the Bible and that puts it in doubt: "The Bible may then abound in contradictions" because it "reflects in its literary form the inscrutable mystery of the ways of God."[73] The result of this critique of orthodoxy is that, even among those thinkers who are believers and integrate certain conclusions from the scientific criticism of the Bible, the imagination is given a greater value and reason is not at the center of the relationship with God. The critique of orthodoxy and the fact of separating religion from knowledge has a consequence, which is to reevaluate the reinterpretation of religious experience itself, which is that of a Call: "something undesired, coming from the outside, going against man's grain."[74]

The critique of orthodoxy not only preserved the interest in Revelation and determined the true ground of the debate, which is not theory but life, which concerns existence, in Kierkegaard's sense. It also permitted the reconsideration of the essential question of religious experience. This experience, attributed by Spinoza and later on by Freud to man's experience of his own impotence, is asserted by Rosenzweig and Buber as constituting the irreducible meaning of Revelation: it is first of all "the fact that God reveals himself to man, that he addresses himself to man" and "is not only known through traditions going back to a distant past and which are now 'mere objects of belief' but is truly known by present experience of which every human being is capable if they do not close themselves off from it."[75]

It is experience precisely that will be the beginning point for Rosenzweig, who speaks of "God, man and the world as forms of experience, as realities that are irreducible to each other" and who opposes philosophical systems, and efforts of traditional philosophy of a reductionist kind, which seek a reality independent of the experience of man and the world. Strauss suggests that unbelief can be the result of a refusal and reverts to the notion of atheism as a model of lucidity and courage, of probity, while faith is a sign of weakness. In deriving religion from human fear, did Spinoza not extinguish those characteristic experiences that are connected to the interest in Revelation?[76]

Spinoza perhaps refused to recognize the radical nature of certain experiences, such as human vulnerability and weakness, and this refusal, which goes hand in hand with his assertion of the adequacy of human reason, determines his critique of religion, which is a theoretical critique of which the "inadequacy is built into its very nature." The interest for *theoria*, the certainty that "the theoretical attitude is capable of judging the truths of religion," and the resolution to affirm that which enhances the *conatus* precede the critique of religion and make atheism a position that, morally or existentially, is not more courageous than that of faith.

The Challenge of Philosophy

The antagonism between philosophy and orthodoxy thus leads to two conceptions of the right way of life. And it is just this aspect that is understood by the Enlightenment according to Strauss, who discusses their presentation of a Napoleon-like strategy: instead of continuing to directly refute orthodoxy, it "left the impregnable fortress of orthodoxy in the rear . . . it devoted itself to its own proper work, the civilization of the world and of man."[77] If this effort had been successful, if the diffusion of reason, science, and technology had shown that a world without transcendence was possible, then the Enlightenment would have won the day with the idea that religion had been superseded. But the successes of civilization are not as obvious as they might have seemed in the eighteenth century. And "doubts about the success of civilization soon enough became doubts about the possibility of civilization. . . . What is left in the end of the success of the Enlightenment?"[78]

Is it that, with the "final collapse of rationalism, the perennial battle between reason and Revelation . . . has been decided in principle, even on the plane of human thought, in favor of Revelation"?[79] Nothing is less sure. But the issue is joined, and the notion of a critique of the critique of religion becomes relevant. Cohen, putting in doubt the outcome of the Enlightenment, inaugurates a movement of turn toward the tradition that will be continued by Rosenzweig and that signifies that religion has not been definitively put to rest. Moreover, the legacy of the Enlightenment shows that a new way of thinking is needed. And if the common denominator of these two representative thinkers is that they have internalized the impasse of classical rationalism and systematic philosophy, it nevertheless remains no less true that, between Rosenzweig and Heidegger, the debate is related to an alternative between belief in supernatural redemption and the thought of resoluteness, which belongs to the affirmation of our radical finitude and the denial of the beyond: the "difference between Rosenzweig and Heidegger . . . was not unconnected with their difference concerning Revelation."[80]

This "controversy can easily degenerate into a competition as to who offers less security and more terror," a contest where we will rediscover the same argument as at the time of the struggle of the Enlightenment against orthodoxy, that is, that religion is a consolation and that atheism is related to man's courage in the face of his aloneness and mortality. Be that as it may, "the new thinking is the challenge of philosophy," not only because atheism appears as a form of belief, no less than theism, "which is a catastrophe for thought," but also because the new orthodoxy is not an unconditional return to Revelation and differentiates between the experience of the believer today and that which is known through the tradition. It has integrated some of the results of the critique of religion by the Enlightenment. One must recognize that the Enlightenment has finally ended up victorious if it is true that any return to the tradition is impossible, or one could well wonder whether the self-destruction of reason is not the inevitable result of modern rationalism and if it is not through new thought that is itself the heir of this rationalism but of a return to pre-modern rationalism that one can get out of the crisis. It is a matter of rediscovering what was forgotten by the Moderns in their concept of reason, as if the reality of the present were linked to a late recovery of ancient wisdom. "If finally 'orthodoxy or atheism,' and if on the other hand the need for an enlightened Judaism is urgent, then one sees oneself compelled to ask whether Enlightenment is necessarily modern Enlightenment. Thus one sees oneself induced—provided that one does not know from the outset, as one cannot know from the outset, that only new unheard-of ultra-modern thoughts can resolve our perplexity—to apply for aid to the medieval Enlightenment, the Enlightenment of Maimonides."[81]

The Debt of the New Orthodoxy to the Enlightenment and Religious Liberalism

The hesitations of Cohen, Buber, and Rosenzweig in relation to traditional faith originate from the Enlightenment. "Rosenzweig is in agreement with religious liberalism concerning the necessity to choose among traditional beliefs and rules," but his principle of selection is different: the liberals maintained an objective distinction between what is essential and inessential, while for Rosenzweig, the choice is a purely individual one.

This conscious and radical historicization of the Torah, which is compatible with the notion of the Jews as the chosen people, which is ahistorical, goes hand in hand with Maimonides's way of proceeding, which understands the Torah itself as constitutive of the Jewish nation. Rosenzweig first considers Israel's chosenness "the truly central thought of Judaism."[82] He seeks a Jewish analogue for the Christian doctrine of Christ and imagines Judaism from a Christian perspective. But Rosenzweig's main debt to the Enlightenment is indicated by his refusal to believe in all the miracles of the Bible and his interpretation of the Law as a gift, not a prohibition. He constructs his own teaching, central to which is the notion that the mission of Judaism is to implant universalism in the heart of other nations, in light of scientific-biblical criticism, which replaces the principle of allegiance to the tradition with that of personal conviction. The tradition did not make the individual experience of the believer the criterion of the truth of Revelation, but rather truth was communicated in whole form by Revelation to the believer in his interpretation. Philosophy was not a rival of Revelation but its complement. For Rosenzweig, the new orthodoxy is a *philosophy* of Judaism. "Whereas . . . the *Guide of the Perplexed* . . . is primarily not a philosophic book, but a Jewish book, Rosenzweig's *Star of Redemption* is primarily not a Jewish book but a 'system of philosophy.' "[83]

There is a clear break between traditional Judaism and modern Jewish thought. The latter is not superior to medieval thought: it is defined by the problem of the Jew who is lost in a non-Jewish world, but this transformation of Judaism in liberal Judaism is not invulnerable to critiques of the Enlightenment's successors. The God of Cohen is hardly indistinguishable from a mere idea, and in Rosenzweig one has the sense that "the return to the tradition is accomplished exclusively by disputing the post-Enlightenment synthesis, in particular Hegel." Is the nineteenth-century critique of the internalization of the content of religion anything but a "rehabilitation of the Enlightenment"?[84]

Is Cohen not vulnerable to the critique of a religious liberalism that reduces the content of religion to a morality that prepares the attack of Nietzsche? If the content of religion reduces to moral values, then religion itself, considered in relation to a society and a particular time, becomes an autonomous domain of culture, and its utility is suspect. It is even susceptible to being attacked as a device serving to domesticate the aggressive and creative nature of individuals and to curb the strongest. The latter do not dare any longer to affirm their instinct for domination, because the habit of demonizing egoism and identifying self-sacrifice with the good works more effectively than civil laws in creating or developing that organ of self-censure, the moral consciousness. There is but a small distance between the denunciation of the guilt-ridden ideal of Christian morality and the affirmation that Christianity represents the cunning of the weak, who have *reacted* to the situation in which they find themselves in order to assert their Will to Power and take revenge on those who have dominated them. This leap is taken when one defines man as a being beyond good and evil, whose humanity is achieved not in community life but in self-overcoming and the liberation from morality.

For its part, is Rosenzweig's philosophy of Judaism not questionable both from the point of view of the Enlightenment, to the extent that it presupposes an *external* content to philosophy, and also from the perspective of those seeking a real return to orthodoxy, who will think that the manner in which the nation precedes the Torah is a betrayal of the specific character of Revelation? Is the new orthodoxy itself not an attempt to reconcile philosophy and Revelation, while truth supposes a preservation of the tension between Jerusalem and Athens?

Thus, Strauss, who seeks to overcome the impasse of the new orthodoxy, suggests a return to the articulation of philosophy and Law that one finds in Maimonides. In maintaining the heteronomy of the Law and in affirming the right of reason to operate within its own domain, Maimonides permits us to depart from the way of thought presupposed by the modern Enlightenment and to overcome the critique of religious liberalism as an internationalization of the content of faith. The return to the rationalism of Maimonides is the conclusion that Strauss draws from his examination of the fate of the modern Enlightenment. It is thus a matter of imagining the complementarity of two opposite poles, in permanent tension, in relying on what Maimonides says about philosophy when grounded in the Law and the Law when grounded in philosophy. This, according to Strauss, is the path toward a genuine recovery of the tradition. On this road, Strauss encounters Gershom Scholem. A debate occurs between the rationalism of Maimonides, representative of enlightened Judaism, and mysticism. This debate takes up again, at a different level, the question of the legacy of the Enlightenment, because with Maimonides it is an alternative to the modern Enlightenment that is being proposed. The problem once again resurfaces in the controversy between Strauss and Scholem.

Chapter 3

The Return to the Tradition

If there is the common thread in the notion of a return to the tradition in Scholem and Strauss, as well as in Cohen and Rosenzweig, there remains the question of which of these thinkers see reason, and which see experience, as the fundamental basis for such a return. Our emphasis in considering the engagement of Strauss with these contemporaries is to underline the originality of a thinker who, in designating Maimonides as the figure to whom we must return, is, with Cohen, alone in defending the rights of reason against the required appeal, in the midst of the crisis of rationalism, to experience. Effectively, most of the contemporaries of Strauss distance themselves from modernity and interpret the tradition beginning from the failure of the system to explain our relation to a living God, transformed by reason into a mere object or subject. They have thus incorporated the limits of the critique of religion in the Enlightenment, but have not drawn the same implications as Strauss. While Scholem asserts that the philosophers "converted the concrete realities of Judaism in a bundle of abstractions,"[1] Cohen adopts a moral orientation, and Rosenzweig invokes lived experience, anticipating the philosophy of the face and the ethics of Levinas, Strauss defends rationalism and asserts that philosophy is political philosophy.

Cohen, Rosenzweig, and Levinas interpret the Law beginning from a human standpoint and in relation to human experience in the first instance, including when that experience is thought in light of Revelation, as with Rosenzweig. Similarly, they interpret the past as if the truth were more accessible today. By contrast, Strauss and Scholem conceive the return to the tradition as beginning with the givens of that tradition. They disagree concerning the tradition to which one returns, but they affirm that it is necessary to understand a writer of the past on his own terms and that the modern interpreter does not have a more enlightened standpoint than the writer of the past.

We begin with the confrontation between Scholem and Strauss, who are both advocates of a return to the tradition, and not merely an appropriation of the tradition. Then we examine the specific link between Strauss and Cohen. The latter is the spiritual father of Strauss. He put Strauss on the path of return to Maimonides, but his interpretation of the past and his orientation toward moral philosophy, which had inspired Rosenzweig and Levinas and explains their non-political account of the messianic concept, are also at the root of Strauss's break with the neo-Kantian Cohen. Maimonides is at one and the same time what unites Cohen and Strauss and what divides them. Similarly, it is the question of the enlightened Judaism of Maimonides which opposes Strauss to the religious philosophy of the author of *The Star of Redemption* and which leads him, in his questioning of the relationship between reason and Revelation, to prefer the pre-modern Enlightenment. All of this implies a rational critique of reason that allows one to escape from the theoretical and practical impasse that follows from the modern Enlightenment.

Rationalism and Mysticism

Allegory and Symbol

According to Scholem, the necessity to turn God into a living reality depends on a renewed interest in the Kabbalah, which transformed, like philosophy did, "the structure of ancient Judaism" and is not, contra Grätz, a mere reaction against rationalism.[2] Philosophy and mysticism are two modes of *reflection* on Judaism. The Kabbalah offers a symbolic interpretation of the classic themes of Judaism, for example the story of the creation, while philosophy produces an "ideology of Judaism," which can come to the aid of the tradition but, not being as profoundly "in connection" with "the principal active forces of Judaism," is unable to rekindle the enthusiasm of the believer or offer to the Jewish people the means with which to understand their own history. Scholem reverts to the Kabbalah in order to resolve the inherent difficulty of monotheism: How to preserve the purity of the idea of God while at the same time allowing the believer to connect to a living God, not an abstraction?

This is where the symbol plays a role. It integrates a reality and affords it a transmutation that conserves what is living, elevating it to another plane of experience. Thus Luria's Kabbalah, which is evolved after the principal categories of Jewish mysticism have already been elaborated, provides an original interpretation of the story of creation and, in addition to a reflection on the nature of evil, integrates important elements of Jewish history, in particular after the expulsion of the Jews from Spain in 1492.[3] The expression of spontaneous religious sentiment, reflection on the meaning of evil, and the absorption of those elements of experience specific to the Jewish people, such as exile, are lacking in philosophy. Only myth is able to express such realities: mysticism represents a "revival of the mythical consciousness."[4]

Contra Cohen, the truth of Judaism is not that it represents, as monotheism, the victory of reason over paganism and mythic religion, but is in the hidden tradition of symbolic interpretation. Mysticism, far from constituting a regression to myth or an irrationalist reaction, has its own internal coherence and its own principle of interpretation. While the philosophical encounter with the Law, as represented by Maimonides, turns it into an allegory, that is, an abstraction, the Kabbalah provides the key for "building the wall of history according to a symbolic design." Philosophy is unable to render comprehensible the living connection between the Law and narration, the *Halakkah* and the *Haggadah*. Maimonides's analysis and interpretation of *mitzvot* is historically important, but it is unable "to augment . . . immediate appeal to religious feeling."[5] For the Kabbalists, the *Halakkah* does not belong to the domain of thought. Religious commandments are not intellectual allegories or pedagogical measures, but the achievement of a secret rite or of a mystery understood in the manner of the Ancients. Instead of converting them into abstractions, the point is to provide a symbolic interpretation.

> This opposition of allegory and symbol is derived from Benjamin. The symbol is not only the expressible representation of something that is located beyond the sphere of expression and communication. . . . For the Kabbalist, each existing thing is constantly in connection to the entire creation. . . . He discovered something that is not covered by the web of allegory: a reflection of genuine transcendence. The symbol does not "stand" for anything nor communicate anything, but rather it renders transparent that which is outside of all expression. The symbol is understood immediately by the intuition or it is not understood at all. It is an "ephemeral (transient) totality" that is perceived intuitively in a mystical *moment*. The entire

> world is for the Kabbalist a *corpus symbolicum*. . . . A hidden and inexpressible reality finds its expression in the symbol.[6]

The Kabbalists stand on the shoulders of the philosophers and see farther than they. Thus, the mystical interpretation of the idea of creation *ex nihilo* is a deepening of the idea of an infinite Being, the *En-Sof*. Infinity does not denote a mere negation but a Nothing from which each thing has emerged. Creation *ex nihilo* is a creation outside of God: far from being an extension, it is conceived as contraction. Creation is the exile of God into himself, a movement toward return to one's own interior. This is the meaning of the word *Tsimtsum*, which, rather than the expression of the concentration of God in a single point, illustrates his retreat far from a point. And, besides, this symbol has a particular significance in the world of the Jews. It brings us back, like the "Breaking of the Vessels," to the experience of Exile.

The *Shevirath ha-Kelim* or "Breaking of the Vessels" also allows the enfolding of the question of evil and the determination of man's place in the cosmological drama that is creation as conceived by mysticism, where "God is fully real, but not all reality is god."[7] The forces of evil existed before the "Breaking of the Vessels" and were entangled with the enlightenment of the *Sephiroth* or the residue of the *En-Sof* in the primordial space. The divine light that penetrated into this space liberated the first being, *Adam Kadmon*, and captured in special vases the three highest *Sephiroth*. When the turn came of the last six ones, the light penetrated all at once and the schock was too great for the vessels, which broke. In the *Zohar*, evil is a by-product of the vital process of the *Sephiroth*, particularly of the *Sephira* of strict judgment. According to Luria, when the vessels broke, the light either diffused or flowed back to its source, or flowed downwards. "The powers of evil developed out of the scattered fragments of the vessels which have sunk into the lower depths of the primordial space."[8] "The fiendish nether-worlds of evil, the influence of which crept into all stages of the cosmological process, emerged from the fragments which still retained a few sparks of holy light . . . in this way the good elements of the divine order came to be mixed with the vicious ones."[9] Thus there is an inherent defect in everything that exists. Salvation is restoration, the reintegration of the original whole or *Tikkun*. Far from being pantheistic, the teaching of Luria describes "the theogenic process in God using the terms of human existence" and "represents an attempt to arrive at a new conception of the personal God," even if this leads to a "new form of Gnostic mythology."[10]

Reason and Experience

The study of mysticism can give vitality to the modern religious conscience because it is not cut off from either man's history or his fears. In not paying attention to these fears, which have provided "the material for myths," philosophy has lost contact with the human and established an "arid wisdom." Kabbalah is superior to medieval philosophy because in mysticism religion has remained intact, in direct relation to the experience of the average Jew, while the philosophers of the Middle Ages had "abandoned, to a considerable extent, the biblical ideas of God, world and man in favor of the Greek ideas."[11]

In passing judgment in this way on medieval philosophy, did not Scholem succumb to the same illusion as the modern Jewish thinkers, like Julius Guttmann, who asserted the superiority of modern to medieval Jewish philosophy? Does Scholem understand Maimonides as Maimonides understood himself? Does the author of the *Guide* limit himself to the rational justification of divine commandments or does he rather reveal something essential concerning God and the secrets of creation? In this case, allegory would not simply be a pedagogical device, but a way of unveiling the secrets of the Torah in taking into account the esoteric meaning of the Law. Thus Strauss asserts that the first step "to begin to study medieval philosophy" is to ask if Maimonides does not teach a truth for all time and if one can learn something *from* him, not just about him. What we can learn from Maimonides is connected to his posing the question: why philosophy? While the Kabbalah is a symbolic interpretation of an experience, philosophy investigates "the elementary and inconspicuous presuppositions on the basis of which those sentiments or experiences could be more than beautiful dreams, pious wishes, awe inspiring delusions, or emotional exaggerations,"[12] as Scholem himself recognized, for he did not refrain from speaking of the sabbatarianism of Jacob Frank (1726–1791) as messianism influenced by the hunger for power of its spiritual leader and connected to nihilism.[13]

Not only does religious experience neither offer an adequate basis for determining the truth of religious dogmas nor eliminate "the doctrinal conflicts between the three great monotheistic religions," but it is not "sufficient to quell the doubts raised by science or philosophy."[14] These doubts are one of the causes of the perplexity of the modern enlightened religious consciousness, that is, of the believer who recognizes the claims of reason and who is also a philosopher. Thus, "[n]ow, the superiority of modern philosophy to medieval philosophy is no longer so evident as it seemed to be one or two generations ago."[15] The modern philosophers distinguish philosophy from science, but this distinction, alien to the medieval philosophers, "paves the way for science that is not philosophical and philosophy that is not scientific." The former becomes an instrument for any given end, and the latter declines into mere "intellectual biography" or reduces to "methodology that serves modern science." To give up on the possibility of demonstrable truth, is this not to allow prejudice to triumph over reason? Similarly, to cut off science and technology from all reflection on human ends, to separate know-how from wisdom, is one of the defects of modern philosophy and a symptom of the crisis of our times.

The responsibility of reason characterizes the rationalism of Maimonides, which takes on the questions: Why science? Why philosophy? Does man need Revelation for the conduct of his life, individually and collectively? Underlining the relevance of the quarrel of the Ancients and Moderns, which has once again revived because the superiority of the Moderns is no longer self-evident, Strauss asserts that the pre-modern Enlightenment derives from Plato, who justifies philosophy and science before the tribunal of the city, and from Maimonides, who justifies "philosophy or science before the tribunal of the Law, or the Torah."[16] Pre-modern rationalism is more radical than modern rationalism and philosophy, which no longer pose the question of the necessity of philosophy or science. This is why "it is no longer completely absurd to turn from the modern philosophers towards the philosophers of the Middle Ages"[17] in order to learn from them *for* ourselves. It is no longer absurd to think that we are less enlightened than Cohen, for whom the Enlightenment is not self-evident. It is because he understands in an *original* manner the Enlightenment that Cohen is able to render accessible to us the thought of Maimonides.[18]

Most of Strauss's contemporaries who thought that it was necessary to return to the tradition did so in giving primacy to experience as the link to God. For Strauss, it is necessary to return to the rationalism of Maimonides, who is linked to the idea of the complementarity of religion and reason, reason and Revelation as the means of establishing a healthy relation to the tradition. Strauss is the least modern of the philosophers of his generation. He thinks that no one has really understood Maimonides, because no one has understood what is involved in his rationalism, which would require that one be completely free of modern prejudices concerning reason. But Cohen was not ready to abandon these prejudices, which go along with the return to experience as a means of connection to transcendence; instead, he defended them insistently.

It is as if Strauss sought to continue the work of his spiritual father in pursuing that part of Cohen's oeuvre that the latter had abandoned or left incomplete. Strauss will attempt to accomplish that task, which consists in interpreting Maimonides, bypassing the most known part of Cohen's thought. His understanding of religion as ethics prevented Cohen from understanding the truth of the philosophy of Maimonides, that is, his political philosophy. For Strauss, Cohen is the thinker who leads us to an understanding of the rationalism of Maimonides, but in focusing on morality, he misses the truth of Maimonides and leaves the field open to philosophies that are existentialist humanist interpretations of Revelation and that emphatically assert the primacy of experience over reason. Strauss is a successor to Cohen, and he sets himself apart from all the other heirs of Cohen's neo-Kantianism. His originality and his political philosophy are connected to his specific manner of limiting the influence of Cohen to that which concerns the reference to Maimonides and rejecting almost all the rest. By contrast, Rosenzweig and Levinas take from Cohen his thinking concerning sin and forgiveness, which constitute the self as a person defined in co-relation with God, with the theme of the "other" acquiring the status of a philosophical concept. Like Cohen, they uncover the *human* meaning of messianism, thus connecting to the specific historicity of Judaism without being concerned by the political or nationalist meaning of messianism.

The Human Experience of the Absolute

Religion and Philosophy

Because Franz Rosenzweig and Emmanuel Levinas challenged, like Strauss, the kind of rationality that totalizes natural and social experience, and because, for them, existence is prior to thought, they defend the idea of an articulation of philosophy and religion that is radically opposed to the system of Hegel, but also to all the heirs of Spinoza who establish philosophy as completely detached from any reference to Judaism. Instead of attempting a reconciliation of philosophy and religion, the "new thinking" considers religion as the original horizon of all meaning. There is something beyond thought, and that something is Revelation. Levinas draws from an awareness of the tradition and appropriates the categories of Judaism: one can trace the notion of chosenness to the idea of a subject that is not just a rights holder and the priority of responsibility over liberty. Philosophical discourse is open to Revelation. Religion informs or inspires philosophical discourse. This interest in Revelation goes hand in hand with the overcoming of the ideal, central to the Enlightenment of Spinoza and Kant, of the autonomous self. It also implies going behind the transcendental subject as it is defined by idealism, which "throws down the gauntlet to all philosophy, from Ionia to Jena."[19]

This heteronomous position, which Levinas, Rosenzweig, and Strauss all interpret differently, separates them from Heidegger, who never leaves the horizon of *Dasein*, which refers to a world closed onto itself. If existence is fundamentally openness to transcendence and not simply worldness, if it is in the discovery of otherness that the distinctively human existence is born, then the philosophy of existence is linked to an ontology or overcomes itself to an ontology and is in the first instance the interpretation of a reality beyond subjectivity. The overcoming of Cohen by Rosenzweig and Levinas and the use they make of his distinction between the individual as defined in Law (*Gesetz*)—by moral and social imperatives and the Law—and the self that emerges with the specifically religious experience of sin and redemption are human experiences of the Absolute, or philosophic interpretations of religion.[20] This is the meaning of heteronomy. There is something in the consciousness that is self-overcoming. It is not God's transcendence but that of his commandment (*Gebot*). For Cohen, Levinas, and Rosenzweig, the acceptance of Revelation does not occur in the strong sense through obedience of the ceremonial Law. Rather, what is crucial is to decipher this Revelation, which is the horizon of human life. This commandment, which shatters the autonomy of man, brings into being the consciousness already open to otherness as actual relation to God, to the absolute Other, outside the self. This commandment bids the love of God. Thus, according to Levinas and Rosenzweig, there is an appropriation of the tradition, not a return to it. We see in the extension of the philosophy of Cohen an interpretation of Revelation that uncovers the meaning of human life (Levinas) and a religious philosophy "where philosophy invokes theology as a bridge between Creation and Revelation and succeeds in connecting Revelation and Redemption." Far from being an a posteriori reconstruction of the content of theology, Rosenzweig's philosophy is a preparation for theology and an exposition of the a priori conditions on which its content depends. Rosenzweig and Levinas take up the challenge of the critics of the Enlightenment and indeed of the liberal theology that ignored the Creation and did not allow for the connection that inserts hope between Revelation and Redemption. This relation between philosophy and theology goes hand in hand with a new rationalism, because faith becomes the content of a known truth and this knowledge postulates in its foundation faith. The heteronomy of thought implies the abandonment of the ideal of reason's autonomy and the Kantian idea of the limits of knowledge, which made the move to Hegel almost inevitable, as well as the attempt to think the Absolute. In demonstrating that it is through the most personal experience that man discovers his responsibility for the Absolute, Rosenzweig and Levinas transcend the Enlightenment. They disarm all those who, in order to counter religion, borrow their arguments from Spinoza, Kant, and Hegel. This is evident from the Rosenzweig's interpretation of miracles, a target of the Enlightenment thinkers. When he raises the question of language and the face of man, which bears the visible traces of Revelation, Rosenzweig articulates the possibility of miraculous experience. He restores the miracle and gives it a place in philosophy.

The absolute transcendent truth is constituted within the core of experience. It is when man attains the ultimate limit of his condition of being-in-the-world, of createdness, that he awakens to the sensation of his irreducible unity and discovers his destiny as a being of *logos* (language), embracing experience as personal. This ultimate experience, with which the *Star of Redemption* begins, corresponds to the mystical contemplation of the truth, which is situated at the extreme limit of existence—and at the end of the book also—and cannot be grasped except through flashes of illumination. I have a presentiment of this vision of the truth when I look at the other and see his face. This awareness of the transcendence of the other that is revealed in the face-to-face encounter, where his face opens me to something that escapes the representation I have of him, will be described by Levinas and developed as experience of the Infinite, of God who comes to mind, the ethical relation to the other, and the openness to his otherness recurring to the God, with whom we cannot be on familiar terms. As with Jacobi and the Counter-Enlightenment of which these two Jewish thinkers are, in certain respects, the heirs, thought does not serve to synthesize this experience, but constitutes its acceptance or recognition (Rosenzweig) and its articulation (Levinas). These philosophies represent a deepening of Cohen's theory of double correlation and an original way of extending his legacy, because the dependency on Kant is jettisoned.

Strauss shares with Rosenzweig and Levinas the idea that the rationalism of Kant is inadequate and that a new way of articulating the experience of reason and Revelation is necessary. This reformulation is not anticipated by the Enlightenment, and it also escapes its critics. The new thinking, like the philosophy of Strauss, is at once an appropriation of the tradition and a critique of the Enlightenment. However, the relationship between philosophy and the Law that Strauss proposes in turning to Maimonides sets him apart from Rosenzweig. Strauss advocates a return to Maimonidean thought, the truth of which needs to be recovered. He does not endeavor to construct a philosophy that would be an interpretation of the tradition from a modern point of view. Had Strauss turned his attention to the philosophy of Levinas, he would have made the same criticism that he had leveled at Cohen, that what is at issue is an idealizing interpretation of the past, a way of reading the texts of the tradition while projecting onto them contemporary preoccupations. The idealizing interpretation can give rise to thoughtfulness, but it is partial and lacks the truth contained in the texts of the past. The appropriation of the past presupposes that in the first instance we will return to the past in order to know it and to see how it might illuminate our current situation.

The interpretation by Rosenzweig and Levinas of Revelation or of the Call that constitutes the self gives rise to philosophies where the relation to the other is, like in Cohen, the site of my relation to God, and God comes to mind, as Levinas says, in the trace of the other. This appropriation of tradition gives rises to an ethics. The link between the relationship to God and the relationship to others does not concern the private. The ethical dimension that is at the heart of the philosophy of the face developed by Levinas allows a delimitation of the space and the concept of the political. Here we need to study the transition from this personal experience to the objective religious reality in the reading that Rosenzweig proposes of the relationship of Christianity and Judaism to history. This reflection on the relation between religion, ethics, and politics allows us to appreciate what distinguishes Levinas and Rosenzweig from Strauss, who proposes a different articulation of the relation between philosophy and religion and places the emphasis on a political philosophy as distant from messianism as it is from the philosophy of history.

Ethics and Spirituality

Just as, with Cohen, the correlation between man and God is linked to those experiences where man becomes conscious of his irreducibility to any whole that threatens to assimilate him, the primordial experience that leads to religious intrigue and to Revelation is that of anxiety before death. Man does not find his place in the whole that embraces him. Man, world, and God are in the first instance separated, as one sees in the first book of *The Star of Redemption*, which is the pre-logical or pre-religious, mythic description of this life, alien to any all-encompassing universality, which goes back to the creation, God's approach toward the world. But if the approach of God to man enclosed in his selfhood is Revelation, man, in response to this love of God, turns himself toward the world and others. Revelation is the coming into relation of these elements that were separated in the beginning. Nevertheless, this synthesis, this openness to life, to language, and to time, does not realize itself through being-in-the-world. It is in relation to the perfection of a future world and pertains to the Redemption. Human relations are not at the deepest level the coexistence of isolated egos, because other human beings are the "they" to whom one learns to say "you." Life is not defined essentially by the *conatus* or the quest for preservation of one's being. The isolated individual who, in experiencing the absurdity of war, exclaims his irreducibility to the order of things is led not to the concern with his own preservation but to a relation to the human other. It is not in the transcendental consciousness that God, man, and the world are united, but it is an event that allows man to bridge that absolute break that is Revelation. This fundamental fabric that connects us to others is "the '*dia*' of dialogue, of dia-chrony, of that time that Rosenzweig means to 'take seriously,' the 'binding separation' known by the well-worn name of love."[21] This love of God externalizes itself as love of one's neighbor. Similarly, it is through the face of the other man that he can have a vision of the "face of God."

Rosenzweig, too present in the work of Levinas to be cited, points to the philosophy of the "face" that introduces an ethical relation to the other. Not only is the relation between consciousnesses not essentially a relation of knowledge or representation, because the other as such escapes my objectifications and robs me of my constitutive power in inviting a face-to-face posture, but, in addition, a specific dimension opens up in me when I am in the presence of another being and see his face.[22] "The face tears apart the sensible," as Levinas put it in *Totality and Infinity*. It is this face that I see, and this unity is constitutive of otherness, of the other as transcendent, of the other who is not an alter ego, but an otherness of which the mystery, the difference, and the solitude should be preserved, even in relations that are close and intimate.[23] But the nakedness of the face, its exposition becomes a matter of its unmasking, of its vulnerability as a being exposed to suffering, hunger, and death. There is, in the manner in which the other appears to me, an indication of the ethical relation: to see the other is to hear the appeal that he launches to me not to leave him alone.

In *Otherwise than Being*, Levinas insists on this primordial responsibility that is revealing to me of the face of another. Prior to being, it reverts to a dimension that transcends us and provokes a rupture of time that signals toward something other than merely being, that is to say, toward something that Rosenzweig sought to give a name to in the system of *The Star of Redemption* in articulating Creation, Revelation, and Redemption. In *Otherwise than Being*, Levinas speaks of being a hostage to the other and emphasizes this dimension of heteronomy that gives the encounter its meaning. It is only in responding to the call of the other that subjectivity emerges. It is not a matter of obedience to a law inscribed in my reason and giving me the sense of good and evil. The appeal is to something outside me. Ethics is not the universalization of a maxim. Freedom begins with non-freedom and making by hearing. While morality concerns the values relative to the existing individual or the society to which he belongs, ethics designates the dimension of my primordial relation to the other.

The originality of the philosophy of the face of Levinas stems from the fact that the prohibition of murder and the welcome of the other as such are based on the description of the way in which the other appears to me. There is a "You shall not commit murder" inscribed on the face of the other.[24] I see that the desire to take his life and to appropriate that which escapes my power of power would be an absolute transgression, a murder. Far from being relative to the rules of a society or a religion, the prohibition of murder as Levinas understands it at the core of our daily experience is absolute and applies to everyone. The philosophy of the face underscores our dependence in relation to the other, but also the violence of the good. The other is also the undesirable. It is he who accuses us: "the other is the sole being I can wish to kill."[25]

This sense of the human displays the distance that exists between the Enlightenment of Kant and Spinoza and the human experience of the Absolute in Levinas and Rosenzweig. In defining the human subject by his openness to the other, these thinkers reappropriate the Jewish tradition: I am not alone, which means that my freedom is not that which defines me essentially or primarily, and the consciousness is not identified with consciousness of rights. In *Four Talmudic Readings* (1968), Levinas discerns in the Talmud this sense of the human, while, in his philosophical work, he discovers and describes his idea of the Infinite in human experience. But his philosophy is linked to a Jewish definition of man. The ethics of Levinas is an ethics drawn from Jewish sources. It does not derive from Greek philosophy, where self-sufficiency is constitutive of wisdom, which integrates happiness and virtue, and where at the same time one has the notion of man as by nature a political animal: the

Aristotelian city is the primordial site where the human realizes itself; it is ontologically prior to the family and the collective "we" that proceeds the "you." By his insistence on experiences related to a letting go and to the Call (coming from the other) and constant reference to the ontological solitude of man, which love does not eliminate and which constructs the relation to a particular other, to a "you," the site where the individual gives birth to himself, the thought of Levinas belongs to Jerusalem, not Athens. The fear of God as the beginning of wisdom doesn't mean that one must beware of the warlike and jealous God of the Old Testament, but that this fear derives from man's experience of his fragility and nothingness. By contrast, Spinoza had suppressed and rejected these experiences. This dependence of Rosenzweig and Levinas on biblical thought and their distance from the modern Enlightenment are particularly evident in their interpretation of messianism, in the relationship that Rosenzweig postulates between Judaism and Christianity in his articulation of Revelation and Redemption, and in the way in which Levinas conceives, contra Hobbes, a state based on justice.

Redemption and Politics

The ethics of Levinas grounds a politics characterized by justice and hospitality. This politics, far from being reduced to a pure and simple defense of the morality of human rights,[26] articulates justice in terms of the good, the right of each to fulfill the respect for the duty that he has toward the other who is his brother. This phenomenology of the rights of man, which studies the structure of the conscience or this question of respect for the other, amounts to a putting in question of the Kantian definition of practical reason. It is not on the basis of will, which can have "an incoercible part that cannot be obligated by the formalism of universality,"[27] or freedom, that one can understand human rights, but rather brotherhood, where the duty in respect of the other appears to my conscience at the moment of the encounter: "Should not . . . fraternity . . . be discerned in the prior non-indifference of one for the other, in that original goodness in which freedom is embedded, in which the justice of the rights of man takes on an immutable significance and stability, better than those guaranteed by the state?"[28]

If one insists on freedom alone, the concept of justice that one obtains is reduced to "the norm of pure measure"[29]: relations between individuals display a certain indifference, as if one were dealing with anonymous pawns, interchangeable, and this politics without ethics, justice without goodness, is ineffective. Ethics, which is what we call the relation to the human other thought in the light of proximity, ought to be the foundation of politics and ought to be its *authority*. We find here a critique of the abstractness of human rights, but also of the idea that reason alone is capable of grounding a politics aimed at the respect of others. For Levinas, human rights are not deduced from reason or from the idea of freedom, which is "the potential negation of every other freedom"[30] and should be preceded by responsibility. They are not derived either from religion, but are manifested by the human experience of the Infinite that is the encounter with the other. Levinas opposes the rationalism of the Enlightenment a certain interpretation of the idea of Revelation that equally allows him to distance himself from any reactionary project aiming to base politics and morality on religion.

The idea of thinking human rights in terms of responsibility that I bear in relation to another being, who concerns me even if I do not know him; this implantation of goodness into justice, of fraternity into liberty, of ethics into politics is related to the religious dimension of Levinas's thought, even if one cannot speak of his case in terms of a return to orthodoxy. It is rather a matter of his discovering in the tradition a timeless truth and showing how it is central to our everyday experience. The Moderns, according to Levinas, didn't so much forget this truth as bury it and are no longer in a position to recognize because their very vocabulary is hackneyed. Here the role of phenomenology is identical to that of art in Merleau-Ponty: it is a matter of making these truths visible again, to display their meaning and make them a living reality.

Duty toward the other is equally a matter of relations between citizens and even of peace between communities, that is, states, because one is dealing here with the arrival of the idea of God. In disputing the Kantian idea of free practical reason, Levinas suggests that politics unoriented by religion is doomed to impasse and leads, as he suggests is the case with technology, to the opposite of what it is intended to promote. The heart of the Straussian critique of the modern Enlightenment is that modern rationalism, when it is entirely divorced from Revelation, leads to the destruction of reason. Heteronomy does not have the same meaning in Levinas as in Strauss, but they are equally sensitive to the destructiveness of the modern Enlightenment. One could say that this critique of modernity is connected to this "particular frisson of return"[31] of which Levinas speaks in relation to Rosenzweig in expressing his fidelity to Judaism. But what is Judaism, and what does "fidelity" mean? Do these words carry the same meaning for Levinas and Rosenzweig, who think of God's command as love, as for Strauss, who, seeking to give back to the consciousness a place in the relationship to the Absolute, speaks of an enlightened Judaism?

Such is the difference between the thought of Rosenzweig, who positions himself as the heir of Kierkegaard, and that of Strauss, follower of Maimonides. Rosenzweig places the *mitzvot* within the drama of existence, while for Strauss the interpretation of the Law is able to guide the perplexed reader in a progressive search for a truth that will transform him through Enlightenment. His interpretation of the Jewish tradition, which proceeds by means of a return to the truth of the tradition, distinguishes his political philosophy from the political thought of Levinas and Rosenzweig and thus differs from their philosophy, which is centered on ethics and spirituality and based on love.

It is beginning from this interpretation of the command of God as love, of which the human response is the love of one's neighbor, that Rosenzweig conceives Redemption and the respective roles of Christianity and Judaism in the salvation of humanity. Man, "mediator of Redemption," "indispensible conduit of the movement that comes from God,"[32] has a mission in the world and in relation to other men. He is meta-ethical. "Revelation is at once love" and it "marks off the future."[33] Human love is work itself, effective Redemption. This love is not merely contemplative, but engages a certain political responsibility, that is, the religious stage does not exclude, unlike the case of Kierkegaard, involvement in politics. Religions have a vocation not only with respect to the edification of individuals but also with respect to peoples. It is in this manner that Levinas and Rosenzweig appropriate the theme of the Messiah.

In Levinas, the concept of peace is circumscribed beginning from an ethical view of the Messiah and allows one to go beyond the question of the tyranny of the state or its anonymous universalism. In thinking through the conditions of a specifically political responsibility, Levinas goes beyond politics. This is the meaning of his 1971 reflections on the choice between *the state of Caesar and the state of David*. While the first, which recalls the Hobbesian theory of the state, only knows peace to the extent that individuals, in conflict with one another, are held in check by a third, the state of justice, founded upon fraternity, can engender a peace based on other-regardingness and being-for-the-other. There is more in the state than the state. The anthropology of Hobbes and Machiavelli is arguably more realistic, but it is important to note at the same time the connection and the gap between ethics and politics. This gap is why the thought of Levinas is still not a political philosophy.

The fact that Socrates begins with the opinions of the city and returns to the phenomena themselves, which are neither the concepts of scientific reason nor the *pragmata* of Heidegger, but social relations, could very well reveal that there are beneath consciousness human affections and an experience that Levinas describes when he speaks of the encounter with the other. By contrast, Strauss, in his return to the things themselves, privileges opinions over feelings. And because political philosophy comes from Athens, it thinks of man's humanity as constituting itself in relation to the political community, prior to any transformative encounter. The relations between beings at the heart of the community being characterized as much by conflict as by agreement, political philosophy is closer to Hobbesian pessimism than is Levinas. Having made these distinctions, one must recognize that while the reduction of Husserl does violence to reality because the revealed consciousness is too homogenous, the *epoche* of Levinas is not lacking in radicality. Finally, according to Strauss, politics is prior to ethics, because men are from the outset needful of the idea of the good, and they are, as in Aristotle, determined by passions. When Levinas borrows from Greek philosophy, he is thinking of Plato rather than Aristotle. Like Plato and Cohen, Levinas thinks that the state, morality, philosophy, and religion are in each case the basis for a movement that leads them beyond themselves toward the idea of the Good. This movement is exactly the meaning of messianism for Levinas.

The coming of the Messiah or a better world is based on a promise. *Perhaps* the Messiah will come. This is the expectation of an occurrence one can never predict. Levinas, in refusing to make messianism the ground of politics and in relating the messianic experience to the conception of awaiting, the hope for the impossible, remains in the tradition of Cohen and Rosenzweig. In differentiating sacredness from holiness and in abandoning the vocabulary of rationalism and philosophy in order to learn about what opens up the subject to another whose future he can never be, Levinas speaks of an experience of the other that derives from a gift from a welcoming and not an exchange. It is not a matter of the recognition of the other, which will be the object of a politics based, in the sense of Arendt and Schmitt, on the identification of the enemy.

Temporality is the central theme of *The Star of Redemption*. The truth temporizes itself. Far from being the departure from eternity, time is the relating of God to the world in the *past* of the creation, and also of God to man, in the command to love that which is the *present* of the Creation. In fulfilling this command, man constructs the *future* of a world that prepares the Kingdom of God. In Rosenzweig, as with Levinas, the Messiah has not arrived, and this anticipation of the impossible is constitutive of a non-political messianism, from the notion of a Redemption not through Zionism, even if connected to the concept of chosenness. For Rosenzweig, the Truth is shared between Judaism and Christianity. These religions are no longer considered as creeds or dogmas, but as two expressions of the experience of the Absolute. Thus Rosenzweig reconsiders Judaism and Christianity, including in their social and ritualistic meanings, as primordial structures and categories of his messianic "theory of consciousness." Their meaning and mission, but above all their relation to time, are different. Judaism, where Revelation is identical with commandment, does not signify the yoke of the Law, but attests to the renewal of the love of God for man, his living presence. Remaining outside of history, God is characterized by a specific relation to time, where, in ritual, one constructs the experience of this original commandment. Paradoxically, the wandering Jew has reached his destiny, while the Christian remains on his journey.[34]

The *mission* of Christianity is to bring Redemption to individuals and to accompany peoples in their historical journey until the world recognizes in the collective existence of the Jews the already realized model of ideal humanity. Judaism is thus no truer than Christianity, buts its ahistoricity is largely compensated for by *chosenness.* Offering to all peoples the model of a collective existence always identical to itself and unceasingly renewed, an existence extending from now until the end of time, this is the "passionate heart" of *The Star of Redemption.*[35] Rosenzweig turns on its head the reasoning of Spinoza, which rejects the particularism of a national religion and considers the ceremonial law as a yoke. In articulating religion and history, spirituality and action in the world, love of God, and love of men, and in presenting Judaism in its universalism, Rosenzweig appears to be able to escape from subjectivism and the excessive internalization of the content of religion. He removes the obstacle presented by Spinoza, even if he does not return to traditional Judaism. Is it credible that "the new thinking" and the new orthodoxy offer a solution to the crisis of our times? Or, rather, is the work of Rosenzweig, which begins with a questioning of the politics of the state implied in the philosophy of Hegel, nothing other than "anticipation of great disruptions and a break in thought, which bears responsibility for so many catastrophes"?[36] Strauss opts for the second view: it is not ultramodern thought that can enlighten us, but pre-modern thought, which is timely because it is untimely.

The Jewish Enlightenment of Maimonides

Cohen and Strauss

Maimonides's philosophy possesses a truth that is not simply relative to the Middle Ages and that has not been surpassed by modern Jewish philosophy. Herman Cohen (1848–1918) put Strauss on the path of the return to Maimonides: the return to the tradition is a return to this "classic of rationalism." Thus it is not experience or existence, but knowledge of the Law and its interpretation that constitute the domain of the relation to God. The predicament to which we are led by the modern Enlightenment, in the manner in which it constructs the conflict between religion and reason, can be overcome by the rationalism of Maimonides. This requires a different definition than that to which modern thought has become habituated. And the rationalism of Maimonides, which is open to Revelation and accepts the limits of reason, is not immediately comprehensible to us because we no longer have a sense of the questionableness of the modern Enlightenment; we take it as self-evident.[37] This spurious obviousness explains how Cohen is closer to the truth than we are. Thus we must turn to him in order to understand the Enlightenment of Maimonides and his alternative of enlightened Judaism. This implies a philosophical examination of the end of the Law and prophecy and an interpretation of the content of Revelation.

Cohen is the first to show that enlightened Judaism is more than an application of the Enlightenment to Judaism[38] and to emphasize the Platonic origins of the thought of Maimonides. Strauss is never so close or so far from Cohen than when Maimonides is concerned. Cohen inspires Strauss to draw all the consequences of the specific way in which Maimonides articulates reason and Revelation, but Cohen and Strauss differ in how they understand the core of Maimonides's teaching. The veneration of Strauss by Cohen is not based on a student–teacher relationship but is rather more a matter of filiation, and here the interpretation of Maimonides represents a break. This break appears during the 1930s in Strauss's "Cohen and Maimonides" and *Philosophy and Law*. It leads Strauss to define the core of his thought and inquire into the break of the Moderns with the Ancients concerning the status of politics.

Cohen reinterprets Maimonides and the writings of the prophets as if their truth became apparent in Kantian morality and in the reformulation of this morality, to which Cohen devoted much of his career. Tradition is indeed a source, but its richness is only apparent to us now.

There is continuity between Maimonides and Kant. Cohen presents his thought as extending Maimonides in his effort to rid monotheistic Judaism of idolatrous and mythological elements. Enlightenment consists in purifying Judaism through reason, thus turning it into enlightened Judaism where the God of the prophets is cleansed of anything carnal or tribal, where Judaism itself is comprehended in its most universal aspect, that of morality. The truth of Judaism is enlightened Judaism. This religion of reason is not susceptible to the critique of Spinoza, to the charge of nationalism and the identification of faith with superstition, but this is an idealizing interpretation of Judaism.

Cohen neglects the difference between Kant and Maimonides, that is, the break of the Moderns with the Ancients. He is faithful to the schema of the Enlightenment: he thinks that truth, in the past, has been encumbered, obscured, and that it can be better understood today than in the past. The modern Enlightenment is the handmaiden of ahistorical Judaism, enlightened Judaism. It perfects tradition rather than returning to it. According to Strauss, the return to the tradition presupposes that one considered that Enlightenment is pre-modern and that access to the truth requires a break with modern thought. For the truth is not distorted but rather forgotten. What Maimonides is saying escapes, and our interpretation of his analysis of the Law is wrong. It is modernity that hides this truth. Cohen derives his understanding of the Law as morality from Christianity,[39] rather than the unity or totality of political, religious, and moral life. The return to Maimonides requires that one deconstructs modern prejudices and that one understand the thinkers of the past as they understood themselves.

This rule of interpretation is the reversal of the transcendental dialectic of *Kant's Critique of Pure Reason*. The break with Cohen can be understood as the rejection by Strauss of neo-Kantianism. To understand what is at stake in this disagreement, it is not sufficient to consider the writings of Cohen on Judaism, but rather also his early works on Kant, from Kant's *Grounding of Ethics* (1873) to *The Ethics of the Pure Will* (1904). This dispute between Strauss and the neo-Kantians is central to Strauss's opposition to the Enlightenment in Germany. And even if this is not evident on a first reading of Strauss's works, it is nevertheless one of the driving forces, from his first writings on Jacobi to his debate with Cohen about Maimonides, and including his response to the Davos debate between Cassirer and Heidegger.

Strauss opposes Natorp, who in his *Plato's Doctrine of the Ideas* accords a fundamental importance to the theory of the Ideas and instead insists on the political dimension of Platonic philosophy. At play here is a critique of the neo-Kantian philosophical method: concepts are in the thing itself; they are not transcendental. Finally, the entire Enlightenment project is contested when one puts in question the relevance of this interpretation of Plato constructed out of the theory of Ideas. For in neo-Kantian idealism, the project of the Enlightenment is conceived of as the realization of the Idea. One recalls the disagreement with Cassirer, who, in the *Philosophy of Symbolic Forms*, asserts continuity between myth, religion, and philosophy. Strauss rejects this continuity and emphasizes the heterogeneity between religion and philosophy, a heterogeneity that allows one to speak of two opposed kinds of wisdom. His critique of the modern Enlightenment is clearly a rejection of neo-Kantianism, of its transcendental orientation and idealism, but also of the continuity between myth, religion, and thought that is considered in the framework of the philosophy of culture, where religion, politics, ethics, and the arts are autonomous spheres. To confront the crisis of our time, in particular the crisis of liberalism, which is connected to this autonomy of politics absorbed in society and oscillating between ethics and economy, one must overcome the obstacle represented by neo-Kantianism.

The return to the tradition implies a distancing from the ideas that have shaped our way of reading the history of philosophy. This distancing should allow us access to the thought of Plato, who is the father of the Jewish and Arab Enlightenment of the Middle Ages, as Cohen had seen. Cohen began a project that Strauss sought to continue and to surpass. He had signaled to Strauss that Maimonides was the thinker to turn to, but it is the way Heidegger reads the Ancients that Strauss puts in radical opposition to the interpretative scheme of the modern Enlightenment and to Cohen. It is necessary to read the Greeks without seeking to project on them our modern categories. These categories have not merely hidden the truth; they have constructed an entire history of philosophy characterized by the forgetfulness of what is essential. And we are not even aware of this forgetfulness.

From Morality to Politics

In his 1908 text "Characterizing the Ethics of Maimonides," Cohen shows that the Maimonidean doctrine of negative attributes is the proof that our relationship to God is essentially moral. We do not have knowledge of the essence of God, but only of his ways. The negative attributes of God (God is not without life) are negations of privation.[40] One should avoid merging the Creator and the creation and maintain the unity and transcendence of God. Cohen shows that Maimonides does not deny the possibility that man can relate to God through his reason, but only metaphysics, the knowledge of God by positive attributes. This limitation is the indicia of an essentially moral relation to God. The negation of privations amounts to speaking of God's attributes of action. Revelation thus addresses man as an essentially moral being, and its function is to provide knowledge of God as the model for morality.

Revelation as Cohen conceives it is a fact of reason, which is a practical reason, and indicates the relation between God as the idea of the Good and man as a moral being. Reason is the site of this relation. It is reason that receives the commandment of God. This definition of reason is at once Kantian in its practical orientation while following Jacobi in the emphasis on the dimension of receptivity. Reason in Cohen goes beyond what is understood by the philosophers, but it does not correspond with Jacobi's understanding of faith. Its elaboration owes a great deal to the opening provided by the practical philosophy of Kant, but this opening does not postulate as necessary the heteronomy of the Law. There is nothing of the historical in Revelation. This accords neither with the view of Maimonides nor of orthodoxy. Cohen understands himself as continuing the effort of Maimonides to provide a rational foundation for the 613 precepts of the Law and the classification of the different types of commandments. But this analogy between the neo-Kantianism of Cohen, which represents the synthesis of philosophy and faith, and the enlightened Judaism of Maimonides is false. Maimonides does not reconcile Revelation and reason.

Even if there is a coincidence between idealizing interpretation and the principle of allegory, Cohen and Maimonides have two opposed conceptions of reason. While Maimonides presents a rationalism that is also a critique of the limits of reason, Cohen places all the value of Revelation in reason. Cohen deifies reason. He does not want to put in question the autonomy of man, as is evidenced by the question with which he begins his 1908 study: "Can one reconcile ethics in general with a moral doctrine of the essence of religion, thus with the worship and love of God?" The autonomy of reason goes hand in hand with belief in the capacity of man to work on his own toward his salvation, without recourse to anything but his reason. He rejects an interest in Revelation or the need for a divine Law.

That which is religious in the ethics of Cohen, that which leads him to articulate morality in religious terms, is precisely the Kantian—or Fichtean—distinction between what is and what ought to be, and the idea of an infinite moral progress: because man who ought to progress in his moral effort needs an infinite time, the effort of each individual toward moral perfection ought to be sustained by something other than relative communities, such as the state. This effort requires a dimension that is not really the dimension of hope of which Ricœur speaks in relation to Kant's postulate, but resembles it: it transcends the state and society and derives from the idealized, that is, secularized, interpretation of messianism. Finally, it includes an idea of humanity that eliminates all trace of the particularist or the national in the idea of a chosen people. Religion is thus ethical in essence; its truth is moral. Conversely, morality, as we saw was the case with Rosenzweig and Levinas, requires reconnection with religious notions and the incorporation of what is essential in them, which relates to the intelligence of the dual correlation, to the link between the relation to God and the relation to another.

For Cohen, ethics is the center of all real philosophy. This is why he holds that Maimonides is more directly related to Plato than to Aristotle.[41] Cohen rejects the eudaimonism of Aristotle, which makes contemplation an ideal way of life, while for Plato the philosopher is required to go back down into the cave: he has social responsibilities, like the medieval thinkers who philosophized before the Law, or Cohen himself, in his campaign against the death penalty. Moreover, Aristotle places God outside of the ethical realm: "Whatever respect one owes the God of Aristotle, he is not the God of Israel."[42] This opposition to Aristotle is "deeply rooted in the Jewish Sensibility." For Cohen, who insists on his debt to Plato and Maimonides, God is ethical and is a God for men. And it is just this ethical interpretation to which Strauss will object.

If Cohen is correct in saying that Maimonides is closer to Plato than to the contemplative ideal of Aristotle, he does not grasp all the implications of this claim and does not think through this opposition to its root, that is to say, beginning with Socrates.[43] Socratic questioning is indeed "questioning about the just life," but it is "a questioning-together about living-together" and concerning the common good. "It is essentially *political*." Socrates returns to the opinions that men share in the city. Political philosophy is inseparable from this return, neglected by Cohen as by the Moderns generally. For Strauss, politics is primary in relation to ethics, because the questioning concerning the just life takes place in the first instance in the city. Cohen and Levinas did not reflect on the fact that Socrates preceded Plato.

Along similar lines, Strauss criticizes Cohen for not having asked why Scripture mentions only the moral qualities of God. "The response of Moses is that "these make possible the existence and the rule of men. . . . They are necessary for the operation of the state."[44] The core of Maimonides's thought is not ethics but politics, and this political teaching is contained in his prophetology. Socialization is nowhere so necessary and so difficult as for human beings, who require a ruler. And man requires a revealed law in order to guide him. It is communicated to human beings by the prophet: "The prophet is the founder of a community that revolves around the true perfection of man."[45] Strauss vindicates the interpretation of Cohen to the extent that Maimonides's Enlightenment is Platonic. But Cohen ought to have asked himself why, in Maimonides, philosophy does not suffice to guarantee the existence of a perfect city. What does it mean that the prophet is superior to the philosopher?

The philosopher should be at the same time "prophet, poet and politician all in one person."[46] The prophetology of Maimonides is platonic to the extent that the Law is oriented to the specific perfection of man and that the establishment of the city is not just an exterior form of life but is a revealed Law. Nevertheless, Revelation in Plato is not erased through the brute fact of Revelation. Besides, its understanding and application require more than philosophical qualities: the prophet is superior to the philosopher, because in the prophet both the understanding and the imagination are at the command of the intellect. He possesses at the same time theoretical capacities and the facility of making the commandments of the Law understandable to human beings in general. In sum, he knows how to govern, how to rule human beings, but also to legislate. Does this mean that rationalism leads to a defense of the theocratic state or even to the notion that the good political leader is above all a charismatic chief? Before answering this question and showing that the manner in which Strauss interprets the prophetology of Maimonides leads to the affirmation of political philosophy, it is important to consider what kind of relation between philosophy and the Law follows from Maimonides's critique of reason.

The Rational Critique of Reason

The truth of Maimonides philosophy resides in the way in which it articulates philosophy and religion, reason and Revelation. And, far from being a synthesis of the two, the enlightened Judaism of Maimonides is the affirmation, *from the point of view of reason*, of the interdependence of philosophy and the Law, but also the demonstration of their respective roles, meaning, and domains. When Guttmann asserts a certain superiority of modern to medieval Jewish philosophy, because only the Moderns succeed, by theory of dual truth, to guarantee at the same time the autonomy of the religious consciousness and that of science as well as their relation, he does not see that Maimonides makes a *rational* critique of reason: "human intellect has a limit which it cannot cross: for this reason man is obliged, for the glory of his Lord, to halt at this limit and not to reject teachings of Revelation that he cannot comprehend and demonstrate."[47]

This is the meaning of the superiority of the prophets to the philosophers: "Contemplative knowledge of the "upper world" is possible only for the prophets . . ."[48] This truth, according to which the world was created, transcends philosophy, and it is communicated by the prophets to all human beings because it is necessary for life. The rationalism that is at the same time belief in Revelation is more than the affirmation of the interdependence of philosophy and the Law. This is a matter of philosophy of religion: that which orders the conflict between reason and Revelation is reason. The rationalist Maimonides asserts that reason is limited and that all those truths necessary for life are accessible to man through reason and Revelation.[49] Revelation is a given: that is the meaning of Revelation; instead of knowing God based on man or the religious consciousness, the philosopher submits to the Law. He accepts the answers that Revelation gives to certain questions that cannot be answered theoretically. On the other hand, the Law also means to the philosopher the obligation to philosophize.[50] The task of the philosopher is to inquire into the role of the Law and draw out the implications of prophetology: the prophet being, in Judaism and Islam, a legislator, one may well ask what are the political consequences of this affirmation and consider at the same time the Greek origins of the Maimonidean Enlightenment, its opposition to the Christian world and that which makes enlightened Judaism something problematic for a philosopher. For Plato, the Law is a question: it is not given, and the philosopher has to seek it. The Platonic requirement to put the philosopher back in the cave is realized in medieval Jewish and Islamic philosophy. The prophet is the founder of the Platonic city.

We need to ask whether political philosophy as Strauss understands it presupposes that one retains this *questioning* of the Law or if religion is necessary in the name of an *answer* to the problem of the meaning of life. In the first case, Straussian Enlightenment would be a way of critiquing modern rationalism while at the same time being faithful to a tradition of Enlightenment that goes from Plato to Spinoza through Maimonides and defends the freedom to philosophize. Is not Strauss's critique of the modern Enlightenment a return to the original Enlightenment of Plato, which entails taking seriously the gap between the small number of wise and the many? Is Maimonides not the conduit leading us to Socrates and Plato, or is there a distinct advantage of medieval over ancient rationalism?

The way in which Maimonides conceives the interpenetration of philosophy and religion means that fidelity to his enlightened Judaism would not be secured by modern Jewish philosophy, whether a religious philosophy or the Cohen's religion of reason. The truth of pre-modern rationalism only becomes evident once one reopens the quarrel of the Ancients and Moderns and grasps the implications of Maimonides's prophetology, that is, the theological-political problem. The meaning of enlightened Judaism amounts to a certain conception of the relation of religion to politics, and only by understanding the meaning of the Law is it possible to gauge the political significance of Maimonides's prophetology. The notion of the Law as the unity of social, political, and religious life is central to medieval Arab and Jewish political philosophy. This approaches the ancient understanding and is distant from Christianity and the interpretation of the Law that ensues from the *Epistle to the Romans* I, 20: "It is the notion of Law that united Jews and Greeks . . . this notion which is hidden by the tradition of *Christianity* and natural right, under the spell of which philosophical thought falls silent. By the *Christian* tradition: that which begins with the radial *critique* of the Law by Paul. By the *natural right* tradition, which establishes a system of *abstract* norms, which *positive* law should fulfill and make practicable."[51] Further, our habituation to living in a political order where the public and private spheres are separated desensitizes us to this understanding of the meaning of the Law. Why is it necessary not to understand the Law as morality, but to reformulate the theological-political problem and to conceive the articulation of religion, ethics, and politics, which is the theme and preoccupation of Strauss in respect of Maimonides?

Our hypothesis is that Strauss does not aim at defending theocracy, but at being concerned with the Law understood as a structure. The Law reflects a relationship to transcendent notions (for religion and morality) and transcendental ones (for politics). What is the end of the city, and what kind of society do we want to promote in taking this or that decision? The critique of the modern Enlightenment and the inquiry into premodern rationalism, which implicates at the same time the critique of the limits of reason—thus (which implicates) Revelation—and the need for a Revelation, lead Strauss to take up again the classic questions of political philosophy, that is, to turn toward classical political philosophy: to whom should one confide the task of lawmaking? What is the end of the state?

Should one limit oneself to following custom and tradition, whatever they may be, or act so that the state vindicates its legitimacy and acts with a view to the virtue and happiness of the citizens? Do the laws serve only to protect the rights of the citizens, or do they also serve a pedagogical purpose? These matters of debate are at the core of the difference between ancient and modern political thought. It is attention to the meaning of the Law in Maimonides that inclines Strauss to assert that the solution to the crisis of our times does not depend on the articulation of morality and religion, but rather politics and religion.

The reformulation of the theological-political problem that follows from this critique of modern rationalism leads to an examination of the quarrel of the Ancients and Moderns in the political domain, that is, to the opposition of classical political philosophy, which goes from Plato to Maimonides, to modern political thought, which begins with Machiavelli and Hobbes. The dissection of the modern religious consciousness and the questing of modern rationalism lead to the deconstruction of the presuppositions that ground our conception of the state and communal life. It is a matter of understanding how fidelity to enlightened Judaism can be equated with the advancement of political philosophy. The question of the opposition between Jerusalem and Athens is revisited, and with it that of understanding why revealed religion, in particular Christianity,[52] dug a second cave, burying more and more the meaning of the Law. The affinity of the Straussian approach to phenomenology will become clearer when we examine the status accorded to political philosophy, in particular the Socratic turn and the meaning of the Law in Maimonides. We could equally ask whether it is not fidelity to the enlightened Judaism of Maimonides—and through Maimonides Cohen—that enabled Strauss to propose a non-Heideggerean solution to the crisis of rationalism and the challenge of Nietzsche.

Part II

Dissecting of the Modern Political Consciousness

The theory of liberal democracy, as well as of communism, originated in the first and second waves of modernity; the political implication of the third wave proved to be fascism. Yet this undeniable fact does not permit us to return to the earlier forms of modern thought: the critique of modern rationalism or of the modern belief in reason by Nietzsche cannot be dismissed or forgotten. This is the deepest reason for the crisis of liberal democracy. The theoretical crisis does not necessarily lead to a practical crisis, for the superiority of liberal democracy to communism, Stalinist or post-Stalinist, is obvious enough. And above all, liberal democracy, in contradistinction to communism and fascism, derives powerful support from a way of thinking which cannot be called modern at all: the premodern thought of our western tradition.

—"The Three Waves of Modernity." In *An Introduction to Political Philosophy, Ten Essays by Leo Strauss.* Edited by Hilail Gildin (1975). Detroit: Wayne State University Press, Detroit, 1989, p. 98.

Introduction

The Foundations of Modern Political Thought

To reflect on the political is to reflect not on a natural phenomenon, but on practices that have already been permeated by visions of the world. One must avoid two errors[1] if one is to understand what political philosophy is: the first consists in considering it as a mere branch of philosophy; the second is to reduce it to the expression of opinions, to ideology. Political philosophy is not the application of philosophical categories to the domain of politics. And, distant from the ideal of contemplation, it enters into relations with the non-philosophic: its starting point is the ensemble of opinions that exist in the political community. Political philosophy nonetheless stands in opposition to the natural tendency of commitment or partisanship. The ambiguity of the relationship of the philosopher to the political is coeval with political philosophy, which implies the possibility of putting in question the opinions of the political community. This activity of critique is perceived as a threat against the established order and underlines the original tension between philosophy and the political community. Political philosophy makes the possibility of philosophy its central question. Philosophical inquiry is the attempt to transform opinion into knowledge, but it also is a matter of reflection on the categories that formed our understanding of the world and that may come from philosophy itself. And, beginning with Machiavelli and Hobbes, there is a break with classical political philosophy.

While Plato and Aristotle start from the most familiar themes of political debate in order to ascend little by little to the principles of justice, Hobbes believes to have discovered a perspective in relation to nature that transforms the political into a science. Human nature is knowable, and this from the passions, understood as the basis of political life, from which the moderns elaborate a new political science. In the first instance opposing itself to opinion, this political thought will assimilate with opinion. The relationship of philosophy to the political community, the link between knowledge and power, but also the meaning of philosophy itself change with Machiavelli and Hobbes.

The philosophical reflection of Plato and Aristotle is guided by the consideration of the ends of the political, which means the human good, virtue, and justice. By contrast, the Moderns speak of the material interests that impel human beings toward political order. Far from being a political animal unable to fulfill itself other than in the political community or through laws that educate it and help it develop its *logos*, the human is considered by the Moderns as a needful whose fundamental tendency is self-preservation. The human being is not a rational animal in that reason itself is nothing but the slave of passions. The human being is an asocial animal, a being that sees the good as what is expedient for himself. In order to create a political order and to subject the self-interested individual to rule, one must provide for peaceful coexistence and the fulfillment of the rights of each. The limits posed on the seeking of pleasure are linked to the need to maintain order and not to a higher philosophical ideal where a human being fulfills his nature in combating his passions. The first wave of modernity begins with Machiavelli because he decided to take human beings as they are, not as they ought to be. He chose a "low but solid ground" far removed from the idealism of the classical political philosophers.

This break with classical political philosophy affects all subsequent politics, right up to communist and Nazi totalitarianism, and including as well the problem of representation in our democratic regime. To lay bare the foundations and assumptions of modern political science is to dissect the modern political consciousness, which is blind with respect to its own origins. Modern political philosophy differs from ancient and medieval philosophy in that it is the product of an intellectual revolution. The Moderns take as given or natural categories that are themselves the products of modern philosophy. The separation of politics from religion, pluralism, individual rights, the modern concept of the state, its distinctness from civil society, the question of power, the introduction of equality into all consideration of justice, the priority given to legal justice are the essential givens of *our* political experience, but they were born in a radical break from an earlier manner of thinking. Political philosophy is not only a matter of analysis of the non-philosophic world, but also of a world that is already the product of modern philosophy. There is not only a tension between philosophy and the political community, but political philosophy must also liberate itself from the assumptions of modern philosophy.

Two other points of difference between modern political philosophy and classical political philosophy are worth mentioning. They concern substance more than form. The question of knowing what is the virtue specific to politics is central for the Ancients, to which they respond in speaking of prudence or they reflect on the type of human being, philosopher or prophet, on which the salvation of the political community depends. In modernity, this inquiry is abandoned in the service of a definition of politics as the art of acquiring and preserving power. This notion of power becomes essential from the very founding of modern political philosophy. It goes hand in hand with the amoralism of modern political thought: the human being is self-regarding, and the other is always a potential enemy. War is central to political reflection, whether civil war or war between communities. Morality itself is but an island surrounded by immorality. The political communities that contributed to the progress of civilization, like Rome, were all born in crime. The republic, like international law, should be able to make justice prevail even among a nation of devils, "provided they have common sense," as Kant said, that is, that they have been driven by an enlightened egoism.

Modern thought is characterized by a pessimistic anthropology or a tendency to be suspicious of the virtues of the Ancients, to question their aristocratic ideal, and also to doubt the good. It puts the emphasis in the first instance on institutions, not virtue. One is required to ask whether, instead of representing a greater consideration of evil than the Ancients, these aspects of modern thought do not derive from its prior definition of the human being as an individual, separated from the rest of the universe and other human beings. In defining the social connection by the logic of interests, competition, and contract, does not the first wave of modernity give rise to the second, to the bourgeois? This defining of the human being in terms of his rights does it not lead to the "last man," that is, the individual who becomes further and further removed from the model of humanity represented by the eighteenth-century idea of genius—the synthesis of the universal and the individual—and who is susceptible to every form of barbarism?

When the human being is not dependent on a superior being that has binding force over his conscience, sociability takes its justification solely from the claims of each on the others. This idea of subjective will as the basis for social order will lead, beginning with Hobbes, to contract theory, which goes hand in hand with the theme of the conquest of nature, including human nature. It is a matter of seeing, from the origins of modern thought, that which orients Western civilization toward a civilization marked by the rule of technique. The Enlightenment project led to the uncontrolled development of technology, which is "an amazing process" by which "modern man has ever more expanded and thus become ever more shallow."[2]

The modern definition of reason as calculation and instrument of the passions is again in question in this challenge to the problematic legacy of the Enlightenment. The dissection of the modern political consciousness is an essential chapter of this prolegomena to the political philosophy to which Strauss points. As with the part devoted to the religious question, there are differences that exist between Machiavelli and Hobbes that are more important than their common ground. Similarly, we do not seek to undertake a complete analysis of the philosophers implicated in the three waves of modernity, but to see what Strauss brings to a reflection on the crisis of the West, which goes back to the origin of the sickness in the modern Enlightenment.

Chapter 1

The First Wave of Modernity

Machiavelli, the Originator of the Modern Enlightenment

The End of the Renaissance Humanist Ideal

In the introduction in 1964 to the English translation of his early book on Hobbes's political philosophy,[1] Strauss wrote that it is not Hobbes but Machiavelli who inaugurated the first wave of modernity and broke in a decisive manner with classical political philosophy. This claim is all the more worthy of interest because Machiavelli developed his thought in a country and at a time when the modern state did not yet exist. Machiavelli wrote *The Prince* in 1513 on the Sant'Andrea estate in Percussina, where he was banished after having been arrested, then tortured when the Medici, returned to Florence, put an end to fourteen years of republicanism. This work, which did not come out until 1532, like the *Discourses on the First Ten Books of Titus Livy*, begun in 1514 and published in 1531, and the *Florentine Histories*, is not understandable unless one puts the observations of Machiavelli on how to acquire and conserve power in the context of the wars that had been tearing apart Italy since 1385. One must also take into account the influence and eventual fall of the Medici in November 1494, at the moment when the army of Charles the VIII invaded Florence, Milan, Rome, and Naples. The new Republic in which Machiavelli—at that time second secretary of the chancellery, charged with problems concerning the oversight of the army and sought-out political adviser—participated is based on a conception of history and politics where the violence of the times was the starting point for any credible statement.

Machiavelli writes at the moment when Erasmus is working on his *Christian Prince* (1516), dedicated to Charles V, exhorting the good ruler to defend the peace, which resonates with the ideals of the Renaissance, inspired by the philosophy of the Ancients and an idea of virtue specific to politics. The puzzle is not why Machiavelli based the political art on his analysis of different situations of conquest of power, as he did in *The Prince*. From 1490 to 1510, Italy had gone from being the beacon of Renaissance to a country that was internally divided and occupied by foreigners. The city-states, the territories where there was a common jurisdiction and where political behavior was defined in terms of their independence in relation to outsiders, were rife with corruption. One must thus expect that Machiavelli will bring his political experience into his thought. Nevertheless, most surprising in Machiavellian realism, which goes hand in hand with the abandonment of the question of the best political regime, is not the reasoned whole that supports it but its later success: "Why was political modernity not simply a prolonged and expanded Renaissance?"[2]

In showing how the use of force and fraud could obtain an effective political result, Machiavelli subverted the philosophical genre known as "the mirror of princes." These short works, in which the writers of the Middle Ages and of the Renaissance guided the behavior of monarchs and lords, are preoccupied with articulating the virtue specific to the sovereign. Morality was connected to greatness of political action in these idealized portraits of the sovereign. The idea is that in order to govern others, the sovereign must first know how to govern himself. Machiavelli breaks with that alliance between morality and politics and asserts that what is a virtue in morality can be a vice in politics. A prince cannot practice liberality without harming at the same time his subjects, from whom he must at one moment steal, and himself, in that he will be held in contempt and hated. By contrast, sometimes the use of cruelty can be good.

Machiavelli is radically opposed to the idea of an absolute good or evil. Not only is politics, which resembles war, a matter of the correctness of decisions that avoid mistakes, and not their morality, but, furthermore, there does not exist a fixed meaning of good and evil. Good and evil are not opposites; they resemble each other and are attractive to one another. The political problem is not the opposition of good and evil, but a matter of distinguishing between good and bad combinations of good and evil. The valiant prince understands how to recognize in what circumstances one can, in order to have a good reputation, say good of the good and, when it is useful, condemn the ferocity of those whom he had previously ordered a massacre. Such is the example of Cesare Borgia, who knew how to make himself feared without making himself hated.[3]

The notion of *virtù* designates the quality of new princes who have succeeded in acquiring power and in preserving it. They have managed to operate with the course of political events, which are sometimes unpredictable. *Virtù* is inseparable from the master of men and the mastery of necessity. The first entails an art of manipulation that goes along with the introduction of the question of power in political life and that rests on a particular anthropology. The second is the explication of the connection that brings together *virtù* and fortune. These two questions make Machiavelli into the originator of the Enlightenment. Fortune is the raw material for *virtù*, because politics is inherently situational. It is a matter of directing fortune without letting oneself be disarmed by it. Victory belongs to those who know how to choose what is preferable in the circumstances instead of acting in light of fixed ideas about good and evil. And like a woman with a strong personality, fortune does not disdain the audacity of those who remain resolute in the face of adversity.[4] *Virtù* is not that which is moral, but, being the distinctive domain of the *vir*, it supposes a talent and a virtuosity that allow the valiant prince to use circumstances to his advantage. *Virtù* is the capacity to do what fortune commands in adapting oneself to it. Far from being the enemy of man, it is the raw material of history. It is in this way that one must understand what Machiavelli says about Christianity in Rome: not only the ideals of the Church led to the contrary of what it was seeking to defend, to crime and war, but, moreover, Christianity, with its contemplative ideal, eradicated political *virtù* and made men effeminate. It made them "the prey to criminal men, who can manage it securely, seeing that the collectivity of men, so as to go to paradise, think more of enduring their beatings than of avenging them."[5] The Catholic Church has ruined Italy. It is responsible for the failure to imitate the Ancients.[6]

The amoralism of Machiavelli and the fact that he regards the beginnings of political communities with his eyes turned toward Rome go hand in hand with the idea that one cannot go beyond the passions in the game of politics. While Plato and Aristotle advocated a political order where reason is in charge, Machiavelli shows the ineffective and insidious character of what was considered until then as good politics. This radical break with the humanism of the Renaissance is explained by the conviction that war and violence are inevitable. Fortune is the material of politics, but so also is the corruption of political communities and men, of rulers and ruled. Even if Machiavelli recognizes in the people a certain innocence, he does not believe in the possibility of making men good.

Not only is the individual driven by the desire to acquire early glory and recognition, considered as the greatest of goods, but, in addition, moral virtue and republican virtue do not coincide, that which is good as such is not always compatible with the common good.

This teaching[7] provides the new orientation of modern political thought. The people always prefer the seductive to the virtuous; politics comes down to the art with which the prince is able to manipulate opinion and play with appearances in order to hide his intentions and methods. Machiavelli opens the way to all modern reflection on celebrity politics and on the kind of identification that is at the core of the people's attachment to its leader. Machiavelli substitutes the question of what is the virtue of the good political leader with a reflection on what today would be called populism. This "new morality," which leads one to ask questions about the relationship between power and illusion, inaugurates modern political thought. It is characterized by suspicion of the Good and the idea that because low passions govern men's behavior, only other passions can serve to control them.

This manner of making power depend on the passions rather than reason, and the anthropology that underpins it, would never again be put in question. Solutions will be thought up for resolving the tensions between the contradictory demands of what would become liberal democracy, caught between the equality of citizens and the question of representation, which invokes the idea of the superiority of the representatives to the represented. But neither elections nor democratic political parties suppose that the political relation will be rational and that the end of politics is the virtue of the citizens. Sovereignty itself is the expression of the will, not reason. The executive power takes its legitimacy from the election, a theater of the passions and emotive allegiances.

Far from the humanist ideal of man who fulfills his nature and perfects it in the practice of philosophy, Machiavelli thinks that the end of man is earthly glory in a peaceful political community, where the arts and sciences allowing man to master necessity are able to develop. Philosophically, he destroys humanism. This literary and artistic movement born in Italy during the Renaissance (1330–1520) under the influence of Petrarch (1304–1374) was oriented toward a return to Greece and Rome in order to understand the meaning of the good life. Without projecting onto Machiavelli the later idea of *raison d'Etat*, Strauss believes that the rupture with the past that Machiavelli achieved is of far greater interest than examining what his thought has in common with that of the Renaissance. The author of *The Prince* is the first of the Moderns.

Power, the Mastery of Men, and the Mastery of Nature

"Men must either be cajoled or eliminated," writes Machiavelli in Chapter 3 of *The Prince*. But, far from being reduced to the use of force alone, the art of the prince supposes the capacity to see where the traps are in order to be able to escape from them: "It is necessary for the prince to know how to be both beast and man . . . he must be a fox in order to recognize the snares and a lion in order to frighten the wolves."[8] Cunning is what allows one to endure. It masters and directs force and serves to manipulate men by playing on appearances. Not being naturally oriented toward fixed goods or ends, individuals are malleable. They are driven by fear, which makes its entry into modern politics and will be the principal driver of Hobbes's political theory. Machiavelli replaces the idea of political philosophy that defines the best regime in light of the end and excellence of man with a theory that the good society is possible by the action of men sufficiently capable "to transform the most corrupt people, the most corrupt matter, into an incorrupt one by the judicious application of force"[9] and cunning. Politics becomes the art of avoiding civil war.

These elements are present today in the manner in which one views the state and the role of law: far from being a community based on the good life, as in Aristotle, the state should protect the individual and guarantee the *conditions* of his happiness, looking to his welfare and security. Nothing is said about how to define happiness. Virtue and happiness of the citizens are no longer matters for political inquiry. The question of what kind of man one wants to form in adopting a particular law no longer matters in politics. The state is an instrument in the service of the freedom and happiness of individuals who need it simply to defend themselves and for work, through collective egoism, for the common good. Individuals are free to live as they please and to determine their goals as they wish, on condition that the exercise of this liberty doesn't interfere with that of others or disturb public order. One goes from classical political philosophy to political realism where political philosophy served to enlighten the prince on the means for conserving his power and how to deal with the people.

This tendency is radicalized by Hobbes, who consolidates the rupture of Ancients and Moderns in founding the state on the rights of the individual. The modern political consciousness is characterized on the one hand by the liberalism of Hobbes and on the other by the republican concern about participation that is present in Machiavelli and Rousseau. Today, the experience of democracy is an oscillation between these two tendencies, but the Machiavellian understanding of the meaning of the political is never put in question. Rather, it is considered, along with the view of man and of reason that underpins it, as self-evident.

Finally, the Enlightenment begins with Machiavelli because an account of politics focused on power and control supports the project of mastery of nature. This philosophy depends on a concept of human freedom that goes hand in hand with the rejection of classical natural right. Man's freedom is not limited by any good that is superior to him. The transformation of the matter of politics presupposes a conception of man as "an Archimedian point outside of nature."[10] While for Aristotle man is not the peak of the universe, Machiavelli discovers before Descartes this radical free power of man, which suggests that everything can be conquered.

Strauss, at the end of his book on Machiavelli, raises the question of the uncontrolled development of technology and the "charm of competence that bewitches" peoples, elites, and all of humanity. A radical emancipation from the old order allows for the triumph of this spirit of conquest. It requires a rejection of the difference between philosophers and non-philosophers. The fact that technology develops without reflection on its legitimate use is connected to the disappearance of classical political philosophy, which implies a distinction between the philosopher and other human beings and its replacement by ideology.

It is understandable that technology spreads like a cancer when progress is seen exclusively as material progress and science is no longer oriented toward the question of knowing if innovation is useful or harmful to man, given his ends. The disappearance of classical political philosophy with its focus on the question of the good life goes hand in hand with the disappearance of all limits on science and technology. But, in addition, Strauss asserts that the disappearance of political philosophy leads to the disappearance of any limit imposed on sciences and technologies. The end of the opposition between philosophers and non-philosophers contributes at the same time to the defeat of classical philosophy and to the irrationalism of the modern project, to barbarism.

Philosophy, Propaganda, and Barbarism

The role of the philosopher and the status of the philosopher, and his relationship to power and society, are changed with Machiavelli. Classical political philosophy, of which the typical representative is Xenophon for Machiavelli, understands the political and moral phenomena in light of the perfection of man, that is, in light of philosophy itself and the contemplative life. Philosophy transcends the political community, but the worth of the political community depends on its openness to philosophy.[11] There is an unbridgeable gap between philosophers and other men. Similarly, the philosophers and the *demos* live in a permanent tension because they pursue different ends. Only rhetoric can build a bridge between philosophy and the democratic political community. The philosopher, far from ceding to all men's desires and giving form to their partisan positions, begins with what they say and transforms these opinions into knowledge. The political community as the good life lived in common constitutes itself by the very dynamism of the debate concerning what is just and unjust. Its worth depends on the manner in which it allows its citizens to educate themselves, to develop their *logos*. Reason and the ability to distinguish good from bad is the principle of political community according to the Ancients; the gap between philosophy and the political community subsists, but philosophers should support among other men the desire to transcend the perspective of received opinion and to free themselves from illusion, which is at the same time a deprivation of knowledge and of freedom. Philosophers have always had a way of relating to the world that is different from that of other men. They are more strangers in the world than those who present themselves as revolutionaries or ideologists. They are, as Xenophon said, in a place somewhere around which the political community cannot draw boundaries.

By contrast, with Machiavelli, the philosopher cedes to men's desires and abandons the ideal of the contemplative life, which assumes that action cannot solve all problems. The given world is replaced by the world of which man is the theoretical and practical architect. Pure knowing loses any priority over the situation of man in the world. Machiavelli prepares the rule of those who use newspapers and talk shows and form public opinion. The cave is not something the philosopher leaves and returns to in a permanently paradoxical and conflictual relation that the art of writing rhetoric is intended to moderate, but it has become the essence: "Propaganda is to guarantee the coincidence of philosophy and political power."[12] Philosophy becomes ideology. Its "purpose is to relieve man's estate or to increase man's power or to guide man toward the rational society, the bond and the end of which is enlightened self-interest or the comfortable self-preservation of each of its members."[13]

The consequences of this definition of philosophy are that, void of any consideration of the ends of man and based on a law foundation where the human is understood in purely human terms, it will not be able to oppose itself to the unlimited expansion of science and technology. Today's technologies are able to increase our power, but also to change man himself. Philosophy becomes it own worst enemy, as it encouraged that which leads to its disappearance. Finally, the logic of social relations on which modern thought rests leads to the elevation of the status of the desire for recognition to that of a universal value. While classical philosophy addressed itself, through the esoteric art of writing, to a small number of wise men capable of following and seeing all the consequences of its arguments, while its eyes are fixed on the truth, situated beyond society, the philosopher-ideologist lives, like other men in the cave, in the world of appearance and spectacle; society is the object and subject of the desire of recognition. Recognition comes to be in the hands of the mass media, which becomes an end in itself, leading to the end of freedom of thought, in the name of freedom of expression. Such are the contradictions of the modern Enlightenment, which always becomes radical Enlightenment.

The ultimate reason for the break of Machiavelli with the past was political atheism: "Perfection envisaged by both the Bible and classical philosophy is impossible. But for the same reason for which perfection, and in particular the initial as well as the ultimate Paradise is impossible, there cannot be a Hell. Man cannot rise above earthly and earthy humanity and therefore he ought not even to aspire beyond humanity. Such as aspiration merely leads to the most terrible and wholly unnecessary inhumanity of man to man."[14] Atheistic fervor was at the root of modern natural right in the sense of a right that is completely immanent. It supposes a harmony between man and the world and leads to relativism.

Strauss engages with Machiavelli not only on the ground of natural right and the struggle against religious intolerance, but through a reflection on divine Law. It is because man no longer depends on a superior being who binds his conscience with the force of law that society is defined in terms of the conflict of interests and competition, by the back and forth between the claim to be superior to others and the return, through fear, to a more modest aspiration where each looks to his vulnerability and the equal capacity of men to destroy one another. Vanity and fear of death, supplanting the aristocratic ideal of honor, where self-preservation is not as important as what makes life worth living, will become with Hobbes the principles of politics.

With Hobbes, one grasps the logic that leads the Moderns to the dual temptations of individualism and totalitarianism, economic liberalism and communism being the social manifestations of the priority accorded to vanity (a politics grounded on economic prosperity and the enjoyment of material well-being by individuals) or fear (a politics based on security and respect for order, the order of society above all). Nazism constitutes a reaction to these two phenomena: the struggle against communism and the *total* rejection of a society to which heroism and warrior morality are completely foreign. Finally, the world that would come out of the Second World War will be characterized by an oscillation between the primacy of prosperity and the primacy of security. But in no event would the foundations of modern thought be put in question.

The conception that Machiavelli has of man and his political theory are embodied in a political teaching centered on the individual, who has become the basis for the state and its limits, but also the measure of the true, the good, and the beautiful. Man, in the absence of a consideration of the hierarchy of ends, will be the measure of all things. Free to obey his own gods and demons, he will find in the glorification of his power, in the exercise of a will oriented to itself, without an object but incredibly potent, the possibility of self-affirmation. Barbarism will be the exultation of the Will to Power, the free fall into a liberty without constraint and a systematic denial of the other, which means also of law and symbolic order. Communist and Nazi forms of totalitarianism are succeeded by terrorism and its obsession with uniformity, with the *Oumma* or community of likes, but also by an increase in violence and new pathologies, which in a democratic society bear witness to the difficulty of conceiving the social and the eclipse of the law.

Hobbes or the Founding of the Modern State

Political Science

It is Hobbes who first articulated the categories that determine our political experience. The break he creates in the natural right tradition and his theory of the state make him the father of liberalism. Thus the crisis of liberalism that Strauss confronts in the 1930s leads him to examine the thought of Hobbes, who is the equivalent in politics of what Spinoza represents in the domain of religion. Modernity has become problematic.[15] One must thus return to Hobbes, who is the founder of modern individualism. All the categories of modern political thought rest on individualism, that is to say, on a certain definition of natural right. Hobbes defends the priority of right to positive law. The *jus* that he refused to identify with the *justum*, or to conceive in relation to cosmology or theology, is considered as a natural power of man, as the bundle of capacities necessary for his preservation. This anthropological definition of right is foundational to the modern state and at the core of the theory of sovereignty of all later thinkers, including those who are critics of absolutism. But the primary innovation of Hobbes, analogous for politics to the Galilean revolution in physics and the Cartesian revolution in pure philosophy, is methodological: Hobbes wants to turn political philosophy into political science.

While for Aristotle political existence is a form of knowledge between science and ordinary experience and is connected to prudence or practical wisdom as the required virtue in the political domain, Hobbes asserts that there is no middle ground between rigorous scientific proof on the one hand and unordered experience on the other. Not only can "the names of Virtues and Vices . . . never be true grounds of any raciocination,"[16] but, in addition, it is necessary to begin from principles if one wants to transcend skepticism and lack of precision in political thought. The originality of Strauss's interpretation is to have emphasized the dependence of Hobbes on Euclid while at the same time showing that the foundation of Hobbes's politics is his "moral attitude."[17]

The first steps in the science of political power of Hobbes are not based on the supposition that the order of things can be described as we perceived them but rather on a methodological choice. To know a thing, one must know what it is composed of. We understand in reality only what we make. Hobbes's debt to the theory of the *verum factum*, or that we know what we make,[18] leads to an emphasis on the genesis of the object of production and the adoption of the resolutive-compositive method. And we cannot know human nature because we did not make it. Far from constructing the city from a metaphysical a priori, like Plato, or from the teachings of theology, it is a matter instead of considering the city as it exists and seeing by what mechanisms it was able to be brought into being. What is it that renders men capable of forming political communities, and how should those who wish to come together in a political community conduct themselves? In exposing the foundations of politics, Hobbes sought to articulate the principles of civil power. This project goes hand in hand with the idea, dear to the modern Enlightenment, that there is little that is innate and that man is the product of his own action. In rendering comprehensible the structure of civil institutions, Hobbes sought to show that, being the master of his own fate, man can construct his humanity with a view to a better future, one of security and happiness. The political science of Hobbes is a plea on behalf of civilization. The resolutive-compositive method, where the political "data" like the conception of justice and state are analyzed and broken down into their components (individual wills), goes hand with hand with the idea that the fundamental problem is the good organization of the state, not the question of the just life.[19] Man, the creator of civil society, can solve the problems inherent in man, the material of civil society.

The methodological contribution of Hobbes is thus to make the notion of power central to the doctrine of politics, the *jus* or the *potentia* designate what man is capable of doing, and the *dominum* or the *postestas* what he has the permission to do. Political science moves from the question of "why?" to the question of "how?" and it is in the service of a civilizational project the end of which is the establishment of right. But can one say that "the absolute priority of the individual to the state, the conception of the individual as asocial, or of the relation between the state of nature and the political community as an absolute antithesis, and finally of the state itself as Leviathan" are "determined by and implied in the method"?[20]

Strauss's argument is that the origin of Hobbes's political philosophy is not, contrary to Cassirer,[21] his method but his anthropology. In Hobbes's mechanistic psychology, one finds not so much its foundation as its justification. "This 'pessimistic' view of human nature was evident in Hobbes before he had or could have the least conception of a mechanistic psychology."[22] And this "moral attitude" is characterized by two typical features of the modern Enlightenment that will be decisive for the future: the powerlessness of reason and the interaction of vanity and fear. Even if there were superior men, the others would not obey them. Authority belongs to the one who has sovereign power.

Vanity and Fear

Proceeding in a manner analogous to geometry with its axioms, Hobbes provides a definition of political life in terms of its origins and its constituent elements. Focusing on efficient causes, he claims that the state of nature is the war of all against all. This theoretical fiction allows one to understand what would happen if the civil state did not exist at all and to grasp how man can survive. And the natural condition of man being one of equality, that is, the notion than each individual is capable of physical violence against others, men have a posture of fear toward each other and enter into competition for scarce goods. Conflict has three principal causes: rivalry, or the fact that, despite natural equality, each imagines himself superior to the others; distrust, which means that in an egalitarian world, the question of security becomes central; and vanity or vainglory, which is the universal aspiration to recognition. Before Hegel, Hobbes had seen that man desires the desire of another.[23] Human appetite is, contrary to animal appetite, infinite in itself: it is not a simple reaction to external impressions and does not limit itself to finite objects but is uniquely insatiable. This aspiration to power is not only linked to the fact that, contemplating the future and not only the present, man seeks "power after power" (. . .) "because he cannot assure the power and the means to live well, which he has at the present, without the acquisition of more." There is furthermore "an irrational striving after power," as if this were an end in itself; "men from their very birth, and naturally, scramble for everything they covet, and would have all the world, if they could, to fear and obey them," Hobbes said.[24]

This conception of man depends less on a mechanistic physiology than on knowledge of human nature, deepened and extended by self-knowledge. The anthropology of Hobbes and the way in which he distinguishes human and animal appetite through the notion of vanity, that is, the pleasure that man experiences from his own power, is not derived from naturalism. As Montesquieu noted, vanity depends on society. The *gloriatio*, which one finds in the definition of the state, compared to Leviathan, king of the proud, is the specific contribution of Hobbes to political anthropology.

Machiavelli had taught that politics is the suppression, never definitive, of fear by fear. In making the pairing of vanity and fear the basis for sociability, Hobbes articulates the foundation of modern right. His political philosophy is based on a new foundation for morality,[25] which gives a specifically human sense to the idea of subjective rights. The opposition that serves as his point of departure is between vanity, source of the natural appetite of man, and the fear of violent death, a passion that leads man to reason. It is because men want others to fear them and pay them regard that they enter into conflict. Hobbes does not say exactly that man is bad, and he rejects the idea of sin. He speaks of a *natural* hostility, of a state where men are predators toward each other, where man is dangerous because his passions put him in conflict with others: everyone is fighting everyone for the same thing in a world where each individual thinks only for himself but where he lives within the view of others. Vanity is the foundation of all the human appetites and passions, but fear will temper this unchecked competition and substitute for reason.

In effect, if in Hobbes vanity comes before fear, because man has the tendency, like a *puer robustus*, to dream of conquest and domination over others, fear provides a reality check and inclines him to be more modest.[26] The conversion of Hobbes to Euclid was a distancing from Aristotle and not a return to Plato: political philosophy must begin with *precision* concerning the motivations for human action. But this takes nothing away from the profound disagreement of Hobbes with Plato. Plato asserts the unity of the key virtues (moderation, courage, wisdom, and justice) and thinks that the salvation of the city lies in the coincidence of philosophy and ruling. For Hobbes, reason does not allow man to master his passions, and it is not directed toward a transcendent ideal, the Good. Force and fraud are the key virtues in the state of nature where over time war and fear alone can transform these tendencies into a reasonable competition that characterizes political life.

Hobbes identifies reason with calculation: the fear of violent death makes men lucid, creating a consciousness of their fundamental vulnerability. It is on this that Hobbes bases his theory of the state and the social contract. Honor is replaced by fear of death, which makes men prudent. The philosophy of Hobbes reflects the struggle against aristocratic virtue in the name of the conditions of bourgeois life, which are the guarantee against violent death, security, and the refusal to consider courage a virtue. Man, naturally proletarian, has nothing to lose here and consecrates himself to the exploitation of nature through work. A specifically modern attitude is expressed in this opposition between vanity and fear: "It is to the opposition so understood that one must go back . . . if one wishes to understand the ideal of liberalism, as well as socialism, in its foundations. For each battle against the political in the name of the economic presupposes a preceding depreciation of the political. But this depreciation is carried out in such a way that the political, as the domain of vanity, prestige, the desire for importance, is opposed either in a veiled or in an open manner, to the economic as the world of rational, "matter-of fact," modest work."[27]

The foundation of the political philosophy of Hobbes is a "new morality," which leads to a new conception of sovereignty as the central notion. Thus, on the basis of natural equality, the question becomes under which conditions and within which limits some men can claim to rule over others who are their equals. By contrast, the Greeks "believed in the need for education to tune and harmonize social opinions to the spirit and tone of a fixed and fundamental law."[28] The Moderns developed the notion of representation in order to conceptualize the relationship between sovereignty and authority. The major categories of modern thought flow from a break with ancient rationalism. In Hobbes this leads to social contract theory, the foundation for modern liberalism. But it is a "pessimistic" concept of human nature that leads Hobbes himself to defend absolutism.

Individualism, Liberalism, and Absolutism

The major contribution of Hobbes is the distinction between right and positive law and the theory of sovereignty, of which the foundation is not the good, but the natural rights of the individual. Hobbes asserts individualism in politics and provides the foundations of liberalism, of which one of the definitional traits is that the rights of man are more important than his duties. The law is determinative and binding, that is, obligatory, while right "consisteth in the liberty to do, or to forbeare."[29] The individual, prior to civil society, is the foundation of the state, the mission of which is to protect his life and secure his rights. By contrast, in classical political philosophy, duty has primacy, because man is unable to pursue the perfection of his nature except through civil society, which preexists him. Friendship as the basis for social relations between beings who share common ideas is replaced by a sense of solitude. Man leaves his solitude by necessity. The Moderns, from Hobbes to Rousseau and Kant, believe that individuals need one another in order to live, but social life is no longer a pleasure in and of itself. It is considered as alienating, and one prefers solitary dreaming (Rousseau) or approaches it with a fundamental ambivalence (Kant).[30]

The conception of man that underpins the political thought of Hobbes corresponds to the radical affirmation of subjectivity. Human nature, far from being an abstract ideal, is the reality of every individual (*every man*). Right is the power belonging to each individual taken in his particularity. Natural right, unconditional and secularized, is not a juridical category but a "*necessity of nature*." It is a drive to self-preservation characteristic of the mechanism of the living human being that, because of the complexities of the human machine, cannot but unleash a war of all against all. In and of itself, natural right is alien to all rule. But the contradictions and misery that ensue will make necessary the transformation of right: "Reason suggesteth convenient Articles of Peace, upon which men may be drawn to agreement. These Articles are . . . are called the Lawes of Nature."[31]

Hobbes asserts the natural (ontological) priority of right to positive law and political priority of positive law to right. The natural (ontological) priority of right to positive law, and defining the individual in terms of his liberty and not in terms of submission to an order that transcends him, are the foundations of modern thought. We will rediscover in Rousseau this definition of the nature or essence of man in terms of liberty, as well as the idea that the political community is an absolute sovereign, founded and deduced from the state of nature, which is capable of other interpretations but is linked to the idea of contract. Hobbes establishes a new philosophy of right that responds to this new definition of man as autonomous individual. There is a political agenda implied by this definition of right that is rooted in individual will. Conceptualized as a capacity (power) or freedom (liberty), this right is given over to self-preservation and accords with reason in adapting to this end the totality of means.

Each individual is the judge of the means appropriate to his own survival, but the state of nature leads to war, so it is a matter of determining what form of political order is best for establishing the most certain conditions that allow each to exercise his rights. And security and peace are the minimal conditions of individual liberty. Hobbes is surely the father of liberalism and the distinction between the public and private spheres that it implies. Happiness and liberty belong to the subjective sphere, and the state is but an external framework charged with securing this happiness and, in the first instance, with protecting the individual. The justification of the state is the protection of what we call today human rights. Even if Hobbes himself is inclined toward an absolutist solution of the political problem, his definition of natural right makes him the father of human rights.

The law of nature, which man discovers through awakening to the consciousness of his vulnerability, does not carry the meaning of an imperative. Because this law, which inclines man to work toward peace, opposes itself to natural right and the natural claim over everyone and everything. Man chooses to leave the state of nature and transfer his right to a third. Far from being an abandonment or a gift, this cession of natural right is a transfer. The individual does not give any power to another, but rather commits not to harm others. This is a reciprocal contract: this mutual transfer of the right of each is made to the Leviathan, who is then invested with the power constituted by the aggregate of the rights that everyone has confided in it. It is a matter of the delegation of rights to a third, an artificial person, provided with, like in Bodin, the supreme power allowing him to act in the place of individuals. The sovereign power thus constituted is the essence of the Republic. In Hobbes, this essence is a mortal god, *tremendum et fascinans*, who makes a unity from the plurality of individuals and cannot but be *external* to the individual. Thus Hobbes is an absolutist because he is an individualist.

Hobbes rejects any transfer of will, any representation of it by another, because the will belongs to the individual. But the subject will recognize as his own all the actions of the sovereign: the conferral of authority that constitutes the compact of representation is such that if a man should punish the representative, he punishes another for acts that he himself committed. Hobbes, in making the citizens and the sovereign inseparable, thinks that the external situation of the sovereign, of the Leviathan, is legitimated by a logic of representation that assimilates those represented to the representative. Such is the principal mode that articulates the relation between the people and the sovereign (and makes it similar to the relation between the author and the actor). The personality of the representative connects a source of authorization (individuals, who are the principals and who enact the compact of representation) to an object (the representative or the agent) who formulates the laws as sovereign edicts to his people. The sovereign is the actor: he is conceived as exercising the authority that resides in the ruled, who are the authors.

Hobbes poses a problem that is central to democracy, the existence of absolute sovereignty. But he opposes the idea that sovereignty resides in the nation (which would be dear to the revolutionaries of 1789). He allows only for sovereign *representation*. He believes the laws should be placed beyond any possible disputation and that if men do not cede *authority*, which is a right to act, they will fall back into civil war. This is Hobbes's anthropological pessimism, combined with his distrust in the power of reason to guide human conduct, which explains his rejection of the democratic solution, prone to encourage vanity and conflict. Hobbes, in comparing monarchy, aristocracy, and democracy, is concerned with the best form of state, not from the perspective of fulfilling man's essence but in taking into account the experience of human life: "As far as democracy is concerned . . . the emulation and contention of the demagogues for reputation and glory of wit play a part which is disastrous to the common weal. In an aristocracy, it is still worse. Each aristocrat 'desireth to be the chief' . . . because that is the case, monarchy is the best form of state."[32]

One can conjecture that the political doctrine of Hobbes, where the emphasis is placed on the harm, not the good that men are able to do, is related to the experience of the English civil war. This would culminate in the execution of Charles I in 1649 and in the religious war by Oliver Cromwell and the dictatorship of Richard Cromwell. In fact, history is, for Hobbes, the confirmation of his political principles and his "moral attitude." It is because he thinks that only the omnipotence of the sovereign, rationally constructed, can take man out of his malevolent nature that Hobbes would show his sympathy for the Stuarts, defending the monarchy in his *Elements of Law* and choosing voluntary exile in 1651.

From War to Commerce

Hobbes is the originator of that political form that is known as the state and that appeared in the sixteenth and seventeenth centuries. The state is different from the ancient city and also from empire. This civil authority does not purport to exercise a universal sovereignty but is supreme in its own domain. Sovereignty contrasts with military power, with *imperium* and *potestas*, which designate all power to command in the ordinary sense of the term. It is an elevation of the state and goes along with the idea of a unified legal order of uncontestable authority within a given territory. The foundation of the modern state with Hobbes or political liberalism anticipates a society where individuals are able to peacefully go about their own business. The risk of civil war contained, rivalry and competition reemerge in the sphere of commerce. Political liberalism leads to economic liberalism, and this is evident in Locke and Montesquieu, who reject the absolutist solution, which amounts to men being "so foolish that they take care to avoid what Mischiefs may be done them by *Pole-Cats*, or *Foxes*, but are content, nay think it Safety, to be devoured by *Lions*."[33]

The distinction between civil society, the domain of equal rights, and the state, which assures peace and order, originates with Hobbes. But while Hobbes infuses the state with moral personality,[34] considering it as an artificial person, this reconciliation between the individual and the state, which still maintains the primacy of the political, will gradually disappear. Civil society will become the essential element of political life, the sphere of personal development and morality, and economy replaces politics in a world where the risk of war seems avoided. This result is less due to history than to a certain conception of human nature.

Montesquieu, for whom vanity is not a primary human motive, does not place war at the center of his political reflections. Similarly, Locke's definition of natural right and self-preservation, in terms of hunger and not fear of violent death, makes the sphere of work and economics central to philosophical reflection on civil government. In a world where one lives in the shadow of war and in constant fear, peace and order are the priorities. In a world where men are in competition because of their need for food and where they live interdependently, peace is a condition of prosperity and is achieved through commerce and the division of labor.

Carl Schmitt would emphasize that this forgetfulness of war represents at the same time a lack of clarity about the nature of the political and a proof of its disappearance. Liberal democracy diminishes the specificity of the political in absorbing it into the economic realm and in turning it into a combination of ethics and economics. Even if Schmitt thinks that Hobbes misunderstood the nature of the political, that is, the distinction between friend and enemy that is the basis of war between political communities—and not only between individual men—and makes it the essential question, he asserts that Hobbes is the thinker who came closest to grasping the truth about the political. But Schmitt goes further than Hobbes. He retains Hobbes's pessimist anthropology while giving it a meaning that cannot be reconciled with Hobbes's kind of political atheism. Finally, Schmitt puts in question the foundation of liberalism, the distinction between the private and public sphere that leads to the autonomy of the political, which becomes a mere field of the culture associated with civil society.

The Crisis of Liberalism: The Dialogue between Strauss and Schmitt

From the Rechtsstaat *to the Total State in the Era of Technology*

In his speech titled "The Age of Neutralizations and Depoliticizations," given in Barcelona in 1929 and published in the *Europäische Revue* in December of the same year, and in *The Concept of the Political* (1932),[35] Schmitt presents modern history as a process of ongoing neutralization that leads to the total state, thus to the reverse of what liberalism seeks, in the era of technology. The liberal state is, in principle, neutral and its power should be limited, according to Montesquieu's teaching.[36] It is defined by the separation of powers, the delimitation of the private sphere from the public, the distinction between society and the state, and the affirmation of the fundamental rights of the individual, *terminus a quo et terminus ad quem* of the democratic polity. Yet, according to Schmitt, this liberal state, which, according to Constant, should leave the citizens the largest amount of time possible for their private affairs, leads to a situation where everything is political.[37]

Everything is political because nothing really is. It is this crisis of liberalism that will make manifest, in the disappearance of any difference between the bourgeois and the citizen, a denaturing of the liberal state.

The total state is an administrative state (*Verwaltungsstaat*): required to address more and more of society's problems, the state loses its sovereignty and can no longer draw a line between the matters within its competence and those that are not. This totalization of the political is in reality a socialization of the state and a state-ization of society. And this socialization of the state, for which there is no longer any neutral area beyond its control and which is quantitatively total, leads to the era of technology that replaces the economy as the dominant sphere.

From 1932 on, about a year before he became a Nazi and discovered in a qualitatively total state, like Mussolini-style fascism or the Nazi state, the alternative to the quantitatively total state, Schmitt thought that the process of ongoing neutralization was coming to its end and was legal to an era where, contrary to appearances, nothing is neutral. The era of technology is that moment when the political is attached to no particular domain, such as the economy. According to Schmitt, history is history of a migration of multiple spheres of activity to a dominant sector. Political theology is not only the fact that "all significant concepts of the modern theory of the state are secularized theological concepts,"[38] but secularization is only one instance of the process of neutralization where the center of activity is displaced between the sixteenth and nineteenth centuries, from theology to metaphysics to humanitarian morality and economics. The representations that a given era provides of its political being and of the world are organized around the dominant sector: the principle that organizes the world as it appears has a political tenor. This analogy between the metaphysical image that an epoch has of the world and its representation of what the state should be illustrates how for Schmitt political theology is a philosophy of history. And the end of the process of neutralization coincides with the emergence of technology as the dominant sector. This end of neutralizations and of the assignment of a privileged place to the political is the moment when politics is totalized because "technology is no longer neutral ground . . . ; every strong politics will make use of it. . . . Yet technology can do nothing more than intensify peace or war; it is equally available to both."[39]

Schmitt's analysis of the era of technology connects all the threads of his political reflection on right.[40] The interest of this contemporary engagement with the works of Jünger is that it opens up the question of the political. Schmitt understands that technology can serve either freedom or oppression—it all depends on the way that men use it. When he writes that technology requires that man decide "which type of politics is strong enough to master the new technology and which type of friend-enemy groupings can develop on this new ground,"[41] one may say that his solution, decisionism and warrior morality, is not adequate to his awareness of the genuine problem.

Schmitt has the merit to see the problem of technology as a political problem and to connect this "domination of spiritlessness over spirit"[42] to a certain condition of civilization. Alienation on account of technology is not only defined by what Heidegger would call, in the 1950s, "enframing" (*Gestell*) in order to capture how "modern technology" controls or puts in place its structures at a planetary level and provokes our making as non-making.[43] Schmitt's analysis is political. He shows that the false neutrality of technology, which is an instrument in the service of any chosen end, leads to a world where *everything* is political in the sense of being controlled. Politics as such is then repressed. But, despite appearances, this control is effectuated by powers in conflict with other groups of men. This world is still political because it is characterized by violent struggle and the risk of war. Intellectual, moral, and aesthetic alienation leads to the situation where one has gone from the liberal state to the total state and where "new and even alien masses threatening to traditional education and taste continually arose from . . . cultural and social nothingness."[44] This is the fate of the ideal of the Enlightenment: "the belief in technology is in fact only the result of a certain tendency in the shifting of the central domain—as a belief it is only the result of this shifting."[45]

Like Heidegger, Schmitt relates the question of technology to the fate of the West, but he does not trace the problem back to the origin of metaphysics. In Heidegger, the problem of technology is examined in light of the history of metaphysics and goes back to the manner in which thinking is understood since the beginning of this history, where there is a determination of being by science and where reason is calculation and the taking possession of things, not their reception. Heidegger thinks the essence of technology. For him, it is linked to the notion of *Ereignis*. For Strauss, by contrast, the problem of technology is that of rationalism, of which the crisis manifests itself in the twentieth century and originates in the first wave of modernity, not Plato and Aristotle. The return to the Ancients is not a return to the pre-Socratics but rather to the classical political philosophers, to Plato and Aristotle. And there are the Jewish and Arab philosophers of the Middle Ages, who in the manner in which they understand the relation of reason and Revelation articulate a rationalism that is different from that of the modern Enlightenment, which is oriented to the ideal of the mastery of nature, including human nature. The theological-political problem must thus be rethought in light of the quarrel of Ancients and Moderns so that we are able to illuminate the problem of technology and propose an alternative to that which, in the eyes of Strauss, like Schmitt and Heidegger, constitutes a danger for the West and for man as such.

As for Strauss, technology becomes in Schmitt a problem as soon as theology is replaced by humanist morality, which goes hand in hand with the constitution of the modern state and is coeval with a conception of man where right is self-preservation and earthly happiness and satisfaction are given pride of place. Humanist morality, which supposes that a hedonistic society is possible, encourages "an activistic metaphysics—the belief in unlimited power and the domination of man over nature, even over human nature; . . ."[46] This humanist morality is already based on a technological outlook. From the beginning there was no fixed limit to the power of technology over nature, neither pious fear nor a sense of transcendence. Present-day technologies and weaponry, which appeared between the time when Schmitt published these works and the end of the 1960s, when Strauss published his book on Machiavelli, only give man more means to exploit this possibility and to use his freedom, defined by the infinite will of a being who can act on physical reality and other human beings with ever increasing efficiency. The problem was there from the beginning, as soon as the theological ceased to be the dominant sector and the state itself was rethought in terms of society. The political, for Schmitt, has thus become an instrument in the service of an ideal that is external to it and that concerns the private happiness of individuals. And when these individuals, in a globalized society, themselves lose the autonomy and independence that Constant considered primary, one can say that the era of technology is contemporaneous with a state of affairs where everything is political because nothing is absolutely political or because nothing is neutral.

Schmitt's response is to opt for a defensive position and to make liberalism an enemy, thus for polemics and reaction. Strauss noticed the relevance of Schmitt's analysis of technology, but he distanced himself from Schmitt's solutions. For Schmitt, one must affirm the political against the absurd situation to which the liberal state has led, again irresoluteness and indifference, against the development of technology, which also involves asking who will be the rulers of this pacified and globalized society.[47] For Strauss, the solution lies in examining the *tension* between Jerusalem and Athens, which is the promulgation of a political philosophy that has nothing to do with decisionism and in maintaining, at the core of a rationalism that owes more to Maimonides than the modern Enlightenment, biblical wisdom on the one hand and philosophical wisdom on the other. Is not the idea that the fear of God is the beginning of wisdom and that man, if he forgets his situation, can return to nothingness, to chaos, the only limit to man's power over nature? How can one really prohibit the application of certain technologies to living beings without invoking a divine Law?

There is much at stake in the confrontation between Schmitt and Strauss. Here we see everything that makes the political philosophy of Strauss something different than a reaction against modernity. Here it is a matter of examining Strauss's 1932–33 review of *The Concept of the Political.* Is this critique of liberalism motivated solely by the disgust inspired in Schmitt for a society founded on pure *distraction* and the loss of seriousness? If Strauss himself is not referring to this "order of human things," what does it mean to him to retain, besides the anthropology specific to real political thinkers such as Machiavelli or Hobbes, a certain idea of what is just by nature? It is in examining the polemical motives that drive Schmitt's analysis and in the scrutiny of their anthropological and theological undertones that Strauss achieves a real confrontation with Schmitt over the essential question: that of understanding the responsibility of the Enlightenment and liberalism for the crisis of the state?

War and the Affirmation of the Political

Schmitt opposes liberalism because it has forgotten the dimension of conflict that is constitutive of every human association. He does not seek to glorify war, but to conceive it has the limit-situation that defines the horizon of every human association. Politics signifies not a domain of human activity but the intensity of a given human association: "The specific political distinction to which political actions and motives can be reduced is that between friend and enemy. . . . The distinction of friend and enemy denotes the utmost degree of intensity of a union or separation, of an association or dissociation."[48]

This affirmation of the political explains at once Schmitt's interest in Hobbes, for whom war and the fear of death are central to the reflection on the political, while at the same time indicating his distance from Hobbes. But in the first instance it is a matter of attacking illusions, the fraudulence of the ideal of a globalized society purporting to work toward peace. Schmitt accuses the global, humanist perspective that the Enlightenment had sought to bring to political thought and the vocabulary of *Weltbürgerlichkeit* to deny "the enemy the quality of being human and declaring him an *outlaw of humanity*; and a war can thereby be driven to the most extreme inhumanity."[49]

Constant had claimed that commerce had replaced war.[50] In reality, war subsists. It is even worse. As Hobbes had emphasized, "The rule of a higher order . . . is an empty phrase if it does not signify politically that certain men of this higher order rule over men of a lower order. The independence and completeness of political thought is here irrefutable."[51] The opposition "ethics-economy" to which the liberal state and the international order founded on a pacifist vocabulary have led explained that those who threaten this superior order are declared "outside humanity." So "a war waged to protect or expand economic power must, with the aid of propaganda, turn into a crusade and into the last war of humanity."[52] The temptation to abolish the political out of love for humanity increases inhumanity, writes Strauss,[53] whose thought cannot serve, except by being distorted in nonsensical ways, to counsel a politics of intervention and empire like that directed by the advisers of George W. Bush in justifying the war in Iraq in 2003.[54]

The conceptual criterion (*Begriffsmerkmal*)[55] is for Schmitt the friend–enemy distinction.[56] It is a matter here of the political enemy (*hostis*) and not of an *inimicus* in the broader sense, which could mean anyone who is an object of personal hatred. The successors of Hobbes forgot the state of nature characterized by war. Hobbes himself is responsible for this state of affairs, because he elaborated a political theory concerning the exit from the state of nature, but he is, for Schmitt, a political thinker of unsurpassed profundity because he sets out the foundations of the liberal state and of absolutism in a precise manner. Contrary to his successors, who bet on man being capable in all circumstances of a temperate use of his freedom, Hobbes based his theory on the idea that conflict is inevitable. All political theories are grounded on an anthropology: for liberals, "the goodness of man signifies nothing more than an argument with whose aid the state is made to serve society. This means that society determines its own order and that state and government are subordinate and must be vigilantly controlled and bound to precise limits. Thomas Paine says: society is the result of our reasonably regulated needs, government is the result of our wickedness."[57] All specifically political thinkers, whether Machiavelli or Hobbes or Bossuet; Donoso Cortes, Taine, de Maistre, or Hegel, however each differs one from another, "presuppose man to be evil, i.e., by no means an unproblematic but a dangerous being."[58] For them, man is dangerous and needs to be ruled. And even when men care about the good and the just, it is, said Hobbes, "the conviction of each side that it possesses the truth, the good, and the just [that brings] about the worst enmities, finally the war of all against all."[59]

However, there is certainly in Schmitt disgust for a society where, commerce having replaced war, individuals, ensconced in the private sphere, are incapable of sacrifice and where the liberal state becomes a caricature of itself. According to Schmitt, representative democracy and parliamentarianism are signs of social decline, for which he has contempt that borders on *ressentiment*. It is not only Hobbes's successors who had forgotten war, which Hobbles at least had always maintained as a possibility between nations, but now all of humanity is living in distraction. Strauss emphasizes Schmitt's distaste at the prospect of a society that is completely pacified, where individuals live only for entertainment (*divertissements*).

Politics, as Constant wrote, becomes secondary in relation to private life: "To ask the peoples of our day to sacrifice, like those of the past, the whole of their individual liberty to political liberty, is the surest means of detaching them from the former and, once this result has been achieved, it would be only too easy to deprive them of the latter."[60] This situation makes necessary a representative system of government, which is "an organization by means of which a nation charges a few individuals to do what it cannot or does not wish to do herself."[61] But while Strauss, like Tocqueville,[62] is inclined to express the danger that is associated with modern liberty, Schmitt rejects this system for reasons that are at the same time moral and aesthetic. Strauss himself could have been the author of the following warning by Constant himself: "The danger of modern liberty is that, absorbed in the enjoyment of our private independence, and in the pursuit of our particular interests, we should surrender our right to share in political power too easily."[63] The risks of dictatorship and mass democracy are implicit in Constant's warning. They are also part of Strauss's consciousness. In his essay "German Nihilism," Strauss shows that both communism and Nazism were protests against Western civilization that came from Western man himself. The communists contested the ideal of a universal society based on capitalism and consumer culture, and the Nazis, full of hate for this "cultural bolshevism," wholly rejected Western civilization itself. Much more, the young German nihilists who adhered to Nazism were at the beginning people who could not tolerate the idea of a society based on materialism or its mercenary morality. It is this motive and this movement from contempt to rejection to hate of the liberal state that one finds in Schmitt. This explains, without excusing, Schmitt's adhesion to Nazism, but it also suggests that at the beginning of the 1930s it was not inevitable that he would move in that direction.[64] To avoid that moral fault, he would have needed to develop a philosophical response to the problem posed by liberalism rather than simply react in disgust to liberal society.

In Schmitt, there is a distaste for a certain kind of human being who seeks contests and intrigues—which could be "very interesting"[65]—but who lives in forgetfulness of what really matters. Strauss emphasizes this scornfulness of Schmitt, indicated by the expression "might [be] very interesting," which indicates his alienation from that world and his moral disgust for it.[66] He shows how Schmitt feels alienated from this world and that his distaste is on the plane of morality. Liberal society that is the negation of the political is the negation of the seriousness that makes human life worth living. But Strauss does not notice that there is also an aesthetic element in Schmitt's distaste for a "world of entertainment." In any case, this aspect clearly distinguishes Schmitt's reactionary thought from Strauss's constructive critique of democracy and his Socratically inspired political philosophy.

For Socrates, it is the dialectical inquiry concerning the just life that makes human existence worthy of the name. This is the life of the philosopher, who goes back into the cave after having questioned the Good in order to transform the opinions that dominate in the cave into knowledge or to offer a critique of those opinions in his writings. The latter are the product of an art of writing that reflects awareness of the gap between philosophy and the city. One does not find in Socrates the idea that the political good should be imposed by force or any sense of contempt toward those men who do not have access to the truth. In the place of contempt, there is irony, which is in essence philosophical and of which the philosophers themselves may be the object, to the extent to which they are away of the possibility of falling into delusion. The fact that the philosopher is compelled to go back into the cave and that some human beings are philosophers by nature and others not demonstrates that the need for entertainment, far from being a vice specific to democracy, is an unavoidable reality. Different from contempt for non-philosophers, the elitism of Strauss, to the extent that it does not go beyond the elitism of the Greeks, guarantees the possibility of critical reflection on democracy and is a bulwark against the rejection of democracy, which, prior to going in the direction of extreme solutions, is always prepared by a tendency toward disgust rather than by genuine thinking.

This disgust is aesthetic, because the moral accusation leveled against the world of entertainment that denies the spirit of seriousness is nourished, in Schmitt, by the representation of men as prey to this need for amusements and thrown, without knowing it, on a course that is, more so than (life) in Hobbes, headed toward a cultural and social abyss, towards small pleasures and small vanities, equally repulsive. By contrast, the Straussian critique of mass democracy does not encompass dreams of grandeur and nostalgia for a world where human beings were less driven by material well-being. When Strauss says that without a liberal education that allows us to be genuinely free persons, we are the captives of vulgar fashion, which issues from a lack of experience of the beautiful, at the same time he does not hold out the ideal of a society of great, noble, courageous and proud men. Here Strauss does not follow Nietzsche.

Similarly, Strauss's consideration of the Ancients, the study of whom makes us conscious of forgotten truths, does not represent a longing for a time where women did not have the vote and where slavery existed. While Strauss may occasionally express a sense of civilizational malaise, this sentiment must be distinguished from his philosophical argumentation. The sobriety of his analysis is reflective of his method, his political honesty. Finally, when he considers the notion of human perfection, it is in the sense that it was understood by the Greek philosophers: it is the fulfillment of human nature, which may be divine. The wise man, who is able to be a God among men, is something more than a fellow human in the specific sense that he is aware of his place in the universe.

Strauss is thus closer to Tocqueville than to Nietzsche when he examines the presuppositions of modern thought that have conditioned the evolution toward a global materialist society. It is a matter of understanding why the human type that emerges from the waves of modernity is easy prey for barbarism. But in his consideration of the modern individual, Strauss does not focus on the image of the bourgeois incapable of sacrifice. He is more concerned with the moment where modernity turns against itself. Modern rationalism, which put itself in the service of the ideal of the conquest of nature, including human nature itself, and which made reason an instrument of calculation divorcing it from any transcendent mission, has led to the destruction of reason. As with Tocqueville, the remedies that Strauss proposes entail considering what needs to be preserved in order to prevent modernity from betraying its own aspiration to progress.

It is in confronting both authors, who are at the same time very close and very far from him, that Strauss's originality emerges. In 1932–33, when he reviewed *The Concept of the Political*, Strauss had not yet acquired what would be needed to refute Schmitt. He had not yet learned all that he would learn—between 1934 and 1938, when his thought took a Farabian turn—from his studies of Maimonides and Farabi. The elements[67] that would constitute the foundations of his political philosophy would permit him to provide a response to the problem posed by the crisis of liberalism. In 1932–33, Strauss wrote that Schmitt was still trapped within liberalism; in a sense, he was too liberal. We need to examine that interpretation and the manner in which Strauss articulates the difference between Schmitt and Hobbes.

Decisionism and Political Philosophy

Schmitt and Hobbes do not look at man's dangerousness in the same way. For Hobbes, the badness in human nature is "innocent": it is like that of an animal driven by instinct (hunger, desire, fear, jealousy), even if consciousness of time, vanity, and the importance of signs of one's power make human passions quite different from animal instinct and explain human dangerousness and its consequences, that is war. Schmitt, however, gives man's dangerousness a moral significance.[68] This difference stems from the fact that Hobbes denies the existence of sin: man is not subject to obligation. The fundamental political fact is natural right, which is a legitimate claim of the individual that, at the same time, implies a *subsequent* limit on that claim. Man is bad or harmful merely like the beasts,[69] and "being an animal able to learn from his mistakes," this learning results in the fixing of limitations on the power of each if, like Hobbes, one thinks obligations are necessary in order to secure the respect of others. Or, on the contrary, one counts on education, as in anarchism or in contemporary opinion.

The state of nature is a theoretical fiction that serves the purpose of elaborating the notion of sovereignty and sustaining the liberal state against theocracy. Hobbes needed an anthropology that allowed him to construct his political theory, to reject the earlier political solutions prior to the liberal state, that is, empire, and to struggle against his political enemy, the Church. This is why he defined human badness exclusively in terms of dangerousness and being driven by passions. There is philosophical irony in this anthropological conception, which is at once a methodological starting point and a conceptual tool. By contrast, in Schmitt, the belief in man's badness as moral baseness (evil) is a matter of a profession of faith, and does not have the quality of the "known."[70]

Hobbes's anthropological hypothesis serves as the elaboration of a political theory, but its normative content appears only to support absolutism. Strauss writes that "the affirmation of the political is ultimately nothing other than the affirmation of the moral"[71] but it is not sure that this formula accurately characterizes the thought of Schmitt. Nevertheless, this notion allows Strauss to distinguish his own idea of the tension between Athens and Jerusalem from the Schmittean teaching, where faith, psychological motives, and theological dogma become intertwined with political considerations and determinative of them. Does Schmitt's thought derive from political theology in the sense that it is *due* to his theology, to his Catholicism, and the fact that he believes in original sin?[72] Or is this anthropological pessimism a weapon for doing battle with liberalism?

Schmitt does not leave matters at recognizing man's dangerousness; he affirms this dangerousness. And this affirmation of the political, which is the response to his disgust with a world of entertainment, is the decisionism the origins of which he believes he has found in Hobbes. Citing the formula of the Latin version of *Leviathan*, *Auctoritas, non veritas facit legem*, he writes: "Sovereign is he who decides the exception."[73] This interpretation is not self-evident. If it is true that, in Hobbes, the state is founded on the sovereign decision and is the condition of the effectiveness of law, of which the content presupposes the state, this does not prevent the laws of nature, which are precepts of reason, from being embodied in the civil law. What Schmitt retains of Hobbes is the idea that "there is no distinction between the just and unjust except in the state and by the state," that is, by sovereign command. Contrary to Grotius and to normativist approaches, the decisionist view of law is based on the concept of the decision as prior to any normative content to law, instead of supposing that there is guidance from some prior conceptions of justice. The situation of the exception reveals the foundation of the legal order, that is, that war is the critical test, the moment where there is a true affirmation of the political. Nevertheless, this orientation toward "the decisive conflict" leads to "the affirmation of fighting as such, wholly irrespective of *what* is being fought *for*."[74] Such an affirmation of the political is equivalent to neutrality in the sense that it does not distinguish between the ideals in the name of which one fights. There is not neutrality in the sense that there is decision and action, not retreat within the private sphere, but there is neutrality in the sense that one fights for the sake of fighting. Decisionism does not escape from relativism and nihilism.

Strauss's critique of this form of neutrality that leads to absolute tolerance is related to his condemnation of relativism in *Natural Right and History*, and his reading of Max Weber. Here one sees the common ground between liberalism, the morality of pacifism and human rights, on the one hand, and relativism and decisionism, on the other. All of these partake of what Nietzsche called the second form of nihilism, where all values are placed on an equal footing, where everything is worth the same and therefore worth nothing: "He who affirms the political as such respects all who want to fight; he is just as tolerant as the liberals—but with the opposite intention; . . ."[75] Decisionism is a form of nihilism, because it can be invoked in the name of any cause whatsoever. It encourages reaction against a flat world where men are unwilling to spill their blood to defend their country or their honor. Just as the last man lacks an object for his longing, and thus will be tempted by the most extreme manifestations of the Will to Power, he who affirms the political and is decisionist will quickly become a nihilist. But if he does not have the means to resist nihilism, if he finds in the exaltation of warrior morality the possibility of putting an end to indecisiveness, it is because he is not himself completely nihilistic: as both Löwith and Strauss saw, in Schmitt the decision is not completely unmotivated, but it is not derived either from normative rationality.

Schmitt's political theory is inadequate to propose any alternative to liberalism except dictatorship. As is the case today, Schmitt and the young German nihilists believed themselves to be facing a spiritual void. The only alternative to the bourgeois social vision was the struggle against capitalism and the market or that paradoxical alliance between individualism and that struggle against the injustices of the world, which suggests that citizens are divided between the perfection of their private happiness and the collective pursuit of an abstract humanitarian ideal. In facing the spiritual void of his times, where liberalism and communism were the alternatives, Schmitt, who saw the modern world as the enemy of Catholicism, chose reaction.

Schmitt's affirmation of the political and his decisionism are thus both moral and aesthetic. Schmitt sought to escape from the infinite regress of normativism and contingency because he was repulsed by a world of entertainment. This revulsion, together with his inability to propose a real alternative to liberalism and his inability to overcome nihilism, led him to decisionism and then to National Socialism. But one cannot say, as Strauss is often read to say, that Schmitt was a decisionist because he was too liberal. He was a decisonist because, like the liberals and to the same extent, he was a nihilist. He wanted to react against the nihilism of the liberals, indecisiveness and normativism. In this sense, his critique of normativism is itself normative. But this break with the rationality of the liberals, this refusal to ground the decision in rational norms has something of the aesthetic in it, reflecting a vision of the world quite widespread in the Germany of the 1920s and 1930s. This vision has elements of political romanticism and of reaction against the will to nothingness that is perceived as the basis of decadence.

When Strauss writes that "the affirmation of the political is ultimately nothing other than the affirmation of the moral," he cannot be taken to mean that Schmitt is too moral, but that his critique of liberalism is linked to his conception of "the seriousness of life." This expression has a moral resonance, but to the extent that Schmitt does not have a philosophy that gives it content, we can say that his decisionism is a halfway house between morality and aesthetics.

The debate between Strauss and Schmitt on the crisis of liberalism takes place in the shadow of Weber and Nietzsche. But the true successor of Nietzsche is, in Strauss's view, Martin Heidegger. Strauss avoided a direct confrontation with Heidegger, instead choosing to carve his own path apart from Heidegger. This is why Strauss's silence is eloquent, above all when one is aware that Löwith considered Schmitt in light of his interpretation of Heidegger, linking decisionism with the theme of resoluteness in Heidegger.[76]

Resoluteness in Heidegger

In paragraphs 60 and 62 of *Being and Time*, Heidegger refers to resoluteness (*die Entschlossenheit*) in order to designate the privileged mode of the openness of Being-in-the World (*Dasein*). And resoluteness being in each case that of an active *Dasein*, of which the essence is existence, it does not "exist" except as decision that understands and projects itself. But to what does *Dasein*, in its resoluteness, open itself? About what must it decide?

"Resoluteness exists only as a resolution [*Entschlossenheit*] which understandably projects itself. But on what basis does *Dasein* disclose itself in resoluteness? On what is it to resolve? Only the resolution itself can give the answer. . . . *The resolution is precisely the disclosive projection and determination of what is factically possible at the time.* To resoluteness, the *indefiniteness* characteristic of every potentiality-for-Being into which *Dasein* has been factically thrown, is something that necessarily *belongs*."[77]

This passage illustrates the common ground between Heidegger and Schmitt. The content of "liberal metaphysics" is indecision, to which decisionism opposes itself. But, at its core, Schmitt's conception of the political suffers from the same indeterminacy as the thinking that it opposes—as Strauss suggests in his discussion of neutrality—if, as Löwith thinks, decisionism is an occasionalism and remains impotent before the event, to what extent is this criticism also addressed to Heidegger?

For Heidegger, "'resoluteness' signifies letting oneself be summoned out of one's lostness."[78] "The call of conscience summons us to our potentiality-for-Being, it does not hold before us some empty ideal of existence, but call us forth into the situation."[79] Oriented toward pure possibility, toward the possibility of the impossibility of existence that is death, resolute *Dasein* does not simply act in any old way. One cannot address to Heidegger the same critique that Strauss addresses to Schmitt. Resoluteness, because it is primary and characterizes the way in which *Dasein* acts in thinking itself beginning from the possibility of *its* death, implies a temporalization of its temporality that does not allow us to assimilate repetition to decisionism. Heidegger is closer to Kierkegaard than Schmitt, who misappropriated Kierkegaard. Religion confronts an absolute dilemma that makes the individual being committed in his singularity and goes beyond any general determination of ethics and politics.

Strauss, in his commentary on the *Concept of the Political*, does not address Heidegger. He considers that Heidegger's thought offers no escape from nihilism, but at the same time he does not believe that Heidegger can be simply identified with decisionism or the encouragement of warrior morality. The silence of Strauss is above all a reflection on the fact that he constructs his own thought in the shadow of Heidegger, in facing the challenges of nihilism and technology, which Heidegger did not know how to solve. This is the nihilism of which Nietzsche made the diagnosis. Technology is a manifestation of the crisis, of the moment that makes necessary a rupture with the prevailing philosophy, with the thought of the Moderns, for Strauss, and for Heidegger all metaphysics since Plato.

Strauss undertakes an archeology of nihilism and dissects the modern political and religious consciousness, while Heidegger deconstructs metaphysics. Both Strauss and Heidegger conceive the crisis of contemporary rationalism as the crisis of the West and examine it starting from the philosophy of history. The crisis is characterized by a forgetting that needs to be addressed. This requires a return to the Greeks. But, according to Heidegger, metaphysics has overlooked ontological difference and has thought Being in terms of the entity; the forgetting is a forgetting of the question of being. According to Strauss, the Moderns had believed, from the beginning of the Enlightenment, that the theological-political problem had been resolved: the forgetting is a forgetting of the meaning of Law for the Greeks as well as for the Jewish and Arab philosophers of the Middle Ages. One must return to Socrates and Maimonides and abandon the categories of thought established and determined by the modern Enlightenment and Christianity. According to Heidegger, one must return to the pre-Socratics and abandon onto-theology in thinking the divine without reference to God or monotheism. Finally, this forgetting of Being, which is the retreat of Being, is connected to the *Ereignis*, and one must situate oneself within the history of Being in order to conceive a different relation to the *Gestell.*

What is it that disturbs Strauss in Heidegger's notion of resoluteness, and why does he claim that it explains Heidegger's adhesion to Nazism? "Anticipating resoluteness" is not persuasive for Strauss. Is this because it is conceived in relation to the question of death, in the context of an atheistic teaching? Heidegger thinks, like Hobbes and Hegel, that death is what animates consciousness, which previously was comprehended in terms of thingness. Death is the ultimate possibility that concerns me as such, in my *Jemeinigkeit*. The awareness of its finitude removes the consciousness from indifference. "One dies" from the fact that there are always others who die. It takes the consciousness away as well from life in the *One,* in the decadence of a purely worldly existence, where I either lose time or always lack time, because despite all the business, I am escaping and remaining in distraction. The thought of my death introduces seriousness into my life, inciting me to bring to life that which is most personal, with a sense of urgency that comes from the sense that my days are numbered. But "anticipating resoluteness" is not linked to the desire to transcend the human condition and is unrelated to the cult of heroism: "it brings one without illusions into the resoluteness of "taking action." . . . "[I]it springs from a sober understanding of what are factically the basic possibilities for *Dasein*."[80]

Heidegger, who establishes on the plane of immanence the connection between the consciousness of one's finitude and the mastery by each of his liberty, seems then to encourage a life dedicated to creation rather than a life of flight and clash, where one makes war in order to affirm one's Will to Power. But there are no transcendent ideals that allow an individual to construct his life in a particular way. The teaching of resoluteness doesn't encourage each one to obey his own god or demon in the sense that it encourages each to affirm with the greatest force possible his will, but it does not prohibit obedience to a demon and does not allow for resistance to the violent affirmation of the will. Heidegger's thought, like all thought that consists in secularized theological concepts, does not allow for resistance to nihilism. It has, ultimately, the same starting point as that of liberalism, namely the passions, and, in Hobbes, death—seen as the absolute master. Yet, according to Strauss, reason is not determined by the passions, and even less by the fear of death or by the consciousness of one's finitude. Wisdom is not a matter of choosing between Jerusalem and Athens, but of letting each of these types of wisdom remain in tension with one another. And the fear of God does not reduce to a consideration of our mortality. It is rather a matter of the limits on my action and my autonomy. What prevents the *Gestell* from being that in which and starting from which man and being encounter each other is political philosophy, which is the consideration of the Law and the relationship between reason and Revelation that underpins it.

For Strauss, the thought of Heidegger leaves a void. This void is all the more significant in an era of technology. When he writes that the young German nihilists did not encounter in the thinkers of the period any resistance to nihilism,[81] his severity toward Max Weber and his condemnation of Heidegger "implicated in National Socialism" should be understood in terms of the awareness of the problem: he is conscious of the urgent need to escape from confusion, but the greatest thinkers of the time are incapable of proposing a solution that permits the overcoming of nihilism. Strauss and Heidegger share an orientation in the critique of modern rationalism. They are aware that they live in the world as described by Nietzsche, but Heidegger is the direct heir of Nietzsche, while Strauss sets himself apart: he has a different diagnosis of the origins and meaning of the crisis of our time, and his response has nothing to do with the doctrine of the eternal return. Finally, even if he is aware that one cannot simply return to the faith of one's ancestors, he does not conceive the death of God in the same way as Heidegger, for whom there is no place for God the Creator: "one cannot speak of anything being prior to man in time . . . the question as to what is responsible for the emergence of man and of '*Sein*' of what brings them out of nothing . . . is a very big question for Heidegger. He says, '*Ex nihilo omne ens qua ens*' [out of nothing every being comes out]. This could remind one of the Biblical doctrine of creation out of nothing, but Heidegger has no place for the Creator God."[82]

Heidegger conceals the theological origins of his thought. By contrast, Strauss's reopening of the theological-political problem is a contestation of the Nietzschean legacy and of what Heidegger fails to question, including when he speaks of the divine under the inspiration of Hölderin and envisages the last god or the extreme god as the solution for the *Gestell*. The notion of the sending of Being and the idea of destiny that one finds in the concept of the *Ereignis* that Heidegger would expound later would not turn out to seduce Strauss. Beginning in the context of the 1930s, when he would discover that the core of medieval Arab and Jewish philosophy is the concept of Law, Strauss thinks that he is more capable of addressing the crisis of our times than Heidegger. The two central aspects of his though are his devotion to an enlightened Judaism, which distances him from Heidegger, and his promotion of political philosophy. This entails the study of Hobbes, who introduces the principal notions of modern political thought, in particular those of contractarianism and representation. But it is Hobbes's successors who will develop these notions in the context of a political reflection on republicanism (Rousseau) or philosophy of history (Hegel), compelling the reconciliation of the contradictory demands of the liberal state. This is the significance of the second wave of modernity, that beginning with Rousseau, and the philosophy of history of Hegel, which is a matter of contention in the dialogue between Strauss and Kojeve.

One needs to understand the extent to which the totalitarian experiences of the twentieth century are already anticipated by Hegel. Thus, in the following chapter, which addresses both the second and third waves of modernity, we undertake that dissection of the modern political consciousness that issues from a critical reflection on the modern Enlightenment. Hobbes, who swallows morality into the state and breaks with the traditional conception of natural law, with Grotius, in suggesting that there is no natural right prior to the establishment of human society, anticipates Hegel. For Hegel, acts of virtue are defined in relation to the state. Thus, to understand Rousseau and Hegel, who each in his own way battles liberalism, that is to say the engulfing of the state by society, the emergence of abstract morality, but also, linked to commerce, the defense of a "serpentine wisdom,"[83] is to understand that the Enlightenment gave rise to thinkers who took issue with the Enlightenment.

Rousseau, who sets forth a critique of the Enlightenment and its ideal of progress through science and technology understood as enhancing the power of man, represents "in the first place . . . a return from the world of modernity to premodern ways of thinking."[84] Nevertheless, Rousseau will lead to a radicalization of modernity. Similarly, even if the Hegelian solution of a reconciliation between the state and civil society allows one to take into account the Schmittean critique of liberalism without succumbing to Schmitt's decisionism, it remains the case that the philosophy of history, which is the legacy of the second wave of modernity, contains the assumptions and illusions that will characterize communism. It recovers the high ideal of classic philosophy, but, instead of bringing about the just society through shared reflection on the ends of human life, it wagers on a synthesis of theory and practice that is completely alien to what Strauss calls political philosophy, which is inseparable from the notion of a gap or tension between philosophy and the city. It is thus that the philosophy of history will come to legitimate a politics that imposes a certain social order that it deems just. In examining the three waves of modernity, we attempt to make clear what Strauss understands as political philosophy and the relationship between the thought and the action that it implies.

Chapter 2

The Second and Third Waves of Modernity

The Rousseauian Moment

The Paradoxes of Rousseau

We are familiar with Jean-Jacques Rousseau as a lover of paradoxes. This is particularly pertinent to Rousseau's place in the history of political thought. On the one hand he denounces the modern corruption endangered by the arts and sciences and questions the concept of progress central to the Enlightenment, and on the other "he accepts Hobbes' premise. . . . natural law must have its roots in principles which are anterior to reason, i.e., in passions which need not be specifically human."[1] Rousseau will go even further than Hobbes: "usurping the place of reason and indignantly denying her libertine past, passion began to pass judgment, in the severe accents of Catonic virtue, on reason's turpitudes."[2] Rousseau never ceased to claim that "the adventure of modernity is a radical error" and to oppose Hobbes—his concept of the state of nature, his definition of social relations in terms of calculation, and his absolutism. He sought a solution for this "error" in turning toward the ancient city, but "his return to antiquity was, at the same time, an advance of modernity. While appealing from Hobbes, Locke, or the Encyclopedists to Plato, Aristotle or Plutarch, he jettisoned important elements of classical thought which his modern predecessors had still preserved."[3]

Rousseau reflects the first crisis of modernity. "The Rousseauian moment" displays the contradictions of the modern project and the impossibility of completing it. The paradoxes of Rousseau are thus our own paradoxes, whether they are a matter of defining liberty as autonomy or the conflict between the individual—complete and solitary—and "society," which absorbed the state and civil society and returns by contrast to the hypothetical state of nature from which man has exited. And this opposition between individual liberty and the common good is the heart of the political problem to which Rousseau responds with his theory of the general will, and it is a given of the modern political experience. Never again after Rousseau would men forget the sublime sentiment of liberty, which they claim against society, either through becoming the conscience of society, like the artist[4] or a revolutionary, who seeks to actualize this ineffable liberty. Yet maintaining at the same time "the very indefiniteness of the state of nature as a goal of human aspiration leads to the following consequence: "the individual claims such an ultimate freedom from society as lacks any definite content."[5] And this disproportion between undefined and undefinable liberty and the demands of civil society" will not be well understood by the successors of Rousseau, whether as philosophers or citizens.

Rousseau thus leads to a form of modernity even more distant from classical thought than that of the seventeenth- and eighteenth-century philosophers. It embodies the passionate protest of a philosopher against the illusions of the Enlightenment, against the Enlightenment belief in the omnipotence of reason understood as augmenting the mastery of nature by man, but also against the ideal of civilization, which leads to depravation and corruption. Rousseau's critique, and his invocation of the ancient city, are motivated by his reactions against that lowering of man that goes from the desire for glory—central for Machiavelli—to the quest for power and competition, which in Hobbes is "businesslike" and anticipates acquisitive desire and the right to property in Locke. The critique of economism as "Machiavellianism come of age"[6] is the central thread of the Rousseauian critique of the first wave of modernity. His opposition to Locke is based on the struggle to remake the bourgeois into a citizen.

The return of Rousseau to pre-modern thought is linked to his condemnation of social inequality. Founded on conquest, society entrenches inequality between rich and poor: political power and economic power are entwined. But Rousseau is a Modern: he understands the return to the ancient city in terms of the Hobbesian conception of the right to self-preservation and actually radicalizes the break with classic natural right, which is oriented toward transcendence or man's perfection in light of a higher law. From this break and the difficulties that follow from it in deriving justice from immanent criteria results a formal definition of liberty, a delineation of the relation between the individual and the community and a consecration of history that will be characteristic of the French Revolution. These same principles can be found in the theory according to which ideas should be actualized historically. If the rational is the real and the real is the rational, violence is legitimate: it brings about the just social order and allows a people, a nation, or all of humanity to achieve its destiny. Revolution becomes salutary.

Such is the movement that needs to be followed in order to understand the link that exists between the first two waves of modernity and the acceleration of history that begins with Nietzsche. It is a matter of more and more radical modernity that comes from the fact that the heroes of the seventeenth and eighteenth centuries broke, in their theological-political treatises, with an essential dimension of human life. And the teaching of those who in the beginning sought to put an end to wars of religion and lay the foundations of modern liberal democracy is considered self-evident today. Men today are no more enlightened in that they accept the conclusions of the philosophers of the Enlightenment as given, and these conclusions, often in a caricatured form, have become prejudices. Finally, the men of today who have, at least in the West, accepted civil equality no longer make the effort, as Tocqueville observed, to cultivate the sense of liberty. This, beginning with Rousseau, becomes the essence of man, who no longer has a nature. He is alone and unjustified. There is nothing external to his subjective consciousness that can orient him in light of a fixed end. This is the reason why Sartre rejects every notion of human nature.

One might think that Sartre's existentialism is the radicalization of the Rousseauian definition of man and liberty. Existentialism, which is a kind of historicism, represents an acceleration of the destructive dialectic of Enlightenment. Sartre's existentialist atheism, which Strauss does not identify with Heidegger's existentialism,[7] has a Christian origin that is most often forgotten: Kierkegaard. The destruction of reason through historicism goes hand in hand with the emptying of the notion of nature in modernity, even if this forgetting expresses, but does not *explain*, the crisis of our times. Thus, it is in examining the "Rousseauian moment" that one understands what Strauss means when he says: "He (Nietzsche) is as little responsible for fascism as Rousseau is responsible for Jacobinism. This means, however, that he is as much responsible for fascism as Rousseau was for Jacobinism."[8]

Society and the Rich

"Machiavelli's discovery . . . of the need for an immoral or amoral substitute for morality became victorious through Locke's discovery . . . that that substitute is acquisitiveness."[9] "But this egoistic passion that does not require the spilling of blood" inspires Rousseau's indignation. This is because the modern system, which replaces virtue with commerce, makes wealth the criteria of human value. Virtue is forgotten. The foundation of human relations becomes calculating self-interest. It is not only against this enfeebled citizenship that Rousseau protests, but also against the fact that the greatest number do not enjoy the security for the sake of which they entered society. The majority is required to "give up their own wills to work for the satisfaction of the few . . . who control the laws . . ."[10] Politics is the extension of economic domination. The modern state, founded on self-preservation, is directed toward the satisfaction of it subjects, but it forgets true human happiness, and consecrates inequality, the gap between rich and poor.

The hopes of the Enlightenment, which saw in the arts and sciences the conditions for social progress and political emancipation, are deceptive: the arts and sciences do not perfect morals, but rather they lead to corruption. They require luxury and leisure; they will increase inequalities and bring about vices connected to the emergence of new needs that are impossible to satisfy. This is because many workers are required for this system, and a great deal of money to defray the cost of the arts and sciences. Moreover, the man who appears in such a society "nourishes in the soul the miserable taste for oneself and impotent hatred for others. In such a society, man lives only for the gaze of others, whom he hates."[11] The rich man embodies a society based on comparison. Modern man, having become bourgeois, has, on account of his contradictions, ceased to be a citizen. He is too dependent to be really free and to avoid the omnipotence of public opinion, and too individualistic to imitate the ancient citizen. Alienated, he thinks that his interests and those of the city are in tension.

The problem is that of establishing a society on the basis of the individual while at the same time assuring social cohesion without resorting to despotism. Rousseau returns to the ancient city not in order to find a substitute for liberalism, but in order to condemn modern society, which has made men bad in developing in them anti-natural passions. *Amour-propre*, the basis of vanity, is born only with society. It supposes comparison and it vanishes as soon as man, in his solitude, recovers the immediate sentiment of existence, which is true happiness, different from pleasures that alienate his soul and leave him with a sense of emptiness.[12] Man described by Hobbes is civilized man. In his *Discourse on the Origin and Basis of Inequality Among Men*, Rousseau will thus search for natural man in the most simple operations of his soul. And this kind of man, who resembles the statue of Glaucus, because society has made him almost unrecognizable, is characterized by self-love [*amour de soi*]. But instead of clinging to the desire to dominate others, as in Hobbes and Nietzsche, the egoist tendency of self-preservation is counterbalanced by natural pity or the revulsion that everyone feels in seeing a living and sensitive being suffer needlessly. The nature of man is that he does not have a nature. But inasmuch as he is the product of his acts, he is perfectible.

Membership in society, far from being natural, is the result of geographical accident, which constrained men to coexist in the face of an increasingly harsh natural world. Coexistence and dependence will bring into being new sentiments leading to the denaturing of this naturally good but amoral being and transform him into an individual capable of the most noble sentiments. But the state of war obliges men to leave the state of nature and establish by contract the rules of their life in common. The collectivity of individuals becomes an association, a state. The political problem addressed by Rousseau's *Social Contract* is to reconcile the interest of each with the interest of all. It is a matter of establishing social cohesion while respecting the nature of man, free and independent, while leading him to identify with the common good and acquire the civic virtue that he does not possess by nature. This is the role of the general will. And this notion will represent an acceleration of the process of modernity. It is at the same time Rousseau's answer to the "error" of modernity, an expression of his nostalgia for ancient virtue, and the opening for revolution and the philosophy of history. Rousseau elaborated this notion, like social contract theory with its republican orientation, because he saw in political institutions the continuation of the inequality of rich and poor that originates with the institution of private property.

Property, which embodies the contradictions of the human world, gives rise, as in Locke, to labor, but the latter does not provide the basis for *right* to property. It is society and law that transform possession, which is a matter of usurpation according to Rousseau, into property. Inequality of property is based in the first instance on inequality of power. But the strongest, possessing more than others, is more threatened than others and more dependent on society for his self-preservation, including the preservation of his property, and this requires foresight. Political society, which presupposes language and the ability to plan for the future, thus reason, serves to make up for the weakness of the rich and give them the power of the many. The laws are the means by which the power of the many ends up serving the rich. Rousseau, in setting forth his republican conception of the state, grounded on self-legislation—the people are both subject and object of the laws—seeks to correct this inequality to prevent economic inequality from becoming legal inequality. For Rousseau, who rejects the principle of legislative representation and who confines the role of delegates of the sovereign, such as ministers and officials, to the application of the laws, the poor have civic rights, and this mitigates inequality of property but does not eliminate it.

Revolution, History, and the General Will

The general will is the site where particular wills identify, not the sum of those wills. The individual who has adhered to the social contract sees through generalization that the common good is his own good, or that his private good cannot be guaranteed without the state. In his way of conceptualizing the relation between the individual and the collectivity, Rousseau goes further than any definition founded exclusively upon self-preservation or need. He speaks of citizens as the *members* of a *body* that designates the state in which the individual deciphers his will, once it is liberated from the narrow and egoistical perspective that stifled the voice of the universal in him. And in order for each individual to identify with the new whole of which he is a part, or so that the general will is able to express itself without erring, one must have a good society where people have not been corrupted to the point that the divine instinct that guides them to the good is extinguished. It is thus necessary that morality remains the basis of social cohesion. The task of the legislator, who is the founder, that superior man[13] who is able to give commandments as if they were of divine origin, and then the natural theology of Book IV of *Emile* are the means by which Rousseau furnishes morality with a stronger and more effective support than calculation. More aware than his successors of the necessity to find a realistic substitute for traditional natural law, he elaborates his theory of the general will in order to close the gap between nature and law that ensues from modern natural law, the ground of which is immanent.[14]

According to Strauss, Rousseau accepts Hobbes's "reduction of virtue to social virtue"—"Do good to yourself with as little evil as possible to others."[15] Nevertheless, if his doctrine of the general will and his idea of the generality of law that anticipates the categorical imperative of Kant allow a reconnection to an ideal higher than "the low but solid foundation" chosen by Machiavelli and Hobbes, Rousseau remains no less a Modern. He accepts the break with classical natural right and refuses to conceive man on the basis of a *telos* that he must achieve through education, laws, and philosophy. The gap between nature and law is, on the contrary, exacerbated by his definition of man in terms of liberty. He could thus come to be overwhelmed by history. Rousseau opens the way for those who, believing they possessed the truth and that they incarnated the sovereignty of the people, thought they had the right and the duty to impose it, even by terror.

The general will never errs inasmuch as it is directed to the good of the people, but the people do not always see what is their good. And the successors of Rousseau do not rely on the same guide that he does in order to conceive the transition from individual to citizen. We have evoked the Terror in the French Revolution, but we could also refer to the communists. In order to install the dictatorship of the proletariat, the communists created a party and methods of control destined to repress all those who opposed progress in justice as they themselves conceived it. To the extent that the successors of Rousseau will dispense with the idea of political representation and prefer revolution to the reforms and middle courses that serve, as with Hegel's civil servants, to close the gap between civil society and the state, we can say that Rousseau's concept of the general will is in essence juridical. It leads to a political impasse or an incoherent account of how, in a society based on such premises, it is possible to have clarity concerning the general will. With Rousseau, modern natural right is in crisis because "his conception of the state of nature points toward a natural right teaching which is no longer based on considerations of man's nature. . . . My desire transforms itself into a rational desire by being "generalized."[16]

Rousseau does not want to return to the idea that man is sociable by nature, because he insists on affirming the independence of the individual. His theory of the state of nature allows him to conserve this independence of the individual, who can always recover his natural liberty by leaving civil society. Liberty is superior to life in Rousseau, who has a moral seriousness in contrast to Hobbes: man is fundamentally himself when he obeys his conscience and acts rightly.[17] This is why Rousseau will make up for the modern foundations of his thought by the advocacy of a society of which the criterion of legitimacy will be the respect of man's original goodness. The just society is the society that, while denaturing man, will respect what is best in his original nature. This is the reason for the paradoxical admiration that Rousseau has for the Ancients, an admiration for their practice, not their theory, because he breaks with the classic definition of justice based on the end of man and his place in the universe. Everything is related to the complex origins of the word "nature" and the Moderns' polemical use of this word to condemn society while emptying it of all content. Rousseau, in extending the tendency to secularization of the natural right inaugurated by the first wave of modernity and in making liberty the essence of man and the highest value, superior even to life itself, is at the origin of the "philosophy of freedom." He thus opened the way to a legal definition of political liberty and the general will and to German idealism, which at the same time denies the natural sociability of man and posits "the being of the individual as the first and highest thing,"[18] thus contradicting the two fundamental propositions of Aristotle.

Rousseau thus continues the rejection of the idea that man is naturally oriented toward the ends of political life. But this rejection of the notion of ends already signifies the supremacy of history. The legitimate state that Rousseau, in the *Social Contract*, deduced from the nature of the political problem and the definition of man as a free individual, equal to every other man by nature and in dignity, is a human construction. Man is the product of history. And to the extent that the criterion of legitimacy ought to entail the respect for his nature, that is, for his liberty, human action to promote a state that conforms to this ideal of justice is to be encouraged. But this "possibility" opened up by the revolutionary act is so indeterminate that no politics could ever dispense with it or realize it. There remains the belief in history after the nations have tried, provisionally, to master it.

After Rousseau and the French Revolution, political theories will be oriented toward liberty or toward history. Liberals after the French Revolution, for example, Guizot and Constant, work to construct the institutions appropriate for a free society. Tocqueville will seek a counterweight to the passion of equality in the rediscovery of the meaning of liberty through education, human associations, and all that conduces to the individual becoming a citizen. His particular concern will be representation. After the Revolution, liberals oppose themselves both to reactionaries who want to return to the Ancien Régime and those who wish to continue in the name of the revolution "and hence make impossible the stabilization of the liberal institutions implied by its principles."[19]

Everyone has acquired the historical sense. Those who think that the end of human history is the establishment of a just society based on perfect equality seek the most effective means for getting rid of what they consider the vestiges of an archaic society, private property and the status of the individual who is nothing beside the party, the true whole. The conflict between East and West, between communism and capitalism, which marked history when Strauss was in the United States, and the reign of ideology are already in play from the moment when, beginning with "the French Revolution and Rousseau," political philosophy as such is dead.

Mass democracy and the appearance of the last man derive equally from the legacy of Rousseau, as Strauss suggests when he says that the transition between the second and third waves of modernity has the character of an acceleration, not a further rupture. The rupture will be historical. It will make impossible the assimilation of communism and Nazism. There is a certain continuity between Rousseau and Nietzsche, but after Nietzsche a more violent movement takes modernity to an extreme point. This is why the return to a pre-modern ideal and the reaction of the German nihilists of the 1930s are different from the anti-Enlightenment and Romanticism. Irrationalism after Nietzsche has nothing to do with Romanticism and Rousseau because contemporary irrationalism is the destruction of reason, not its submission to feeling. For the original goodness of man, his compassion, and the immediate sentiment of existence, which is a pure happiness where man is self-sufficient, is substituted a tragic vision of existence and the sentiment that life is Will to Power. Man has unlimited desire. This desire for self-affirmation is expressed through domination of others because this domination is, along with violence, the most exuberant expression—or the refuge—of a will that has not other object but its own affirmation. It seeks only to will *itself*, instead of abandoning itself to solitary dreaming and communion "with those celestial intelligences whose number it hopes shortly to augment."[20] One the one hand, it is a politics of power, earthly glory, and blood; and on the other, the paradoxes of a man divided between individual self and citizen, the materialism of the wise man, and the hopes of the believer, philosopher and literary artist. On the one hand, the Eternal Return is willed by the Superman, and on the other, it is the desire to be exemplary of a man who, confessing *intus et in cute*, addresses himself to posterity.

It is worth stressing another ambiguity in the Rousseauian legacy. Rousseau did not teach that history should do what man himself cannot do by nature, that is, give himself completely to the state. In insisting that man has the right to take back his natural liberty, he resists the temptations of his successors, that is, the temptations of totalitarianism. On the one hand, Rousseau permits everyone to complain about everything and the fact that society is not respectful of nature and individual freedom, and on the other he opens the path to the temptation to alienate the individual to the collectivity. He authorizes and at the same time avoids these two excesses of modernity that are communism and the despotic degradation of democracy, where individuals are blinded by the passion for equality. This is above all the vindication of an imaginary equality, and, in alliance with an individualism that Rousseau denounced before Tocqueville, it leads each to complain about everything, to demand everything, including to distinguish one's individuality from the mass.

Modern Tyranny, Marxism, and Capitalism

The Dialogue between Strauss and Kojeve

The consequence of the first two waves of modernity is communism. Modern political thought represents the break of modern natural right from the ancient natural right teaching but also a break with the Ancients concerning the relation of theory to practice. Whereas the perfect political order articulated by Plato is understood as realizable in practice, the Moderns think that it is possible for human beings to guarantee the realization of the ideal order.[21] In his dialogue with Kojeve, Strauss shows that this change leads to a new kind of tyranny that is different from ancient tyranny in that its basis is technology and ideology and it threatens to become permanent and universal.[22] Like technology, the ideal of a universal and homogenous state goes hand in hand with a collectivization of man and of human thought. It is not a mere manifestation of modernity, but its ultimate implication. Communism reflects the logic of the West since the Enlightenment. This understanding of communism in light of its philosophical origins goes to explain the possibility of a dialogue between Kojeve and Strauss, despite the enormous gulf between their two positions. Kojeve asserts that the universal and homogenous state is the end of history and that "there is indeed a wisdom that prescribes that one does everything that leads to this end and that condemns everything that impedes it . . ."[23] All men will be satisfied in such a state, which he identifies explicitly with the direction of Stalinism. The (true) philosophy (of Hegel) will be actualized. Strauss, who considered that in his time no one "had made the case for modern thought as brilliantly [as Kojeve],"[24] objected to communism and Stalinism, which are modern forms of tyranny, and argued that the coming of the universal and homogenous state would be the coming of the last man and the death of philosophy.

For Kojeve, the universal and homogenous state is the end of history, an end for which the philosopher should work, instead of thinking like Socrates and like Strauss that the realization of the best regime is improbable. In this state, the conquest of nature is brought to completion. There will be neither work nor struggle. The achievement of the Enlightenment is the conquest of nature and the end of history after the revolution. But will not this Hegelian-inspired philosophy lead to a contradiction?

> This end of history would be most exhilarating but for the fact that, according to Kojeve, it is the participation in bloody political struggles as well as in real work or, generally expressed, the negating action, which raises man above the brutes. The state through which man is said to become reasonably satisfied is, then, the state in which the basis of man's humanity withers away, or in which man loses his humanity. It is the state of Nietzsche's would be most exhilarating but for the fact that, according to Kojeve, it is the participation in bloody political struggles as well as in real work or, generally expressed, the negating action, which raises man above the brutes. The state through which man is said to become reasonably satisfied is, then, the state in which the basis of man's humanity withers away, or in which man loses his humanity. It is the state of Nietzsche's "last man.[25]

In such a state, would one ever encounter an individual such as Kojeve?

When he addresses the *Hiero* of Xenophon, Kojeve interprets the final response of Simonides, who appears to defend benevolent tyranny in suggesting that this notion is realized by the regime of Salazar in Portugal, that today's tyrants are good tyrants in Xenophon's sense,[26] and that the improvement of tyranny along the lines of Simonides's suggestions includes " 'Stakhanovistic' emulation." Not only is Strauss not convinced by this interpretation of the government of Salazar, but above all he suggests that "Stalin's rule would live up to Simonides's standards only if the introduction of Stakhanovistic emulation had been accompanied by a considerable decline in the use of the N.K.V.D. or of "labor" camps."[27]

What is really at stake in Xenophon's dialogue is the distinction between the philosophical way of life and the others, whether that of the gentleman or the statesman, the tyrant or king.[28] Certainly, the *Hiero* is "silent about the status of wisdom."[29] But if one compares this dialogue with the other works of Xenophon, and if one understands that Simonides's praise of pleasure and honor is directed at leading his interlocutor to a certain place in the argument, one realizes that there is a "profound agreement between Plato and Xenophon." This agreement concerns the nature of wisdom and the distinction between the ordinary conception of justice and justice in its highest form, which coincides with philosophy.[30]

This distinction relates to the opposition between a way of life based on the desire for truth and a way of life based upon pleasure, whether luxury and the pleasures of the table or of love or recognition. The benevolent tyrant to whom Simonides refers seeks to be loved and uses wisdom as a means of self-preservation and in order to lead a life of pleasure. The difference between the benevolent tyrant and the tyrant who fears being assassinated because he has committed too many injustices is one of degree. The contrast between such a man and the philosopher is such that Hiero cannot stop himself from believing that Simonides covets power. He does not understand his love of the truth and experiences a combination of fear and suspicion in the presence of Simonides. Aware of this gap between philosophers and the rest of mankind, Simonides, when he advises the tyrant, presents himself as "an utterly unscrupulous man. The greatest man who ever imitated the *Hiero* was Machiavelli."[31]

Nevertheless, if it is the case that the philosopher is able to govern better on account of his rhetoric, Simonides does not exploit the despondency of Hiero, who wonders whether suicide would not be a solution in his case. Because the philosopher is not interested in the same thing as the tyrant, the political philosopher necessarily has an ambiguous relation to politics. The notion that, for the Ancients, the coincidence of philosophy and kingship is improbable goes back to their understanding of the specific character of philosophy, and thus the status of political philosophy. Philosophy does not find its justification in the consequences it may have for action. It is zetetic: "the philosopher ceases to be a philosopher at the moment at which the 'subjective certainty' of a solution becomes stronger than his awareness of the problematic character of that solution. At that moment, the sectarian is born."[32]

This statement makes sense of the many places where Strauss does not conceal his contempt for "ideologues." Kojeve is not for Strauss among this category of opportunistic intellectual: he is a philosopher.[33] But Strauss challenges his modern Hegelian conception of the relation of theory to practice. For Kojeve, not only does the ancient point of view represented by Strauss and the Socratic ideal lead to utopianism, but it also goes hand in hand with a selfish life,[34] for the philosopher, who in his "Garden" only has to worry about the competition in the republic of letters, lives removed from the stage of historical action. Ancient philosophy is irrelevant and contrary to the vocation of the philosopher, which is commitment, even if the conflict between theory and practice, the philosopher and the political man is, in the Christian and bourgeois world, a tragic one, a problem without a solution. To renounce the active life in order to philosophize and to renounce philosophy in order to act is to be untrue to Socrates and the Greeks, whose irony and art of writing Kojeve nonetheless emphasizes, a vivid illustration of the tension between philosophy and society.

For Strauss there can be no *Aufhebung* that resolves this tension. Thought and action cannot be reconciled. The tension between philosophy and the city is the very subject matter of philosophical reflection. The philosophy of history is an illusion, a reconstruction of the meaning of history that can be attractive in theory, but that is false in practice because it abstracts from an essential dimension of political life. In his dialogue with Kojeve, the necessity to return to a conception of philosophy that is prior to modern rationalism remains Strauss's principle and method. This is the basis of Strauss's skepticism toward the philosophy of history, which puzzled most of his contemporaries. But it is also because he was not seduced by these grand Hegelian Marxist conceptions that Strauss possesses the means to think through modern tyranny. Is it not after all the tension between philosophy and society that allows us to recognize modern tyranny? "When we were brought face to face with tyranny—with a kind of tyranny that surpassed the boldest imagination of the most powerful thinkers of the past—our political science failed to recognize it."[35]

This impotence of modern political science is the consequence of the crisis and alienation of modernity. It is no accident that problems Strauss raises about the monstrous development of technology are precisely those that Kojeve does not understand.[36] For this monstrous development of technology is not only required by totalitarianism because it is a means, a weapon, but is itself the manifestation of that other form of modern tyranny that can insinuate itself in the shadow of democratic institutions. It is this fruit of liberty, this instrument of the democratic diffusion of science and innovation that comes back to haunt democracy and destroys it while at the same time making use of it.

Modern tyranny, whether it is in the form of communism or Nazism or a new kind of dictatorship where economic coercion replaces military coercion, is the point of contention in this confrontation between the Hegelian point of view, represented by Kojeve, who remains enclosed in the modern concept of history, and the pre-modern perspective, which Strauss considers the only way out of the crisis. In this dialogue that lasted for more than three decades, the two men reflected on the relationship of philosophy (or wisdom, according to Kojeve) and society. They shared the same concern, which was to know how thinking or wisdom, in Kojeve distinct from philosophy, can still be possible in the universal and homogenous state.

This debate is interesting not as a contest between two philosophical or "ideological" positions, as one could have by opposing a Marxist and a defender of liberalism who lived in the United States at the height of McCarthyism, or who took up the defense of liberal democratic constitutionalism, even if he did not hide his reservations concerning capitalism. The interest in this confrontation between Kojeve, who is charmed by Stalinism, the first complete account of the universal and homogenous state, and Strauss derives from the radicality of the position of the one and the originality of that of the other who shows the common ground between capitalism and Marxism, in particular, in his interpretation of Locke. Finally it is the irreducible opposition between the philosopher (for Strauss) or the man of absolute wisdom, the sage, who dwells in the eternity of the *logos* (for Kojeve) and society that determines the meditation on the city, thus the meaning of "political philosophy." Despite their differences, which can be traced to Hegel, these two thinkers push each other to think outside of modern categories and dichotomies. In this sense, Strauss and Kojeve form a trio with Carl Schmitt: the critique of modernity is a trialogue where the recourse to Hobbes and Hegel is decisive, that is, it determines the nature of the alternatives to modern liberalism. Despite ideological differences, and whether they chose Hobbes or Hegel, all three thinkers share the same concern about a contemporary world that does not encourage men in living a life worthy of the name. But Strauss reveals the contradictions of Schmitt and Kojeve: just as decisionism becomes nihilism, the universal and homogenous state makes inexplicable how someone like Kojeve could be possible.

More radical than the opposition between Marxism and capitalism is the opposition between Ancients and Moderns. This opposition, in light of which one can say that Marxists share with the adherents of liberalism most of the essential presuppositions of modern thought, is the opposition between, on the one hand, the foundations of modern right and the Enlightenment ideal of civilization, and, on the other hand, the definition of man and the status of philosophy that follow from a return to the Ancients or the revival of pre-modern thought. More profound than the opposition between Soviet totalitarianism and representative or liberal democracy is the opposition between a certain attempted reconciliation of theory and practice and the idea of a conflict between the philosopher or sage and the rest of mankind.

Philosophy and Politics

The most important passage in the *Hiero* is that where the tyrant expresses his fear of the philosopher.[37] The tyrant "fears . . . the brave and the just because their virtues or virtuous actions might bring about the restoration of freedom or at least of nontyrannical government."[38] Strauss, who thinks that Xenophon is suggesting that "the same experience which Socrates had had under a democracy would have been had by him under a monarchy,"[39] analyzes this suspicion as the result of a lack of understanding of wisdom. This ignorance signifies that it is not only because the sage can be a tyrant that he is an object of suspicion for other men.[40] Similarly, "Simonides' refraining from acting like a man who wants to do away with a tyrant, or to deprive him of his power, is the decisive reason for the change in Hiero's attitude [toward Simonides]."[41] But that does not mean that the problem evoked by Strauss has disappeared.

The theme of this work is liberty. There cannot be liberty if men of knowledge are condemned. And power is threatened by the philosophers, because their manner of counseling the tyrant to be benevolent in order to be loved is ironic. The philosophers address themselves to political men, in particular to tyrants, in awareness that they are not dealing with wise men and in pretending to adopt their cynicism. But, as with Simonides, they do not dissimulate completely their superiority nor their awareness that tyranny, however benevolent, is not liberty and that the tyrant, even if benevolent, is not just. Simonides reminds us of Socrates. This interpretation, which emphasizes the tension between philosophy and the city and evokes the status of political philosophy, is already a refutation of the philosophy of Kojeve.

Kojeve understands immediately that he must respond to Strauss's nonpolemical views, which constitute a devastating attack against the Hegelian dialectic. Kojeve wants to demonstrate that if the advice of Simonides is to amount to anything more than utopian or "general" or "abstract ideas," it is necessary that "whoever is a master of discourse or 'dialectic' . . . become master of the government."[42] Philosophers should take power: they will allow government "to be better because of a relative absence of *prejudices* and the relatively more concrete character of [their] thought."[43] Moreover, he will encounter less resistance, because his thought is in step with the march of history: "[He] knows that what has to be reformed or opposed is nothing but 'prejudices,' that is to say something unreal and hence relatively unresistant."[44]

The philosopher, the enlightened conscience of the spirit of his times, is able to bring about what other men wish for, but in an unconscious and abstract manner and while still adhering to certain prejudices. Kojeve states in the conclusion that what he has supposed right from the outset of "Tyranny and Wisdom" is that there is no fundamental opposition between philosophy and the rest of mankind, but simply a different degree of consciousness. Kojeve is a child of the Enlightenment: liberty is desired by all, and everyone, whether consciously or not, is working toward it. The only obstacle, as in Marxist ideology, is the dominant class, which wants things to stay the same. This obstacle, along with the necessity of enlightening the proletariat, justifies recourse to violence. Kojeve is consistent when he suggests that in Marxism, there are no major obstacles to this liberation that forms part of the movement of history. Strauss, on the contrary, does not think that liberty and truth are desired by everyone. Tyranny can mean a soft and orderly servility that characterizes not only a particular social class, but all individuals.

Kojeve is incapable of understanding modern tyranny because he considers the teaching of Hegel as definitive. He has emphasized the superiority of ancient to contemporary thinking, but he rejects the solution of the classics to the fundamental problems.[45] When he speaks of governmental action of which the philosopher is the master,[46] he supposes that the qualities of the philosopher are the same as those of the man of action. The philosopher simply has more adequate rhetoric and a greater consciousness of what is required by the historical situation. He doesn't reject simply the classics, but rather their ideas. The thought of the Ancients is inaccessible to him.

Kojeve, who speaks here only of the philosopher, not the sage, short-circuits the Aristotelian distinction between the intellectual virtues, cultivated with excellence by the philosopher through contemplation, and the virtues specific to political deliberation. He disregards the distinction between theoretical wisdom (*épistémè*) and practical reason and tends to graft the thought of the philosophers (thus all thought other than that of absolute knowledge) onto technical or poetic reason, which according to Aristotle does not entail the formation of a certain character (*ethos*). The mastery of the emotions is not necessary for the work of *technikos* or artists. The criteria for distinguishing these modes of reason are linked to their object. *Épistémè* is related to objects that cannot be other than they are—nature (*physis*)—while practical reason and *techne* are concerned about what can be otherwise, whether because it is an artifact made by man, or, like the judiciary and the police, it concerns future contingencies. The understanding of those things that can be otherwise requires a particular *ethos* or attitude, but it also perhaps marks the difference between the virtuous man and the political man.

Unlike morality or the private conduct of man, which concerns his own well-living, politics, or the art of guiding *others*, requires prudence. It is the virtue specific to politics that distinguishes certain men who are able to deliberate and to choose the best moment and means for action. Good politicians are not necessarily great philosophers, and moral qualities are not sufficient to make good heads of state. And Kojeve says nothing about the formation of the character required to be the head of a just state or about the capacity to direct other men that allows this head of state to be effective. Does he think along Hegelian lines that the encounter between a man and an epoch suffices to shape a statesman who is a providential man that history in its rationality cannot fail to bring forward?

The major obstacle to the understanding of pre-modern thought but also modern tyranny is the religion of history, which is more complex in Kojeve than in most historicists. Kojeve recognizes the superiority of classical to contemporary thought, which demonstrates a naive conception of the relation between thought and action. He is conscious of Plato's *Seventh Letter* and notices the silence of Hiero after Simonides has described to him the good tyranny. Finally, he is contemptuous of the social science of his time, which is unable to understanding modern tyranny and what is really at stake in politics. The problem is that he denies that this is the inevitable outcome of modern philosophy. According to him, present-day social science is merely "the inevitable product of the inevitable decay of that modern philosophy which has refused to learn the decisive lesson from Hegel."[47]

Kojeve cannot accept the classical solution to the fundamental problems and cannot "return" to Socrates because "he regards Hegel's teaching as the genuine synthesis of Socratic and Machiavellian (or Hobbeian) politics . . ."[48] In other words, he "regards unlimited technological progress and universal Enlightenment as essential for the genuine satisfaction of what is human in man."[49] Nonetheless, this belief in history gives birth to a form of tyranny that is more violent than classic tyranny on which it depends. "But in the absence of absolute rule of the wise on the one hand, and on the other hand of a degree of abundance that is possible only on the basis of unlimited technological progress with all its terrible hazards, the apparently just alternative to aristocracy open or disguised will be permanent revolution, i.e., permanent chaos in which life will be not only poor and short but brutish as well."[50]

In the face of this alternative, liberal democracy represents for Strauss a wiser choice and one more in accord with classical thought. The regime of representation, which assumes that not everyone is capable to conduct affairs of state, is in effect closer than one might think to the ancient conception of aristocracy.

But if liberal democracy is opposed to the philosophy of history that seeks to eliminate the gap between theory and practice through revolution, can one nevertheless really say that the break between liberal democracy and communism is a radical one? While one returns to the Ancients in order to protect the meaning of political liberty that it is the vocation of liberal democracy to defend, this does not mean that there is not a difference with ancient thought that both liberal democracy and communism have in common. This brings us back to the quarrel of Ancients and Moderns and the foundation of all modern political thought on modern natural right and the Enlightenment ideal of civilization. It is important to examine the foundation that communism and capitalism have in common in order to see how the former, which condemns the economic and political exploitation perpetuated by the latter, never really puts in question the principal presupposition of modern thought.

It is in expounding Strauss's interpretation of the thinker who is considered the apostle of modern liberty and the defender of the right to property that we will be able to see at the same time what makes the Ancients so inaccessible to the Moderns and what makes the history of modern political thought an oscillation between the defense and the condemnation of liberalism. It is as if the contradictions of capitalism, the failure and then the end of ideologies, were the admission of a profound crisis of modern political thought. It is as if liberal democracy was itself afflicted by a sickness that radically distanced it from its essence and made it susceptible to modern tyranny, whether because it is vulnerable to dictatorship or because it is threatened from the inside.

Locke's Liberalism

In making self-preservation the first need and thus the fundamental right of man, John Locke extends the teaching of Hobbes and opposes the tradition, whether the Greeks, Cicero, or Christianity, in particular Thomism. Locke's natural law doctrine is different from that of Hooker, the protestant disciple of Aquinas. As with Hobbes, natural right is prior to the law of nature and to civil obligation. Reason itself is not prudence,[51] and Locke aims to oppose political tyranny otherwise than through *phronesis*. The problem for Locke is to expand on Hobbes's teaching while rejecting the solution of absolutism. In order to do this, he will interpret the state of nature differently than Hobbes, which will lead him in the *The Second Treatise of Government* (1690) to a doctrine where property and political liberty are inseparable and to replace the question of the best regime with a reflection on government and representation.

What makes Locke a Modern and leads Strauss to consider his philosophy as akin to that of the materialist and atheist natural philosophers, if not to exaggerate his "atheism,"[52] is his rejection of nature as a source of value. As is evident from Locke's conception of the right of property and his labor theory of value, it is man, not nature, who creates value.[53] This theory, which, at the very same time, prepares capitalism and the Marxist critique of the exploitation of man by his fellow man, is central to the *Second Treatise*. It goes hand in hand with a conception of the barrenness of nature.[54] The evolution of money and interest rates, where Locke encourages a commercial society based on an expansion of finance that the political authorities should support, invites an examination of the relationship between the social economic and political conditions of liberalism. Locke's constitutionalism and his defense of liberty thus must be understood in light of the individualist conception of man that underlies his thought. Locke does not avoid the contradictions of liberalism. The study of his thought allows us to see the contrasting strengths and weaknesses of liberalism, the former relating to the defense of political liberty and the latter to liberal economy. And this essential link between the economy, morality, politics, and society as well as the tensions in liberalism are understandable beginning from the Lockean conception of the state of nature and the natural law.

Man as understood by Locke is simpler and poorer than in Hobbes, where he is driven by the desire for power. If hunger is what threatens man in the first place in the state of nature, the evil that must be fled from is not linked to other men. The state of nature in Locke is not defined in the first instance by fear, and man is even more alone than in Hobbes. He is distant from his fellows and relates only to his own body and the natural world. This conception allows Locke to attribute the rights of man to the isolated individual. And the first right that follows from the necessity of self-preservation is the right to appropriate the food that one needs. The man who is hungry picks the fruits he sees and eats them. This appropriation is legitimate and does not require the consent of others. The right to property belongs to the individual alone and is prior to the establishment of society. Property is natural, not conventional. It is linked to the need of self-preservation, not to political justice. It is not a social right.

This fundamental right is an attribute of the individual alone. Man is a worker-owner. The relationship between man and nature is defined through work, and it is by his work that man becomes an owner, without this right being constrained by law. This conception has important implications if one only thinks of Marx's definition of man in terms of work. But the opposition between Lockean thought, which is emblematic of economic liberalism, and the critiques of those whom he calls "quarrelsome and contentious" because they argue that the law should control the right to property in the name of what we would call today social justice, is obvious.

According to Locke, justice and political institutions should guarantee property and encourage the productivity of those who exploit nature. When he elaborates the two obligations that are to limit the right of property, namely to avoid waste when one takes more than one can consume and not to threaten the survival of humanity by preventing other human beings from having access to resources, Locke is still defending a philosophy as much oriented toward political economy and the defense of utility as toward the respect of the rights of man. The principal form of property is the earth. He who works the land and becomes a landowner does not commit a theft, because in making it yield more than in its natural state, he *adds* something. He gives to humanity the fruits of earth that owe their existence to his work. His exploitation is not merely legitimate, but is necessary for the survival of humanity. Property even permits men to be independent of the community and gives them the leisure required for virtue.[55] Finally, from the moment that money[56] permits wealth to be stored in a form that does not spoil, the natural right of the individual to property has no limits, because waste is avoided.

Money, which is a convention, requires an agreement among individuals, so that, from the state of nature, one sees society born. Society that comes into being before the state is characterized by economic exchange. Individuals are united by economic interests in a society oriented toward utility. Work is but the beginning of the institution of property, its origin, which means that property becomes separate from the right of the worker and attaches to the fruits of his work. A legitimate owner can be someone who lives by selling goods that conserve their value when exchange is free and when the disposable wealth of society is in circulation. The worker is not harmed because the specific character of his work is the production of value and not the right to property itself. And what belongs to property is the conservation of that value. Thus in deindividualizing work, in considering it as the quantity of labor of the society as a whole, Locke "embodies that moment when liberalism becomes fully aware of its foundation in the individual right to property."[57] This is the ultimate implication of the establishment of a society based on the right to self-preservation as the first "sacred" law of nature.

The predominant strand of this development of individualism is the consecration of the egoist passions. In the absence of a *summum bonum* or moral direction for man, each individual is preoccupied with the avoidance of hunger, poverty, and insecurity in order to live freely, comfortably, and in peace. One sees clearly what divides the individualism of Locke, which is constitutive for his liberalism and makes comprehensible the transition from natural right to political economy, and the thought of Kant. As Marx said, the categorical imperative puts in question the capitalist exploitation of man, while Locke's theory of rights requires that one endorses it. The liberalism of Locke is not simply a defense of human rights. Political liberty is the very condition of economic liberty and an incentive for individual initiative, considered to be advantageous for the entire society.[58]

Locke's constitutionalism is closely linked to this individualist conception and to the orientation of liberalism toward political economy. When he says that the state of nature is not a state of war but rapidly deteriorates into one and that laws are needed to settle disputes between individuals, he makes the institutions of politics the guardians of property. The role of the law is not to educate the citizens to virtue. Of course, according to Locke, individuals are not vicious and their passions seem moderate. In fact, their spirit of independence is tempered by their need for security. Besides, the substitute for wisdom in a system where the end of politics is not virtue, but the pursuit of utility, is the guarantee of freedom and civil peace. The end of men and government is happiness. Political power is representative of the people and has their trust. This indicates a kind of consent that reflects the cautious, calculating spirit of a man entrusting a bank with his deposit.[59] Locke's system is "judicious," but was Swift not right to compare his regime to that of Lilliput?

Far from being oriented toward human excellence, the Lockean regime encourages the allure of acquisitiveness, that is, economic competition and the restlessness that consists in working more and more or dedicating one's time and energy to the acquisition of material goods, which, as Tocqueville said, flood the soul with small and vulgar pleasures.

The consequence of this individualism and materialism is that people no longer tend to their souls or cultivate that which makes them human, rather than merely industrious beasts. Leisure, one of the advantages that property was supposed to provide, is lacking for these men who are looking only, in their free time, to entertain themselves, because, as Marx said, the man who is alienated in work is also alienated in leisure. Free time, where human beings are no longer subject to necessity (to work in order to live) is merely a means for restoring the energy necessary to work or for satisfying animal needs. Man remains prisoner of his needs. And what is true of the assembly line worker is equally true of the businessman, who is no more internally free than the laborer. The difference is merely that the latter does not have the means to vary his pleasures, while the rich man, thanks to the products offered by the consumer society and commodity fetishism, he can choose his escapism *à la carte*, giving him the illusion of being an interesting man. But the most serious danger is that human beings will lose interest in the public sphere: "the place of government is almost empty. If, at this critical moment, an ambitious, able man comes to take possession of power, he finds the way open to every usurpation."[60]

How does Locke, in his theory of power, avoid the risk of usurpation? How is it that the representatives of the people really represent citizens and deliberate in their stead without robbing them of their sovereignty? Is representation not that which confers its unity upon a people, or does the nation preexist the representative? And how, in that case, to take into account the diversity of opinions and interests while embodying political unity? These questions, which are ours today, are at the heart of Locke's constitutionalism.

The transfer of all rights to an absolute sovereign according to Locke worsens the state of war. On the other hand, Rousseau's rejection of popular representation is incompatible with the foundation of political theory in Locke on the right to property and the commercial society that must be supported for the good of all. Citizens should be able to tend to their affairs in peace and accumulate goods and wealth. The solution is to institute a supreme power that has a right to require obedience and that represents the members of society: it speaks in their name without destroying their rights. It thus should itself be subject to the laws that it enacts. This is the role of the sovereign and representative legislative body. The latter should not always be in session; otherwise, its own interest might become separated from those of the common good. But "the laws must be continuously applied. Hence the necessity of another power subordinate to the first, the executive power."[61] The latter should be equally charged with adapting the laws to different situations that cannot be predicted ex ante, and this is the logic of the prerogative accorded to it. Finally, Locke calls the federal power the third power, which is concerned with external relations. Most of the time, this domain is confided to the executive for reasons of convenience[62] and perhaps because, in principle less important than the legislative and subordinate to it, it in fact embodies the unity of the people and the greatness of the nation.

The legislative power is linked to the natural desire for self-preservation. It is thus the natural site for national representation. But it is the civil executive that, because it is irreducible to the law, embodies "the essence of man's political condition."[63] This paradox explains in part that we have a strong executive. It arises from the tension between economic interests, the foundation of society and the cause of its heterogeneity, and the idea of the nation, which transcends these interests and the divisiveness they engender. Finally, because the modern representative body, unlike the Athenian assembly or the Roman senate, "confines itself to the law and leaves action to the executive, its deliberation is always radically incomplete."[64] But is it necessary to believe that the link between deliberation and action, which is essential to political direction, will carry the day in the executive power? Does the slowness of decision making in our democracies explain itself exclusively through the tension between representation and politics? Or, rather, is the impotence of politics the consequence of a more profound malady that is correlative to the dominance of the economy but not identical to it?

The Contemporary Form of Tyranny

It is as if the real site of decision making is neither the executive nor the legislature and that it eludes citizens and peoples and even most states. The role of the representatives tends to be limited to the competent management of middle-level policies, the more or less equitable or unpopular defense of the groups or corporations that compose civil society. One doesn't forget to conjure up the symbolism of a glorious past and to bring together, on the occasion of a public holiday, a people composed of the aggregation of individuals who live removed from their fellow citizens and which the uniformity of society discourages or crushes. Parliamentarism, impotence of the executive, and the defects of the constitutionalist regime are perhaps not simply systemic faults. Along the same lines, if money rules, if the important decisions for a country, a continent are taken without any social, moral, or political consideration and solely for economic reasons, this is not essentially attributable to capitalism. The conflict between capitalism and communism, the condemnation of the political economy produced by liberalism, from which its most passionate adversaries borrow their vocabulary and their morality, do they not get both the diagnosis and the remedy wrong?

The contemporary form of tyranny, which affects capitalism and communism alike, is it not linked to the fundamental choice made by the West in the first wave of modernity? The rule of money, the autonomous development of technology and the subordination of politics to economics are the manifestations of the new tyranny. It is permanent and universal, global, because it benefits from modern means of communication and the integration of science and technology. Yet is this not simply the logical implication of the establishment of society on the basis of self-preservation? If one grounds the laws on individualism, if they are not understood as educating human beings, assisting them in achieving an end that is higher than mere preservation, then how can one avoid the instrumentalization of politics and its subordination to economic growth alone, which is something that in itself has no limit?

How, beginning from such a philosophical basis, is it possible to establish a limit not only to the exploitation of men by other men, but also to the transformation of men through biotechnology? Of course, one could introduce bioethics committees, but precisely because one consigns the problem to ethics and the argument advanced for limiting the application of certain technologies is human dignity understood as the autonomy of the subject means such that authorities are destined not to be effective. And it is not because these questions have an ethical dimension that they should be relegated to ethics, understood as a separate realm.

In political philosophy, ethical questions are *integrated* within reflection on the good life and the meaning of human excellence. This reflection ought to be at the center of political debate. Politics cannot exclude the philosophical or Socratic questioning, which is the constant and timeless reminder of this reflection on where the laws, but also science and technology, are related to the meaning of human life and living well. When human excellence no longer constitutes the horizon of the laws, the laws lose their educative and symbolic function that supposes the gap between what is and what ought to be, the rejection of relativism, the reestablishment of the notion of duty, and the ontological priority of positive legal obligation to right. But this affirmation of political philosophy requires a philosophical revolution, because it is a matter of claiming that man is not in the first instance freedom and instead thinking man in terms of his *telos*.

After all, beginning from the foundations of modern political thought, it became impossible to justify a government preventing the modification of human nature "for the sake of man," the conservation of whose life is considered as a sacred law, an end that transforms cloned embryos into mere means from which one can harvest organs usable by other human beings who will rejuvenate their skin and be able to stay longer on the pleasure market. How, starting from such a ground, to avoid capitalism, better adapted to individualism than collectivism, becoming the sole model of society? The mistake would be to think that it is the origin of the evil rather than simply the logical conclusion of political individualism. Similarly, the disappearance of the political and its replacement by the total state that coincides with the era of technology is a logical consequence of the definition of the political relation by the egoistic passions of the individual, which in principle have no limit, except that imposed by nature on a mortal being. The freedom of the individual is to conquer nature, to transcend it, to defy it more and more and at any price, without any consideration for generations to come and for other peoples, without any consideration for other species, and with a frenzy or a religion of the moment, living for instant gratification.

The work of Strauss is, in its critique of historicism, relativism, and the deconstruction of modernity in three waves, but also in its study of pre-modern texts, an attempt to understand that it is possible to reconsider the foundations of our society. It is a matter of supplementing liberalism, which has allowed the promotion of subjective rights—of which Strauss does not contest the legitimacy but only the absoluteness—by the idea that the end of man is not reduced to his preservation. And, without thinking in terms of the ideal of a perfect society imposed by force or history, Strauss suggests that the remedy is in the first place internal. One must support philosophy, because it is the modern definition of man itself that is necessary to contest and to rectify. Only through the exercise of philosophy can one put in question the modern definition of man in terms of egoistic passions and self-preservation.

To the revolutionary action of Kojeve, Strauss prefers pedagogical action. The modesty of this task is merely apparent when one recalls that the most violent attacks against liberal democracy and the West have come from within the West, from Communists and Nazis. Independently of whatever Nazism owes to the personality of Hitler, it reflects the meaning of the third wave of modernity. It takes to its highest point the crisis of rationality, because the questioning of reason and the nostalgia for a pre-modern ideal are turned against reason, in a rage to destroy that applies to everything, including religious and cultural traditions.

Nihilism According to Nietzsche and after Nietzsche

Friedrich Nietzsche challenges rationality through putting in question the entire history of philosophy. There is a continuity between Rousseau and Nietzsche.[65] However, for these two thinkers, the cause of man's denaturing is not the same, and the word "nature" does not have the same meaning. For Nietzsche, it is a matter of affirming life, which is Will to Power, joy, and innocence. This does not exclude the idea of domination over others, which is absent from the Rousseauian ideal of happiness. Besides, the search for natural man supposes opposition to Christianity, understood as nihilism. The transvaluation of values envisaged by Nietzsche requires that one abandon all moral determination of man and all providence.

This characterization of the Nietzschean project of transvaluation of values does not resolve all the difficulties in his critique of modernity, nor does it hide the ambivalence of this critique. In order to address the issue of Nietzsche's responsibility for irrationalism and even Nazism, one must first understand his thought. What is his diagnosis of nihilism, and what is it that makes him our contemporary, first among the thinkers of the third wave of modernity? What are his assumptions? Did he succeed in transcending nihilism, as he claimed to do with his theory of the Eternal Return? Finally, is he, as Heidegger said, the last of the metaphysicians? And what of his attempt to "repeat antiquity at the peak of modernity"?[66] Is it a failure, because Nietzsche is still too modern to have access to the Ancients?

There are the relevant questions for an examination of nihilism according to Nietzsche and after him. Nihilism means at the same time the nihilism that he diagnoses and seeks to transcend and that which he accelerates. His return to antiquity in fact leads to a definition of man even more distanced from the Greek conception than that of his predecessors. His repetition of antiquity is a radicalization of modernity. It is the demonstration of the limits of Greek *philosophy* and is accompanied, as with Heidegger, by a new determination of being that Strauss counters with a return to Socrates.

The Repetition of Antiquity at the Peak of Modernity

Strauss devoted only one of his writings to Nietzsche[67] despite a fascination with Nietzsche that lasted from the time he was twenty-two to the time he was thirty.[68] In studying Spinoza and Hobbes, which allowed him to "understand better certain aspects of Heidegger and Nietzsche"[69] that he had not grasped from reading their own works, he saw that Nietzsche's suppositions were those of the Moderns. Nietzsche is right to want to return to the Greeks, but his interpretation of Socrates is wrong. He cannot return to the Greeks, even to the pre-Socratics, because he shares with those he rejects a certain number of preconceptions inherited from Christianity: he is paradoxically too Christian and too moral to succeed in transcending nihilism and embracing the natural man, who is the Greek man.

Nietzsche says that nihilism is of Christian origin, because Christian morality is life denying. The message of Christ, denatured by the depiction of Christ on the cross, is the expression of a cruelty and a vengeance that have transformed men into sublime aborted creatures, moral invalids.[70] Nietzsche calls for liberation from the "Judeo-Christian hope for a *providentia particularis*."[71] That which can bear the heaviness of the thought of the abyss and want to repeat it all, without hope of reward in the beyond and without believing in the resurrection of the body, is the one who will give men back faith in themselves. Having understood the teaching of Zarathustra, he could be called the Overman. But it is not certain that this "yes" to everything is really neutral. Moreover, "what is ambivalent in the Nietzschean doctrine of the Eternal Return . . . is the extraordinary pathos that is necessary for him to justify a truth that had been asserted calmly and without emphasis by the Greeks; in this—and this alone—he reveals to what extent he is in negative relation to the Christian hope of *providentia particularis*."[72]

Nietzsche betrayed his own intention to repeat antiquity because he was the prisoner of his polemic with Christianity and of certain modern notions such as the Will to Power. This becomes the will to will, without the possibility of reconciliation between Nietzsche and the philosophy of the eighteenth century. Nietzsche is the heir not only of the Protestantism of Luther, who left his mark on the modern doctrine of subjectivity, but also of the Christianity of St. Paul, where Christ is the end of the Law.[73] The will that desires itself leads to the era of technology and the exaltation of force by the individual who acts solely in order to feel his own power. This sickness of European man is the ultimate result of Christianity.

But if the determination of the essence of man and the world as Will, which culminates with Schopenhauer, is of Judeo-Christian, not Greek, origin, this means that the accomplishment of metaphysics does not only lead back to the Greek beginning of the thought, but that one needs a philosophy of life that avoids the reactive Will to Power. Will the doctrine of the Eternal Return, which Nietzsche presents as an antidote to the death of God, be able to avoid the *circulus vitiosus deus*?[74] Is the philosophy of life really beyond good and evil? And is it true that after the death of God and the risk that man himself steps into this void to establish the rule of technology, "only a God can save us now," that there is a divide that separates the faith in the God of Abraham, Isaac, and Jacob from the Dionysos of Nietzsche? What must one think of the will to eternity that gives the world a value that Christianity had refused it: Does it not "[make] atheism religious"?[75]

Strauss picks up the reflection of Nietzsche on the kind of man who corresponds to the final form of nihilism, and he takes up his critique of Christianity as an obstacle to true thought. Strauss and Nietzsche agree on the manifestations of nihilism but their diagnoses of its origins and meaning are different. The mention of St. Paul in the struggle of Nietzsche against Christianity is more important than the notion of Law—of which Christ, for the apostle, is the end—that is at the heart of Strauss's thought. It is on the basis of this notion that Strauss connects the Greeks with the medieval Jewish and Muslim philosophers and that leads him to consider Christianity as a phenomenon of modernity. The quarrel between the Ancients and Moderns becomes more complex and turns into the quarrel between, on the one side, Athens and Jerusalem, and on the other, Christianity and the Moderns.

For Nietzsche, the constitutive character of the Law in Judaism is the result of denaturing, of a Will to Power turned on itself. Judaism and Christianity, which display a degree of cruelty toward oneself that makes the latter more questionable than the faith of Moses, are his targets. Their destruction is the condition of the possibility of the transvaluation of values that Nietzsche seeks to deploy with the aim of transcending nihilism. For Strauss, on the contrary, the Law is not a symptom of the decline of the West, and it was not fulfilled by Christianity. It should be rethought as a structure or a whole in order to understand the crisis of our times, which is a crisis of political philosophy, and to estimate the role and responsibility of the moderns and Christianity in contemporary nihilism. This notion of Law allows Strauss to claim that Nietzsche failed in his return to the Greeks and that, rather than transcending nihilism, he radicalized modernity.

The Law as Denaturing and the Religious Atheism of Nietzsche

This denaturing of God and history that led to the Jewish transvaluation is, according to Nietzsche, an inversion of the relation between the covenant and justice, and it implies the turning on itself of the Will to Power. It is the reaction of the Jews to their plight after the destruction of the Second Temple and the conquest of Jerusalem by the armies of Nabuchadnezzar. The result of this denaturing is the birth of Judaism as Law. The priests falsified the Bible in translating the history of Israel into religious terms and in moralizing everything. The consequence is the subordination of all aspects of life to a single Law. The Will to Power turned against itself, and the introduction of anti-natural values is what Judaism has in common with this "creation of resistance or priestly values that constitutes the true birth of Europe."[76] The Jewish priest, the true originator of Christianity, is the inventor of the force of resistance.

If one agrees with Nietzsche on the causes of nihilism, one thinks the doctrine of the Eternal Return, far from being just one more religion, is a life-enhancing philosophy that allows one to escape from sanctimonious values and resentment. The Law, the result of denaturing, must be fulfilled and transcended. But it is not certain in these circumstances that Christianity is *in principle* more nihilistic than Judaism, even if the emphasis on the unity of humanity or the brotherhood of men before God, charity, and the "demonization" of pride contributes in *fact* to the development beyond the Jewish Law of the moral conscience and individual guilt. It may well be the case that the vehemence of the Nietzschean critique is inspired by contempt for a morality that weakens the strong and permits the weak to triumph. Nevertheless, the harm is not born with Christianity: the denaturing began with the birth of Judaism as Law. In reality, what Nietzsche cannot bear is the type of man that Christianity has engendered: "a smaller, almost ridiculous type, a herd animal, something eager to please, sickly, and mediocre has been bred—the European of today—."[77]

It is because Christianity promotes values that are those of the last man, who is a pacifist and more democratic than the priestly Jews, that Nietzsche singles it out as his main target. This link between Christianity and the "last great slave uprising" that begins with the French Revolution leads him to be enraged. The values of Christianity make men effeminate and are the cause of injustice: there is an inversion of values because the strong are weakened while the weak, victorious, drag Europe toward decline. Finally, Christianity represents a particularly heightened degree of religious cruelty: it is not living beings but the strongest instincts of man, his nature, that have been sacrificed to God. The Christian derives a perverse satisfaction from this sacrifice. Nietzsche attacks this abomination and thinks that Christianity leads to the sacrifice of God to nothingness. It leads to the death of God, and the death of God leads to the last man or the superman.

Nietzsche seeks to transform the idea that God is dead into a living truth. The overman is he "who has not only come to terms and learned to get along with whatever was and is, but who wants to have what was and is repeated into all eternity . . ."[78] If one accepts Nietzsche's diagnosis of nihilism, understood as the denaturing of man that begins with Judaism, which is radicalized in Christianity and reduces man to a midget because he is too moral, then one thinks that the doctrine of the Eternal Return is not a new religion but a life philosophy. If, like Strauss, one thinks that nihilism is not linked to the Will to Power turned on itself, but rather that the human will is cut off from all reflection concerning its ends and on its nature, then one will say that Christianity has some responsibility for nihilism because it obscured the meaning of the Law as a totality and made faith the guiding principle and the criterion of the good, the fine, and the true. In that case, the doctrine of the Eternal Return is a religious atheism. It is unsure whether it will allow for the transcendence of nihilism and avoid the emergence of its most extreme forms. Does it not prepare a nihilism where everyone is able to obey his own god or demon?

The Radicalism of the Straussian Critique of Christianity

For Strauss, it is not resentment but the forgetfulness of the meaning of the Law and of the understanding of politics in terms of the question of the good life that leads the West to self-destruction. Christianity has a share of the responsibility for nihilism. Contrary to appearances, Strauss's critique of Christianity is more radical than that of Nietzsche. For Nietzsche, Christianity is merely a form of hostility to reality, a more abstract form of existence even than Judaism. His polemical tone should not conceal the fact that it is the same logic that goes from Judaism to Christianity to the French Revolution. This history, which is that of a "long error," encompasses Socrates-Plato, Jesus, and all the philosophers, with the exception of Nietzsche. Zarathustra alone can deliver us from nihilism. For Strauss, by contrast, there is a break between Judaism and Christianity. To speak of the Judeo-Christian is incoherent.

There is thus, for Nietzsche, a continuity between Judaism and Christianity, but the latter is crueler and nastier than the transvaluation of values accomplished by Judaism. The solution is to affirm life, which is always Will to Power, without hiding behind the mask of religion and morality. By contrast, for Strauss, there is a radical break between the Ancients, on the one side, and the Moderns, on the other, among which he includes the three waves of modernity as well as Christianity. Socrates-Plato and Maimonides are divided from Machiavelli, Rousseau, and Nietzsche by Christianity. Christianity is the first "error." The Moderns allied themselves with the Ancients against the Christians, but they had broken with the Moderns on the basis of Christian categories: they began from the conscience and not the cosmos or nature in order to conceive being, interpreting everything in moral terms and forgetting the meaning of the Law. This deployment of Christian categories in a non-Christian way leads to a situation of crisis and even, as suggested Bernanos,[79] to a kind of diabolical inversion of Christianity.

The rule of the last man and the false prophets or the most insane dictators is not linked to the revolt against life. It is not Dionysius against Christ on the cross, but the turn to Socrates that is the solution to the problem of the crisis of the West. The latter is not a decline, a degeneration, or a weakening of man by the violence he has done to his own instincts, but it is a fleeing, a lack of substance, and a tumescence that takes him away from himself. St. Augustine used this expression to explain the dialectic of evil, the solidarity between suffering and sin and the vicious circle in which the sinner is enclosed, who goes from destruction to self-destruction. The crisis of the West resembles more a falling into hopeless and darkness than a physical malady. The ill stems from the fact that man has been estranged from his core, which is not defined, in Strauss, by God, but by philosophical questioning of which Socrates is the unsurpassable example and which culminates in the interpretation of the Law by Maimonides.

The self-destruction of the West, of which technology and contemporary irrationalism are the most obvious symptoms, results from an estrangement from what makes life worth living. This self-destruction gives rise to a loss of self-confidence of the West. This means also that the crisis gives rise to an occasion to put in question the erroneous presuppositions that have grounded the modern political and religious consciousness, the relations of men with each other, to nature, to their nature, and to life. There is the notion of a return to the Greek origins.

This does not mean the pre-Socratics: Plato and Socrates were not the first "errors." Metaphysics is not the source of the problem. It is not the onto-theo-logical structure that explains how modern rationalism is a destruction of reason, because there were examples from the Greeks to Maimonides and to Jacobi of a rationalism welcoming to Revelation—and to revealed religion.

To get out of the crisis, it is thus necessary to examine the presuppositions that originate from Christianity. It is not the *content* of the difference between ancient and modern natural right that is at stake, but rather the status of the Law, which encompasses the totality of life. For this structure, which is irreducible to the individual consciousness, tends to disappear in modern right at the same time as the symbolic value of the laws. It is replaced by the morality of respect and the religion of love. Christianity as the end of the Law cannot but lead to the death of political philosophy and its replacement by modern political thought and ethics. The latter represents a separate discipline, because the question of the ends of man has been carved off from political reflection. The emergence of ethics as a separate discipline and the reduction of religion to morality are the consequences of Christianity. Strauss's distance from Christianity interests *us* because when seeking to reopen the quarrel of the Ancients and Moderns and to confront modern with ancient rationalism, the Christian mode of thinking does not allow us to recover what has been forgotten. Strauss's objection is not to Christianity as a religion but to the categories it introduced into philosophy. More radical than a return to ancient natural right and to nature, which could well be achieved on Christian terms, the return by Strauss to Socrates and Maimonides is a way of rethinking the concept of Law and of reaffirming political philosophy.

Chapter 3

Political Philosophy as First Philosophy

The Return to Socrates

"It is not self-forgetting and pain-loving antiquarianism nor intoxicating romanticism which induces us to turn with passionate interest . . . toward the political thought of classical antiquity. We are impelled to do so by the crisis of our time, the crisis of the West."[1] In this return to antiquity, the emphasis is in the first place on Socrates as the founder of political philosophy. The inquiry concerning the status that Socrates conferred on political philosophy and its constant tendency to return to commonsense opinion are, according to Strauss, ways of employing the phenomenological reduction while at the same time differing from Husserl and Heidegger. The problems examined through the figure of Socrates lead to the elaboration of a political philosophy. The Straussian reduction, which is situated in the extension of the Socratic return to the opinions of the city, is the method of political philosophy and gives rise to political phenomenology. The concept of Law as elaborated by Plato and reinterpreted by Maimonides is what gives to political philosophy its determinate content.

This chapter, which elaborates the constructive contribution of Strauss to philosophy, thus focuses on his two major discoveries. The first of these allows us to understand the meaning of his return to the Ancients as a return to Socrates and demarcates the status of political philosophy. The second permits us to understand what Strauss is referring to when he speaks of the medieval Enlightenment. What is at stake is defining the task of philosophy today when, as Nietzsche said, we are at the moment of the greatest danger, and for this reason the greatest hope.[2] But the solution proposed by Strauss is in opposition to those of Nietzsche and Heidegger.

Political Philosophy as the Fulfillment of Phenomenology

Edmund Husserl explained to the young Strauss that, contrary to the thinking of the neo-Kantians, our understanding of things, including our scientific understanding, is derived from our natural understanding, our everyday understanding of the world.[3] Husserl put Strauss on the path of a phenomenological reduction that determines the task of philosophy as the transformation of opinions into knowledge. Nevertheless, Strauss will diverge from the Husserlian reduction. He will retain the notion according to which philosophy distinguishes itself from ideology or *Weltanschauung* through its concern with the pure truth, but Strauss will radicalize the phenomenological definition of the return to the things themselves. The first move brings Strauss close to Husserl, while distancing him from Heidegger. The second move permits him to see that the understanding of things cannot be simply natural. For the historicism of Heidegger, Strauss substitutes the notion of the understanding of things within the horizon of the political community, which goes back to Socratic questioning.

Strauss presents himself as concerned with the achievement of what phenomenology aspires to, once one understands fully its implications, as did the Husserl at the end of his life: in 1911, when he published his essay "Philosophy as Rigorous Science," he did not grasp the place of politics, but the distinction he would later draw between every *Weltanschauung* and philosophy "is close to constituting the contribution of Husserl to political philosophy."[4] Philosophy, conceived as rigorous science, is linked to the requirement of satisfying the highest theoretical needs in matters of ethics and religion and makes possible a life governed by purely rational norms. This aspiration was never at any time in the past fully achieved,[5] but this takes nothing away from its necessity; in its constant task of clarifying consciousness and its acts, philosophy is irreplaceable even if it will always be persecuted.[6] Philosophy transcends the "reigning naturalism" and prevents the "so-called exact psychology" from "constantly mak[ing] use of concepts that stem from every-day experience without having examined them as to their adequacy."[7]

Husserl accepted the modern separation between science and wisdom and related to philosophy the task of "render[ing] possible in regard to ethics and religion a life regulated by pure rational norms."[8] Strauss does not subscribe to this separation of science and wisdom that is the consequence of the end of political philosophy, that is, the exclusion of the question of the best way of life from political reflection. He also does not share Husserl's confidence in reason. Husserl thinks that the crisis of

Western humanity is a crisis of method.[9] The rationalism of the *Crisis of the European Sciences*, and the hope expressed there for philosophy as rigorous science, which would provide to the universal society or at least to the West rational rules of living evokes a kind of confidence that Nietzsche and the historical shocks of the twentieth century had destroyed. Strauss praises Husserl for having refused to identify philosophy to a *Weltanschauung*, which would be "some kind of system to live by" and would respond to our need of "exaltation and consolation."[10] *Weltanschauung* is the other possible solution, the alternative to philosophy. It is for the Moderns what poetry was for Socrates and Plato, that is, an imitation of the opinions of the city and—when it is controlled by the legislator—a deception for the sake of the many. Strauss equally presents himself as the defender of philosophy. But for him, philosophy is political philosophy, because the understanding of the world through sense experience as Husserl understands it is not primary but itself derivative.

Here Strauss for his own purposes takes up the Heideggerian critique of the Husserlian reduction—that it is not sufficiently radical. "The full thing is what it is not only in virtue of the primary and secondary qualities as the value qualities in the ordinary meaning of that term but also of qualities like sacred or profane: the full phenomenon of a cow is for a Hindu constituted much more by the sacredness of the cow than by any other quality or aspect."[11] Heidegger asserts that our understanding of the world is historical and opens the way to what, applied to any other philosopher, would be called his philosophy of history. It leads to an eschatology where it is a matter of rediscovering a *Bodenständigkeit* or preparing a new kind of *Bodenständigkeit* beyond the most extreme *Bodenlosigkeit*, a being at home that surpasses the most extreme lack of at-homeness. Is this solution not a *Weltanschauung*? The recourse to poetry and to a way of thinking that welcomes the *Sage* (the *Saying*)[12] responds to our need for "exaltation and consolation." It appears as a compensation for nihilism, which the discrediting of reason intensifies, but it offers no escape from nihilism. For Strauss, the critique of the Husserlian reduction implies that our understanding of the world goes back to the community from which one must start in order to philosophize: the return to the things themselves is the return to the opinions of the city.

The Socratic turn implies that the investigation of nature as a whole, thus also of man as a part of the whole, begins with the diverse opinions that are current in the city. Socrates, in his confrontation with the natural or pre-philosophical world of politics, morality, and faith, proceeds with a philosophical examination of opinions that is precisely the task of philosophy as opposed to *Weltanschauung* thinking. This life world (*Lebenswelt*) is neither the homogenous world described by Husserl nor the world of a particular historical epoch in Heidegger, but rather it is constitutively political. No science can "reach clarity about its doings if it does not possess a coherent and comprehensive understanding of what is frequently called the common sense view of political things, . . . as they are experienced by the citizen or statesman; only if it possess such a coherent and comprehensive understanding of its basis or matrix can it possibly show the legitimacy . . . of scientific understanding."[13] The commonsense understanding of political things comes first because the city is where human beings form their experience of things in general. Their opinions are the primary *data* from which it is necessary to begin, and politics is the context or horizon where all understanding arises. Science and philosophy, which will often break with the opinions of the city, are thus secondary or derivative from this foundation.

Political philosophy is first philosophy in the sense that political life is the beginning point. The phenomenological reduction is a reduction to the opinions of the city, and political phenomenology corresponds to the Socratic turn. Because it is the conscious form of the commonsense understanding of political things, classical political philosophy, which was inaugurated by Socrates and elaborated by Plato and above all by Aristotle, can serve as a refutation of the assumptions of modern political thought and social science. Political philosophy is concerned with the natural attitude and the opinions that it criticizes, but also with the results of the various sciences and, today, with the categories derived from modern philosophy. The poetry with which Socrates is in opposition is at the same time a synthesis of the opinions of the city that the philosopher is to examine and the symbol of the resistance of the city to philosophy, the institutionalization of this resistance.

The Conflict between Poetry and Philosophy

Socrates conceived of the decision to pose the "what is?" question as a return to common sense: the things that are "first in themselves" are in some sense first "for us," and "the things which are 'first in themselves' are in a manner, but necessarily, revealed in men's opinions. . . . The highest opinions, the most authoritative opinions, are the pronouncements of the laws. . . . Even Socrates is compelled to go the way from the law to nature, to ascend from law to nature. . . . He must show the necessity of the ascent by a lucid, comprehensive, and sound argument . . . by 'dialectics.' "[14] If Socratic philosophy is not science in that it supposes the knowledge of ignorance and the incompleteness of all human knowledge, if one must abandon Husserl's aspiration for philosophy as rigorous science, at the same time the wisdom in question has nothing to do with poetry. The disagreement between Socrates and the Sophists is less radical and less profound than the conflict between philosophy and poetry.[15] It is this conflict that informs the tension between the philosopher and the many in the city who decide on the laws of Athens. The representations of Socrates by Plato and Xenophon are in fact responses to the Socrates of Aristophanes's *Clouds* and *Assembly of Women*.

The works of Plato and Xenophon have among their aims that of responding to the powerful attack on philosophy by Aristophanes, who presents philosophy as speculation concerning nature and as political rhetoric and ridicules Socrates as someone who is unable to understand political matters.[16] Far from being a royal or political art, Socratic dialectic exploits the discoveries of science and interacts with the diverse society of non-philosophers. Xenophon, in his *Oeconomicus*, showed the break of Socrates with natural philosophy. The *Republic*, which is the examination of the strengths and weaknesses of rhetoric, is "the reply par excellence to Aristophanes"[17] because the philosopher plays the role of the Just Speech, like Socrates in the face of Thrasymachus. Socrates required in the name of justice that the unregulated poets be banished from the city because poetry is an obstacle to philosophical education. And this permits the individual to attain a perfection "which the city never reaches,"[18] but which it should, if it is just, encourage or at least permit. The criterion of justice is the openness of the city to philosophy.

Contrary to Aristophanes, poetry is not the key to wisdom, because the poets consecrate the passions of the many and merely imitate their opinions. Poetry belongs entirely to the city and is connected to the charm that imprisons human beings within it. This is why it is used by rhetoricians who are lacking in scientific understanding but use their skill to influence the opinions of the many. Poetry prevents human beings from taking distance from opinions that some have an interest in maintaining. "Poetry praises and blames what the city, what society, praises and blames."[19] Plato does not mean that poetry is useless. On the contrary, it has a role in the city because philosophy is not accessible to the many; the idea of justice that philosophy implies may be different from the justice that is supported by the laws. But this necessity of noble lies, which implies that poetry is necessary for persuading the multitude, in no way detracts from the fact that philosophy *should* be possible. And poetry, which imitates the opinions of the city and presents them as oracular wisdom, constitutes the greatest obstacle to the exercise of thought. In the end, its prestige and success are such that they attract the most gifted, who would be capable of becoming philosophers, to take an easier path more satisfying to their vanity, which philosophy would require them to abandon.

There is thus a problem that is not susceptible to a compromise solution: if poetry is allowed into the city, it will make it impossible to leave the cave. But this condemnation of unregulated poetry and the fact that the ideal city cannot accept it except to the extent that it is reduced to a facsimile of the opinions necessary for ordinary morality is not the last word of Plato. The poets accuse the philosophers "as bitches barking at their masters"[20] because the philosophers contest their authority. But this means as well that poetry can be the expression of truth in a form other than that of a treatise or discursive writing. Is the vocation of poetry not to serve that which, in its truth, transcends discourse, as Plato himself did in writing dialogues and in transforming, with unrivaled art of dramatization and narration, the material of traditions, mysteries, and tales?

The poetry that Plato attacks is thus a deluded poetry, complicit with the intellectual delusion of the city. The public is more a creature of habit than of taste. Poetry comforts human beings in some of their passions and some of their vices. The poetry that Plato denounces is official poetry, not because, like the other that it pretends to recognize, it serves to maintain morality, but because it is the ally of those who seek to manipulate souls. The latter, sometimes close to tyrants, are also as questionable as tyrants. In a democracy, the poets act as intermediaries between the rulers and the people. They have the greatest power that one can have in this type of society, namely, the power of public opinion, which Plato and Tocqueville observed had the potential to persecute philosophy. Official poetry is not what one thinks. It is viewed as extraordinary or original by the sophists and the media, and it comes between man and man. Finally, it serves to ridicule or to censure philosophy or any other kind of poetry that, far from being the enemy of truth, finds its place in the wisdom to which philosophy remains the key.

The old quarrel between poetry and philosophy illuminates the situation of literature in our democracies. We are dealing with a literature gone astray, far from its first vocation, which is to liberate the soul and develop sensibility in a manner not predetermined by society. The conflict between poetry and philosophy, as Plato understands it, is relevant to the cultural symptoms of the crisis of our time, that is, in fact, to the disappearance of political philosophy and to the situation of philosophy that has been split up into various domains or identified with a *Weltanschauung*. Thus the task of thought is not to invent a new philosophy, another system of philosophy that consoles or elevates us, but to reaffirm political philosophy. This is first because common sense is first and the matrix of experience is the city. Conversely, "philosophy is primarily political philosophy because political philosophy is required for protecting the inner sanctum of philosophy, which transcends the city."[21]

Wisdom and Moderation

Socrates's wisdom is inseparable from the knowledge of his ignorance. But this "is more than the insight into the worthlessness of human wisdom."[22] For Socrates "knew a great deal. He knows that for example the greatest sons of Athens, Themistocles and Pericles, did not in truth help Athens, contrary to what everyone believed."[23] Above all, Socrates "remains in the question," but this questioning is "the questioning that opens on to what is *problematic*, which is *vital*, it is questioning in order to know how one should live, questioning that concerns the just life."[24]

At the same time, Socrates knows that one cannot teach non-philosophers. He is aware of the "gap" between the few who maintain that an unexamined life is not worth living and that one should not return harm with harm, and those who maintain the contrary.[25] He sees that it is not right to address human beings in the manner of Thrasymachus, who persuades his listeners by terrifying them. This is why Socrates speaks but does not write. His dialectic art is appropriate only for gentlemen who are able to philosophize. Also, the wisdom of Socrates is inseparable from moderation. This is "the recognition of essential differences and noetic heterogeneity."[26] This finds its expression in the distinction between two ways of life: the political life and that which is higher and transcends politics. This moderation, inseparable from the limits Socrates imposes on his questioning, explains in part his attitude toward his death sentence. Aware that the city is more closed than genuinely open to philosophy, he asks whether it is not better for the Athenians to preserve their prejudices intact.[27] It would not be wise to challenge, through escaping, an authority that Socrates recognized as necessary throughout his life. Here is an indication of the paradoxical relationship of philosophy and the city: the latter is not just, and Socrates stung it like a gadfly, but his "action" did not cause him to rebel against the city or those who condemned him.

This relation between Socrates and the city of Athens sizes up what Strauss calls liberal education: one should not flatter democracy, but rather expose the dangers it poses for itself and for human excellence. Liberal education, which is inseparable from the Socratic way of thinking, including when we are required to create a dialogue between the great thinkers who engage in monologues and contradict each other on the most important questions, is "the counterpoison to mass culture, to the corroding effects of mass culture, to its inherent tendency to produce nothing but 'specialists without spirit or vision and voluptuaries without heart.' "[28]

Socrates is more threatened by the multitude who make the laws than by the sophists who profit from their rhetorical superiority to flatter the many. He shows that one cannot separate wisdom from moderation and thus from obedience to the laws of the city. Similarly, the consciousness of an irreducible gap between the philosopher and the city and the specific role of the former leads Strauss to reject the extremes of communism and fascism, which are temptations for those struck by the imperfections of liberal democracy: "wisdom requires loyalty to the cause of constitutionalism."[29] The political action of the philosopher is thus of an indirect nature and addresses itself to individuals or small groups rather than to society at large. But in learning to listen to "small voices" instead of "loudspeakers," liberal education "shuns the limelight"[30] and is hardly condemned to have no consequence or legacy.

As for Plato, he combines the way of Socrates—his dialectical art—with the way of Thrasymachus, who is capable of persuading those who are resistant to dialectics.[31] While the daimon of Socrates, which relates to the defensive side of his nature, prevented him from engaging in political activity and conversing with certain personages, his whole being is characterized by Eros, leading him to question himself in questioning others concerning the just life. Plato, who possesses a gift that Socrates lacks, will write texts, dialogues where, as he says in his *Seventh Letter*, he will articulate only a part of the whole. Socrates's not writing is a direct consequence of his not engaging in political activity.[32] In this sense, there is a kernel of truth in Aristophanes ridiculing Socrates for being inept at politics. Nevertheless, what is important is to grasp the Socratic legacy.

We ought to wonder that someone like Plato could have existed. Because, as for the Greeks, we should not forget, as Castoriadis observes, that they are closer to Homer than to Plato. That there is a phenomenon like the Platonic dialogues, which present the figure of Socrates and defend philosophy, is admirable. Even where the *Metaphysics* of Aristotle and the platonic theory of the forms break with the teaching of Socrates, the essential Socratic message is preserved: this concerns the status of political philosophy and the relationship between philosophy and the city. And this is what Farabi retains. The return of Strauss to political philosophy is thus a return to the Arab philosophers of the Middle Ages, whose impact on Maimonides was considerable. In effect, these philosophers who had access to the *Republic* and *Laws* of Plato but not the *Politics* of Aristotle were more sensitive than the Christian writers[33] to the Platonic politics of philosophy, that is to say the Socratic legacy.

Strauss reveals that which distances us from Socrates in Plato and above all in Aristotle in opposing it to the Socratic questioning concerning the just life as "*the questioning-together concerning the just life together in the interest of just living together*."[34] Especially toward the end of his life, Strauss gave his full effort to extracting Socrates from what hides and separates him from us. Not only the Moderns, beginning with the first wave of modernity, have closed off access to most of the questioning that was fundamental for the Ancients, but in addition they substituted their own categories, which are the root of the misreading we make of Plato and Aristotle. Strauss never ceased to turn toward thinkers who would deconstruct the modern illusions and make accessible to us the questioning of the Ancients. After all, his return to the Ancients is not driven by nostalgia or antiquarian interest, but for the sake of recovering forgotten truths. These were buried in the first wave of modernity, but they are also masked by Plato and Aristotle if we do not know how to read them. This is why it is necessary to focus on Socrates. Strauss thus turns to Maimonides and Farabi, who enlighten *us* concerning what is true in the thought of the Greeks. And to the extent that Farabi and Maimonides are confronted with the brute fact of Revelation, their Enlightenment is our Enlightenment and part of our universe, that of the Occident as determined by Athens *and* by Jerusalem. The medieval Enlightenment is particularly relevant for us. But is there a specific contribution of the Jewish and Arab Middle Ages in addition to the decisive contribution of the Greeks, or rather is the medieval Enlightenment simply a means to show the path to Socrates? In either case, the medieval Enlightenment serves as a model for the application of the wisdom of Greece to a situation, an example that we ought to imitate. For the horizon of Strauss remains that of the crisis of our times. "[A]n adequate understanding of the principles as elaborated by the classics may be the indispensable starting point for an adequate analysis, to be achieved by us, of present-day society in its peculiar character, and for the wise application, to be achieved by us, of these principles to our tasks."[35]

The Medieval Enlightenment

The Platonism of Farabi and Maimonides

The Straussian interpretation of Farabi and Maimonides is fundamentally political. The *Republic* and the *Laws* are authoritative political texts for those whom we customarily classify as Jewish and Muslim Aristotelians. Not only was the *Republic* not translated into Arabic, but this was probably a deliberate choice.[36] Revelation, which presented itself as the Law, was interpreted in the framework of Platonic political philosophy as the ideal political order. While the Christian philosophers of the Middle Ages, like St. Thomas Aquinas, thought of Christian society as governed by two powers and two different legal codes—one canonical or ecclesiastical and the other civil and temporal—the Jewish and Muslim thinkers viewed religion as a comprehensive social order. The divine Law thus governs the public and private life of the members of the community, excluding any sphere of activity where reason can be exercised independently of it. The highest science in Islam is the science of the Law (*fiqh*), the task of which is to interpret, apply, and adapt the prescriptions of the divine Law to which dialectical theology (*kalam*) is subordinated. In interpreting politically the Mosaic Law and considering in the manner of Farabi the prophet lawgiver as a philosopher king in the Platonic sense, Maimonides is able to find a home for philosophy, the condition of true perfection, in explaining the foundational and purely philosophical opinions upon which the Law is based. Wisdom is not a matter of morality but of true knowledge of God. This knowledge is neither accessible to everyone nor communicated without precaution. Also, one of the functions of the interpretation of the Law will be to show that it contains beliefs that, while not being true, are necessary for the proper ordering of the city.

By interpreting Revelation through Platonism, Farabi and Maimonides show that the study of the moral virtues is not the study of the happiness or the true end of man. Ethics does not merit the central place,[37] which belongs to true knowledge or philosophy. It is necessary for what Maimonides calls "the true Law . . . the end of this Law in its entirety is the achievement of [the] two perfections."[38] It is less a matter of the perfection of a corporal nature—health, wealth, social order—than perfection of the soul. The latter comprises moral virtues and intellectual perfection or active intelligence.[39] For Maimonides, who modified Psalm 19, verse 9 concerning the praise of the perfection of the Law of the Lord, perfection consists in acquiring, thanks to the Law and its purifying virtue, sound opinions, for example, free from idolatry, and for those who are able, true opinions as such. The latter allow human beings to "become rational in actu, I mean to have intellect in actu; this would consist in . . . knowing everything concerning all the beings that it is within the capacity of man to know in accordance with his ultimate perfection. It is clear that to this ultimate perfection there do not belong either actions or moral qualities and that it consists only of opinion toward which speculation has led and that investigation has rendered compulsory."[40]

Paradoxically, it is in "choosing" Plato, not Aristotle, with whose political thought the Jews and Arabs of the Middle Ages were familiar through *The Nicomachean Ethics*, that Farabi and Maimonides defend the idea, dear to Aristotle, according to which blessedness resides in knowledge. By contrast, Thomism is the modification of Aristotelianism under the influence of Christianity and stoicism. This modification is linked to the fact that Thomas no longer defines human excellence in terms of political life but by the knowledge of the natural law, of which God is the author. By his participation in the natural law, the individual "finds himself a member of a universal community or cosmopolis ruled by divine providence and whose justice is vastly superior to that of any human regime."[41] This transpolitical character of the Thomist doctrine goes hand in hand with the division between morality and political science, the separation between spiritual and temporal power, and the fact of judging civil society from a higher perspective embracing all nations at the limit, that is to say the kingdom of God and the redemptive grace of the Creator.[42] "[T]he very structure of Christian society, with its clear-cut distinction between the spiritual and temporary spheres, bore an obvious affinity with the restricted and somewhat independent manner in which political matters are treated in Aristotle's *Politics*."[43]

Plato in *The Republic* considers the question of the best political order and suggests that the salvation of the city depends on the coincidence between philosophy and the ruler. But to the extent that this coincidence is very unlikely and the extent to which he saw that "neither the perfect philosopher nor the perfect prince could use his acts in the nations and cities that existed in his time . . . he then began to investigate whether we should settle for the ways of life he finds among the citizens of his city or nation."[44] This inquiry is the task of the *Laws*. This work is "the principal source of the opinions that Maimonides and his teachers" had concerning the relation between philosophy and the Law.[45] It is also one of the most ironic works of Plato, as it does not disclose on the surface its entire teaching concerning perfection. Combining the pedagogy of Socrates with the method of Thrasymachus, Plato writes this work with a view to the members of the city changing their way of life and their opinions. In his *Letters*, Plato described "his own views on the form of government that should be employed" to arrive eventually at virtuous ways of living and correct laws.[46] This inquiry is the subject matter of the *Laws*. This work is "the primary source of the opinions Maimonides and his teachers held concerning the relation between philosophy and Revelation, or, more exactly, between philosophy and Law."[47]

Similarly, Maimonides wrote both the *Misneh Torah* and the *Guide*. The first work is a rehearsal of the Torah, an interpretation for those who are not perplexed, and the second is a treatise for believers who have been influenced by philosophy. But each of these works transcends in the way it is written this division between believers and perplexed people. The *Guide*, an interpretation of the Torah that is at the same time exoteric and esoteric,

> is a most ingenious combination of opinions of the people of the excellent city, i.e. of a strictly demonstrative discussion of the beliefs which are common to philosophy and Law, with a defence of the Law, i.e. with a rhetorical discussion of the unphilosophical beliefs that pertain to the Law. Thus not only the Law itself, but also Maimonides' philosophical interpretation of the Law, has two different meanings: a literal meaning, addressed to the more unphilosophic reader of philosophic education, which is very near to the traditional Jewish beliefs, and a secret meaning, addressed to true philosophers, which is purely philosophical.[48]

Maimonides finds in the *Laws* the relation between philosophy and Law that allows him to write the *Guide* and defend the Law philosophically but also to execute his work of codification. Strauss summarizes the three concepts that Maimonides and his predecessors borrowed from Plato. These allow us to understand what is meant by the medieval Enlightenment. Of Platonic provenance, they were applied to the Jewish and Muslim worlds of the Middle Ages, where religion governed all of society in such a manner that freedom of thought was compatible with the maintenance of social order. The three ideas are: "(1) Law is based on certain fundamental beliefs or dogmas of a strictly philosophical character, and those beliefs are, as it were, the prelude to the whole Law.

(2) Law contains, apart from those rational beliefs, a number of other beliefs which, while being not properly true, but representing the truth in a disguised way, are necessary or useful in the interest of the political community. (. . .) (3) Necessary beliefs," which only belong to the Law, and which "are to be defended (. . .) by probable, persuasive, rhetorical arguments, not recognizable as such to the vulgar; a special science is to be devoted to that defence of the Law."[49]

Farabi and Maimonides are men of Enlightenment; they are rationalists who defend philosophy as human perfection. This depends on the acquisition of true opinions. This acquisition is gradual and requires the entirety of the sciences.[50] The love of God entails the knowledge of the universe. Metaphysics is physics for Maimonides, which combats idolatry and any reading of the commandments that attributes to God a body and passions of the kind that human beings experience. But Maimonides also distances himself from apophatism. His rationalism and intellectualism, the fact that the wisdom concerning God is the key to understanding the divine commandments, well reflects what we call Enlightenment.

The Enlightenment of Maimonides

God does nothing that is not governed by his wisdom. It is by considering the intention or purpose of the laws that their divinity is manifest: contrary to al-Juwanyi, who puts the emphasis on the origin of the Law and tends to arbitrary obedience to the commandments, Maimonides shows that the divine commandments possess an internal rationality, a wisdom by which God intends well by human beings. The Mosaic Law of which God is the author is aimed at the perfection of man. It is for the sake of man, and it is not the means by which God manifests his omnipotence. The sacrifice of Abraham benefits Abraham and not God because God has no need to test the human heart. But it permits Abraham to try the steadfastness of his faith.

The commandments of Moses, even those that seem strange, like not mixing certain food groups, have a preventative aim: they serve to wean human beings from idolatry. Maimonides makes reference to the religion of the Sabeans, which has the features of all idolatrous cults practiced by the contemporaries of Moses.[51] He uses this religion, more or less fictitious, to contrast idolatry and the divine Law. Certain commandments, which prohibit practices that were widespread in the time of Moses and among the Egyptians, have the sole purpose of combating these practices, preventing the people from turning away from the one and only God.

The ultimate aim of the Law, the intellectual perfection of man, can only be achieved by a truly wise man. This is the meaning of the love of God. It is not emotional. Similarly, Providence[52] depends on the intelligence and prudence of the man in question: the more a man concentrates his thoughts on God, the more he purifies his soul and his image of God will be pure. This is how God exercises his Providence on men. Maimonides identifies the knowledge we have of God with the knowledge God has of us. It is one and the same illumination. This conception, which is linked to the doctrine according to which God pours his intellect into us, allows one to speak of Maimonides as an enlightened Jew. The fullest treatment of this is in his prophetology. The imagination, which can lead us to believe illusions, is not what in the first place makes the prophet superior to the philosopher. It is by his direct and immediate grasp of the divine that his whole mind and imagination are taken. Unlike the philosopher, he is able to communicate these truths to human beings in a concrete way, guide them politically, and predict the future. The prophetology of Maimonides, far from being in contradiction with his rationalism, deepens it and distinguishes it from modern rationalism.

In interpreting the commandments beginning from the principle of the wisdom of God, Maimonides in the *Guide* modifies the Jewish tradition that precedes him and combats the *kalam*. Plato and his Arab teachers, in particular Farabi, aid him in purifying Judaism of whatever is carnal and idolatrous. But at the same time, Maimonides defends the Law *philosophically* and applies the Enlightenment of Plato to Judaism and in the interests of Judaism.[53] If there are several levels of comprehension of the Torah and if the interpretation that Maimonides gives to the story of the chariot, far from mystical, tends toward the cosmological, this does not prevent him from maintaining that the purifying virtue of the Law and the concord between the end of the Law and human intellectual perfection does not orient the Enlightenment toward atheism. Does Strauss turn toward Maimonides because Plato does not allow, when he proposes the noble lie, to avoid that "dialectic of Enlightenment" where "the critique of ideals in the name of the seeking of the truth at any cost ends up in a critique of the very ideal of truth?"[54] Why did Strauss emphasize the medieval Enlightenment? Was the Greek Enlightenment not adequate to his purposes?

The way in which Maimonides explains that the Law contains opinions that are not true but that are indispensible to the life of the community recalls the minimalist credo and the *pia dogmata* of Spinoza. This approach goes back to book X of the *Laws*, where Plato shows that the role of the lawgiver is to ensure that certain beliefs concerning the gods are not propagated. The difference between Ancients and Moderns is here above all a difference between Maimonides and the successors of Spinoza, who ignored the political dimension of religion in believing in the unbounded diffusion of the truth. However, there is also a break between Spinoza and Maimonides. There is something very distinctive about the Jewish and Arab Middle Ages.

The modern Enlightenment considers that the theologico-political problem is soluble and has a conception of reason that excludes Revelation and particularly biblical Revelation. It ignores completely the third idea that Maimonides and his Islamic masters borrowed from Plato, namely the idea that there can be beliefs specific to the Law, that must be defended by a special science, where one makes use of rational argumentation but where reason is in the presence of something that transcends and requires a specific instruction akin to oral teaching and lessons addressed to a small group. The modern Enlightenment considers with Spinoza that there is nothing that cannot be grasped by reason. What the tradition refers to as the secrets of the Law are, for Spinoza and the modern Enlightenment, lies and superstition. The modern religious consciousness, favoring an internalization of the content of religion that is in part the consequence of the primacy of experience over knowledge, doesn't value these secrets, today revealed without precaution or discernment to the public in books that are above all commercially successful vulgarizations. This gives support to those skeptics who see in religion the refuge of the ignorant and weak.

It is thus a rationalism that is open to revelation (Plato) and completed by Revelation (Maimonides) that distinguishes medieval from modern Enlightenment. And this rationalism can be understood in its full depth when one studies it in light of the notion of Law as understood by the Platonic Jewish and Arab philosophers. One sees equally that the key to the medieval Enlightenment is prophetology, which takes the place of what in Platonism is a political interpretation of Greek philosophy.

The natural conditions of prophecy, the capacity of the prophet to communicate truths to the people, and the relation between imagination and intellect that characterizes the prophet constitute the most important elements of understanding that the medieval Enlightenment represents for Strauss. The awareness of the relation between theory and practice specific to the pre-modern Enlightenment depends on the examination of the status and specific qualities of the prophet. Maimonides borrows the definition that Farabi has of true perfection and practical intelligence, but, in his philosophical defense of the Law, as in his art of writing, he leaves room for the understanding of truths that do not derive from philosophy alone. Farabi is closer to an intellectualism that anticipates that of Spinoza than the Enlightenment of Maimonides, which represents the tension between Athens and Jerusalem. Not only do Farabi and Spinoza recognize the superiority of philosophy to the royal art, but in addition one may well ask whether for Farabi the philosopher is not superior to the prophet himself.

Farabi is a representative of Platonic Enlightenment, which he applies to Islam in order to defend the freedom to philosophize before the religious authorities, who are capable of persecuting philosophy where it asserts itself openly. In Maimonides, in addition to this Platonism, there is a specific dimension to medieval Enlightenment that is linked to the dual allegiance to Athens and Jerusalem. What Strauss writes concerning the *Guide* underlines the difference between Maimonides and Farabi: "Philosophers are men who try to give an account of the whole by starting from what is always accessible to man as man: Maimonides starts from the acceptance of the Torah. A Jew may make use of philosophy and Maimonides makes the most ample use of it; but as a Jew he gives his assent where as a philosopher he would suspend his assent."[55] Thus, Maimonides is the exemplary figure of medieval Enlightenment and the specific rationalism that Strauss sought to promote since his first writing on Jacobi.

What is it that allows Strauss to claim that we can obtain from a type of pre-modern thought solutions for thinking the crisis of our times and preserving liberal democracy, while there are no more prophets and philosophy of history is dangerous? Does invoking Maimonides's philosophy of Law signify a return to tradition? Or rather is the interpretation of Maimonides for Strauss the core of his elaboration of political philosophy where Maimonides serves as the "paradigm for a perfectly contemporary project?"[56] Given Strauss's paradoxical relation to modernity, Maimonides, because of his thinking about the Law, allows Strauss to challenge the status of the consciousness and to affirm that the task of thinking is the rebirth of philosophy and the return to Socratic-Platonic questioning.

The Natural Conditions of Prophecy

One and the same light illumines human beings, whether they are philosophers, prophets, or rabbis. In the place of the theory of dual truth,[57] there is in Maimonides, as with his Muslim predecessors, considerable usage of the distinction between exoteric teaching, based on rhetorical arguments, and esoteric teaching, based on demonstration. Human beings in general do not receive the light with the same degree of intensity and immediacy as the prophet.[58] Strauss returns through Falqera to Farabi, who, true to the Platonic source, expresses himself in the following way: "there are three ranks of men: the first is the rank of the multitude; the multitude know the intelligible things only in material forms . . . they are like those who dwell in a cave . . . The second rank is the rank of the philosophers; these know the intelligible things, but only indirectly, as one sees the sun in the water; the third rank is the rank of the blessed, . . . they see, as it were, the light itself, . . . they themselves become what they see."[59]

The difference between the prophet and the philosopher resides in the fact that the former receives the truth immediately: he receives an emanation of God that acts, through his active intellect, on the rational faculty of the prophet and then on his imagination. This allows him to be, at one and the same time, philosopher, holy man, and political leader. He then can communicate the truth to other men through the use of images.[60] The mistake would be in thinking that prophecy derives from the superiority of the imagination to the understanding. It is, on the contrary, because the prophet sees more and more immediately than the philosopher, "because he is blinded by a too direct light, to which he is not habituated, that he presents what he knows through images" and that he sometimes seems disturbed. The imagination itself is not involved in prophetic knowledge, in particular in the case of Moses, who attained the highest degree of prophecy.[61] The imagination does not explain the prophecy, but rather is "completely seized *from above*, completely taken." Instead of disrupting knowledge, as would be the case with the philosopher, the imagination allows the prophet to present God and the angels in a visible and corporal manner. It is only the exposition of what the prophet knows that involves images, and this faculty of communicating truths to other human beings, of guiding them, is the fruit of his perfect intellectual faculties.[62]

The imagination of the prophet does not take him beyond what reason obliges him to accept. Immediate, "without premises or conclusions," the knowledge of the prophet is superior to that of the philosopher "on the philosopher's own ground." This is why Maimonides advises the philosophers to follow the prophets, who can guide them in their philosophical activity.[63] The prophets possess intellectual perspectives that are not accessible to purely philosophical knowledge but that can nourish it.

There are thus natural conditions of prophecy, even if God can refuse it to someone who possesses these qualities, which are perfection of the understanding, morals, imagination, boldness, faculty of divination, and capacity to lead. The prophetology of Maimonides in no way compromises his rationalism. Rather, it is an important dimension of that rationalism.

Revelation consists not so much in receiving a truth but in communicating it. The philosopher, who is required to use demonstrative arguments and proceed systematically, does not possess this faculty of communication. The prophet has flashes of insight. He understands immediately and can transmit what he sees in an effective manner. But someone who does not possess true knowledge and active intellect cannot be a prophet; he would merely be some kind of visionary. Maimonides's reading of the Torah is not orthodox. His political interpretation of prophetology, which is of Platonic origin, is also completely original. The fact that he is inspired largely by the Arab philosophers in his definition of the prophet-lawgiver should not obscure the specificity of his conception of the relation between the philosopher and the community. This question, which goes back to the examination into the relationship of theory to practice, concerns the engagement of Maimonides with his community and his instruction of it.

The prophet is consumed with longing to know the upper world. His superior knowledge, combined with his ability to communicate, makes him a guide and a political leader. He is able to educate the masses, teach them, and direct them. Maimonides follows the doctrine of his Arab predecessors and does not appear to distinguish himself from them except in leaving out the gift of working miracles when he enumerates the natural faculties of the prophet. Like Farabi, who links theology with politics and asserts the identity between the political leader, imam, and lawgiver, he insists on the necessity for human beings to have a divine Law and a guide; the differences among human beings are such that they are not able to conduct themselves in a virtuous manner and attain perfection without a divine Law, centered on the good of the soul. Human laws, related solely to welfare, can only guarantee external peace, not justice, which requires, in addition to legality, morality and a certain number of beliefs establishing the interest of the citizens for something other than their personal pleasure. This idea of the necessity of a divine Law, which goes hand in hand with the recognition of the incapacity of human beings to attain perfection on their own and which is a critique ahead of its time of any purely secular morality, goes back to the *Laws* of Plato but does not imply theocracy.

Esoteric Teaching and the Enlightenment

According to Farabi in his *Treatise on the Opinions of the Inhabitants of the Ideal City*, a city that is not governed by a prophet is an unjust city where human beings have little opportunity for the good life. He who seeks philosophy and wishes to practice it even risks being killed. Maimonides returns to the idea that the philosopher-king does not suffice for the founding of the just city and establishes, with the figure of the prophet, an additional condition: the leader of the city must know how to address himself to the masses, communicating truths concerning God such that each, according to his level and abilities, is able to understand. Prophecy is a natural phenomenon. Only the divine refusal to make into a prophet someone gifted with these qualities is miraculous. But where to find such a human being? And if he existed, would he be accepted by the others? Maimonides was writing in a time where there were no more prophets. Inasmuch as there is not for the human species a king, as with bees, one has to have recourse to the law as a second sailing in the Platonic sense. But for Maimonides, the divine Law is given. It is not a second best: God is its author and it is perfect. It is the given from which Maimonides starts, in depending on the Revelation that Moses transmitted.

He who pursues the teaching of the philosopher will thus be the rabbi-philosopher. He is gifted with qualities that one finds in the philosopher to a higher degree. But to the extent that Maimonides insists on the fact that prophecy is a natural phenomenon, to the extent that the end of the Law is the perfection of man himself and that the prophet guided men in helping them, through the Law, to perfect themselves, then one can conceive of the *Guide* and the *Mishnah Torah* in the continuation of this teaching. And this is the reason for which the *Guide* is at the same time exoteric and esoteric and only reveals the secrets of the Torah with precautions.

It is necessary to draw all the implications of the Maimonidean doctrine of prophecy, in particular that it depends on natural conditions in showing that the interpreter of the Law should possess the qualities of the prophet. If Maimonides had said that prophecy was miraculous, this would have meant that he awaited the coming of another prophet or was returning to the notion of a lawgiver making wise laws and using religion as a lie suited to the encouragement of virtue, as in Plato's *Republic* or book X of the *Laws*. Such is the view of Farabi, for whom there is no distance, no intermediary between the prophet-legislator and the philosopher. He suggests that in unjust cities the philosopher will keep to himself certain of his opinions and not put his superiority on display. Like Plato, he will practice irony and not reveal that for him philosophy is superior to the life of simple virtue. This solution anticipates Spinoza: if Spinoza in his *Theologico-Political Treatise* counsels the separation of theology and politics, he suggests that religion, understood as morality supported by beliefs that accord a divine origin to it, is useful for the establishment of a lasting civic peace, which is good for human beings and for the *solitary* exercise of philosophy.

The position of Maimonides is different from that which starts from the *Republic* and book X of the *Laws* and leads to a hybrid where religion is invoked as the complement of morality, where the philosopher lives separated from other human beings and for himself. In Maimonides there is a more subtle and complex relation of philosophy to the world. The truth should not be divulged, and Maimonides transgresses the prohibition of writing down the oral Law, because he thinks that the end of the Law is to help human beings acquire salutary opinions and, eventually, true opinions concerning God. The knowledge of God, but also of everything that is, is a commandment of God. It is the commandment par excellence. This is why if one does not orient human beings in this direction and one holds to a view of religious opinions as mere beliefs, human beings will make themselves remote from the true basis of the relation to God, which is knowledge, rather than experience or morality. Obedience to God cannot be blind, because a wise God cannot but wish that human beings augment their wisdom and understand His Commandments. Some of them make use of philosophy to study the Torah. For others a guide is necessary, and the teaching of Maimonides is intended to aid in this task. It is the link to prophecy in a world where there are no more prophets and where the opinions of the philosophers may leave the believers perplexed. He enlightens others.[64] And to the extent that Maimonides begins from the Torah as a political fact and realizes what in Plato could only be hypothesized, he does not have to seek the divine Law, which has been given; thus it is a matter of interpreting the Law such that its proper end is realized. The secrets of the Torah should only be divulged to a perfect human being.[65]

The esoteric teaching and the art of writing of Maimonides, far from being elitist, are thus an integral part of his commitment as a Jew and as a philosopher. They are made necessary by his project of a teaching concerning the Law. The art of writing is a condition of the enlightened Judaism of Maimonides and an essential condition of his rationalism. In effect, if Enlightenment is esoteric, in the sense that it entails keeping secret certain truths rather than divulging them carelessly, then Maimonides's project without doubt is that of an enlightened man. He thinks that the knowledge and the acquisition of just opinions concerning God are the conditions of justice and progress, understood as individual and collective perfection. Maimonides does not concern himself with the justice of the city solely because it makes possible the solitary exercise of philosophy. He is concerned with the justice of the city *and* the perfection of individuals.

Strauss turns upside down the received wisdom contrasting the darkness of the Middle Ages with the progress attained by the Moderns. The latter have betrayed Enlightenment and lost sight of what it truly means to enlighten human beings. Instead of preserving the idea of human progress through reason while being attentive to the efforts and steps required to attain individual perfection, they are blind to the positive aspect of natural inequality and the openness to diversity of human types, orientations, gifts, and challenges. This is why they identified Enlightenment with the wide diffusion of knowledge. The goal of Maimonides's Enlightenment and the modern Enlightenment are the same: it is a matter of illuminating the masses to educate them to rational understanding. However, the first is essentially esoteric, the second exoteric.[66]

The determination of the eighteenth-century thinkers to propagate their teachings does not mean they expected they would be understood by everyone. By contrast, Maimonides "had in mind a *certain* Enlightenment of all men."[67] The superiority of the Enlightenment of Maimonides to that of the Moderns derives from the fact that in the former, truth and knowledge are preserved, whereas the latter leads to relativism. This tendency of modernity, which becomes fully evident in Nietzsche and which is one of the reasons for Strauss's return to Maimonides, is linked to the modern ideal of dissemination of knowledge and action of equality, which becomes a passion, and of the consciousness, which goes from the principle of principles—whether of Descartes or Husserl—to that of a credo: elevated to the measure of all things, subjectivity becomes a basis for rejecting any contestation of the distinction between opinions and underpins a cult of genius where what matters is whatever is done, not justice or truth.

Finally, the Enlightenment of Maimonides is superior to that of Farabi, who returns to the solution of Plato in book X of the *Laws*. The exercise of philosophy in the *Guide* does not exclude faith. Strauss makes Maimonides the model to imitate because his rationalism best represents the *tension* between Athens and Jerusalem. And the preservation of this tension is the condition of the vitality of the West. But we still need to determine whether Maimonides is the medieval model of a successful application of the Socratic-Platonic thought or if he has something original that we must take into account in applying Greek philosophy to the current situation.

The Task for Thinking and the Rebirth of Philosophy

Phenomenology and the Meaning of the Law

To say that the prophetology of Maimonides has a political meaning and to rediscover, thanks to the way in which he rethinks the Platonic legacy, the meaning of the Law is not the equivalent in political philosophy of defending theocracy, but rather is to connect politics to the question of the good life and to restore of the symbolic function of human laws. The state is no longer a mere framework for cooperation but a community in the good life, of which the end is the virtue specific to human beings. The disappearance of political philosophy being with the first wave of modernity and the separation of the temporal and the spiritual, which is a function of Christianity and leads to the foundation of civic life on purely secular values, leads to contradictions: freedom turns against itself and rationalism destroys reason as soon as human beings lose sight of the end to which their lives are directed, and reason becomes an instrument in the service of power over things and beings. Modern philosophy, which is faithful to the Pauline interpretation of the Law and could be considered as the secularization of biblical morality, self-destructs: it inaugurates the rule of technique, which denies its authority and legitimacy, and becomes the indirect accomplice of new forms of tyranny and against which one lacks the means to struggle.

Strauss says that no political regime, including democracy, can suppress human excellence without at the same time threatening individual and collective freedom. And this reference to human excellence as the horizon of politics, but also of science, depends on a rationalism and an Enlightenment that are closer to Maimonides than to modern thought. At the core of this Enlightenment is the notion of the Law. To say that the Law constitutes a whole of which the content is at the same time religious, social, and political is to say that philosophy is political. This means challenging the absolute status of subjectivity. To begin from the Law as given and to end up conferring on it an interpretation that postulates as its end the perfection of the human being themselves is to give up on considering subjectivity as the condition of the objectivity of all things.

For Socrates, the world of human things is the key to the understanding of the whole, but the knowledge provided by phenomenology is limited by what is perceived by human beings and the way in which it is perceived.[68] This knowledge, in order to be less objectifying than that of the sciences and even human sciences, is too limited to allow us to ascend to the truth. Strauss does not suggest a return to cosmology, but his choice of Maimonides as a representative of the genuine Enlightenment is a way of putting in question the modern approach, which is to start from consciousness. Not only is man perhaps not, as Aristotle suggested, what is greatest in the universe, but humankind is not an empire within an empire. And the analysis of phenomenology is limited by its commitment to subjectivity. At once it cannot avoid the fragmentation of knowledge or the juxtaposition of descriptions, which to be valid for a particular domain and capable of revealing the things themselves through our use of them and our social representation of them is nonetheless limited by the solitary experience of the individual. The individual can share this experience and communicate it, but it is only true to the extent that it resides in the meditation of the individual.

The way that phenomenology restores that which belongs to us does not tell us how we must act. Phenomenology succeeds only in the realm of theory or contemplation. It is successful as a meditation but falls short as philosophy. It results in frustration, because that which is brought to light by the description and restored to consciousness after the reduction is necessarily missing or elusive in the real. Phenomenology fuels a desire for purity that cannot be found in any object in the world. It gives rise to a desire for that which is ideally itself after the reduction, but which is always mixed or other in the world. Phenomenology is in deeper agreement with Aristotle than with Plato, from which it retains the theory of the forms, uninteresting to Maimonides and Strauss.

The phenomenologist leaves the cave, but he does not return except to the extent that he offers the fruits of his work to isolated individuals. This is why phenomenology, which might have encompassed a political teaching and contributed to altering the choices of the West, in particular concerning the relation between science and technology, remained impotent. By contrast, Strauss seeks to construct a political philosophy with a phenomenological approach that encompasses both a taking account of the human being in the community and the consideration of human ends. And this is where Socrates and Maimonides together constitute the example. Far from merging technology and ethics, political philosophy integrates them in a more radical reflection where ethics is not accorded the central place, but where it is not a separate sphere either, isolated or so to speak exiled from philosophical, political, cultural, or scientific fields of activity.

Phenomenology is thus lacking in the ability to be open to different horizons, different perspectives on the things that are not reducible to the experience of consciousness. This is because it is confined to subjectivity, the concern of modern philosophy, but which foundationalist metaphysical thought had in view from the outset such that being eluded it, according to Heidegger. It remains hidden.[69] For Strauss, the unthought is not the meaning of Being, but rather that which can be attained by reason, assuming that it has a correct conception. This unthought instead signifies the Law. A certain conception of reason and Enlightenment has been obscured: the notion that reason is the interpretation of something that does not derive from itself and that can illuminate it more or less directly or with more or less intensity. This idea, of which there are traces in Jacobi, is at the core of Maimonides's prophetology. Modern philosophy forgot the significance of the Law and obscured Enlightenment. It is confined to subjectivity, a preoccupation also of Christianity but not of Greek philosophy, as one sees once one understands the political dimension of their philosophy.

The Conception of Truth in Maimonides

In order to transcend phenomenology, one must return to the question of the whole. How today is that possible? How to begin from the human things, as did Socrates, at the same time as avoiding that knowledge has that partial and limited character that relegates phenomenology to a collection of analyses and descriptions each of which is individually focused on a particular domain but lacks a general orientation? Husserl, who in any case consigned his project of philosophy as a rigorous science to a distant and hypothetical future, related the project to that of the Encyclopedists. There is a division of knowledge, a dispersion of philosophy into specialized domains. And if phenomenology is to achieve its objective, it must bring together those insights that allow man to live rationally in the domains of religion, ethics, and so forth. It is methodology alone that unifies knowledge. Phenomenology lacks a unified substance. One understands that Husserl saw a grand temptation to fill this gap with *Weltanschauungen*. It is to this division that Heidegger objects as a symptom of philosophy ending. He does not believe that phenomenology can play the role that Husserl had hoped it would play after him. For Heidegger, the rise of the sciences replaces phenomenology, and this event belongs to the end of philosophy; "philosophy turns into the empirical science of man, of all that can become for man the experiential object of his technology . . ."[70]

The result, which is the dominance of the technological way of thinking, is evident from the starting point. But it is not philosophy in the original sense that is responsible for this type of objectifying thought. This division of knowledge and destruction of reason, reduced to the rank of an instrument of measurement and control, are not connected to the fact that philosophy in its beginning was a metaphysics even if one can see, in the theory of the forms or in the *Metaphysics* of Aristotle, this onto-theo-logical structure that underpins the conception of truth as *aletheia*. The recovery of the political dimension of the philosophy of Plato and Aristotle and the emphasis on the figure of Socrates is what leads to this treatment of the original contribution of Strauss to philosophy: the way in which Maimonides uses philosophy to interpret the Law, but also in explicating it in a manner that gives it an intrinsic rationality, and his art of writing grounds a rationalism that is open to everything human, from the truths concerning God and the angels to the science of all beings.

Reason is not the origin of enlightenment, but it is, as Jacobi would have it, that which is illumined by it. Reason is a mode of explanation and expression of that which is so received and certainly does not lead to calculation and representation where one thinks being in molding it. Like the rhetoric that Maimonides deploys in interpreting the Law, the principle of reason is one tool among others for thinking, but it is not that which defines its essence. One should not conflate understanding and reason (Jacobi), the cognitive faculty, which permits logical reasoning in syllogistic fashion, and those intellectual operations, which are analogous to a vision and which allow us to grasp according to our level a truth that is not reducible to logical deductions (Maimonides). When it fixes itself on something and grasps the truth, the intellect communicates on its level the truth that it has received. But this expression of truth is an adaptation of the truth to our faculties, because there also exists an immediate vision of God. Maimonides's rationalism presupposes Revelation. Far from being relative to the way in which things are presented to consciousness, which in itself cannot be the source, truth presents itself in a more or less direct manner and with a different degree of intensity. Maimonides does with the Torah, but also with Aristotelian physics and with opinions and dogmas, what philosophy must do for real thought.

Maimonides is faithful to the return to the opinions of the city, because it is in beginning from the Law that is given to the community that he ascends toward the truth. But this should not be mistaken with the Law, which is the Revelation given by God to Moses, who has direct contact with the Creator. The Law is at the same time the starting point and also the vehicle by which Maimonides is led to confront other opinions, even if he is required to reject them. In the end, in being in this situation, unknown to the Greeks, where he has to explain himself before both Athens and Jerusalem, Maimonides presents the model of rationalism appropriate for us. It is by imitating him that we can apply classical political philosophy to the current situation, succeed in returning to the opinions of the city, embrace the diverse elements that constitute our tradition, and become enlightened. Philosophy does not become human science, nor does it cede its place to the sciences. Rather, its task is to integrate without thereby synthesizing the diverse findings of the sciences, in particular those such as quantum physics and biology that recall that man is not an empire in an empire. To the tension between Jerusalem and Athens is added the tension between philosophy and contemporary sciences, which, in their application as technology, present problems that give rise to the need for political philosophy.

It is in beginning from the same view as Heidegger concerning the technological world and phenomenology that Strauss conceives the rebirth of political philosophy as the task of thought. The critique of rationalism led Heidegger to turn toward Parmenides, seeking a discourse that is open to Being and safeguards the clearing (*Lichtung*) of Being. This discourse, in essence poetic, marks the end of philosophy. In Strauss, the critique of the modern Enlightenment leads to a rationalism linked to a conception of truth that is open to Revelation. The core of the true Enlightenment is philosophy. And while Maimonides in his treatment of prophecy does not exclude that there is an access to truth that is superior to that of the philosopher, political philosophy may contain a strategy for integrating that which is other for political philosophy, namely poetry. It is indeed because philosophy is political that it is open to poetry. Far from being mere escapism, art can be a means of expression and communication of a truth that philosophy "in its premises and conclusions" proposes and only for a reader who already possesses a certain culture.

What Is Called Thinking?

Heidegger asks: "But is the end of philosophy in the sense of its evolving into the sciences also already the complete actualization of all the possibilities in which the thinking of philosophy was posited? Or is there a first possibility for thinking apart from the last possibility which we characterized (the dissolution of philosophy in the technologized sciences), a possibility from which the thinking of philosophy would have to start, but which as philosophy it could nevertheless not experience and adopt?"[71] Heidegger believes that there is still a task that is held in reserve for thinking. This task is to care for Being instead of "moving within the prevailing attitude belonging to technological, calculating representation."[72] It is an overcoming of metaphysics and an exit from the *Gestell*. The latter is characterized by the forgetfulness of Being, "sets itself above the thing, leaves it, as thing, unsafeguarded, truthless."[73] The *Gestell* hides what the world is for us and what we are in the world, that is what belongs to the fourfold of heaven and earth, mortals and the divine.

The technical mode of thinking, "though veiled . . . is not a blind fate in the sense of a completely ordained destiny." The state of non-concealment—or *aletheia*—that is conveyed by the Open, thus that man is in charge, is not thought. And neither phenomenology nor the sciences can say what is involved in "the nearness of world that nears in the thing."[74] Man cannot safeguard Being except if he, "as the mortal, looks out toward the divine."[75] It is a flashing glance: that which "is" is not "being," but Being comes to language. Thus poetic discourse articulates this correspondence of man to the call of the glance. It cannot be understood except when it is clarified as *Gestell*, the essence of *techne*, that is, when we see how, in the putting at our disposal of being as an available resource and in the mode of technological thought, the thinking or taking into one's care of Being, is rejected. We are thus ready—or called—to pass to a new beginning, which counters, in its ambivalence, the *Gestell*.

Poetry evokes "man's belonging within the wholly mutual interrelating of the fourfold of sky and earth, divinities and mortals."[76] It is the site of this clarification where the truth can reveal itself because man responds to what calls him instead of considering it as being, connected to the use that he can make of it. Poetry and all discourse that corresponds to it realizes the task of thinking, which is the true action (*Handeln*) because, if we are really thinking, we lend a hand (*Hand*) to the essence of Being in order to build in the middle of being the domain where it carries its essence to language.[77]

Thought is the initial correspondence between Being and man. On the contrary, philosophy, up to the present, has made truth the agreement between knowledge and Being. This is why the philosophers were never able to investigate the non-retreat of *aletheia*, non-retreat that alone makes possible that there be truth. Parmenides alone spoke of the expanse of the Open, that is, what lets Being and thinking arrive in their presence one to the other and one for the other. And in order to be able to investigate that which makes possible the evident, it is necessary to have the experience of *aletheia* as *Lichtung* (Clearing) to experience the expanse of the Open. Heidegger refers to the experience of Parmenides, who calls "the perfect roundness" this state of Being without retreat. But in order to reflect upon that which is called "Being and thinking" and not interpret it as correctness of speech, another conception of truth than that of Greek metaphysics and theories of knowledge is necessary. In sum, one needs "a thinking outside the distinction of rational and irrational."[78] And this is precisely what Strauss finds in Maimonides.

If Heidegger had reflected on Maimonides's conception of truth as it is derived from prophetology and if he had not refused the idea of Revelation that is constitutive for the rationalism of the medieval Enlightenment, he could not have maintained that the end of philosophy occurred with the emergence of the sciences. Nor could he have affirmed that the task of thinking requires the overcoming of philosophy considered as metaphysics, theory of perception, and then the will to will. He would not have done the *Gestell*, which is the accomplishment of onto-theological thinking, the passage to the other beginning, and the discourse that appropriates man to that which he looks at and pronounces his essential attachment to the *Geviert* (the fourfold). Poetry would not have been for him the sole site of revelation and the alternative to philosophy, because he would have understood that that which is the unthought in philosophy is the unthought of modern rationalism, that is, of a conception of truth that is reduced to the correspondence between my representation and being (*Seiende*).

The metaphysics that is constituted after Plato and Aristotle but also once one had recovered Socratic questioning on the basis of doctrines in which Plato himself perhaps did not fully believe is characterized by the obscuring of the relation between reason and Revelation. This relation is implicated in the notion of truth revealed in the allegory of the cave and is suggested in Plato's *Letters*. And the medieval Enlightenment interprets this conception of truth within the framework of a rationalism where reason appeared as a means of comprehension and expression of a truth that could be seized immediately and communicated other than by premises and conclusions. We have seen that this idea of Revelation takes nothing away from the intellectualism of Maimonides, which brings together human and divine knowledge. And it is the same light that is the source of the knowledge of God and illuminates human reason, from the prophet to the philosophers and to other human beings. Which means that Maimonides posed the question of how to know that which makes possible the truth. Moreover, the brute fact of Revelation, the gift of the divine Law, is, to the extent that Maimonides in the *Guide* begins from this fact and accepts it, the non-retreat that makes possible the truth and the way in which it can be what it is. Man himself appears, in Maimonides, in the expanse of the Open.

Heidegger's reading of metaphysics is thus determined by the presuppositions of the Moderns, who do not have access to the meaning of the Law as it is understood in the rationalism of Maimonides. If philosophy were what Heidegger says that it is, he would be right to think that it is finished and that the task of thinking supposes its overcoming. And certainly Strauss would have followed him in this. But metaphysics, which leads to *techne*, is an erroneous interpretation of Socratic-Platonic philosophy. The task of thinking implies the rebirth of philosophy, that is, the revival of that which, in the West, has remained unthought. And this is the meaning of the Straussian project of a return to Maimonides.

"The genuine understanding of the political philosophies . . . may be said to have been rendered possible by the shaking of all traditions; the crisis of our time may have the accidental advantage of enabling us to understand in an untraditional or fresh manner what was hitherto understood only in a traditional or derivative manner. . . . However, we cannot reasonably except that a fresh understanding of classical political philosophy will supply us with recipes for today's use."[79] What then is the program of this philosophy? What is the task of thinking once the unthought of philosophy has been identified and we have a model of true Enlightenment? What does it mean to be enlightened today?

Surpassing Heidegger on His Own Ground

Like Heidegger, Strauss seeks to "[awaken] a readiness in man for a possibility."[80] These two thinkers view the history of the West in light of the history of philosophy and the alternatives that characterize the West. "We are thinking of the possibility that the world civilization that is just now beginning might one day overcome its technological-scientific-industrial character as the sole criterion of man's world sojourn."[81] The task of thinking is to take charge of this unthought. Strauss and Heidegger have a sense of the danger and the way in which the problem is posed today with an acuteness unprecedented in prior epochs. But the interpretation of Maimonides is for Strauss the means of surpassing Heidegger on his own ground. This is the rational critique of reason that, from Jacobi to Maimonides, Strauss opposes to the temptation of irrationalism.

The way in which Heidegger turns toward poetry is more a solution to avoid irrationalism than an adequate expression of a new beginning that he summons from his will. Heidegger said that poetry was the alternative to philosophy as metaphysics but not to thinking. Poetry takes account of that which is the task of thinking, but it is not this task. This is why Heidegger does not totally reject philosophy. He hesitates between the appeal to a discourse suited to prepare us to think and the idea that, philosophy being at its end, poetry should take over and avoid the complete domination of the technologized sciences. Is it because Heidegger did not find an alternative to this ultimate possibility that he turned toward poetry? Is it because he does not know how to resist this ultimate possibility that would deny to thinking any chance of a new beginning that he maintains faith with poetry?

Heidegger calls for "a thinking which is more sober-minded than the incessant frenzy of rationalization and the intoxicating quality of cybernetics," but he never succeeds in naming this thought, because his notion of rationalism is too limited, too modern. If he had had at his disposal the concept of truth in the medieval Enlightenment, of Platonic origin, then art, instead of being the other—and the rival—in relation to philosophy, as it still is for the sophists of the *Republic* who make Socrates exclude it, would have found its place at the side of philosophy and not against it. It would have become the expression of truth through different means than those of philosophy. As Heidegger recognized, art and philosophy are not from two different sources, but are two means of expression of the truth, two types of revelation.

Seen in light of the rationalism and prophetology of Maimonides, art and philosophy collaborate in the task of thinking. But, as for Plato, it is philosophy that is the key to this wisdom, because it maintains in view the end without human action is fated to a fragmentation in diverse domains of culture where ethics, religion and art itself are merely value choices. Only Socratic questioning as questioning together of the good life in common can confer on knowledge the unity that it would otherwise lack and orient human action in light of the meaning of human being-and be open to the question of the meaning of Being as such. The forgetting of the meaning of the Law and the notion of truth that underpins the relation of Reason and Revelation in the pre-modern Enlightenment encompasses as well the loss of the meaning of Being. The task of thinking as Strauss defines it allows the fulfillment of what Heidegger aspired to, the transcendence of the *Gestell* toward a true beginning where the question of Being is thought.

It is thus in rescuing the notion of Law—as understood by the Jewish and Arab philosophers of the Middle Ages in the wake of Plato—from the oblivion in to which it fell with Christianity and modernity that one can begin to think. Like Heidegger, Strauss considers that "thinking means to give attention to what must be preserved in thought." He knows that we seek and desire something that desires us and seeks ourselves. And that is all he truly knows. To think is to question in the sense that Socrates meant it. It is to be a philosopher, a lover of wisdom. It is to orient oneself in thought in beginning from the city as the context for all opinions and experiences, and to act such that "what we do and do not do is the echo every time of the revelation of the essential" which does not exclude the revelation of the whole (Plato) nor biblical Revelation (Maimonides).

Hence philosophy is political philosophy. It is within the city that which never ceases to remind of what transcends the city. The elaboration of a political philosophy for the future requires that preparatory work that orients research and devises an entire program of scientific and humanistic activities that are not divorced from wisdom or the consideration of the end of man. But in its content, this political philosophy is descriptive and requires the collaboration of several disciplines. As with Maimonides, heterogeneous elements are derived from the sciences and our dual allegiance to Athens and Jerusalem. Art, as the art of writing, is with the teaching of dialectic or philosophical argumentation among the most powerful means of expression for the application of ancient wisdom and the pre-modern Enlightenment to the present situation. And while at the same time considering some problems urgent, like that of technology, political philosophy remains more than the solutions it proposes. In its interpretation of truth, which becomes more and more direct, political philosophy, which integrates philosophy in its own program, taking nothing away from the zetetic character of Socratic questioning, never ceases to remind that thought is openness and it transcends politics and every *Weltanschauung*. But this is also the reason why there is a place for a type of expression of truth and description of the world, which is by nature resistant to instrumental or technological thinking.

In the program that is animated by political philosophy, poetry, visual arts, and literature are all brought together. And, even if Maimonides says that the rabbi-philosopher possesses to an inferior degree the qualities of the prophet, we are able to think that, with the intuitions of genius, it is a little this flash of truth that penetrates in a sudden, perceptible, and overwhelming manner. Strauss surpasses Heidegger on his own ground, if it is true that his critique of modernity and return to the Enlightenment of Maimonides are a way of defining the task of thinking as the rebirth of philosophy, that is, as political philosophy as the Ancients understood it.

Conclusion

The Straussian Enlightenment

Strauss's Radical Questioning

If the choice of a philosophy is determined by character,[1] then Strauss is more original and countercurrent than either his detractors or those who use his thought to justify the imposition of a political orthodoxy would suggest. Rather than leading to a condemnation of the Enlightenment, Strauss's critique of modernity leads to a different Enlightenment. But to understand in what sense Strauss is a thinker of Enlightenment and to understand his invitation to revive classical thought, it is useful to emphasize the true distinction between Ancients and Moderns and to consider the break that occurred at a certain moment in Western history. This radical questioning surpasses the successors to Strauss and most of his contemporaries. Instead of claiming that modernity has provoked a relativism that renders democracy incapable of struggling against tyranny, instead of seeing in the quarrel of the Ancients and Moderns an opposition between a society based on classic natural right and a world based on the morality of human rights, we should go to the heart of the matter, the question of rationalism itself. In its radicalism, Strauss's critique of the modern Enlightenment is a philosophical critique. He thinks through the crisis of the West by putting in question the definition of reason that brings forth the liberal state and the era of technology, a civilizational project driven by the faith that science will lead to more freedom and happiness but result in hatred of reason and self-destruction. What is the definition of reason and of man that is at the origin of the reversal of the Enlightenment into its opposite?

Strauss poses the question of the meaning of reason. This question leads from Jacobi to Maimonides. Maimonides offers the solution to the problem that Jacobi poses. Strauss diverges from his contemporaries, breaking off from the path traced by the great philosophers who, beginning in the eighteenth century, were considered as those who had narrowed the scope for reflection. He follows neither Kant nor Hegel. He is prepared to confront Nietzsche's challenge of nihilism. He brings to light that which is too modern in Nietzsche, where the latter does not have sufficient distance from his times. He stands up to Heidegger, rejecting the notion that technology is the fate of the West, from which we can opt out as individuals but that we cannot change. Why did Heidegger, who engaged in the destruction of metaphysics, showing that it is characterized by the forgetfulness of Being, fail to see that he was using a derivative and erroneous notion of reason? How could he ignore that part of the Western tradition that proposes another kind of rationalism than that which, from Plato to Husserl, he rejects?

This questioning concerning reason, which leads Strauss to return to the Ancients and speak of the tension between Athens and Jerusalem, explains his obsession with Maimonides, who suggests a relationship between reason and Revelation that corresponds to the kind of rationalism and Enlightenment that Strauss wants to advance. But, far from being an enemy of Spinoza and Hobbes, it could well be that Strauss is also their heir, in that he borrows from the great figures of the seventeenth and eighteenth centuries what their successors were unable to retain. Here it is a matter of noticing, in this paradoxical thinker, that the two attitudes that constitute the radicalism of his reflection, the originality of the project and the distancing from his own times, give birth to a single position: that of the moderate, whose stance is never exactly predictable.

On the one hand, Strauss is able to take to heart the expression of Bossuet that God laughs at those who deplore the effects while admiring their causes. He tars with the same brush the advocates and the enemies of liberalism in showing that capitalists and Marxists share the same individualist conception of man, separating reason from any reflection on the end of man and making it the mere instrument of his needs. Along similar lines, he brings to light the contradictions of those who on the one hand defend the rights of man and on the other loudly denounce market society and the reign of profit, which, however, is the achievement of the liberal state based on the defense of individual rights. But Strauss himself seems to be in neither camp: as a philosopher, he is skeptical and lives in a space not confined by the political community. He is ironic and thus distinguishes himself from the partisan or the ideologue. This irony and skepticism must be taken into account in his critique of the modern Enlightenment, in particular when it is a matter of returning to the original credo of Enlightenment in such a way that afterward the theological-political problem was buried and religion overcome. Strauss shows that the quarrel between the Ancients and Moderns has not been decided in favor of the Moderns and that the struggle of the Enlightenment against orthodoxy has not destroyed the interest in Revelation. But the tenor of his critique of Spinoza is such that, once he raises the obstacles to a return to the pre-modern way of thinking, he can say that the foundation of a liberal state on the natural right of the individual—and not on transcendence—does not mean that religion has no use for society. Not only does the "Christianity" of Spinoza return us to a reflection on the limits of a purely secular morality, but it also suggests that thinkers of the radical Enlightenment had a political sense that their successors lost, as they were blinded by the idea of equality and a certain starry-eyed idealism.

The radical Enlightenment is superior to the moderate Enlightenment, but also to the thought of the twentieth century, which seems less enlightened than that of Hobbes or of Spinoza. The utilization that Strauss makes of Maimonides does not amount to the defense of theocracy, and neither does it entail espousing religious orthodoxy. Rather, it serves to advance a kind of rationalism and Enlightenment to which the modern conception of reason and of man prevents access. And it may be that a form of rationalism that is accommodating to Revelation, whether or not linked to the God of the Bible, and a conception of truth that does not exclude the supra-rational were present in certain thinkers at the beginning of the modern Enlightenment but got lost or overwhelmed by its main tendency. Further, is not the way of defining political philosophy as reflection on commonsense opinion, and placing description before abstraction at the same time as a critique of the ineffectiveness of human rights, the opportunity to rediscover the idea of the public world that one finds in Husserl[2] and that Leibniz[3] expounds in his image of the same city seen from different points of view? Are not Strauss's critique of the modern Enlightenment and his journey through the pre-modern Enlightenment an opportunity to rediscover the modern Enlightenment itself?

Because Strauss goes to the roots, to the heart of the matter, which is that of knowing what is reason, because he is original and not a child of his times, his critique of the modern Enlightenment is both positive and negative. We are dealing here with a constructive critique of modernity. It is at the same time intransigent and severe yet moderate. It is linked to a precise diagnosis of what ails the West and the conviction that unless we break from some modern assumptions, we are condemned not to decadence but to destruction. Nevertheless, instead of appealing to history, or an improbable return of the divine, Strauss sketches a project of the philosophy of the future. We follow this path, which goes from Jacobi to Maimonides and to the Enlightenment of Strauss himself, in order to identify and spell out the questions that Strauss inspires us to pursue.

From Jacobi to Maimonides: Neither Kant nor Hegel

Strauss is viewed as a historian of ideas, but he is above all a truth seeker who sees in the history of philosophy the key to understanding the logic that leads to the crisis of our times. This way of using the philosophers in light of his own problematic is particularly evident in his relation to Jacobi. This is where Strauss began, because Jacobi wrote, in the eighteenth century no less, that the rationalism of the Enlightenment is a false rationalism; instead of considering reason as the site of the revelation of Being, as a means of knowledge of given realities, one turned it into a faculty that itself produced the ideas. This "illuminating flame" is the source of justice and truth. And not only did this erroneous concept of reason lead to the privileging of abstraction as opposed to beginning with experience and its description, but, in addition, this "insolent" reason "without heart or guts" makes philosophy into a philosophy of representation, incapable of speaking about the real and blind to everything that escapes its constructions. Thus the philosophers of the Enlightenment established a theory of right based on mere thinking, on the subject, contemptuous of experience and traditions, and they denied what transcends sense experience, the strong meaning of Revelation.

The internal critique of rationalism undertaken by Jacobi allows Strauss to radicalize the conflict between the Enlightenment and orthodoxy and to reopen the quarrel between the Ancients and Moderns. The conflict puts the Enlightenment and atheism in the opposition. That is, the moderate Enlightenment is shunted aside. Moreover, the real problem is to confront the conception of man and of reason that underpins, respectively, the thought of Spinoza and pre-modern rationalism. And the conception of reason that Strauss discovers in discovering Maimonides's manner of interpreting the Law and his theory of the natural conditions of prophecy corresponds to the kind of rationalism that he wishes to advance. Jacobi allowed him to show the error of the modern conception of reason and to reject the Kantian solution that makes religion the handmaiden of morality. It allowed him to affirm that the Law is heteronomous and to set himself apart from the neo-Kantians and the philosophy of Cohen, of which the center is ethics, but Strauss does not leave matters there.

In effect, he discovers in Maimonides what he had already found, but imperfectly, in Jacobi. The latter led him to see the error of the modern Enlightenment at its root, making no mistake about the real adversary: Strauss thus turned to Hobbes and Spinoza and studied their treatment of the theological-political problem. But Maimonides is the model, given his particular way of conceiving the relationship between reason and Revelation and his rational critique of reason: he represents the *tension* between Athens and Jerusalem, refusing to choose one over the other and also rejecting the possibility of a synthesis. The Enlightenment of Maimonides is the true Enlightenment. Unlike Jacobi, Strauss is not an enemy of Enlightenment. He finds in Maimonides the solutions to the problems raised by Jacobi. Thus he focuses on medieval philosophy, and having broken with the Kantian critical philosophy thanks to Jacobi, he is able to dispense with Jacobi himself. It is no longer a question of a philosophy of anti-Enlightenment once the quarrel of the Ancients and Moderns has been reopened and the focus shifts to the scrutiny of Spinoza's critique of religion, of which Strauss articulates the limits but also the influence. Strauss is, however, always mindful of the critique of modern rationalism unleashed by the pantheism debate. It is thus that he demonstrates the contradiction that is at the heart of Spinoza's system. And this contradiction resurfaces in Hegel. In other words, "the problem of Jacobi" allows Strauss equally to reject Hegel and to oppose the Hegelian *Aufhebung*, his idea of a tension or a vital dialogue between two distinct kinds of wisdom represented by Jerusalem and Athens.

While the two philosophies that have framed the history of ideas beginning with the Enlightenment are those of Kant and Hegel, Strauss advocates an approach and a style that are neither critical in the Kantian sense nor a Hegelian philosophy of history. The philosophers who situate themselves in the tendency of Kant or Hegel have a conception of the relation between theory and practices that renders them incapable of thinking through the theological-political problem and facing the crisis of our times. They also lack the resources to confront Nietzsche's questioning of rationality itself. This is why, with the exception of Cohen, who put him on the way to Maimonides, and Kojeve, who shares Strauss's concern for the future of wisdom, neo-Kantian and neo-Hegelian philosophers are not among Strauss's interlocutors. By contrast, he engages in a confrontation with Heidegger and takes up in his own way the approach of phenomenology to which Jacobi's empiricism opened up the path, and he finds a precedent for this approach in the manner of Socratic questioning.

The Kantian critical philosophy and Hegelian synthesis were never persuasive for Strauss. It is not only that Hegelian reason, understood as grasping the totality of the real, does not correspond to his conception of reason or to his sensibility and experience, related to the shocks of twentieth-century history, but, more important, he does not believe that the synthesis is superior to the distinct opposites that constitute it. For the thought of contradiction and its resolution and overcoming Strauss substitutes the thought of tension, which preserves both of the opposites without trying to make a synthesis of them. Just as Maimonides does not reconcile Aristotle and the Bible, but uses philosophy to defend the Law and justifies philosophy before the Law, Strauss similarly retains the two sources of wisdom in the West. Rather than needing to be effaced, the differences have a positive and creative meaning. This is an original way of thinking, obviously opposed to the way of Marxism and philosophy of history, which are based on a linear conception of progress through the synthesis of opposites, the overcoming of contradiction, and the advent of a conflict-free society. For Strauss, rather than a revolution being needed to deal with the contradictions, the vitality of a civilization, like the creativity of a human being, depends on the tension between elements that, if reconciled, are neutralized, resulting in a faded version, common to the Moderate Enlightenment and all those who have been unable to know how to recognize modern tyranny.

Similarly, to the idea of a reconciliation between the rational and the real, thought and action, Strauss opposes the idea, equally un-contemporary, of an irreducible gap between philosophy and the city. This tension underpins the art of writing between the lines. Most of Strauss's interpreters, whether friendly or hostile, see this esotericism as a reflection of Strauss's elitism. However, the esoteric Enlightenment, of which Maimonides is the model, is related to a teaching that has as its purpose to guide human beings in the knowledge of the Law. Far from excluding the vulgar, Maimonides holds that knowledge brings about their salvation and improvement. But this supposes gradualism, and certain matters cannot be studied without precaution. The art of writing between the lines and esotericism are related to the idea that the diffusion of the truth should not entail its deformation and that religious secrets are transmitted orally, with the aid of a guide and depending on the degree of progress of the pupil or disciple. Like Maimonides, Strauss thinks that the truth ought not to be hidden, because the perfection of man occurs through understanding. However, to be "enlightened" means in the first instance to be guided in knowledge and to accede to the truth step by step. The path that leads to truth is a steep one, and truth itself, which is unique, is revealed, that is, communicated, by different channels and with a degree of intensity that is not the same in the case of the ordinary man, the philosopher, and the prophet. The Moderns thus had a conception of reason, but also of truth, that is erroneous. And these notions are used and considered as self-evident in the expression "Enlightenment."

Strauss puts in doubt the idea that there is no censorship. We have repeatedly raised the Tocquevillian motif in his critique of mass democracy and downward leveling and the all-powerful nature of public opinion ("political correctness"). This does not exclude manipulation by the media and the censure of human beings who have retained their critical sense. But this censure goes back at a deeper level to the problem of an irreducible gap that has always existed between the philosopher and the city. The philosopher is obliged to have recourse to the art of writing and to take into account that suspicion of the representatives of the established order or the resistance of other human beings.

This idea, which supposes that the philosopher practices irony and does not seek consensus, does not nevertheless imply that the philosopher will have no impact on the world or that salvation is self-enclosure or erudition, that is, an egoistic mode of living. There is, in political philosophy, a notion of the engagement of philosophy that constitutes the very meaning of the Straussian Enlightenment. But this engagement and this Enlightenment go back to the person of Socrates and the example of Maimonides. They provide an antidote to the confusion between philosophy and propaganda that Strauss traces to the early modern Enlightenment and that culminates in the phenomenon of the intellectual. Indulging his inclination to judge everything, this kind of man, "impulsive and impatient," lacks at the same time radicalness in his questioning and moderation in his commitment: he is an ideologue, not a philosopher. Where the philosopher is rigorous, the ideologue is overstated. He is quick to take up causes, so long as they make him more visible, while the philosopher, who knows that the ideal regime is a regulative ideal, tends to support the least bad of the existing regimes. Strauss's elitism is inseparable from his irony. It reflects the gap between the philosopher and other human beings and the very division that is at the heart of philosophy itself, to the extent that thought, essentially questioning and living, always risks being converted into a fixed position or a comfort.

This Is Not an Ethics

Strauss is thus an *Aufklärer*. The true Enlightenment is that for which Maimonides furnishes the model. This is a model relevant not only for the Middle Ages, because, contrary to the historicists, there is truth to be found in the thought of the Ancients. This is an always-living, relevant truth: the pre-modern Enlightenment enables us to think through the crisis of our own time and is the soul of liberal democracy, that which can preserve it against itself. It is in being not of his times that Strauss is able to think through the crisis of our times and see the dangers that threaten modern democracy. In being un-contemporary, he is contemporary. For Strauss, this is a matter of applying to our situation the lessons of Maimonides. This renewal of the wisdom of Maimonides requires at the same time boldness and moderation. Boldness is the condition for moderation.

Through the interpretation of the Maimonidean idea of the Law and its application to the modern situation, which relates the divide between theology and politics, Strauss avoids the pitfalls of traditionalism, reaction, and entrenchment in purely modern solutions to the question of the problematic fate of religion. This is the orientation of his political philosophy. It is not merely a critique of the thought of the Moderns, in which, since Machiavelli, the question of the good life is excluded from politics, but it invites a reflection on the challenge of a society preserving democracy on the basis of a purely secular morality. This reflection, of which the core is the reevaluation of the symbolic or pedagogical function of laws, today overly subordinated to the defense of subjective rights and private interests, equally emphasizes the limits of ethics.

Ethics is the touchstone of most contemporary philosophies. It seems to have been born in the ruins of political philosophy. In other words, the disappearance of the question of the good life from the domain of political reflection has led to the evolution of ethics as a separate field. It is considered peripheral, while classical political philosophy considered it central, and an *integral* part of its own enterprise, and also in its understanding of reason. It is thus that, supporting the distinction between facts and values, scientific objectivity became the sole criterion for knowledge, while action and power are governed on the basis of *techne*. It is thus that ethics is constituted as a separate discipline. It is called on to compensate for philosophical relativism—without great effectiveness, depending on the philosophy of human rights, and reviving the morality of Christ. The problems that politics cannot or does not want to deal with are confided to ethics, whether the dehumanization of society, technology, or the loss of social connectedness. And like politics, which is no longer the site of the decisions that determine the future of nations and civilizations, ethics is impotent in the face of the problems and only proposes, by way of solutions, unprincipled compromise and prevarication. But individualism and the autonomy of the subject—the categories of bioethics that often use a self-referential definition of the person[4]—are never put in question. By contrast, the idea of a tension between Jerusalem and Athens allows us to enrich our *philosophical* reflection on contemporary problems, such as biotechnology and the question of how to think about social connectedness, through an appropriation of religious traditions. The notion of Revelation and the idea of a rationalism friendly to Revelation, does this not allow us to proceed, on the basis of the separation of theology and politics, of secularism, to a questioning of the individualist credo and a relativization of the notion of the autonomy of the subject? This questioning is nonetheless impossible except within the frame of political philosophy, and not of an ethics that transforms knowledge based on the study of a tradition into a question of values.

The existence of ethical questions does not mean that ethics can solve them or even think them through. In order to understand the eclipse of politics in a world where money rules and to confront the unprecedented challenges of biotechnology, it is not a matter of recovering morality but of reconstructing the philosophical options chosen at a particular moment of Western history and evaluating them, which is to put them to the test. This is the meaning of the dissection of the modern political consciousness and the analysis of the preconceptions at the origin of our notion of politics. The first of these is the "low but solid" standard chosen by Machiavelli. It is a matter of a definition of the human being as driven by his passions: in the first instance desirous of glory and still republican or even patriotic, he becomes with Hobbes an asocial individual animated by vanity and fear, and then by the love of gain. And this world of Lilliput, in which reason is cut off from any connection to transcendence, and where the individual, defined by his rights, is less and less aware of what connects him to other human beings, other species, and other generations, institutes the rule of the last man.

The last man is at home both in a state of war and in a state of peace, capable of either glorifying violence or seeking security, able to live in a Marxist regime or a liberal economy or under democratic institutions that participate in one or the other, using slogans from one to compensate for defects of the other, ideology in one case and the market in the other. This kind of man, defined by a certain ideal of liberty as a break from nature and self-affirmation and fashioned by centuries of individualism, has neither the means nor the will to resist tyranny. He does not see it.

As an alternative to ethics, Strauss offers the defense of political philosophy. This requires a questioning of individualism and the conception of man that is at the foundation of modern thought. In order to save modern liberal democracy from self-destruction, to preserve its soul, and to return to what Tocqueville understood by liberty, Strauss partially opposes the philosophy that led to the creation of liberal democracy. This opposition is revolutionary, but it is so with respect to philosophical principles, not democratic institutions. It concerns the concept of man underpinning the philosophy of the Enlightenment, which built the modern West on the project of the mastery of nature by man. For Strauss, the reconsideration of Plato, Aristotle, and the Jewish and Islamic thinkers of the Middle Ages is a way of challenging the primacy accorded to subjectivity from the origins of Christianity to the Enlightenment. It is a matter of revaluing the place of man not in relation to the cosmos, but in relation to the Law in its full Maimonidean sense, that is, in relation to nature and what transcends it.

To recover the full meaning of the Law, and to interpret it in light of our current situation, is to say that duty and law, reason and Revelation are linked. In restating the theologico-political problem, Strauss invites his contemporaries and his followers to relate the religious, the political, and the ethical in a manner that is appropriate to our situation and applicable in a liberal democracy. This method of returning to the Ancients to make evident the suppositions of the Moderns and to examine the truth or falsehood of their notions, this refusal to consider as self-evident categories that pertain to a specific historical moment, leads Strauss to ask what needs to be altered in modern political philosophy in order that the liberal democracy that it brought into being can be preserved. Such is the meaning of moderate or conservative thought, which does not appeal to reaction or a return of the ancient social order. The radicalism of Strauss, who questions modern philosophical assumptions, and the boldness with which he does so in showing that the pre-modern Enlightenment provides guidance in this task, are constitutive of his moderation. This paradoxical spirit requires the abandonment of a linear conception of historical time that is characteristic of historicism and progressivism, but also of the philosophy of history, revolutionary thought, and even Heidegger's notion of the fate of the West. To speak of the tension between Athens and Jerusalem implies a real conversion.

But if the tension between reason and Revelation is what the West depends on for its vitality, it also means that the Enlightenment critique of religion had consequences for society at large that the great thinkers of the seventeenth and eighteenth centuries were not able to foresee. Right from his early studies of Spinoza, Strauss never ceases to pose the question of on what basis one can pass from religion to a purely secular morality. This idea, which underlines the superiority of the radical Enlightenment to the thinkers of the twentieth century and takes account of a certain continuity through Farabi between the Enlightenment of Plato and that of Spinoza, has often been considered as indicative of the ambiguity of Strauss, whom most commentators take for an atheist. Nevertheless, the kind of rationalism that he aims to espouse, of which Maimonides was for him until the 1930s the model, means that Strauss, while not orthodox, is also not an atheist in Spinoza's sense. His reflection on the social role of religion does not reduce it to a useful lie solely for the well-being of the vulgar. For it is reason itself that one must not sever from transcendence, whether or not recovered through the givenness of Revelation through God. The Straussian Enlightenment, like that of Maimonides, is of Platonic origin, and evokes the allegory of the cave and the notion of a truth of which there is a unique source, but the communication or expression of which is variable. It supposes a notion of reason that is something other than *ratio* or calculation. Similarly, a purely secular morality is not adequate to instill citizen virtue; while the individual human being with his subjective rights is the measure of all things and loses the sentiment that there is something greater in the universe, when he does not think of himself as profoundly or ontologically linked to others, is it not difficult to avoid the logic that follows from liberty defined as mastery of nature according to will of will and of the idea of man as the possessor of the whole of being?

Is one forced to conclude that man cannot avoid religion or that he should create structures giving him back the sense and the taste of transcendence? This is the problem of culture and goes to the role of art, which Victor Hugo and Kandinsky understood as having the function of *spiritually* elevating human beings. For Strauss, it is a matter of liberal education, which supposes an engagement with the great minds and an experience of the beautiful of which the absence condemns human beings to vulgarity. Whatever the chosen solution—and the philosopher does not have to decide on a solution or conclude his reasoning in faith—the essential is to realize that, without the recollection of the questions that orient the acts and activities of human beings in light of their proper ends, what the Ancients called perfection, which is the realization of the nature of man, democracy is threatened from the inside.

Finally Strauss is not a moralist, and his thought cannot be identified with that of some of his disciples, who look only at the consequences and see in moral relativism the essential problem, while it is merely one consequence of modern rationalism. But he is also to be distinguished from other Jewish thinkers of his generation who prepared a return to orthodoxy. We have confronted Strauss's thought with that of Rosenzweig and Scholem, but also with that of Levinas, with whom he never engaged, because these thinkers, beyond their individual richness, allow the originality of the Straussian approach to emerge. While for Scholem, Rosenzweig, and Levinas, experience is the site of the relationship to God and reveals in human existence the meaning of the Absolute, Strauss, faithful to the Enlightenment of Maimonides, thinks that the ultimate end of the Law is the perfection of the understanding. It is through true beliefs that man pleases God or accomplishes the Law. Similarly, Maimonides begins from the Torah and not the Jewish nation and addresses himself to believers whom philosophy has left perplexed, taking into consideration cosmology and the philosophical opinions prevalent in the time. This approach consists in integrating all the forms of knowledge and opinion, all the traditions that are present in the city in a given period, with a view to studying them and proposing an interpretation—often heterodox—that corresponds to the manner in which Strauss thinks one should philosophize.

The philosopher who begins, like Socrates, from the political things because they are the key to the understanding of the whole and who transforms commonsense opinion into knowledge is using a phenomenological method. Philosophy is reflection on the pre-given opinions of the community and an examination of what might be missing or not thought through. This rigorous undertaking belongs to science and is even, for Husserl as for Strauss, its peak. Philosophy cannot abstract from the phenomena and enclose itself in subjectivity or think that the truth is lived experience, the experience of a human being in relation to the Absolute. It is in this sense that, distinguishing himself from his Jewish contemporaries, Strauss reconnects with the phenomenology of Husserl and Heidegger. But in bringing in the political dimension that they avoided, he grounds a political philosophy that is the fulfillment of phenomenology.

Strauss's Legacy

Strauss never ceased to engage with and confront the thought of Heidegger. And he never ceased to address in his own way Nietzsche's challenge concerning nihilism. But neither Heidegger nor Nietzsche was able to overcome nihilism. Their conception of reason is too modern; it is linked to Christianity and the first wave of modernity. While Nietzsche opposes the morality derived from Christianity and offers as an alternative the joyful affirmation of life for which he is nostalgic, Heidegger sees technology as the destiny of the West. Neither of these two thinkers, who are the two who certainly impressed Strauss the most, was untimely enough to be timely. Neither knew how to be sufficiently attentive to what the Greek philosophers had said about man and his openness to truth. This is why, instead of seeing what is distinctive in the thought of Plato and Aristotle and seeking the authentic Socrates behind the interpretations provided by his disciples, these thinkers set aside the political dimension of Greek thought.

This forgetfulness is connected, according to Strauss, to that which in Nietzsche remains too Christian. This makes sense if we consider Christianity as a particular way of thinking rather than as a religion. Modern philosophy has its origin in the Pauline interpretation of the Law, which has habituated us to the separation of the political and the theological and to reserve matters of belief to the sphere of private morality. The perplexity of the modern religious conscience is linked to this internalization of the content of religion, which is at the heart of the critique by Rosenzweig, but also by Karl Barth, of liberal religion. This is the context for Strauss's confrontation with Spinoza. It is equally this way of putting religion into morality that explains Nietzsche's contempt for Christianity, which he does not separate *in essence* from Judaism. But Strauss shows that the idea of the Law as structure or as a religious, political, and social whole is the specificity of the Jewish and Arab Middle Ages and that it is a sign of the Platonic origin of the medieval Enlightenment. This is the real demarcation line between Ancients and Moderns: the latter are, in a certain way, all Christians.

The Jewish and Arab thinkers of the Middle Ages knew how to conserve that which was essential in Plato and Aristotle—the political teaching of Socrates. While St. Thomas was informed by the philosophy of Aristotle, his *Metaphysics*, Maimonides and his Islamic masters chose Platonic Politics, the *Republic* and the *Laws*. And once one is aware of the political dimension of the Greek philosophers, through the character of

Socrates gaining access to their complete teaching, and one fully understands the notion of Law common to Plato and Maimonides, one can no longer say with Heidegger that the history of the West is determined by the forgetfulness of being. Neither can one say that the history of the West is a history of metaphysics nor be convinced by the thought of *Ereignis* as an illumination of the retreat of Being and the essence of technology.

Strauss, like Heidegger, claims that the crisis of our times is the crisis of the West and that this has to be understood in terms of the history of thought. But for Strauss, the crisis of our times is a crisis of political philosophy; it is linked to the disappearance of political philosophy, to the forgetfulness that man is embedded in a community that is pregiven, and to the exclusion from the domain of politics of the question of the good life. The first forgetfulness is linked to the status conferred on consciousness, which becomes first foundation. The Moderns became blind to the problem of consciousness being in a world that transcends it but of which it is a part, including in its comprehension of the whole and the highest truths.

The second dimension of the death of classical political philosophy is thus the disappearance of the end of man as the horizon for inquiry. This dimension is also linked to a forgetting, but is above all the result of the history of modern thought. It is for this reason that the disease, present from the beginning of the Enlightenment, leads to a situation that is worse in its heirs. The question of the good life, constitutive for the practice of philosophy and engendered by reason itself, was excluded from politics, leading to its disappearance. This rupture, beginning with Machiavelli, was intentional. One can even say that it was motivated by the will of the philosophers to defend freedom of thought and to emancipate human beings from the tutelage of authoritative institutions that dictated their obligations. These institutions, in the time of Hobbes and Spinoza, are both religious and political. The Church being the enemy, a radical break was needed with the manner of thinking that could justify the entanglement of theology and politics and that led to war and misery. But, sooner or later, this separation of religion and politics and this exclusion of the question of the good life from the domain of political reflection and even of knowledge altogether would lead to relativism and a rationalism that is no longer connected to ancient rationalism. Everything happens as if this forgetting, at the beginning intended by the thinkers of the seventeenth century, became unconscious in their successors, leading ultimately to the self-destruction of modernity. Destruction and self-destruction are linked in this process, which recalls the dialectics of evil, where sin and despair are interconnected. Reason, reduced to a mere instrument of the passions, becomes calculation, ratiocination. On the one hand, one has a relativism of values, which does not permit the critique of certain practices and apparently places everything on the same level. On the other, one has a technological reason, which becomes the norm in all things. It is thus that modern rationalism leads to the contempt for reason.

And this contempt for reason figures in the way that Heidegger reconstructs the logic of the West. Not only is his conception of reason derived from a history that begins after Plato, but, moreover, he says that philosophy is unable to get over the crisis, and he appeals to poetry. Heidegger does not allow the possibility of struggling against nihilism, but he is not an apologist for irrationalism. He shares with the Moderns their erroneous conception of reason and sees in technology the destiny of the West. There is, in his reading, a fatalistic account that goes back to that faith in history that is, according to Strauss, the astrology of the Moderns. For Strauss, the self-destruction of the West is not a predetermined outcome. The conception of reason that reduces to calculation, the rationalism that leads to irrationalism, are not the logical fulfillment of Greek philosophy, but the consequence, more or less foreseeable, of breaking points that occurred at certain moments in the history of the West. Surely, the philosophers who brought about the break in question with classical rationalism are responsible for the disappearance of political philosophy and thus for the crisis of our times. But not only the categories that they developed in order to solve the problems related to religious conflict led to liberal democracy, which is a good, but, moreover, on various points, the philosophies of Spinoza and Hobbes are superior to those of their successors and truly belong to the Enlightenment. The political judgment and anthropology of Hobbes, the reflection on the social function of religion in Spinoza, his idea that knowledge is the site of human self-perfection, and the need to defend freedom of thought are strengths that Strauss does not put in question. The problems and misadventures of democracy do not come from *this* heritage of the modern Enlightenment. The difficulty is elsewhere: it is a matter of going back to before the conception of man as individual defined by his need for self-preservation and of integrating the question of the good life not only into political reflection, but within reason itself. Reason means openness to truth, as evidenced by the Maimonidean doctrine of the natural conditions of prophecy. The Enlightenment of Maimonides bids us not to neglect the question that permits us to understand *how* man is open to the truth, even if, for him, the Law is given, and it is not to be questioned *why* it is so.

The dialogue that Strauss pursued throughout his career with the modern Enlightenment led him to return to the Ancients and Maimonides in light of Heidegger's question about truth. The question of Being is integrated within the Straussian reinterpretation of the notion of Law. Strauss then transcends Heidegger on his own ground in claiming that he is inattentive to one of the traditions that determines the West and in accusing him of not wanting to be also of Jerusalem. Strauss's loyalty to his spiritual father, Cohen, who showed him the way toward the enlightened Judaism of Maimonides, permitted him to confront Heidegger. This confrontation is also ours to the extent that, in suggesting that Heidegger did not know how to overcome nihilism, because he did not see the truth contained in monotheism, Strauss leaves, in his legacy, a certain number of open questions.

If it is impossible to overcome nihilism except in reference to the biblical tradition and if this is within the framework of political philosophy, considered as first philosophy, where the religious, the political, and the ethical can be interrelated in a manner that preserves liberal democracy, how to make the religious traditions that determine together our world get along with one another, without having to confer authority on the representatives of only one of them? Similarly, if it is the mission of political philosophy to preserve the tension between Jerusalem and Athens, one must include within its program not only the various traditions, but also scientific knowledge, in order to produce something other than a religious philosophy or a synthesis that would be just one more *Weltanschauung*. How could this enterprise issuing from the Straussian Enlightenment and its reactualization of the true meaning of reason be possible other than in the form of a collective undertaking, in the sense in which Husserl and the philosophers of the eighteenth century understood it?

Further, if the domain of application of philosophical reflection is, in the first instance, technology, the ultimate destination of modernity and the weapon of modern tyranny, how is one able to pose again the question of the best political regime? This regime is a regulatory ideal, and not a reality or an existing regime. Its content is nevertheless determinate, to the extent that it is perceived to provide opportunity to a type of human being open to his own perfection and the fulfillment of his humanity, which occurs through knowledge, by the acquisition of healthy opinions, and, in the best case, true opinions. The question is how to know how to reintroduce into political reflection this philosophical notion of the best regime while avoiding the risk that political action and ideology impair this philosophical task through imposing with violence an order that will have been declared as universally just, but that is a cover for a hegemonic will and that will do nothing for the struggle against the real problem. This touches the whole world in the era of technology. Wars between capitalists and Marxists, supporters of economic liberalism and critics of globalization, West and East, and today the West and Asia, but also the United States and Europe, are the consequence of certain number of choices and assumptions linked to a conception of man that becomes widespread at the end of the Renaissance. This does not mean that medieval Spain was a golden age or that the Ancients were incapable of barbaric conduct. But the malady that characterizes the West and explains the protests against it comes both from outside and inside and must be thought through in radical terms. It is a matter of going to the principles on which our civilization rests and asking what needs to be altered in order that its vitality and richness be conserved.

In a world where, increasingly, not only perplexity but also confusion reigns, one can ask if the legacy of Strauss is not to invite the philosopher to become an engaged observer, a "*spectateur engagé*," as Raymond Aron said. This designated a task that is at the same time less intoxicating and less discrete than would think either Kojeve, who saw only engagement, and Husserl, who considered himself a mere spectator.[5] Is it not for such a human being, who has constantly in mind the spirit of Plato's *Seventh Letter*, to remind us that there is a gap or an incompatibility between thought and action, philosophy and politics, which is positive and which one cannot eliminate without at the same time destroying all creativity? Does not "being enlightened" mean to place oneself where several shafts of light converge, which communicate an aspect of the truth and which convey the light with a degree of intensity that varies? Because the political philosopher knows that the cave is not only the realm of illusion, but a world the center of which opens the possibility of a reflection that can be a reflection in common, because the world of daily life transcends or overcomes the particular perspectives. The phenomenological reduction achieved by political philosophy, far from leading the thinker turning inward on himself and leaving the public space to mere ideologues and opportunists, renews the idea of a public world that appears the same across the diverse perspectives of the individuals who inhabit it. Does not the Straussian Enlightenment give a voice to Leibniz, who was, in addition to a philosopher, active in the world and a metaphysical poet? "And just as the same town, when looked at from different sides, appears quite different and is, as it were, multiplied in perspective, so also it happens that because of the infinite number of simple substances, it is as if there were as many different universes, which are however but different perspectives of a single universe in accordance with the different points of view of each monad."[6]

Notes

Introduction

1. L. Strauss, "What Is Liberal Education?," in *Liberalism Ancient and Modern* (University of Chicago Press (1968), pp. 7–8.

2. L. Strauss, "A Giving of Accounts: Jacob Klein and Leo Strauss," *St. John's College Review* (Annapolis and Santa Fe), vol. 22, n°1, April 1970, p. 1.

3. Ibid., p. 2.

4. Ibid.

5. L. Strauss, "Das Erkenntnisproblem in der philosophischen Lehre Fr. H. Jacobis," (1921), in *Gesammelte Schriften*, Bd. II, Hrsg. Von H. und W. Meier (Stuttgart: J.B. Metzler Verlag, 1997), pp. 236–297.

6. L. Strauss, Brief an Löwith, 2. II. 1933, *Gesammelte Schriften*, Bd. III, Hrsg. Von H. und W. Meier (Stuttgart: J.B. Metzler, 2001), p. 621.

7. L. Strauss, *Thoughts on Machiavelli*, Phoenix Edition (The University of Chicago Press, 1078), p. 173.

8. L. Strauss, "Notes on Carl Schmitt, *The Concept of the Political*," in Carl Schmitt, *The Concept of the Political*, trans. G Schwab, expanded ed. (Chicago: University of Chicago Press, 2007).

9. L. Strauss, "The Crisis of Our time" (1962), in *The Predicament of Modern Politics* (Detroit: University of Detroit Press: 1964), p. 42.

10. L. Strauss, "Preface to the English Translation of Spinoza's Critique of Religion," in *Liberalism Ancient and Modern*, op. cit., p. 224.

11. L. Strauss, "Preface to the English Translation of Spinoza's Critique of Religion," op. cit., p. 257.

12. L. Strauss, "Jerusalem and Athens. Some Preliminary Reflections," in *Studies in Platonic Political Philosophy* (Chicago: University of Chicago Press, 1983), p. 168.

13. L. Strauss, "An Introduction to Heideggerian Existentialism, in *The Rebirth of Classical Political Rationalism*, Essays and Lectures by Leo Strauss, selected by T. L. Pangle (Chicago: University of Chicago Press, 1989), p. 28.

14. Ibid., pp. 29, 43.

15. Strauss, "The Crisis of Our Time," p. 42.

16. Ibid., p. 43.

17. L. Strauss, "German Nihilism," *Interpretation*, 26/3 (1999), p. 360.

18. L. Strauss, "What Is Political Philosophy?," in *An Introduction to Political Philosophy: Ten Essays by Leo Strauss*, ed. H. Gildin (Detroit: Wayne State University Press, 1989), p. 56

19. A. de Tocqueville, *Democracy in America*, part IV, chap. 6.

20. See the article "Democracy" in the *Encyclopedia*, where the author expresses the common understanding of the Enlightenment. In the *Federalist Papers*, James Madison responded to opponents of the Constitution who conflated democracy and representative republicanism. This was also the sense of the debates of 1789–1991 concerning the constituent assembly.

21. L. Strauss, "Liberal Education and Responsibility," *Liberalism Ancient and Modern*, op. cit., p. 10.

22. See, generally, the writings of Strauss beginning in the 1930s. See also the correspondence between Strauss and Klein from 1929 to 1969, *Gesammelte Schriften*, Bd. III, op. cit., pp. 455–605.

23. Scholars typically distinguish three phases in the development of Strauss's thought. See, for example, Allan Bloom, "Leo Strauss September 20, 1899-October 18, 1973," in *Giants and Dwarfs: Essays 1960–1990* (New York: Simon & Schuster, 1990), pp. 246–250.

24. L. Strauss, "Cohen und Maimuni" (1931), *Gesammelte Schriften*, Bd. II, op. cit., p. 395.

25. Strauss, "The Crisis of Our Time," op. cit.

26. L. Strauss, *Philosophy and Law, Contributions to the Understanding of Maimonides and his Predecessors,* trans. Eve Adler (SUNY, Press, 1995), pp. 37–38. Strauss writes, after Nietzsche, concerning an atheism from probity in a rather different context, but it is equally a question of the gap between the situation of today's philosophers and that of their predecessors.

27. Edmund Husserl, *The Crisis of European Sciences and Transcendental Phenomenology*, trans. D. Carr (Evanston: Northwestern University Press, 1970).

28. Ibid., p. 299.

29. L. Strauss, *Natural Right and History* (Chicago: University of Chicago Press, 1953), p. 45.

30. For an examination of this interpretation of Heidegger by Strauss, see Part II, Chapter 1 of this book.

31. M. Heidegger, *Contributions to Philosophy (From Enowning)*, trans. Parvis Emad and Kenneth Maly (Bloomington: Indiana University Press, 1999).

32. L. Strauss, "The Crisis of Political Philosophy," op. cit., p. 96.

33. Heidegger, citing Holderin in "The Question of Technology," in M. Heidegger, *Basic Writings*, ed. D. F. Krell (London: Harper Perennial Modern Thought, 2008), p. 333. There is a pun on the word for save, Retten, which can mean to rescue from danger but also to assist, "to fetch something home into its essence, in order to bring the essence for the first time into its proper appearing."

34. L. Straus, "Philosophy and Law," op. cit., p. 25, footnote of Strauss, pp. 135–136.

35. Ibid., p. 73.

36. L. Strauss, "Cohen und Maimuni," op. cit., pp. 393–436.

37. Seth Benardete, "Leo Strauss: '*The City and Man*,'" *Political Science Reviewer* 8 (1978):11.

38. To borrow an expression that Husserl used with respect to the neo-Kantians. Strauss uses it as well in "A Giving of Accounts: Jacob Klein and, Leo Strauss," op. cit., p. 2. See also L. Strauss, "An Introduction to Heideggerian Existentialism," op. cit., p. 29; and "Philosophy as Rigorous Science and Political Philosophy," in *Studies in Platonic Political Philosophy*, op. cit., p. 31.

39. This interpretation differs from that of Shadia Drury in *Leo Strauss and the American Right* (New York: St. Martin's Press, 1999). She considers Strauss as an enemy of liberal democracy who is haunted by the ghost of Weimar. She misses the essential point that Strauss engages in a constructive critique of democracy, which is developed through a critical examination of the modern Enlightenment, the questioning of its conception of human nature and reason, and far, from being one-sided, this critique goes hand in hand with the superiority of Hobbes and Spinoza to their successors. Strauss wishes to advance another Enlightenment and presents himself as a philosopher more faithful than the Moderns to the Enlightenment of Platonic origin.

40. B. Constant, "The Liberty of the Ancients Compared with That of the Moderns," speech given at the Athénée Royal in Paris in 1819, in B. Constant, *Political Writings*, trans. B. Fontana (Cambridge: Cambridge University Press, 1988).

41. M. Heidegger, "Die Gefahr" ("The Danger"), in *Bremer und Freiburger Vorträge, Gesamtausgabe*, Bd. 79, op. cit., pp. 49–50.

42. L. Strauss, Brief an Scholem, 2. X. 1935, *Gesammelte Schriften*, Bd. III, Hrsh. von H. und W. Meier (Stuttgart: J.B. Metzler, 2001), p. 716.

Part I, Chapter 1

1. L. Strauss, "Progress or Return?," in *The Rebirth of Classical Political Rationalism: An Introduction to the Thought of Leo Strauss,* selected and introduced by Thomas Pangle (Chicago: University of Chicago Press, 1989), pp. 227–237.

2. F. Rosenzweig, "Atheistic Theology," in *Philosophical and Theological Writings*, trans. P. W. Franks and M. L. Morgan (Indianapolis: Hackett, 2000), pp. 10–24.

3. ". . . the contemporary return to Judaism succeeds a break with Judaism which eventually, or from the beginning, understood itself as a progress beyond Judaism. That break was effected in a classic manner by a solitary man—Spinoza." L. Strauss, "Progress or Return, p. 230.

4. L. Strauss, "Why We Remain Jews?," in *Political Philosopher and Jewish Thinker*, ed. Kenneth L. Deutsch and Walter Nicgorski (Lanham, MD: Rowman & Littlefield, 1994), p. 49.

5. K. Löwith, *Mein Leben in Deutschland vor und nach 1933* (Stuttgart: Metzler, 1986).

6. In the sense of B. Constant. See "The Liberty of the Ancients Compared with that of the Moderns," in B. Constant, *Political Writings* (Cambridge: Cambridge University Press, 1988).

7. L. Strauss, "Das Erkenntnisproblem in der philosophischen Lehre Fr. H. Jacobis," *Gesammelte Schriften*, Bd. II, p. 261. See "The Dissertation" (1921), in *The Problem of Knowledge in the Philosophical Doctrine of Friedrich Heinrich Jacobi.* An extract in English translation is available in M. Zank, *Leo Strauss: The Early Writings (1921–1932)* (Albany, NY: SUNY Press, 2002), pp. 54–55.

8. F. H. Jacobi, *Werke*, Bd. II, op. cit., pp. 516–517.

9. This notion of reason in Jacobi renders illegitimate the criticism that he adheres to an illuminism that his concept of belief is unable to support. See F. H. Jacobi, ibid.

10. L. Strauss, "Preface to the English Translation of *Spinoza's Critique of Religion*," in *Liberalism Ancient and Modern*, op. cit., p. 239.

11. L. Strauss, *Thoughts on Machiavelli*, op. cit., p. 173.

12. L. Strauss, "Das Erkenntnisproblem in der philosophischen Lehre Fr. H. Jacobis," op. cit., p. 248.

13. Elise Reimarus served as an intermediary between Jacobi and Mendelsohn. It is to her that Jacobi, on July 21, 1783, revealed the Spinozism of Lessing. On September 1, she transmitted to Jacobi Mendelsohn's questions. Finally, in his letter of November 4, Jacobi gave a summary of his interview with Lessing. Until April 1785, Mendelssohn and Jacobi corresponded regularly. Elise Reimarus was the system of Johann Albert Heinrich. He thought it would be imprudent to make this a matter of public record, and Elise passed on this advice to Jacobi in a letter dated December 5, 1783, less than two years before the publication by Jacobi of *Letters to M. Mendelssohn on the Doctrine of Spinoza,* which appeared at the end of September 1785. Jacobi had decided to publish this correspondence when he learned in June 1785 that Mendelssohn was working on a book on pantheism, which would appear in October 1785 as *Morning Hours: Lectures on God's Existence.*

14. Mendelssohn died on January 4, 1786, three days before having sent to the editor the manuscript of his response to Jacobi, *To the Friends of Lessing*, which would appear with a preface by Engel that accuses Jacobi of having precipitated Mendelssohn's death. This accusation would be repeated in the *Hamburgische Korrespondant* and the *Königliche Zeitung* and would result in a hardening of the tone of philosophical exchange and debate.

15. G. E. Lessing, *Nathan the Wise*, Act III, Scene V, in G. E. Lessing, *Nathan the Wise, Minna von Barnhelm, and other Plays and Writings*, ed. P. Demetz (New York: Continuum, 1991), p. 230.

16. They need tradition, not necessarily religion. This ambiguity is at the core of Strauss's interest in Maimonides. It also explains the fact that his interpretation of Maimonides has the appearance of evolving: when one compares the early writings, like "Philosophy and Law," where Maimonides appears as a *Jewish* thinker, with his letters to Jacob Klein, where Strauss compares the *Guide of the Perplexed* to *Also Spake Zarathustra* and dares to say Maimonides is an atheist, one is surprised. See, for instance, the letters of July 3, 1938, and February 16, 1938, *Gesammelte Schriften*, Bd. III, op. cit., p. 533 and pp. 549–550. However, this surprise and the paradox diminish once one has understood that Revelation or heteronomous Law in Maimonides refers to tradition and is used to put in question the self-sufficiency of reason or the modern conception of reason and of man, that is to say, the modern conception of politics. Such a critique of modern assumptions does not lead to the opposition that faith is redemption and that one has to submit to the God of the Bible to give meaning and direction to one's life.

17. L. Strauss, *Spinoza's Critique of Religion*, trans. E. M. Sinclair (New York: Schocken Books, 1965), p. 29.

18. *Immanuel Kant, Theoretical Philosophy after 1781*, ed. Henry Allison and Peter Heath (Cambridge: Cambridge University Press, 2002), pp. 431–445.

19. The other reason is related to Strauss's opposition to the neo-Kantian idea of method. See Chapter III, "Cohen and Maimonides" on the debates between Strauss and Natorp, and Cohen and Cassirer.

20. For Cohen, reason has need of Revelation or of the idea of God, because Revelation is connected to practical reason, which is, in Kantian morality, an imminent form of transcendentalism, whereas divine Revelation is dispensed with heteronomy.

21. L. Ferry, *Philosophie politique* (Paris: PUF, 1984), vol. 2, p. 41.

22. Über das Verhältnis der Metaphysik zu der Religion" (1787), in *Sämtliche Schriften* (Hannover, 1828). For his critique of the French Revolution, see *Untersuchungen über die französische Revolution*, Hannover and Osnabrück, cited by Alain Renaut and Lukas Sosoe in *Philosophie du droit*, "Recherches politiques" (Paris: PUF, 1991).

23. G. W. F. Hegel, *Elements of the Philosophy of Right*, ed. A. W. Wood (Cambridge: Cambridge University Press, 1991), pp. 161–162.

24. Edmund Burke, *Reflections on the Revolution in France* [1790] (London: Penguin Classics, 1986); and see the preface of P. Raynaud in E. Burke, *Reflexions sur la revolution francaise* (Paris: Hachette, 1989), p. xlviii. See also Hannah Arendt, *The Origins of Totalitarianism*, rev. ed. (New York: Schocken, 2004); *On Revolution* (New York: Viking, 1963).

25. Jacobi, *Werke*, Bd. II, op. cit., pp. 516–517. This is from the famous unfinished letter of Jacobi to French academician La Harpe, dated May 5, 1790.

26. Strauss, *Natural Right and History*, Introduction, pp. 1–8.

27. Jacobi, Letter to La Harpe, op. cit.

28. Letter to La Harpe, in A. Renaut and L. Sosoe, *Philosophie du droit*, op. cit., pp. 311–312.

29. Cited in A. Renaut and L. Sosoe, *Philosophie du droit*, op. cit., p. 314.

30. Cited in ibid., p. 317.

31. Strauss, Letter to Löwith, June 1933. See also the references to Kierkegaard in later correspondence: "Karl Löwith and Leo Strauss: Correspondence." *Independent Journal of Philosophy* 5/6 (1988), pp. 177–192. The position of Strauss toward Kierkegaard is ambiguous yet revealing. In a letter of July 19, 1951, he tells Löwith that Kierkegaard is a greater thinker than Pascal. But in a letter of February 23, 1950, he agrees with Heidegger that Kierkegaard was a man of the nineteenth century. According to Strauss, Kierkegaard's point of departure is wrong: it can lead neither to political philosophy nor to a true awareness of the Greeks.

32. Strauss, Letter to Löwith, ibid.

33. This does not exclude the understanding of discontinuity or ruptures in tradition. To the contrary, Strauss is critical of Cohen's conservatism for his not having seen that "the continuous and changing tradition which he cherishes so greatly would never have come into being through conservatism or without discontinuities, revolutions, and sacrileges . . ." Preface to the English Translation of *Spinoza's Critique of Religion*, op. cit., p. 258.

34. K. Barth, *Protestant Theology in the 19th Century*, trans. B. Cozens and J. Bowden (London: SCM Press, 1959).

35. S. Kierkegaard, *The Sickness unto Death*, trans. H. V. Hong and E. H. Hong (Princeton: Princeton University Press, 1980).

36. In particular in the commandment to love our neighbor, which derives from the first commandment, that is, the love of God, because it is above all the love of God that leads us to the love of our neighbor. See the *First Epistle of St. John* 4. Kierkegaard radicalizes this idea in showing that faith alone as love of God makes interhuman love possible and pulls us away from despair, that is, from melancholy. See "Guilty, Not Guilty," in *Stages on Life's Way*, trans. W. Lowrie (New York: Shocken, 1967) and *The Sickness unto Death*, op. cit.

37. S. Kierkegaard, *The Concept of Anxiety*, trans. R. Thomte and A. B. Anderson (Princeton: Princeton University Press, 1980).

38. Kierkegaard, *The Sickness unto Death*, op. cit.

39. Strauss, *Gesammelte Schriften*, Bd. II, op cit., pp. 455–456.

40. F. Kafka, "Before the Law," in Nahum N. Glatzer, ed., *Franz Kafka: The Complete Stories and Parables* 3–4 (New York: Quality Paperback Book Club, 1971).

41. Strauss, "Progress or Return?," op. cit., p. 229.

42. Zunz created the rabbinical seminar of Breslau in 1854. He edited the *Monthly for Jewish History and Science.* Grätz, the author of the eleven-volume *History of the Jews Since Antiquity*, joined the seminar. It brought together the leading names in Jewish studies in Berlin in 1872, including thinkers who had already set out on a different course. Hirsch found the seminar too liberal while Geiger found it too orthodox, and in 1872 in Berlin he founded the Academy for Jewish Studies, which included Julius Guttman, Leo Beck, and others. Its orthodox rival was the Orthodox Rabbinical Seminar, established in Berlin in

1873 by Azriel Hildesheimer. See P. Mendes-Flohr, *German Jews: A Dual Identity* (New Haven: Yale University Press, 1999).

43. Strauss, "Progress or Return?," op. cit., p. 227.

44. Zunz's "Something Regarding Rabbinical Literature" was written in the context of the Jewish Cultural and Scientific Union, created in 1821 after the failure of the scientific circle that was in operation in Berlin between November 1816 and July 1817 and which already brought together scholars, among them Zunz, whom one would find in Jewish Studies (*Wissenschaft des Judentums*), which is aimed at improvement and renewal in Judaism. The first volume of the *Review of Jewish Studies* (*Zeitschrift für die Wissenschaft des Judentums*) appeared in 1822–1823.

45. Strauss, "Progress or Return?," op. cit., pp. 229–230.

46. Amos Funkenstein, *Theology and the Scientific Imagination from the Middle Ages to the* 17th *Century* (Princeton: Princeton University Press, 1986). See also Funkenstein, *Maimonides: Nature, History and Messianic Beliefs* (Tel Aviv: Israel Ministry of Defense Publishing House, 1998).

47. Strauss, "Progress or Return?," op. cit., p. 229.

48. M. Maimonides, *The Guide of the Perplexed*, trans. S. Pines (Chicago: University of Chicago Press, 1963), vol. I, chap. 26. Thanks to P. Bouretz for this reference.

49. In the discussion that follows, the Moderns are not so much Spinoza and Hobbes as their successors, who take the Enlightenment for granted. In effect, Strauss discovered in the thinkers of the beginning of the Enlightenment an art of writing that permitted them to escape persecution. In all cases, what is hidden in their works relates to their atheism. By contrast, in the case of certain premodern thinkers, there are truths about God that must be hidden, not because they are contrary to political order, but because they concern secrets that not everyone is able to absorb. See Part II, chapter 3 of this book.

50. Maimonides employs the term *talattuf*. According to Remi Brague, this term, which suggests the idea of something generous and subtle, is used by Maimonides and other writers in the same context, where the succession of generations is the device by which God establishes continuity within the living. In Averroes and Halevi, one finds it also as a designation for the elegant solution that permits God to establish continuity where there should be discontinuity.

51. It should be stressed that until the end of the First World War, very few German Jews were Zionists.

52. "Preface to the English Translation of Spinoza's Religion," op. cit., p. 230.

53. Strauss, "Preface to the English Translation of *Spinoza's Critique of Religion*," p. 227. Strauss cites a passage of Goethe, *The Travels of Wilhelm Meister*, book III, chap. 11: 'we do not tolerate any Jew among us; for how could we grant him a share in the highest culture, the origin and tradition of which he denies?"

54. J. Halevi, *An Argument for the Faith of Israel, The Kuzari* (New York: Schocken, 1964), pp. 226–227.

55. Cited by Strauss, "Preface to the English Translation of *Spinoza's Critique of Religion*," p. 228.

56. "Preface to the English Translation of *Spinoza's Critique of Religion*," ibid.

57. "Preface to the English Translation of *Spinoza's Critique of Religion*," ibid.

58. "Preface to the English Translation of *Spinoza's Critique of Religion*," ibid., p. 229.

59. "Preface to the English Translation of *Spinoza's Critique of Religion*," ibid.

60. "Why We Remain Jews?," op. cit., p. 319.

61. "Why We Remain Jews?," ibid.

62. "Preface to the English Translation of *Spinoza's Critique of Religion*," op. cit., pp. 229–230.

63. "Why We Remain Jews," op. cit., p. 320.

Part I, Chapter 2

1. L. Strauss, "Testament of Spinoza," in Leo Strauss: *The Early Writings (1921–1932)*, op. cit., p. 217.

2. L. Strauss, *Hobbes' Critique of Religion*, in L. Strauss, *Hobbes' Critique of Religion and Other Writings*, ed. G. Bartlett and S. Minkov (Chicago: University of Chicago Press, 2011), p. 24.

3. Ibid., p. 23.

4. Strauss uses the word "Epicureanism" (*Epikureertum, Epikureismus*) when he speaks of the Epicurean interest of the critique of religion. This is different from the doctrine of Epicurus.

5. L. Strauss, *Hobbes' Critique of Religion*, ibid., pp. 65–66.

6. Strauss, *Spinoza's Critique of Religion*, op. cit., p. 61.

7. Ibid., p. 90.

8. Ibid., p. 91. See Hobbes, *Leviathan,* chaps. XI, XII.

9. L. Strauss, *Hobbes' Critique of Religion*, op. cit., p. 66.

10. Ibid., p. 26, emphasis in original.

11. Strauss, *Spinoza's Critique of Religion*, op. cit., p. 95.

12. Ibid., p. 97.

13. L. Strauss, *Spinoza's Critique of Religion*, op. cit., pp. 101–102. See Hobbes, *Leviathan*, chapter VIII.

14. And even when he refers to Abraham, it is to say that "he . . . owes his sovereignty not to God but to a purely human relationship." See Strauss, *Hobbes' Critique of Religion*, op. cit., p. 47.

15. Ibid., p. 32.

16. Ibid., p. 34.

17. Ibid., p. 35.

18. Ibid., p. 36.

19. Ibid., p. 37.

20. L. Strauss, *Spinoza's Critique of Religion*, op. cit., p. 65.

21. L. Strauss, *Hobbes's Critique of Religion*, op. cit., pp. 71–72.
22. Ibid., pp. 68–69.
23. Ibid., p. 69.
24. Ibid., p. 72.
25. *Spinoza's Critique of Religion*, op. cit., p. 66.
26. Ibid., p. 67.
27. Ibid., chap. IV.
28. L. Strauss, *Hobbes' Critique of Religion*, op. cit., pp. 111–112.
29. Ibid., p. 113.
30. Ibid., p.108.
31. Ibid., p. 108.
32. Ibid., p. 109.
33. Ibid., p. 113.
34. F. Nietzsche, *Thus Spake Zarathustra*, trans. W. Kaufmann (New York: Random House, 1954), prologue.
35. L. Strauss, *Hobbes' Critique of Religion*, op. cit., p. 69, n. 154.
36. L. Strauss, "Preface to the English Translation of *Spinoza's Critique of Religion*," op. cit., p. 239.
37. A. Matheron, *Le Christ et le salut des ignorants chez Spinoza* (Paris: Aubier Montaigne, 1971), chap. III, p. 172.
38. Hermann Cohen, "Spinoza über Staat und Religion, Judentum und Christentum," in Bruno Strauss, ed., *Hermann Cohens Jüdische Schriften*, 3 vols. (Berlin: C.A. Schwetshke, 1924), pp. 290–372.
39. Strauss, "Preface to the English Translation of *Spinoza's Critique of religion*," op. cit., p. 244.
40. "Preface to the English Translation of *Spinoza's Critique of Religion*," op. cit., p. 245.
41. "How to Study Spinoza's Theologico-Political Treatise," in *Persecution and the Art of Writing* (Westport, CT: Greenwood Press, 1973), p. 184.
42. Ibid.
43. Strauss, *Spinoza's Critique of Religion*, op. cit., pp. 222–223.
44. Spinoza, *Ethics*, I, Proposition XVII, scolie.
45. L. Strauss, *Spinoza's Critique of Religion*, op. cit., p. 247. That is, to prevent acts of violence, form good character, and perfect the understanding.
46. Ibid., p. 256.
47. Ibid., p. 261.
48. Ibid., p. 262.
49. Ibid., p. 263.
50. B. Spinoza, *Theologico-Political Treatise*, trans. M. Yaffe (Newport, MA: Focus Publishing, 2004), chaps. XIX, XIII.
51. Ibid., chap. XIV.
52. S. Pines, "Le *TTP* de Spinoza, Maimonides, et Kant," in *La liberté de philosopher*, trans. R. Brague (Paris: DDB, 1997), p. 365.
53. Spinoza, *Theologico-Political Treatise*, op. cit., chap. IV.

54. Ibid, chap. XIV, p. 164.
55. Maimonides, *Guide of the Perplexed*, op. cit., III; 58, 28.
56. Ibid., p. 166.
57. "Preface to the English Translation of *Spinoza's Critique of Religion*," op. cit., p. 230.
58. Ibid., p. 225.
59. A. de Tocqueville, *Democracy in America*, op. cit., book II, part 2, chap. 2, p. 484.
60. Strauss, *Natural Right and History*, chap. 5.
61. A. de Tocqueville, *Democracy in America*, op. cit., book II, pp. 201–202
62. M. Gauchet, *Le désenchantement du monde, une histoire politique de la religion* (Paris: Gallimard, 1985).
63. A. de Tocqueville, *Democracy in America*, op. cit, book II, part I, chap. 7, p. 426.
64. Ibid., book II, part I.
65. A. de Tocqueville, *Democracy in America*, op. cit., book II; part IV, chap. 6I, pp. 661–665.
66. Nietzsche, *Thus Spake Zarathustra*, Prologue 3, op. cit., p. 330.
67. L. Strauss, "Preface to the English Translation of *Spinoza's Critique of Religion*," op. cit., p. 231.
68. Ibid., p. 254.
69. "Jerusalem and Athens," in L. Strauss, *Jewish Philosophy and the Crisis of Modernity: Essays and Lectures in Modern Jewish Thought*, ed. K. H. Green (Albany, NY: SUNY Press, 1997), pp. 379–380; "On the Interpretation of Genesis," in ibid., pp. 359–361.
70. L. Strauss, "On the Interpretation of Genesis," in ibid., p. 360.
71. L. Strauss, "Jerusalem and Athens," in ibid., p. 402.
72. "On the Interpretation of Genesis," in ibid., p. 374.
73. "On the Interpretation of Genesis," in ibid., p. 375.
74. L. Strauss, "Preface to the English Translation of *Spinoza's Critique of Religion*," op. cit., p. 232.
75. Ibid., p. 232.
76. L. Strauss, "On the Bible Science of Spinoza and his Precursors," in *Leo Strauss: The Early Writings* (1921–1932), op. cit., pp. 173–200.
77. L. Strauss, "Philosophy and Law," op. cit., p. 32.
78. Ibid.
79. L. Strauss, "Preface to the English Translation of *Spinoza's Critique of Religion*," op. cit., p. 233.
80. Ibid., p. 234.
81. L. Strauss, *Philosophy and Law*, op. cit., p. 38.
82. L. Strauss, "Preface to the English Translation of *Spinoza's Critique of Religion*," op. cit., p. 238.
83. Ibid., p. 237.
84. L. Strauss, *Philosophy and Law*, op. cit., p. 28.

Part I, Chapter 3

1. G. Scholem, *Major Trends in Jewish Mysticism* (New York: Schocken, 1946), p. 26.

2. Ibid., p. 23

3. Ibid., chap. VII, pp. 244–286.

4. Ibid., p. 22

5. Ibid., p. 29.

6. Ibid., p. 25.

7. Ibid., pp. 265–268.

8. Ibid., p. 267.

9. Ibid., p. 268.

10. Ibid., p. 269.

11. L. Strauss, "How to Begin to Study Medieval Philosophy," op. cit., p. 215.

12. Ibid., p. 215.

13. Scholem, *Major Trends in Jewish Mysticism*, op. cit., pp. 315–320.

14. L. Strauss, "How to Begin to Study Medieval Philosophy," op. cit., p. 215.

15. Ibid.

16. Ibid., p. 217.

17. Strauss, "Cohen und Maimuni," Vortrag zu halten am 4 May 1931, Berlin. *Gesammelte Schriften*, bd. II, pp. 393–436, pp. 396, 406.

18. Strauss, "Cohen und Maimuni," op. cit., p. 395.

19. F. Rosenzweig, *The Star of Redemption*, trans. W. Hallo (New York: Holt, Rinehart and Winston, 1970), introduction.

20. Cohen gave two-thirds of his manuscript of *The Religion of Reason* to Rosenzweig in 1918, before its publication. The distinction between the Me and the Individual, the issue of forgiveness, and the paradigmatic function of the Day of Atonement will reemerge in Rosenzweig in his analysis of Revelation and of the relation between the connection to God and to other human beings, the first relation, as Cohen said it, expressing itself in the second, in my relation to the other considered as neighbor.

21. E. Levinas, preface to *Système et Révélation, La philosophie de Franz Rosenzweig*, de S. Mosès (Paris: Le Seuil, 1982), p. 16.

22. This is the passage of Husserl's *Cartesian Meditations* that Levinas transferred to his philosophy of the face in *Totality and Infinity.*

23. E. Levinas, "La fécondité," in *Le temps et l'autre* (Paris: PUF, 1983), pp. 86, 89.

24. E. Levinas, *Totality and Infinity: An Essay on Exteriority*, trans. A. Lingis (Hague: Nijhoff, 1969), p. 199.

25. Ibid., p. 198.

26. "The Rights of Man and the Rights of Another," in E. Levinas, *Outside the Subject*, trans. M. B. Smith (Palo Alto: Stanford University Press, 1994).

27. Ibid., p. 122.

28. Ibid., p. 125.

29. Ibid., p. 124.
30. Ibid., p. 123.
31. F. Rosensweig, "Une pensée juive moderne," in *Hors Sujet* (Paris: Le Livre de Poche, 1997), p. 71.
32. Ibid., pp. 77–79.
33. Ibid., pp. 76, 78–79.
34. Ibid., p. 83.
35. Ibid., p. 88.
36. Ibid., p. 73.
37. L. Strauss, "Cohen und Maimuni," op. cit., pp. 395–396.
38. Ibid., p. 399.
39. Ibid., p. 418.
40. Ibid., pp. 416–420.
41. Ibid., pp. 416–420.
42. Ibid., pp. 416, 421.
43. Ibid., pp. 410–411.
44. Ibid., p. 412.
45. Ibid., p. 424.
46. Ibid., p. 424.
47. Strauss, *Philosophy and Law*, op. cit., p. 91.
48. Ibid., p. 66.
49. Ibid.
50. Ibid., p. 90.
51. L. Strauss, "Cohen und Maimuni," op. cit., p. 418.
52. Strauss, "Die Geistige Lage der Gegenwart" (1932), in *Gasammelte Schriften*, Bd. II, op. cit., pp. 455–456.

Part II, Introduction

1. Strauss, "What Is Political Philosophy?," op. cit., pp. 3–52.
2. L. Strauss, *Thoughts on Machiavelli* (Chicago: University of Chicago Press, 1958), p. 298.

Part II, Chapter 1

1. L. Strauss, *The Political Philosophy of Hobbes: Its Basis and Its Genesis*, trans. M Sinclair (Chicago: University of Chicago Press, 1963), p. xv
2. P. Manent, *An Intellectual History of Liberalism*, trans. R. Balinski (Princeton: Princeton University Press, 1995), p. 11.
3. N. Machiavelli, *The Prince*, trans. H. Mansfield (Chicago: University of Chicago Press, 1998), chap. VII.
4. Ibid., chap. XXV.

5. N. Machiavelli, *Discourses on Livy*, trans. H. Mansfield and N. Tarcov (Chicago: University of Chicago Press, 1996), book II, chap. II, p. 131. See also book III, chap. 30.

6. Ibid., preface.

7. Strauss, *Thoughts on Machiavelli*, op. cit., chap. IV.

8. Machiavelli, *The Prince*, op. cit., chap. XVIII, p. 69.

9. Strauss, *Thoughts on Machiavelli*, op. cit., p. 297.

10. Ibid.

11. Ibid., p. 296.

12. Ibid., p. 297.

13. Ibid., p. 296.

14. Ibid., p. 167.

15. L. Strauss, *The Political Philosophy of Hobbes: Its Basis and Genesis*, trans. E. Sinclair (Chicago: University of Chicago Press, 1952), p. 168.

16. Hobbes, *Leviathan*, part I, chap. IV.

17. Ibid., p. 129.

18. L. Strauss, *Hobbes' Critique of Religion*, op. cit., p. 113.

19. L. Strauss, *The Political Philosophy of Hobbes*, op. cit., p. 152.

20. Ibid., p. 2.

21. Ibid.

22. Ibid., p. 3.

23. Hobbes, *Leviathan*, chap. XIII.

24. Quoted by Strauss, *The Political Philosophy of Hobbes*, op. cit., p. 10.

25. Ibid., p. 9.

26. L. Strauss, "Some Notes on the Political Science of Hobbes" (1932); Strauss, *Hobbes' Critique of Religion and Related Writings*, ibid., pp. 134–135.

27. Ibid., p. 135.

28. L. Strauss, *The Political Philosophy of Hobbes: Its Origins and Genesis*, op. cit., pp. 159–160.

29. Hobbes, *Leviathan*, chap. XIV.

30. See I. Kant, *Idea for a Universal History with a Cosmopolitan Purpose*, in *Kant, Political Writings*, trans. H. B. Nisbet, edited with an introduction and notes by H. Reiss (Cambridge: Cambridge University Press, 1991). Fourth Proposition. This idea can be refined once one takes into account the notion of sympathy in Hume and the *Theory of Moral Sentiments* of Adam Smith. In Hume, nevertheless, sympathy is limited to a small group of individuals, and there is no concept of world citizenship or the cunning of reason allowing the establishment of peace between nations beginning from an unsocial sociability. Smith, who trusts in institutions, considers that it may be possible to extend sympathy to other men. In all cases, if these thinkers allow for a moderation of modern individualism, they do so within a framework of individualism, that is, a definition of man as an individual oriented toward utility and earthly happiness, which can be that of the nation or the collectivity, of the liberal system, but which does not have as its horizon either a metaphysical ideal or an idea of the good. There is thus a break

with the Ancients. We should not neglect the diversity of the Enlightenment, varying by national character, which allows one to differentiate, for example, the Scottish Enlightenment of Reid from the French Enlightenment of Voltaire. But the present work is a critique of modernity on the basis of a reconstruction of the Enlightenment as it was addressed by Strauss, emphasizing those aspects that represent a radical break with the Ancients. This is why the focus is on those thinkers who have broken radically with classical ideas.

31. Hobbes, *Leviathan*, chap. XIII.

32. L. Strauss, *The Political Philosophy of Hobbes: Its Origins and Genesis*, op. cit., pp. 110–111.

33. J. Locke, *Second Treatise of Civil Government*, Sec. 93.

34. L. Strauss, "On the Basis of Hobbes' Political Philosophy," in *What Is Political Philosophy?*, op. cit., pp. 170–196.

35. C. Schmitt, "The Age of Neutralizations and Depoliticizations," in *The Concept of the Political*, expanded ed., trans. G. Schwab (Chicago: University of Chicago Press, 2007).

36. Montesquieu, *The Spirit of the Laws*, ed. A. M. Cohler, B. C. Miller, and H. S. Stone (Cambridge: Cambridge University Press, 2008), book XI, chap. 6.

37. "The Concept of the Political," op. cit., p. 69.

38. Schmitt, *Political Theology: Four Chapters on the Concept of Sovereignty*, trans. G. Schwab (Chicago: University of Chicago Press, 2005), p. 36.

39. "The Age of Neutralizations and Depoliticizations," op. cit., pp. 94–95.

40. J.-F. Kervégan, *Hegel, Carl Schmitt, le politique entre spéculation et positivité* (Paris: PUF, 1992), p. 105.

41. "The Age of Neutralizations and Depoliticizations," op. cit., p. 95.

42. Ibid., p. 93.

43. Heidegger, "The Question of Technology," in *Basic Writings*, op. cit.

44. "The Age of Neutralizations and Depoliticizations," op. cit., p. 93.

45. Ibid., p. 85.

46. Ibid., p. 94.

47. "The Concept of the Political," op. cit., p. 57.

48. Ibid., pp. 26–27.

49. Ibid., p. 54.

50. B. Constant, "The Liberty of the Ancients Compared with That of the Moderns," in *Constant: Political Writings*, ed. B. Fontana, p. 313.

51. "The Concept of the Political," op. cit., p. 67.

52. Ibid., p. 79.

53. Strauss, "Notes on Carl Schmitt, *The Concept of the Political*," in *The Concept of the Political*, ibid., pp. 116–117.

54. Not only is it for Strauss that the best regime cannot exist in deed and still less be extended to all peoples, but in addition Strauss seems in agreement with Schmitt in rejecting the use of human rights and humanitarianism for military and economic ends. One can wage war and conduct a foreign policy of expansion

in the name of human rights and declare that it is a struggle of good against evil, against an enemy who is outside the law because he opposes the rule of law that one holds to be superior and that is in fact the order one is seeking to impose. What Strauss does not contest in Schmitt and what he says elsewhere of natural right (in *Natural Right and History*), of which the function of critique is evident but the content of which should not be identified with human rights, would seem to preclude any justification for the political philosophy of George Bush. However, Strauss would have shared with the American neoconservatives a concern for the security of the United States and the defense of Israel. See my article "Leo Strauss et George Bush," *Le Banquet*, No. 19–20, fev. 2004, pp. 281–292.

55. And not his definition of essence (*Wesensbestimmung*).

56. "The Concept of the Political," op. cit., p. 26.

57. Ibid., pp. 60–61.

58. Ibid., p. 60.

59. Ibid., p. 65.

60. Constant, "The Liberty of the Ancients Compared with That of the Moderns," op. cit., p. 323.

61. Ibid., p. 325.

62. A. de Tocqueville, *Democracy in America*, op. cit., vol. II, book IV, chap. 6.

63. Constant, "The Liberty of the Ancients Compared with That of the Moderns," op. cit., p. 326.

64. As is shown by Schmitt's first writings on Nazism, and even if, once he joined the Nazi Party, the fateful process had begun that would lead him to the intellectual folly displayed in his *Leviathan*.

65. "The Concept of the Political," op. cit., p. 35.

66. Strauss, "Notes on Carl Schmitt's *Concept of the Political*," op. cit., pp. 116–117.

67. Namely the Socratic turn, the tension between Athens and Jerusalem, and above all the significance of the Law that resulted from his investigation of this notion in Maimonides. See Chapter III in this part of the book.

68. Strauss, "Notes on Carl Schmitt's *Concept of the Political*," op. cit., p. 114.

69. It being borne in mind that man possesses vanity and that the natural right articulated by Hobbes is a specifically human right and not, as with Spinoza, a right pertaining to every living being. Vanity and fear of death are specific to human natural right. But the "badness" of man in Hobbes does not imply that his nature is depraved. Evil does not imply the notion of sin.

70. Strauss, "Notes on Carl Schmitt's *Concept of the Political*," op. cit., p. 111.

71. Ibid.

72. See H. Meier, *The Lesson of Carl Schimtt: Four Chapters on the Distinction Between Political Theology and Political Philosophy*, trans. M. Brainard (Chicago: University of Chicago Press, 1998); *Leo Strauss and the Theologico-Political Problem*, trans. M. Brainard (Chicago: University of Chicago Press, 2006).

73. C. Schmitt, *Political Theology: Four Chapters on the Concept of Sovereignty*, op. cit., p. 5.

74. Strauss, "Notes on Carl Schmitt's *Concept of the Political*," op. cit., p. 120.

75. Ibid, p. 120.

76. K. Löwith, "The Occasional Decisionism of Carl Schmitt," in R. Wolin, ed., *Karl Löwith, Martin Heidegger and European Nihilism* (New York: Columbia University Press, 1998).

77. M. Heidegger, *Being and Time*, trans. J. Macquarrie and E. Robinson (New York: Harper and Row, 1962), p. 345.

78. Ibid.

79. Ibid., p. 347.

80. Ibid., p. 358.

81. L. Strauss, "German Nihilism," *Interpretation* 26:3 (1999), pp. 361–362.

82. L. Strauss, "An Introduction to Heideggerean Existentialism," in *The Rebirth of Classical Political Rationalism*, op. cit., p. 46.

83. L. Strauss, "What Is Political Philosophy?," op. cit., p. 51.

84. Ibid.

Part II, Chapter 2

1. Strauss, *Natural Right and History*, op. cit., p. 266.

2. Ibid., p. 252.

3. Ibid., p. 252.

4. Ibid., p. 293.

5. Ibid.

6. Strauss, "What Is Political Philosophy?," op. cit., p. 51.

7. As is evident in Strauss, "Introduction to Heideggerean Existentialism," and from his correspondence with Kojeve, published in L. Strauss, *On Tyranny*, ed. V. Gourevitch and M. Roth (Chicago: University of Chicago Press, 2000).

8. "The Three Waves of Modernity," in L. Strauss, *An Introduction to Political Philosophy: Ten Essays by Leo Strauss*, ed. H. Gildin, op. cit., p. 98.

9. Strauss, "What Is Political Philosophy?," op. cit., p. 50.

10. A. Bloom, "Jean-Jacques Rousseau," in L. Strauss and J. Cropsey, eds., *History of Political Philosophy*, 3rd ed. (Chicago: University of Chicago Press, 1987), p. 560.

11. P. Manent, An *Intellectual History of Liberalism*, trans. R. Balinski, op. cit., p. 70.

12. J.-J. Rousseau, *Reveries of the Solitary Walker*, trans. R. Goulbourne (Oxford: Oxford University Press, 2011).

13. L. Strauss, *Natural Right and History*, op. cit., p. 287.

14. Ibid.

15. Ibid., p. 267.

16. Ibid., p. 276.

17. J.-J. Rousseau, *Emile or On Education*, trans. A. Bloom (New York: Basic Books, 1979), p. 280: "I am enslaved because of my vices and free because of my remorse."

18. L. Strauss, *Natural Right and History*, op. cit., p. 213.

19. P. Manent, *An Intellectual History of Liberalism*, op. cit., p. 83.

20. J.-J. Rousseau, *Reveries of the Solitary Walker*, op. cit., p. 47.

21. L. Strauss, *On Tyranny*, op. cit., pp. 205–207.

22. Ibid., p. 211.

23. Letter of Kojeve to Strauss dated October 29, 1953, in *On Tyranny*, op. cit., p. 262.

24. Letter of Strauss to Kojeve dated August 22, 1948, in *On Tyranny*, op. cit., p. 236.

25. L. Strauss, *On Tyranny*, op. cit., p2. 08.

26. A. Kojeve, "Tyranny and Wisdom," in *On Tyranny*, op. cit., p. 139.

27. L. Strauss, *On Tyranny*, op. cit., pp. 188–189.

28. Ibid., p. 79.

29. Ibid., p. 85.

30. Ibid., p. 87.

31. Ibid., p. 56.

32. Ibid., p. 196

33. Ibid., p. 186.

34. A. Kojeve, "Tyranny and Wisdom," op. cit., p. 150.

35. L. Strauss, *On Tyranny*, op. cit., p. 23.

36. A. Kojeve, letter to Strauss dated April 6, 1961, in *On Tyranny*, op. cit., p. 304. "[T]he book is first class. I am naturally not in agreement with the conclusion suggested at the end. But that is not important."

37. L. Strauss, *On Tyranny*, op. cit., p. 43.

38. Ibid., p.41.

39. Ibid., p. 42.

40. Ibid., p. 43.

41. Ibid., p. 59.

42. A. Kojeve, "Tyranny and Wisdom," op. cit., p. 148.

43. Ibid., p. 149.

44. Ibid.

45. L. Strauss, *On Tyranny*, op. cit., p. 186.

46. A. Kojeve, "Philosophy and Wisdom," in *On Tyranny*, op. cit., p. 149.

47. L. Strauss, *On Tyranny*, op. cit., p. 186.

48. Ibid.

49. Ibid.

50. Ibid., pp. 193–194.

51. J. Locke, *Essay on Human Understanding*, book II, chap. XXI, paras. 14–33.

52. As in *Natural Right and History*, where Strauss makes more radical the positions of the thinkers he discusses. I would be more inclined to see Locke as a Socian than as an atheist.

53. J. Locke, *Second Treatise on Civil Government*, chap. V, sec. 40–43.

54. Ibid., chap. V.

55. Ibid., chap. V, secs. 34, 40–51.

56. Ibid., secs. 45–51.

57. P. Manent, *An Intellectual History of Liberalism*, op. cit., p. 46.

58. Contemporary liberal and libertarian theorists are the heirs of Locke. The difference between Locke and the advocates of the minimalist state is that the political has not disappeared in Locke, as his concept of legislative power demonstrates.

59. T. Marshall, "John Locke et la theorie constitutionelle," *Revue de Synthese* 118–119 (1985), p. 365.

60. A. de Tocqueville, *Democracy in America*, op. cit., book II, part II, chap. 14, p. 516.

61. P. Manent, *An Intellectual History of Liberalism*, op. cit., p. 48.

62. Locke, *Second Treatise of Civil Government*, op. cit., chap. II, secs. 11–14.

63. P. Manent, An *Intellectual History of Liberalism*, op. cit., p. 51.

64. Ibid., p. 52.

65. L. Strauss, "The Three Waves of Modernity," op. cit., p. 95.

66. Strauss uses for his own purposes this expression of Löwith (*Wiederholung der Antike auf der Spitze der Modernitaet*). See the letter of June 23, 1935, to Löwith, "Karl Löwith and Leo Strauss: Correspondence," op. cit., p. 183.

67. L. Strauss, "Note on the Plan of Nietzsche's *Beyond Good and Evil*," in L. Strauss, *Studies in Platonic Political Philosophy*, pp. 174–191.

68. Letter to Löwith of June 23, 1935, op. cit., p. 183.

69. Letter to Löwith of February 2, 1933, *Gesammelte Schriften*, Bd. III, op cit., p. 620.

70. F. Nietzsche, *Beyond Good and Evil: A Prelude to the Philosophy of the Future*, trans. J. Norman (Wilder Publications, 2008).

71. L. Strauss, Letter to Löwith of June 1933, undated, in *Gesammelte Schriften*, Bd. III, op cit., p. 632.

72. L. Strauss, Letter to Löwith, June 1933 (undated), op. cit., p. 632.

73. *Epistle to the Romans, X,4.*

74. F. Nietzsche, *Beyond Good and Evil: Prelude to the Philosophy of the Future*, op. cit., p. 68.

75. L. Strauss, "Note on the Plan of Nietzsche's Beyond Good and Evil," op. cit., p. 181.

76. D. Franck, *Nietzsche et l'ombre de Dieu* (Paris: PUF, 1988), pp. 453–454.

77. F. Nietzsche, *Beyond Good and Evil: Prelude to a Philosophy of the Future*, op. cit., p. 76.

78. F. Nietzsche, *Beyond Good and Evil: Prelude to a Philosophy of the Future*, op. cit., p. 68.

79. G. Bernanos, "L'esprit européen et le monde des machines," *La liberté pour quoi faire?*, in *Essais et écrits de combat II* (Paris: Gallimard, 1995), p. 1362.

Part II, Chapter 3

1. L. Strauss, *The City and Man*, op. cit., p. 1.
2. L. Strauss, "Philosophy as Rigorous Science and Political Philosophy," in *Studies on Classical Political Philosophy*, op. cit., p. 33.
3. Ibid., p. 31.
4. Ibid., pp. 36–37.
5. Ibid., p. 36.
6. Edmund Husserl, *The Crisis of the European Sciences and Transcendental Phenomenology*. op. cit., pp. 335–341.
7. L. Strauss, "Philosophy as Rigorous Science and Political Philosophy," op. cit., p. 35.
8. Ibid., p. 36.
9. E. Husserl, *The Crisis of the European Sciences and Transcendental Phenomenology*, op. cit., p. 299.
10. L. Strauss, "Philosophy as Rigorous Science and Political Philosophy," op. cit., p. 36.
11. Ibid., p. 31.
12. M. Heidegger, *On the Way to Language*, trans. P. Hertz (New York: Harper and Row, 1971), "A Dialogue on Language between a Japanese and an Inquirer," pp. 1–56.
13. Strauss, *The City and Man*, op. cit., pp. 11–12.
14. Ibid., p. 20.
15. L. Strauss, "On the Euthydemus," in *Studies in Platonic Political Philosophy*, op. cit., p. 88.
16. L. Strauss, "The Problem of Socrates," in the *Rebirth of Classical Political Rationalism*, op. cit., p. 133.
17. Ibid., p. 125.
18. Ibid., p. 162.
19. Ibid., p. 177.
20. Ibid., citing Plato, *Republic*, 607b.
21. Ibid., p. 133.
22. L. Strauss, "On Plato's *Apology of Socrates* and *Crito*," in *Studies in Platonic Political Philosophy*, Introduction by T. L. Pangle (Chicago: University of Chicago Press 1983), pp. 38–66.
23. L. Strauss, "Cohen und Maimuni," op. cit., p. 411.
24. Ibid., pp. 411–412.
25. L. Strauss, "Plato's Apology of Socrates and Crito," in *Studies in Platonic Political Philosophy*, op. cit., p. 59.
26. L. Strauss, "The Problem of Socrates," in *The Rebirth of Classical Political Rationalism*, op. cit., p. 133.
27. L. Strauss, "On Plato's Apology of Socrates and Crito," in *Studies in Platonic Political Philosophy*, op. cit.
28. L. Strauss, "What Is Liberal Education?," in *Liberalism Ancient and Modern*, op. cit., p. 5.

29. L. Strauss, "Liberal Education and Responsibility," in ibid., p. 24.

30. Ibid., p. 25.

31. L. Strauss, *On Plato's Symposium* (Chicago: University of Chicago Press, 2001), pp. 246–247. See also L. Strauss, "Introduction," in *Persecution and the Art of Writing*, op. cit., p. 16.

32. Strauss, *On Plato's Symposium*, op. cit., p. 247.

33. The *Republic* and *Laws* were not known to medieval Christian thinkers until the fifteenth century. See Strauss, "How to Begin to Study Medieval Philosophy," op. cit., p. 223.

34. L. Strauss, "Cohen und Maimuni," op. cit., p. 412.

35. L. Strauss, *The City and Man*, op. cit., p. 11.

36. R. Brague, "Note sur la traduction arabe de la Politique d'Aristote, drechef qu'elle n'existe pas," in *Aristotle politique: études sur la Politique d'Aristote* (Paris: PUF, 1993), pp. 424–425, 432. The author relies on S. Pines, "Un texte inconnu d'Aristote en version arabe," *Archives d'Histoire doctrinal et littéraire du Moyen Age* 23 (1956); English version in *Studies in Arabic Versions of Greek Texts and Medieval Science, the Collected Works of S. Pines*, vol. II (Jerusalem: Leyde, 1986), pp. 157–195. See also "Leo Strauss et Maïmonide," *Archives Internationales d'histoire des idées,* no. 144 (1986):248. Brague indicates in footnote 9 that the idea that the *Politics* of Aristotle had not been translated into Arabic, "that Strauss seems to have taken without critical consideration from Steinschneider, should be qualified. The theory of a deliberate refusal to translate is present in Pines . . . and Vajda." See G. Vajda, *Introduction à la pensée juive du Moyen Age* (Paris: Vrin, 1947). See Strauss's essay "On Abravanel's Philosophical Tendency and Political Teaching," in *Isaac Abravanel*, ed. J. B. Tren and H. Lowe (Cambridge: Cambridge University Press, 1937), pp. 93–129. This work is the clearest articulation of the way in which Strauss conceives Jewish and Arab medieval philosophy as the product of this period, thus essential for his studies on Maimonides from 1931 to 1937. It is "the study of the sources of the prophetology of Gersonides that led Maimonides to Islam" according to Brague, "Leo Strauss and Maimonides," p. 248.

37. L. Strauss, "Maimonides' Statement on Political Science," *Proceedings of the American Academy for Jewish Research* 22 (1953):115–130.

38. Maimonides, *Guide of the Perplexed*, op. cit., vols. II, III:27, p. 511.

39. Ibid, vol. III:54, pp. 632–638. Here, Maimonides follows Ibn Bajja and articulates four kinds of perfection. In chapter 27, he spoke only of the perfection of the body and the soul. The latter is more important and first in itself and makes men immortal, but it is acquired after the perfection of the body, or health.

40. Ibid., vol. III:27, p. 511.

41. E. Fortin, "Thomas Aquinas," in *The History of Political Philosophy*, 3rd ed., op. cit., p. 258.

42. Thomas Aquinas, *Summa Theologica*, I–II, question 72 a–4.

43. E. Fortin, "Thomas Aquinas," op. cit., p. 251.

44. Al-Farabi, "The Philosophy of Plato, Its Parts, The Ranks of Order of Its Parts, from the Beginning to End," in Al-Farabi, *Philosophy of Plato and Aristotle*, ed. and trans. M. Mahdi (Ithaca: Cornell University Press, 2001), p. 63.

45. L. Strauss, "On Abravanel's Philosophical Tendency and Political Teaching," in *Isaac Abravanel*, op. cit.

46. L. Strauss, "Farabi's Plato," in *Louis Ginzberg: Jubilee Volume* (New York: American Academy for Jewish Research, 1945), pp. 357–393.

47. L. Strauss, "On Abravenel's Philosophical Tendency," op. cit., p. 99.

48. Ibid., p. 101.

49. Ibid., pp. 99–100.

50. Maimonides, *Guide of the Perplexed*, op. cit., introduction, vol. I.

51. Maimonides, The *Guide of the Perplexed*, op. cit., vol. III:29, 30.

52. Ibid., beginning of vol. III and chap. 52.

53. L. Strauss, "Cohen and Maimonides," op. cit., p. 245.

54. R. Brague, "Leo Strauss et Maimonide," op. cit., p. 260. While Brague thinks that Strauss is, at least at the beginning of his career, an atheist who does not want to admit that as such, my own view is that Strauss is at least as close to Maimonides as to Plato, even if he says that atheism from probity is of biblical origin. Nietzsche wrote that absolute probity would result in disgust and suicide if there were no antidote—which is, for Nietzsche in the *Gay Science*, art (*Gay Science*, vol. II, 107). According to Brague, for Strauss, the antidote is the art of writing, the noble lie. But the religion in Maimonides, or perhaps the fact that knowledge is where one is in relation to God, implies something other than the noble lie of disguised atheism. This is the kind of rationalism and philosophy that Strauss has in mind and that he considers not just in a polemical or negative manner—to overcome the destructive character of the modern Enlightenment—but in a positive way. This rationalism open to Revelation does not exclude that "Mr. Strauss" was estranged from Orthodox Judaism and that he did not even personally believe in the God of the Bible. But it is hard to think of Strauss as an atheist in Spinoza's sense.

55. L. Strauss, "How To Begin To Study The Guide of the Perplexed," in The *Guide of the Perplexed*, op. cit., p. xiv.

56. R. Brague, "Leo Strauss and Maimonides," op. cit., p. 260.

57. One belonging to philosophy, the other to theology, as in the common view of Latin Averroism.

58. Maimonides, Guide, introduction, vol. I.

59. L. Strauss, *Philosophy and Law*, op. cit., p. 127.

60. Strauss, ibid., p. 112.

61. Maimonides, *Guide*, vol. II, chaps. 23 and 38.

62. L. Strauss, *Philosophy and Law*, op. cit., p. 107.

63. Here Strauss cites Maimonides, *Guide*, vol. II, chaps. 23 and 38.

64. "Quelques remarques sur la science politique de Maimonide et de Farabi," *Revue des Etudes Juives* 100 (1936):1–37.

65. Ibid.

66. L. Strauss, *Philosophy and Law*, op. cit., pp. 102–103

67. Ibid., p. 103.

68. E. Husserl, *Ideas*, vol. I, sec. 24.

69. M. Heidegger, "The End of Philosophy and the Task of Thinking," op. cit.

70. Ibid., p. 434.

71. M. Heidegger, "The End of Philosophy and the Task of Thinking," in *Basic Writings*, op. cit., p. 435.

72. M. Heidegger, "The Turning," in *The Question of Technology and Other Essays*, trans. W. Lovitt (New York: Garland, 1977), p. 48.

73. Ibid, p. 46.

74. Ibid., p. 46.

75. Ibid., p. 47.

76. Ibid., p. 49.

77. M. Heidegger, "The End of Philosophy and the Task of Thinking," op. cit.

78. M. Heidegger, "The End of Philosophy and the Task of Thinking," ibid., p. 449.

79. L. Strauss, *The City and Man*, op. cit., pp. 9, 11.

80. M. Heidegger, "The End of Philosophy and the Task of Thinking," op. cit., p. 436.

81. Ibid., p. 437.

Conclusion

1. J. G. Fichte, "First Introduction to the Wissenschaftslehre," in *Introductions to the Wissenschaftslehre and Other Writings*, trans. D. Breazeale (Indianapolis: Hackett, 1994), pp. 17–20.

2. E. Husserl, *The Crisis of the European Sciences and Transcendental Philosophy*, op. cit., §49, §50, §51, where Husserl articulates the distinction between the life world, understood as the natural world and the life world understood as native soil. The first is that which nourishes the sciences and presupposes activities specific to a culture, while the second is common to all men. The suspension of the natural world opens up activities through which we create the meaning of what we are making. There is the idea of a common world, which can constitute the public world.

3. G. W. Leibniz, "Monadology," in *Philosophical Writings*, trans. M. Morris and G. Parkinson (London: Dent, 1973), §57.

4. In considering the person as a subject of right, as an autonomous person, and rarely as an object of right, that is as an absolute value, which would imply some limits to certain medical practices and require the recognition that the notion of the person is connected to a certain ethical *content*.

5. E. Husserl, *The Crisis of the European Sciences and Transcendental Philosophy*, op. cit., p. 285: "Man becomes gripped by the passion of a world-view and world-knowledge that turns away from all practical interests and, within the closed sphere of its cognitive activity, in the times devoted to it, strives for and achieves nothing but pure *theoria*. In other words, man becomes a nonparticipating spectator, surveyor of the world; he becomes a philosopher."

6. G. W. Leibniz, *Monadology*, op. cit., 57, pp. 187–188.

Bibliography

Books by Strauss

For a complete bibliography, see John A. Murley, ed., *Leo Strauss and His Legacy: A Bibliography*. Lanham, MD: Lexington Books, 2005; and Heinrich Meier, *Die Denkbewegung von Leo Strauss, Die Geschichte der Philosophie und die Intention des Philosophen*. Stuttgart: J.B. Metzler, 1996, pp. 47–63, and his edition of the volumes of Strauss's work.

Gesammelte Schriften, Bd. I: *Die Religionskritik Spinozas und zugehörige Schriften*. Edited by H. Meier. Stuttgart: J.B. Metzler, 1996.

Gesammelte Schriften, Bd. II: *Philosophie und Gesetz. Frühe Schriften*. Edited by H. Meier. Stuttgart: J.B. Metzler, 1997.

Gesammelte Schriften, Bd. III: *Hobbes' politische Wissenschaft und zugehörige Schriften*. Edited by H. Meier. Stuttgart: J.B. Metzler, 2001.

Gesammelte Schriften, Bd. 4, *Politische Philosophie. Studien zum theologisch-politischen Problem*. Edited by H. Meier. Stuttgart: J.B. Metzler, 2010.

Natural Right and History. Chicago: University of Chicago Press, 1953.

Thoughts on Machiavelli. Phoenix Edition. Chicago: University of Chicago Press, 1958.

What Is Political Philosophy? And Other Studies. Glencoe, IL: Free Press, 1959.

The Political Philosophy of Hobbes: Its Basis and Its Genesis. Translated by M. Sinclair. Chicago: University of Chicago Press, 1963.

"The Crisis of Our Time" (1962). In *The Predicament of Modern Politics*. Detroit: University of Detroit Press, 1964.

Spinoza's Critique of Religion. Translated by E. M. Sinclair. New York: Schocken Books, 1965.

Socrates and Aristophanes. New York: Basic Books, 1966.

Liberalism Ancient and Modern. Chicago: University of Chicago Press, 1968.

"A Giving of Accounts: Jacob Klein and Leo Strauss." *St John's Review*, April 1970.

Xenophon's Socratic Discourse: An Interpretation of the Oeconomicus. Ithaca, NY: Cornell University Press, 1970.

Xenophon's Socrates. Ithaca, NY: Cornell University Press, 1972.

Persecution and the Art of Writing. Westport, CT: Greenwood Press, 1973.

The Argument and the Action of Plato's Laws. Chicago: University of Chicago Press, 1975.

"The Three Waves of Modernity." In *An Introduction to Political Philosophy: Ten Essays by Leo Strauss.* Edited by H. Gildin. Detroit: Wayne State University Press, 1975, pp. 81–98.

The City and Man. Chicago: University of Chicago Press, 1978.

Studies in Platonic Political Philosophy. Introduction by T. L. Pangle. Chicago: University of Chicago Press, 1983.

History of Political Philosophy. With J. Cropsey. Chicago: University of Chicago Press, 1987.

Strauss, Letter to Löwith, June 1933. "Karl Löwith and Leo Strauss: Correspondence." *Independent Journal of Philosophy*, vol. 5–6, 1988.

The Rebirth of Classical Political Rationalism, Essays and Lectures by Leo Strauss. Selected and introduced by T. L. Pangle. Chicago: University of Chicago Press, 1989.

On Tyranny: Revised and Expanded Edition—Including the Strauss-Kojève Correspondence. Edited by V. Gourevitch and M. S. Roth. New York: Free Press, 1991.

Faith and Political Philosophy: The Correspondence between Leo Strauss and Eric Voegelin 1934–1964. Edited and translated by P. Emberley and Barry Cooper. University Park: Pennsylvania State University Press, 1993.

Philosophy and Law, Contributions to the Understanding of Maimonides and his Predecessors. Translated and with an introduction by Eve Adler. Albany: SUNY Press, 1995.

"Jerusalem and Athens." In L. Strauss, *Jewish Philosophy and the Crisis of Modernity: Essays and Lectures in Modern Jewish Thought.* Edited and with an introduction by K. H. Green. Albany: SUNY Press, 1997.

"German Nihilism." *Interpretation*, vol. 26, n°3, 1999, pp. 361–362.

On Plato's Symposium. Edited and with a foreword by S. Bernardete. Chicago: University of Chicago Press, 2001.

The Early Writings (1921–1932). Translated by M. Zank. Albany: SUNY Press, 2002.

Reason and Revelation." In H. Meier, *Leo Strauss and the Theologico-Political Problem.* Cambridge: Cambridge University Press, 2006, pp. 141–180.

Hobbes' Critique of Religion. In L. Strauss, *Hobbes' Critique of Religion and Other Writings.* Edited by G. Bartlett and S. Minkov. Chicago: University of Chicago Press, 2011.

Articles and Lectures

Most of them are reprinted in the three volumes of H. Meier's edition (*Gesammelte Schriften*) and in the books mentioned above.

Das Erkenntnisproblem in der philosophischen Lehre Fr. H. Jacobis, Dissertation zur Erlangung der Doktorwürde der philosophischen Fakultät der Hamburgischen Universität, Hamburg, 1921. *Gesammelte Schriften*, Bd. II, pp. 237–297. Reprinted in part in *The Early Writings*, pp. 53–61.

"Antwort auf das Prinzipielle Wort der Frankfurter." *Jüdische Rundschau* 28, Nr. 9, Februar 1923, pp. 45–46. *Gesammelte Schriften*, Bd. I, pp. 299–306.

"Das Heilige." *Der Jude*, 7 Jg., Heft 4, April 1923, pp. 240–242. *Gesammelte Schriften*, Bd. II, pp. 307–310.

"Anmerkung zur Diskussion über 'Zionismus und Antisemitismus.'" *Jüdische Rundschau*, 28 Jg., Nr. 83–84, Oktober 1923, pp. 501–502. *Gesammelte Schriften*, Bd. II, pp. 311–313.

"Der Zionismus bei Nordau." *Der Jude*, 7 Jg., Heft 10–11, Oktober–November 1923, pp. 657–660. *Gesammelte Schriften*, Bd. II, pp. 315–321.

"Paul de Lagarde." *Der Jude*, 8 Jg., Heft 1, Januar 1924, p. 8–15. *Gesammelte Schriften*, Bd. II, pp. 323–331.

"Soziologische Geschichtsschreibung." *Der Jude*, 8 Jg., Heft 3, März 1924, pp. 190–192. *Gesammelte Schriften*, Bd. II, pp. 333–337.

"Cohens Analyse der Bibel-Wissenschaft Spinozas." *Der Jude*, 8 Jg., Heft 5–6, Mai–Juni 1934, pp. 295–314. *Gesammelte Schriften*, Bd. II., pp. 363–386. Reprinted in Leo Strauss, *The Early Writings* (1921–1932). Translated and edited by Michael Zank, pp. 140–172.

Besprechung von A. Levkowitz: Religiöse Denker der Gegenwart. Der Jude, 8 Jg., Heft 7, Juli 1924, p. 432. *Gesammelte Schriften*, Bd. II, p. 338.

"Zur Auseinandersetzung mit der europäischen Wissenschaft." *Der Jude*, 8 Jg., Heft 10, Oktober 1924, pp. 613–617. *Gesammelte Schriften*, Bd. II, pp. 339–349.

"Biblische Geschichte und Wissenschaft." *Jüdische Rundschau*, 30 Jg., Nr. 88, November 1925, pp. 744–745. *Gesammelte Schriften*, Bd. II, pp. 357–361.

"Zur Bibelwissenschaft Spinozas und seiner Vorläufer." *Korrespondenzblatt des Vereins zur Gründung und Erhaltung einer Akademie für die Wissenschaft des Judentums*, 7 Jg., 1926, pp. 1–22. *Gesammelte Schriften*, Bd. I, pp. 389–414. Reprinted in *The Early Writings*, pp. 173–200.

"Ecclesia Militans." 1925. *Gesammelte Schriften*, Bd. II., pp. 351–361.

"Franz Rosenzweig und die Akademie für die Wissenschaft des Judentums." Jüdische Wochenzeitung für Kassel, Hessen und Waldeck, am I3. Dezember 1929. *Gesammelte Schriften*, Bd. II, pp. 363–364.

"Religiöse Lage der Gegenwart." Referat, zu halten am 21. Dezember 1930, Berlin. *Gesammelte Schriften*, Bd. II, pp. 377–391.

"Pope ein Metapyhsiker!," "Sendschreiben an den Herrn Magister Lessing in Leipzig," "Kommentar zu den" termini der Logik "des Moses ben Maimon," "Abhandlung über Evidenz," XV–XXIII–XLVLIII. In Moses Mendelssohn, *Gesammelte Schriften: Jubiläumsausgabe*, Volume 2. Berlin: Akademie verlag, 1931. *Gesammelte Schriften*, Bd. II, pp. 465–527.

"Cohen und Maimuni" Vortrag zu halten am 4 Mai 1931, Berlin. *Gesammelte Schriften*, Bd. II, pp. 393–436.

"Review of the book of Julius Ebbinghaus." *Über die Fortschritte der Metaphysik*," *Deutsche Literaturzeitung*, 52, am 27. Dezember 1931, col. 2451–2453.

"Die geistige Lage der Gegenwart." Vortrag, 1932. *Gesammelte Schriften*, Bd. II, pp. 441–464.

"Einleitungen zu Phädon," "Abhandlung von der Unkörperlichkeit der menschlichen Seele," "Über einen schriften Aufsatz des Herrn de Luc" et "Die Seele." In Moses Mendelssohn, *Gesammelte Schriften*: Jubiläumsausgabe. Berlin: Akademie-Verlag, 1932, Bd. III, 1, pp. XIII–XXXIV–XXXVIII, XXXVIII–XXXIX, XXXIX–XLI.

"Anmerkungen zu Carl Schmitt, *Der Begriff des Politischen*." *Archiv für Sozial-Wissenschaft und Sozialpolitik*, 67, 6, August–September 1932, pp. 732–749, reprinted in Heinrich Meier, *Carl Schmitt, Leo Strauss und* "Der Begriff des Politischen." *Zu einem Dialog unter Abwesenden; Mit Leo Strauss' Aufsatz über den* "Begriff des Politischen" *und drei unveröffentlichten Briefen an Carl Schmitt aus den Jahren 1932–1933*. Stuttgart: J.B. Metzler, 1988, 143 pp.

"Das Testament Spinozas." *Bayerische Israelitische Gemeindezeitung*, München, 8 Jg., Nr. 21, 1. November 1932, pp. 322–326. *Gesammelte Schriften*, Bd. I, pp. 415–422. Reprinted in *The Early Writings* (1921–1932). Translated by M. Zank, pp. 216–223.

"Quelques remarques sur la science politique de Hobbes. À propos du livre récent de M. Lubienski." *Recherches philosophiques*, Bd. II, 1933, pp. 609–622.

"Maimunis Lehre von der Prophetie und ihre Quellen." *Le Monde Oriental* (Upsala), vol. 28, 1934, pp. 99–139. *Gesammelte Schriften*, Bd. II, pp. 87–122.

"Quelques remarques sur la science politique de Maïmonide et de Fârâbî." *Revue des Études juives*, vol. 100, 1936, pp. 1–37. *Gesammelte Schriften*, Bd. II, pp. 125–158.

"Eine vermisste Schrift Fârâbîs." *Monatsschrift für Geschichte und Wissenschaft des Judentums*, 80 Jg., 1, Januar–Februar 1936, pp. 96–106.

"Der Ort der Vorsehungslehre nach der Ansicht Maimunis." *Monatsschrift für Geschichte und Wissenschaft des Judentums,* 81 Jg., 1 Januar–Februar 1937, pp. 93–105.

"On Abravanel's Philosophical Tendency and Political Teaching." In *Isaac Abravanel, Six Lectures*. Edited by J. B. Trend and H. Lœwe. Cambridge: Cambridge University Press, 1937, pp. 93–129.

"Review of the Edition by Moses Hyamson of Maimonides, *The Mishneh Torah*, Book 1." *Review of Religion*, vol. 3, May 1939, pp. 448–456.

"Persecution and the Art of Writing." *Social Research*, vol. 8, n°4, November 1941, p. 488–504. There is a modified version in *Persecution and the Art of Writing*, pp. 22–37.

"The Literary Character of The Guide of the Perplexed." In *Essays on Maimonides*. Edited by S. W. Baron. New York: Columbia University Press, 1941, pp. 37–91. *Persecution and the Art of Writing*, pp. 38–94.

"The Law of Reason in the *Kuzari*." In *Proceedings of the American Academy for Jewish Research*, vol. 13, 1943, pp. 47–96. *Persecution and the Art of Writing*, pp. 95–141.

"Farabi's *Plato*." In *Louis Ginzberg Jubilee Volume*. New York: American Academy for Jewish Research, 1945, pp. 357–393. Reprinted with modifications in the introduction of *Persecution and the Art of Writing*, pp. 7–21.

"On a New Interpretation of Plato's Political Philosophy." *Social Research*, vol. 13, n°3, September 1946, pp. 326–367.

"On the Intention of Rousseau." *Social Research*, vol. 14, n°4, December 1947, pp. 455–487.

"On Husik's Work in Medieval Jewish Philosophy." In *Isaac Husik's Philosophical Essays: Ancient, Medieval, and Modern*. Oxford: Basil Blackwell, 1952, pp. VII–XLI.

"On Collingwood's Philosophy of History." *Review of Metaphysics*, vol. 5, n°4, June 1952, pp. 559–586.

"Maïmonides' Statement on Political Science." In *Proceedings of the American Academy for Jewish Research*, vol. 22, 1953, p.115–130. *What Is Political Philosophy?*, pp. 155–169.

"On a Forgotten Kind of Writing." *Chicago Review*, vol. 8, n°1, Fall–Winter 1954, pp. 64–75. *What Is Political Philosophy?*, pp. 221–232.

"How Farabi Read Plato's Laws." In *Mélanges louis Massignon*, Institut français de Damas, Damas, 1957, vol. 3, pp. 319–344. *What is Political Philosophy ?*, pp. 134–154.

"An Epilogue." In *Essays on the Scientific Study of Politics*. Edited by Herbert J. Storing. New York: Holt, Rinehart and Winston, 1962, pp. 307–327. *Liberalism Ancient and Modern*, pp. 203–223.

"Replies to Schaar and Wolin." *American Political Science Review*, vol. 57, n°1, March 1963, pp. 152–155.

"How to Begin to Study *The Guide of the Perplexed*." In Maimonides, *The Guide of the Perplexed*. Chicago: The University of Chicago Press, 1963, pp. XI–LVI. *Liberalism Ancient and Modern*, pp. 140–184.

"*The Crisis of Our Time*" and "*The Crisis of Political Philosophy*." In *The Predicament of Modern Politics*. Detroit: University of Detroit Press, 1964, pp. 41–54, 91–103.

"Preface to the English Translation." In *Spinoza's Critique of Religion*. New York: Schocken, 1965, pp. 1–31. Reprinted with some modifications in *Liberalism Ancient and Modern*, pp. 224–259.

"Natural Law." In *International Encyclopedia of the Social Sciences*. Vol. 2. Edited by David L. Sills. London: Crowell Collier and Macmillan, 1968, pp. 80–90. Reprinted in *Studies in Platonical Political Philosophy* with the following title: "On Natural Law," pp. 137–146.

"Jerusalem and Athens. Some Preliminary Reflections." The First Frank Cohen Public Lecture in Judaic Affairs, *The City College Papers*, n°6, 1967, The

Library, The City College, The City University of New York, New York, 28 pp. *Studies in Platonical Philosophy*, pp. 147–173.

"A Giving of Accounts: Jacob Klein and Leo Strauss." *St. John's College Review* (Annapolis and Santa Fe), vol. 22, n°1, April 1970, pp. 1–5. Reprinted in *Jewish Philosophy and the Crisis of Modernity: Essays and Lectures in Modern Jewish Thought,* pp. 457–466.

"Philosophy as Rigorous Science and Political Philosophy." *Interpretation*, vol. 2, n°1, Summer 1971, pp. 1–9. *Studies in Platonic Political Philosophy*, pp. 29–37.

"Introductory Essay." In Hermann Cohen, *Religion of Reason Out of the Sources of Judaism*. New York: Frederick Ungar, 1972, pp. XXIII–XXXVIII. *Studies in Platonic Political Philosophy,* pp. 233–247.

"Note on the Plan of Nietzsche's *Beyond Good and Evil*." *Interpretation*, vol. 3, n°2–3, Winter 1973, pp. 97–113. *Studies in Platonic Political Philosophy*, pp. 174–191.

"Einleitung zu 'Morgenstunden' und 'An die Freunde Lessings,'" 1937–1974. Moses Mendelssohn, *Gesammelte Schriften: Jubiläumsausgabe; Schriften zur Philosophie und Ästhetik*, Bd. III, 2, Stuttgart/bad-Canstatt: Froman-Holzboog, 1974, pp. XI–XCV, XCVI–CX.

Gesammelte Schriften, Bd. II, pp. 528–605. *Leo Strauss on Moses Mendelssohn*. Translated and with an introduction by Martin D. Yaffe. Chicago: University of Chicago Press, 2012.

"The Three Waves of Modernity." In *Political Philosophy: Six Essays by Leo Strauss*. Edited by Hilail Gildin. Indianapolis: Pegasus/Bobbs-Merrill, 1975, pp. 81–98. Reprinted in *An Introduction to Political Philosophy: Ten Essays by Leo Strauss*. Detroit: Wayne State University Press, 1989, XXIV–365 pp.

"Correspondence with Hans-Georg Gadamer concerning *Wahrheit und Methode*." *The Independent Journal of Philosophy/Unabhängige Zeitschrift für Philosophie*, vol. 2, 1978, pp. 5–12.

"Letter to Helmut Kuhn." *The Independent Journal of Philosophy/Unabhängige Zeitschrift für Philosophie,* vol. 2, 1978, pp. 23–26.

"An Unspoken Prologue to a Public Lecture at St. John's." *Interpretation*, vol. 7, n°3, September 1978, pp. 1–3. Reprinted in *Jewish Philosophy and the Crisis of Modernity*, pp. 449–452.

"The Mutual Influence of Theology and Philosophy." *The Independent Journal of Philosophy/Unahängige Zeitschrift für Philosophie*, vol. 3, 1979, pp. 111–118. It is a lecture given at the Hillel House, at the University of Chicago, in November 1952. It is reprinted with some modifications in *The Rebirth of Classical Political Rationalism: An Introduction to the Thought of Leo Strauss. Essays and Lectures by Leo Strauss.*

"On the Interpretation of Genesis." *L'Homme: Revue française d'anthropologie*, vol. 21, n°1, janvier–mars 1981, pp. 5–20.

"Progress or Return? The Contemporary Crisis in Western Civilization." *Modern Judaism*, vol. 1, n°1, May 1981, pp. 17–45. These two lectures were given on

November 5 and 12, 1952. They were published with some modifications in *The Rebirth of Classical Political Rationalism*, pp. 227–237.

"Correspondence Concerning Modernity; Karl Löwith and Leo Strauss." *The Independent Journal of Philosopht/Unabhängige Zeitschrift für Philosophie*, vol. 4, 1983, pp. 105–119. *Gesammelte Schriften*, Bd. III, pp. 607–697.

"Exoteric Teaching." *Interpretation*, vol. 14, n°1, January 1986, pp. 51–59. *The Rebirth of Classical Political Rationalism*, pp. 63–71.

"Correspondence Karl Löwith and Leo Strauss." *The Independent Journal of Philosophy/Unabhängige Zeitschrift für Philosophie*, vols. 5–6, 1988, pp. 177–192. The original version is in German and is accompanied by the English translation of these letters, which date from 1935. *Gesammelte Schriften*, Bd. III, op. cit., pp. 607–697.

"The Problem of Socrates: Five Lectures." These lectures at the University of Chicago (from October 27 to November 7, 1956) are published with some modifications in *The Rebirth of Classical Political Rationalism*, pp. 227–270. For a complete version, see "The Origins of Political Science and the Problem of Socrates: Six Lectures." *Interpretation*, vol. 3, n°2, 1996, pp. 127–207.

"An Untitled Lecture on Plato's Euthyphron." *Interpretation*, vol. 24, n°1, Hiver 1997, pp. 4–23, reprinted with the following title: "On the Euthyphron." In *The Rebirth of Classical Political Rationalism*, pp. 187–206.

"How to Begin to Study Medieval Philosophy." In *The Rebirth of Classical Political Rationalism*, pp. 207–225. It was at the beginning a lecture (May 16, 1944), and the editor shortened it for publication. The original title of the lecture was "How to Study Medieval Philosophy." See also *Interpretation*, vol. 23, n°3, Spring 1996, pp. 319–338.

"The Strauss-Vœgelin Correspondence." In *Faith and Political Philosophy: The Correspondence Between Leo Strauss and Éric Vœgelin*, 1934–1964, pp. 1–19, 35–44, 57–106.

"Why We Remain Jews: Can Jewish Faith and History Still Speak to Us?" This lecture took place on February 4, 1962, at the University of Chicago. It was first published in *Leo Strauss: Political Philosopher and Jewish Thinker*, pp. 311–356. See also *The Review of Politics*, vol. 53, n°1, Winter 1991.

"Existentialism." This lecture took place in February 1956 at the University of Chicago. It was published with the following title: "An Introduction to Heideggerian Existentialism." In *The Rebirth of Classical Political Rationalism*, pp. 27–46.

"The Problem of Socrates." *Interpretation*, vol. 22, n°3, Spring 1995, pp. 321–338. This lecture took place on April 17, 1970, at St. John's College, Annapolis. It was reprinted in part in "Introduction to Heideggerian Existentialism." See *The Rebirth of Classical Political Rationalism*.

"German Nihilism." Edited by D. Janssens and D. Tanguay, 1998. Strauss gave this lecture on February 26, 1941, in a seminar of the Graduate Faculty of Political and Social Science of the New School for Social Research in New York. The text comes from *Leo Strauss Papers* (Box 8, Folder 15) at the Regenstein Library of The University of Chicago. It was published in *Interpretation*, vol. 26, n°3, Spring 1999, pp. 253–378.

Books or Articles on Strauss

Leora Batnitzky, *Leo Strauss and Emmanuel Levinas: Philosophy and the Politique of Revelation*. Cambridge: Cambridge University Press, 2007.

Seth Benardete, "Leo Strauss '*The City and Man*.'" *Political Science Reviewer*, vol. 8, 1978, pp. 1–20.

Allan Bloom, "Leo Strauss September 20, 1899-October 18, 1973." In *Giants and Dwarfs: Essays 1960–1990*. New York: Simon & Schuster, 1990.

Political Philosopher and Jewish Thinker. Edited by Kenneth L. Deutsch and Walter Nicgorski. Lanham, MD: Rowman & Littlefield, 1994.

Rémi Brague, "Oikonomia et Enkrateia." *Archives de Philosophie*, vol. 37, n°2, avril–juin 1974, pp. 275–290.

———, "Radical Modernity and the Roots of Ancient Thought." *Independent Journal of Philosophy*, n°3, 1983.

———, "Leo Strauss and Maimonides." In *Maïmonides and Philosophy*. Edited by Shlomo Pines and Yirmiyahu Yovel. Netherlands: Martinus Nijhoff, Dordrecht, 1986, pp. 246–268. See the English version: "Leo Strauss and Maïmonides." In *Leo Strauss's Thought: Toward a Critical Engagement*. Boulder, CO: Lynne Rienner Publishers, 1991, pp. 93–114.

———, "Athènes, Jérusalem, La Mecque. L'interprétation 'musulmane' de la philosophie grecque chez Leo Strauss." *Revue de Métaphysique et de Morale*, vol. 94, n°3, juillet–septembre 1989, pp. 309–336.

Paul Cantor, "Leo Strauss and Contemporary Hermeneutics." In *Leo Strauss' Thought: Toward a Critical Engagement*. Boulder, CO: Lynne Rienner Publishers, 1991, pp. 267–314.

Joseph Cropsey, "Leo Strauss." In *Biographical Supplement to the International Encyclopedia of the Social Sciences*. London: The Free Press, 1979, t. 18, pp. 746–750.

Kenneth L. Deutsch and Walter Soffer, eds., *The Crisis of Liberal Democracy: A Straussian Perspective*. Albany: SUNY Press, 1987, IX–304 pp.

Kenneth L. Deutsch and John A. Murley, *Leo Strauss, the Straussians and the Study of the American Regime*. Lanham, MD: Rowman & Littlefield, 1999, 472 pp.

Robert Devigne, *Recasting Conservatism: Oakeshott, Strauss and the Response to Postmodernism*. New Haven, CT: Yale University Press, 1994, XIII–268 pp.

Shadia Drury, *Leo Strauss and the American Right*. New York: St. Martin's Press, 1999.

Ernest L. Fortin, *Collected Essays*: vol. I: *The Birth of Philosophic Christianity*; vol. II: *Classical Christianity and the Political Order*; vol. III: *Human Rights, Virtue, and the Common Good*. Lanham, MD: Rowman & Littlefield, 1996. In these volumes the following articles are reprinted:

———, "Christian Political Theory." *Review of Politics*, vol. 41, 1979, pp. 578–582.

———, "Rational Theologians and Irrational Philosophers: A Straussian Perspective." *Interpretation*, vol. 12, n°2–3, 1984, pp. 349–356.

———, "Faith and Reason in Contemporary Perspective." *Interpretation*, vol. 14, 1986, pp. 371–387.

———, "Was Leo Strauss a Secret Enemy of Morality?" *Crisis*, vol. 7, n°12, December 1989, pp. 19–26.

———, "Dead Masters and Their Living Thoughts." *The Vital Nexus*, vol. 1, n°1, May 1990, pp. 61–71.

Marvin Fox, *Interpreting Maimonides: Studies in Methodology Metaphysics, and Moral Philosophy.* Chicago: University of Chicago Press, 1990, XIII–356 pp.

Hillel Fradkin, "Philosophy and Law: Leo Strauss as a Student of Medieval Jewish Thought." In *Leo Strauss: Political Philosopher and Jewish Thinker*, op. cit., pp. 129–141.

———, "A Word Fitly Spoken: The Interpretation of Maimonides and the Legacy of Leo Strauss." In *Leo Strauss and Judaism: Jerusalem and Athens Critically Revisited*, op. cit., pp. 55–85.

Peter E. Gordon and Michael L. Morgan, eds. *The Cambridge Companion to Modern Jewish Philosophy*. Cambridge: Cambridge University Press, 2007.

———, *Continental Divide: Heidegger, Cassirer, Davos*. Cambridge: Harvard University Press, 2010.

Kenneth Hart Green, "In the Grip of the Theological-Political Predicament": The Turn to Maimonides in the Jewish Thought of Leo Strauss." In *Leo Strauss's Thought: Toward a Critical Engagement*, pp. 41–74.

———, "Religion, Philosophy and Morality: How Leo Strauss Read Judah Halevi's *Kuzari*." *Journal of the American Academy of Religion*, vol. 61, n°2, Summer 1993, pp. 224–273.

———, *Jew and Philosopher—The Return to Maimonides in the Jewish Thought of Leo Strauss*. Albany: SUNY Press, 1993.

Stephen Holmes, *The Anatomy of Antiliberalism*. Cambridge: Harvard University Press, 1993, XVII–315 pp.

David Janssens, *Between Athens and Jerusalem*. Albany: SUNY Press, 2008.

Hwa Yol Jung, "The Life-World, Historicity, and Truth: Reflections on Leo Strauss's Encounter with Heidegger and Husserl." *Journal of the British Society for Phenomenology*, vol. 9, n°1, January 1978, pp. 11–25. Reprinted in *Rethinking Political Theory: Essays in Phenomenology and the Study of Politics*, pp. 145–161.

———, "Heidegger and Strauss." *Idealistic Studies*, vol. 17, 1987, pp. 207–218.

Richard H. Kenington, "Bacon's Critique of Ancient Philosophy in New Organon I." In *Studies in Philosophy and the History of Philosophy*, vol. 22. Edited by Daniel O. Dahlstrom. Washington, DC: The Catholic University of America Press, 1991, pp. 235–251.

Jacob Klein, Winfree Smith, Ted Blanton, and Laurence Berns, "Memorials to Leo Strauss." *The College*, vol. 25, January 1974, pp. 1–15.

Laurence Lampert, "The Argument of Leo Strauss in *What Is Political Philosophy?*" *Modern Age*, vol. 22, n°1, Winter 1978, pp. 38–46. See the answer to this article: Steven A. Maaranen, "Leo Strauss: Classical Political Philosophy and Modern Democracy." *Modern Age*, vol. 22, n°1, Winter 1978, pp. 47–53.

Claude Lefort, "Trois notes sur Leo Strauss." In *Écrire. À l'épreuve du politique*. Paris: Calmann-Lévy, 1992, pp. 261–301.

Pierre Manent, "Strauss et Nietzsche." *Revue de Métaphysique et de Morale*, vol. 94, n°3, 1989, pp. 337–345.

Terence Marshall, "Strauss, Leo, 1899–1973." In *Dictionnaire d'éthique et de philosophie morale*, sous la direction de Monique Canto-Sperber. Paris: PUF, 1996, pp. 1467–1472.

———, "Leo Strauss et la question des Anciens et des Modernes." *Cahiers de philosophie politique et juridique de l'université de Caen*, n°23, 1993, pp. 35–86.

———, "Leo Strauss et la morale." *Commentaire*, n°75, automne 1996, pp. 550–557.

———, "Leo Strauss, la philosophie et la science politique." *Revue française de Science politique*, vol. 35, 1985, pp. 605–638.

Heinrich Meier, *Carl Schmitt and Leo Strauss: The Hidden Dialogue*. Chicago: University of Chicago Press, 1995.

———, *Die Denkbewegung von Leo Strauss: Die Geschichte der Philosophie und die Intention des Philosophen*. Stuttgart: J.B. Metzler, 1996.

———, *Leo Strauss and the Theologico-Political Problem*. Translated by Marcus Brainard. Cambridge: Cambridge University Press, 2006.

Horst Mewes, "Leo Strauss and Martin Heidegger: Greek Antiquity and the Meaning of Modernity." In *Hannah Arendt and Leo Strauss: German Émigrés and American Political Thought after World War II*. Cambridge: Cambridge University Press, 1995, pp. 105–120.

Behnegar Nasser, "The Liberal Politics of Leo Strauss." In *Political Philosophy and the Human Soul: Essays in Memory of Allan Bloom*. Edited by M. Palmer and T. L. Pangle. Lanham, MD: Rowman & Littlefield, 1995, pp. 251–267.

Harry Neumann, "Civic Piety and Atheism: An Interpretation of Strauss's *Socrates and Aristophanes*." *The Independent Journal of Philosophy/Unabhängige Zeitschrift für Philosophie*, vol. 2, 1978, pp. 33–37.

David Novak, ed., *Leo Strauss and Judaism: Jerusalem and Athens Critically Revisited*. Lanham, MD: Rowman & Littlefield, 1996, XVI–200 pp.

Susan Orr, *Jerusalem and Athens: Reason and Revelation in the Works of Leo Strauss*. Lanham, MD: Rowman & Littlefield, 1995, IX–245 pp.

Thomas L. Pangle, "The Platonism of Leo Strauss: A Reply to Harry Jaffa." *Claremont Review of Books*, Spring 1985, pp. 17–20; Harry V. Jaffa, "The Legacy of Leo Strauss's Defended," ibid., pp. 21–24.

———, *Political Philosophy and the God of Abraham*. Baltimore: Johns Hopkins University Press, 2003.

Corine Pelluchon, "Leo Strauss." *Dictionnaire de philosophie politique*. Edited by P. Raynaud and S. Rials. Paris: PUF, coll. Quadrige, 2003, pp. 756–762.

———, "Leo Strauss et George Bush." *Le Banquet,* n°19–20, février 2004, pp. 281–292.

———, "Cohen and Strauss: The Question of Enlightened Judaism." *Interpretation: A Journal of Political Philosophy,* vol. 32, n°3, Summer 2005, pp. 219–230.

———, "Strauss and Christianity." *Interpretation: A Journal of Political Philosophy,* vol. 33, n°2, Spring 2006, pp. 185–203.

———, "Leo Strauss: l'impensé des Modernes et les Lumières de Maïmonide." In *Les Lumières médiévales,* 1 vol., collectif sous la direction de Géraldine Roux. Paris: Van Dieren, 2008, pp. 177–201.

———, "Cosmopolitisme, humanitarisme et Etat homogène chez Leo Strauss: une remise en cause des idéaux modernes et de la politique contemporaine." *Le Banquet,* n°25, avril 2008, pp. 171–186.

———, "Ontologie et politique: la tension entre Jérusalem et Athènes et l'alternative straussienne à l'humanisme contemporain." In *Le statut contemporain du théologico-politique*. Edited by Philippe Capelle. Paris: Le Cerf, 2008, pp. 161–170.

Shlomo Pines, "On Leo Strauss." Translated by Aryeh Leo Motzkin. *The Independent Journal of Philosophy,* vols. 5–6, 1988, pp. 169–171.

Paul Rahe, *Republics Ancient and Modern*. Chapel Hill: University of North Carolina Press, 1992, 1 vol.; republished in 3 vols., 1994: vol. 1: *The Ancient Regime and Classical Greece, XXIV–380 pp.; vol. 2: New Modes and Orders in Early Modern Political Thought, XIV–486 pp.; vol. 3: Inventions of Prudence: Constituting the American Regime, XXXII–378 pp.*

Stanley Rosen, "Leo Strauss and the Quarrel Between the Ancients and the Moderns." In *Leo Strauss's Thought: Toward a Critical Engagement,* pp. 155–168.

———, "Politics or Transcendence? Responding to Historicism." In *Faith and Political Philosophy: The Correspondence Between Leo Strauss and Éric Vœgelin,* pp. 261–266.

———, *The Quarrel between Philosophy and Poetry.* New York: Routledge, 1988.

———, *Hermeneutics as Politics.* Oxford: Oxford University Press, 1987, pp. 87–140.

Ellis Sandoz, "Medieval Rationalism or Mystic Philosophy? Reflections on the Strauss-Vœgelin Correspondence," pp. 297–319.

James V. Schall, "Revelation, Reason and Politics—I et II; Catholic Reflections on Strauss." *Gregorianum*, vol. 62, n°2–3, 1981, pp. 349–365, 467–498.

Eliezer Schweid, "Religion and Philosophy: The Scholarly-Theological Debate Between Julius Guttmann and Leo Strauss." *Maimonidean Studies*, vol. 1, 1990, pp. 163–195.

Kenneth Seeskin, "Maimonides' Conception of Philosophy." In *Leo Strauss and Judaism: Jerusalem and Athens Critically Revisited*, pp. 87–110.

Eugene R. Sheppard, *Leo Strauss and the Politics of Exile: The Making of a Political Philosopher*. Waltham, MA: Brandeis University Press, 2007.

Steven B. Smith, "Gershom Scholem and Leo Strauss: Notes Toward A German-Jewish Dialogue." *Modern Judaism*, vol. 13, n°3, October 1993, pp. 209–229.

———, *Reading Leo Strauss: Polemics, Philosophy, Judaism*. Chicago: University of Chicago Press, 2006.

———, ed., *The Cambridge Companion to Leo Strauss*. Cambridge: Cambridge University Press, 2009.

Walter Soffer, "Modern Rationalism, Miracles, and Revelation: Strauss's Critique of Spinoza." In *Leo Strauss: Political Philosopher and Jewish Thinker*, pp. 143–173.

James Steintrager, "Political Philosophy, Political Theology and Morality." *The Thomist*, vol. 32, July 1968, pp. 307–332.

Daniel Tanguay, *Leo Strauss, une biographie intellectuelle*. Paris: Grasset, 2003. *Leo Strauss: An Intellectual Biography*. New Haven, CT: Yale University Press, 2007.

Nathan Tarcov, "On a Certain Critique of 'Straussianism.'" *Review of Politics*, vol. 53, n°1, Winter 1991, pp. 3–18. See also *Leo Strauss: Political Philosopher and Jewish Thinker*, pp. 259–274.

———. "Philosophy and History: Tradition and Interpretation in the Work of Leo Strauss." *Polity*, vol. 16, n°1, Autumn 1983, pp. 5–29.

——— and Thomas L. Pangle, "Epilogue: Leo Strauss and the History of Political Philosophy." In *History of Political Philosophy*, 3rd ed. Edited by Leo Strauss and Joseph Cropsey, pp. 907–938. Chicago: University of Chicago Press, 1987.

James F. Ward, "Political Philosophy and History: The Links Between Strauss and Heidegger." *Polity*, vol. 20, n°2, Winter 1987, pp. 273–295.

Frederick D. Wilhelmsen, *Christianity and Political Philosophy*. Athens: The University of Georgia Press, 1978, 243 pp., chap. 8: "Jaffa, Strauss, and the Christian Tradition," pp. 209–225.

James Wiser, "Reason and Revelation as Search and Response: A Comparison of Éric Vœgelin and Leo Strauss." In *Faith and Political Philosophy: The Correspondence Between Leo Strauss and Éric Vœgelin*, pp. 237–248.

Michael Zank, "Strauss, Schmitt, and Peterson: Comparative Contours of the 'Theological Political Predicament.'" In *German-Jewish Thought Between Religion and Politics. Festschrift in Honor of Paul Mendes-Flohr on the Occasion of His Seventieth Birthday*. Edited by M. Urban and C. Wiese. Berlin: Walter de Gruyter, 2012, pp. 317–333.

Catherine H. Zuckert, *Postmodern Platos: Nietzsche, Heidegger, Gadamer, Strauss, Derrida*. Chicago: University of Chicago Press, 1966.

Catherine Zuckert and Michael Zuckert, "Introduction: Mr. Strauss Goes to Washington?" In *The Truth about Leo Strauss: Political Philosophy and American Democracy*. Chicago: University of Chicago Press, 2006, pp. 1–26.

Thinkers Other than Strauss or Straussians

Al-Farabi, *On the Perfect State*. Translated by R. Walzer. Oxford: Clarendon Press, 1985.

———, *Philosophy of Plato and Aristotle*. Edited and translated by M. Mahdi. Ithaca: Cornell University Press, 2001.

Al-Ghazali, *The Incoherence of the Philosophers*. Translated by S. A. Kamali. Lahore, 1958.

Hannah Arendt, *The Origins of Totalitarianism*. Revised ed. New York: Schocken, 2004.

———, *On Revolution*: New York: Viking, 1963.

Avempace (ibn Bâjja), *El regimen del solitario*. Translated and with an introduction by J. Lomba. Madrid: Trotta, 1997.

Averroes (ibn Rushd), *Averroes On Plato's Republic*. Translated by R. Lerner. Ithaca, NY: Cornell University Press, 2005.

Avicenne (ibn Sînâ), *The Metaphysics of The Healing*. Translated by M. E. Marmura. Provo: Brigham Young University Press, 2004.

Karl Barth, *Protestant Theology in the 19th Century*. Translated by Brian Cozens and John Bowden. London: SCM Press, 1959.

Walter Benjamin and Gershom Scholem, *Briefwechsel* 1933–1940. Frankfurt am Main: Suhrkamp, 1980.

Georges Bernanos, "L'esprit europeen et le monde des machines." *La liberte pour quoi fair?* In *Essais et écrits* de combat II. Paris: Gallimard, 1995.

Martin Buber, *Gottesfinsternis*. Gerlingen: Lambert Schneider, 1994 (1953).

———, *I and Thou*. Translated by S. G. Smith and W. Kaufman. New York: Free Press, 1971.

Edmund Burke, *Reflections on the Revolution in France*. London: Penguin Classics, 1986.

Hermann Cohen, *Jüdische Schriften*. Edited by Bruno Strauss. 3 vols. Berlin: C.A. Schwetshke, 1924.

———, *Religion der Vernunft aus der Quellen des Judentums*. Frankfurt am Main: Fourier, 1929 (1919).

Benjamin Constant, "The Liberty of the Ancients Compared with That of the Moderns." Speech given at the Athénée Royal in Paris in 1819. In B. Constant, *Political Writings*, Translated by B. Fontana. Cambridge: Cambridge University Press, 1988.

Luc Ferry, *Philosophie politique*, vols. 1 and 2. Paris: PUF, 1984.

Johann Gottlieb Fichte, "First Introduction to the Wissenschaftslehre." In *Introductions to the Wissenschaftslehre and Other Writings*. Translated by D. Breazeale. Indianapolis: Hackett, 1994.

Didier Franck, *Nietzsche et l'ombre de Dieu*. Paris: PUF, 1988.

Amos Funkenstein, *Theology and the Scientific Imagination from the Middle Ages to the 17th Century*. Princeton: Princeton University Press, 1986.

———, *Maimonides: Nature, History and Messianic Belief*. Tel Aviv: Ministry of Defense Publishing House, 1998.

M. Gauchet, *Le désenchantement du monde, Une histoire politique de la religion*. Paris: Gallimard, 1985.

Julius Guttmann, *Die Philosophie des Judentums*. Wiesbaden: Fourier, 1985.

———, *Religion und Wissenschaft im mittelalterlichen und im modernen Denken.* Berlin: Philo Verlag, 1922.

Friedrich Hegel, *Elements of the Philosophy of Right.* Edited by A. W. Wood. Cambridge: Cambridge University Press, 1991.

Martin Heidegger, *Bremer und Freiburger Vorträge, Gesamtausgabe*, Bd. 79. Frankfurt: Vittorio Klostermann, 1994.

———, *On the Way to Language.* Translated by P. Hertz. New York: Harper and Row, 1971.

———, *Contributions to Philosophy (From Enowning).* Translated by Parvis Emad and Kenneth Maly. Bloomington: Indiana University Press, 1999.

———, *Being and Time.* Translated by J. Macquarrie and E. Robinson. New York: Harper and Row, 1962.

———, *The Question Concerning Technology and Other Essays.* Translated by William Lovitt. New York: Harper and Row, 1977.

———, *Basic Writings.* Edited by D. F. Krell. London: Harper Perennial Modern Thought, 2008.

Hartwig Hirschfeld, trans. *Kuzari, An Argument for the Faith of Israel.* 1905. Reprint, New York: Schocken, 1964.

Thomas Hobbes, *Leviathan: With Selected Variants from the Latin Edition of 1668.* Indianapolis: Hackett Publishing Company, 1994.

Edmund Husserl, *The Crisis of European Sciences and Transcendental Phenomenology.* Translated by D. Carr. Evanston, IL: Northwestern University Press, 1970.

———, *Ideas: General Introduction to Pure Phenomenology* (Muirhead Library of Philosophy). Translated by W. R. B. Gibson. London: Routledge, 2012.

Friedrich Heinrich Jacobi, *Werke*, Bd. II. Darmstadt: Wissenschaftliche Buchgesellschaft, 1980.

Franz Kafka, "Before the Law." In *Franz Kafka: The Complete Stories and Parables* 3–4. Edited by Nahum N. Glatzer. New York: Quality Paperback Book Club, 1971.

Immanuel Kant, *Idea for a Universal History with a Cosmopolitan Purpose.* In *Kant, Political Writings.* Translated by H. B. Nisbet and edited with an introduction and notes by H. Reiss. Cambridge: Cambridge University Press, 1991.

———, *Theoretical Philosophy after 1781.* Edited by Henry Allison and Peter Heath. Cambridge: Cambridge University Press, 2002.

Jean-François Kervégan, *Hegel, Carl Schmitt, le politique entre spéculation et positivité.* Paris: PUF, 1992.

Sören Kierkegaard, *Stages on Life's Way.* Translated by Walter Lowrie. New York: Schocken, 1967.

———, *The Sickness unto Death.* Translated by Howard V. Hong and Edna H. Hong. Princeton: Princeton University Press, 1980.

———, *The Concept of Anxiety.* Translated by Reidar Thomte and Albert B. Anderson. Princeton: Princeton University Press, 1980.

Gerhardt Krüger, *Philosophie und Moral in der kantischen Kritik*, J. C. B. Mohr, P. Siebeck, Tübingen, 1931.

Gottfried Wilhelm Leibniz, "Monadology." In *Philosophical Writings*. Translated by M. Morris and G. Parkinson. London: Dent, 1973.

Gotthold Ephraim Lessing, *Nathan the Wise*, Act III, Scene V. In G. E. Lessing, *Nathan the Wise, Minna von Barnhelm, and Other Plays and Writings*. Edited by P. Demetz. New York: Continuum, 1991.

Emmanuel Levinas, *Time and the Other*. Translated by R. A. Cohen. Pittsburg: Duquesne University Press, 1990.

———, *Totality and Infinity*. Translated by A. Lingis. Pittsburg: Duquesne University Press, 1969.

———, *Otherness than Being: Or beyond Essence*. Translated by R. Cohen. Pittsburg: Duquesne University Press, 1998.

———, *Outside the Subject*. Translated by M. B. Smith. Palo Alto: Stanford University Press, 1994.

———, Preface to *Système et Révélation, La philosophie de Franz Rosenzweig* de S. Mosès. Paris: Le Seuil, 1982.

Mark Lilla, *The Stillborn God: Religion, Politics, and the Modern West*. New York: Knopf, 2007.

John Locke, *Second Treatise of Civil Government*. Edited by C. B. Macpherson. Indianapolis: Hackett Publishing Company, 1980.

———, *Essay on Human Understanding*. New York: Prometheus Books, 1994.

Karl Löwith, *Mein Leben in Deutschland vor und nach 1933*. Stuttgart: Metzler, 1986.

Niccolo Machiavelli, *The Prince*. Translated by H. Mansfield. Chicago: University of Chicago Press, 1998.

———, *Discourses on Livy*. Translated by H. Mansfield and N. Tarcov. Chicago: University of Chicago Press, 1996.

Moses Maimonides, *The Guide of the Perplexed*. Translated by S. Pines. Chicago: University of Chicago Press, 1963.

P. Manent, *An Intellectual History of Liberalism*. Translated by R. Balinski. Princeton: Princeton University Press, 1995.

Alexandre Matheron, *Le Christ et le salut des ignorants chez Spinoza*. Paris: Aubier Montaigne, 1971.

H. Meier, *The Lesson of Carl Schmitt: Four Chapters on the Distinction Between Political Theology and Political Philosophy*. Translated by M. Brainard. Chicago: University of Chicago Press, 1998.

Moses Mendelssohn, *Last Works*. Translated and commentary by B. Rosenstock. Includes *Morning Hours: Lectures on the Existence of God* and *To the Friends of Lessing*. Champaign: University of Illinois Press, 2012.

Paul Mendes-Flohr, *German Jews: A Dual Identity*. New Haven: Yale University Press, 1999.

Montesquieu, *The Spirit of the Laws*. Edited by A. M. Cohler, B. C. Miller, and H. S. Stone. Cambridge: Cambridge University Press, 2008.

Friedrich Nietzsche, *Thus Spake Zarathustra*. Translated by W. Kaufmann. New York: Random House, 1954.

———, *Beyond Good and Evil: A Prelude to the Philosophy of the Future*. Translated by J. Norman. Wilder Publications, 2008.

Shlomo Pines, *La liberté de philosopher*. Translated by R. Brague. Paris: Desclée de Brouwer, 1997.

A. W. Rehberg, "Über das Verhältnis der Metaphysik zu der Religion" (1787). In *Sämtliche Schriften*, HannoverIt stth, 1828. For his critique of the French Revolution, see *Untersuchungen über die französische Revolution*, Hannover and Osnabruck, cited by Alain Renault and Lukas Sosoe in *Philosophie du droit*, "Recherches politiques." Paris: PUF, 1991.

Rhazes (Abu Muhammad b. Zakariyya al-Razi). Texts edited by Paul Kraus. "Alchemie, Apokryphen, Ketzerei in frühen Islam." In *Gesammelte Aufsätze*. Hildesheim: Georg Olms, 1994.

Franz Rosenzweig, *Kleinere Schriften*. Berlin: Schocken, 1937.

———, "Atheistic Theology." In *Philosophical and Theological Writings*. Translated by P. W. Franks and M. L. Morgan. Indianapolis: Hackett, 2000.

———, *The Star of Redemption*. Translated by Barbara E. Galli, foreword by Michael Oppenheim, and introduction by Elliot R. Wolfson. Madison: University of Wisconsin Press, 2004.

Jean-Jacques Rousseau, *Emile or On Education*. Translated by A. Bloom. New York: Basic Books, 1979.

———, *The Discourses and Other Early Political Writings*. Translated by V. Gourevitch. Cambridge: Cambridge University Press, 1997.

———, *The Social Contract and Other Later Political Writings*. Translated by V. Gourevitch. Cambridge: Cambridge University Press, 1997.

———, *Reveries of the Solitary Walker*. Translated by R. Goulbourne. Oxford: Oxford University Press, 2011.

Carl Schmitt, *The Concept of the Political*. Expanded ed. Translated by G. Schwab. Chicago: University of Chicago Press, 2007.

———, *Political Theology: Four Chapters on the Concept of Sovereignty*. Translated by Schwab. Chicago: University of Chicago Press, 2005.

Gershom Scholem, *Major Trends in Jewish Mysticism*. New York: Schocken, 1946.

Baruch Spinoza, *Theologico-Political Treatise*. Translated by M. Yaffe. Newport, MA: Focus Publishing, 2004.

———, *Ethics*. Translated by E. Curley. London: Penguin Classics, 2005.

Alexis de Tocqueville, *Democracy in America*. Translated by H. C. Mansfield and D. Winthrop. Chicago: University of Chicago Press, 2000.

Georges Vajda, *Introduction à la pensée juive du Moyen Age*. Paris: Vrin, 1947.

Richard Wolin, ed., *Karl Löwith, Martin Heidegger and European Nihilism*. New York: Columbia University Press, 1998.

Index